Rose Elliot's
Vegetarian Kitchen

Rose Elliot's
Vegetarian Kitchen

Rose Elliot

HarperCollins*Illustrated*

First published in 1999 by
HarperCollins*Illustrated*, an imprint of
HarperCollins*Publishers*.

Previously published by
HarperCollins*Publishers* in three
separate volumes – *Vegetarian Fast
Food*, 1994, *Vegetarian Four Seasons*,
1993, *Vegetarian Christmas*, 1992.
The text in this compilation has been
revised and updated.

Text © Rose Elliot 1994, 1999
Rose Elliot reserves the moral right to be
identified as the author of the Work.

Photographs:
pages 16-145 © David Armstrong
1994; pages 150-1, 182-3, 214-5, 246-7
© Jacqui Hurst 1993;
pages 153-179, 185-213, 217-243, 249-
274 © Alan Newnham 1993; pages
281-422 © Martin Brigdale 1992

Home Economist: Lyn Rutherford
Stylists: Róisín Nield, Maria Jacques,
Marion Price
Indexer: Susan Bosanko

A catalogue record for this book is
available from the British Library.

ISBN 0 00 414094 X

Colour origination by Colourscan
Printed and bound in Singapore
for Imago

ACKNOWLEDGEMENTS

Many people have helped create this book, over a period of nearly nine years, and I would like to thank them all. My warmest thanks, then, to my publisher, HarperCollins, and in particular Polly Powell and Barbara Dixon, and the rest of the team to whom I owe both the idea for this book and, of course, the means to make it happen; Sarah Sutton of Thorsons, whose original idea for *Vegetarian Christmas* started it; Robin Wood for his enthusiasm for these books and for all the encouragement and opportunities he gave me while he was at HarperCollins; my agent, Barbara Levy, for the part she played in inspiring this book, in addition to her usual help and support; Lyn Rutherford, who was the home economist for all sections of the book – I'd like to thank her for preparing the food so beautifully; Jane Middleton for editing firstly *Vegetarian Fast Food* and then this book; Susan Bosanko for compiling the index; and Clare Baggaley for making it all look so good.

In addition, I'd like to thank Caroline Hill, design manager for *Vegetarian Fast Food* and *Vegetarian Four Seasons*; also Kelly Flynn, who art-directed *Vegetarian Christmas*. My grateful thanks and appreciation, too, to the brilliant creative teams: photographers Dave Armstrong, Alan Newnham and Martin Brigdale; and stylists Róisín Nield *(Fast Food)*, Maria Jacques *(Four Seasons)* and Marion Price *(Vegetarian Christmas)*. My gratitude, too, to Isabel Moore, who was the original editor for the Cook's Year and Vegetarian Christmas chapters in their first incarnation as individual books and who contributed many ideas.

Finally I'd like to express my love and appreciation to my family – my husband Robert and daughters Kate, Meg and Claire – for being (mostly) willing guinea pigs and for understanding that when the cook is also a cookery writer meals are often unpredictable, depending on publisher's deadlines and on what has to be tested ...

FOREWORD

Welcome to my Vegetarian Kitchen. Like many good things, this book was the result of serendipity. After my books *Vegetarian Fast Food*, *Vegetarian Four Seasons* and *Vegetarian Christmas* had been published it was noticed that they balanced and complemented each other very well. So it seemed natural to combine them in one volume – and that's *Vegetarian Kitchen*! I hope that you will like it and find it useful in your kitchen.

With the vast range of ingredients now on offer, cooking has never been easier or more exciting. Yet the number of convenience meals available is also increasing. I feel sad that many people seem to lack both the time and the confidence to cook their own food and experience the pleasure of preparing and eating real home-cooked meals, especially when these can be so much healthier and more nutritious than convenience foods. I hope that this book will encourage such people into the kitchen. Nearly all the recipes are quick and easy; those in the first section are particularly speedy, and make use of the wonderful fresh produce that is now available. This theme is developed further in section two, which takes you right through the cookery year: using seasonal produce, celebrating traditional festivals, relishing the first of the asparagus, early-summer strawberries, late-summer blackberries, peppers and aubergines; a feast of fungi for autumn, golden pumpkins for Hallowe'en, then chestnuts and cranberries for Christmas. As Christmas is such an important time in the kitchen, when even people who don't cook much during the year are often inspired to have a go, the third section covers the vegetarian Christmas in detail – the facts, the food, the fun, with recipes, tips and plans to make it the best ever So – whether you're a committed vegetarian eating no meat or fish, a vegan eating no dairy produce, an 'almost-vegetarian' or a mostly meat-eater wondering what to cook for a vegetarian or in search of an occasional change, I hope that you'll find something helpful and delicious here; and that *Vegetarian Kitchen* will become a trusty companion, a really useful source of recipes, ideas and inspiration.

CONTENTS

INTRODUCTION

Vegetarian food has a great deal going for it. It tastes terrific. It has wonderful colours and textures. It's very health-giving, as studies have shown: vegetarians are around 30 per cent less likely than meat eaters to suffer heart attacks and some cancers, 22 per cent less likely to be admitted to hospital, and also less likely to suffer from osteoporosis. It's kind to the environment, minimizing pollution and damage to the earth's resources. It makes feeding the whole world completely feasible two or three times over. And last but definitely not least, it prevents the suffering of countless animals. All compelling factors, any of which would be reason enough for becoming vegetarian. In fact they're so logical, and make such common sense, that sometimes I really do find it difficult to understand why everyone isn't vegetarian. Still, the way things are going that may be only a question of time. A Mintel survey demonstrated that vegetarianism is the fastest-growing trend in the UK, and opinion polls show that people in this country are currently turning vegetarian at the rate of 5,000 a week. If that continues, then the whole population would be vegetarian by the year 2030! So what exactly is this vegetarian diet?

WHAT IS A VEGETARIAN DIET?

There are degrees of strictness but generally vegetarians don't eat anything that has been killed – 'anything with a face', as Linda McCartney used to say. So we do eat dairy produce, cheese, free range eggs and milk, but no meat or fish. Vegans take things a step further and don't eat any animal products such as milk, cheese, eggs or even honey. In either case, it's perfectly possible to be really healthy and full of energy, as athletes like Carl Lewis, Martina Navratilova and the vegan marathon runner Sally Eastall demonstrate. The diet appears to be pretty good for the brain too, since Plato, Socrates, Pythagoras, Gandhi and Einstein were all vegetarian.

The main sources of nutrients in a vegetarian diet are:
Fresh vegetables – with particular emphasis on leafy green vegetables and the 'yellow' group, such as carrots, peppers and sweet potatoes, which provide beta-carotene.
Fruit – including dried fruit and avocados.
Beans and lentils (pulses), including all the products made from them – for example, red kidney beans, cannellini beans, brown lentils, split orange lentils; chick peas, including hummus; soya bean products, such as soya milk, tofu and TVP (textured vegetable protein); also peanuts (technically a pulse) and peanut butter.
Whole grains and potatoes – including bread, pasta, noodles, rice, porridge oats, millet, buckwheat and every variety of potato.
Nuts and seeds – almonds, cashews, hazelnuts, brazil nuts, walnuts, pistachios, pecans, pumpkin seeds, sunflower seeds, sesame seeds and tahini (a sesame paste, rather like peanut butter).
Dairy produce – eggs, milk and milk products such as cheese, cream, butter and yogurt; these are included by vegetarians but not vegans.

Vegetarians use vegetable stock cubes and powders such as Marigold bouillon; vegetable gelatine such as agar-agar, vegetable oils and fats, and butter (but not animal fats such as lard). Some margarines contain animal fats so it's important to look for a pure vegetarian or vegan one. If you're interested in health, don't be taken in by margarines that say they are 'high in polyunsaturates':

the word to look for is 'non-hydrogenated' and you'll probably need to go to a health-food shop for this. For shallow-frying, roasting, grilling and salads, I use olive oil; for occasional deep-frying I recommend rapeseed, groundnut or soya oil, as they are chemically stable at high temperatures so there is less chance of free radicals (potentially damaging molecules) being released.

CAN A VEGETARIAN DIET SUPPLY ALL THE ESSENTIAL NUTRIENTS?

I've sometimes thought it ironic that, although studies consistently show the markedly lower incidence of disease amongst vegetarians and vegans, people still worry about whether these diets will provide them with enough nutrients. Truly, a varied vegetarian or vegan diet, based on the foods mentioned above, supplies everything needed for vibrant health and abundant energy. However, since people do seem to need reassurance on this point, we'll look at some of the vitamins and minerals that cause concern:

Riboflavin, also known as vitamin B2 – the major source of this in most people's diet is dairy produce; it's also present in eggs. Vegans or vegetarians eating very little dairy produce need to make sure they regularly consume other good sources of riboflavin. These include almonds, pumpkin and sunflower seeds, buckwheat, millet, quinoa, wheatgerm, cabbage, spinach, sweet potatoes and dried fruit. Fortified soya milk is also a useful source of riboflavin. The one I use, Provamel in the orange packet (labelled Provamel with added calcium and vitamins), is also GM-free.

Vitamin B12 – this is the vitamin that everyone worries about but actually it is now very easy to obtain because so many foods are fortified with it – yeast extracts, breakfast cereals and soya products, for example. The only groups who might like to take a vitamin supplement containing B12, just to be absolutely safe, are pregnant and breastfeeding vegan women and young children. (See *Rose Elliot's Mother, Baby and Toddler Book* for more information on a vegetarian diet before and after childbirth.)

Vitamin D – our intake of this comes mainly from the effect of sunshine on our skin and that, together with the vitamin D in egg yolks, fortified margarine and breakfast cereals, is sufficient for most people. There are some groups for whom a supplement is advisable (check with your doctor first): elderly people who don't get much exposure to sunlight; pregnant and breastfeeding mothers in northern latitudes; infants between six months and three years, when their bones are growing fast and they may not get out in the sun enough for their vitamin D supply to keep up with the demand; people with dark skins living in northerly countries such as the UK – the pigmentation of their skin can prevent the sun's rays from penetrating deep enough for vitamin D to be synthesized.

Calcium – there is virtually no calcium in meat, so vegetarians rely on the same sources as meat-eaters – milk and milk products, which contain plentiful amounts. However, dark-green leafy cabbage, kale and turnip tops are equally good, if not better, sources of calcium. It is also present in molasses, sesame seeds and tahini, tofu prepared with calcium sulfate (read the package), almonds and agar-agar (a vegetarian gelling agent).

Iron – many people, especially women of childbearing

age, are deficient in iron but study after study has revealed that this is just as likely to apply to meat eaters as to vegetarians and vegans. There are plenty of good sources: molasses, pumpkin, sesame and sunflower seeds, pistachio nuts, cashews, almonds, peanuts and peanut butter, fortified breakfast cereals, wheatgerm, wheat (in bread, pasta), soya flour and beans, lentils, red kidney beans, cabbage, spinach, parsley, endive, and dried fruit, especially apricots and peaches.

Protein – getting enough protein is not a problem, neither do you have to 'balance your proteins'. A vegetarian or vegan diet based on the foods mentioned on page 8 supplies plentiful amounts of protein. If you're worried about your protein intake or want to boost it for some reason, there are some particularly high-protein vegetarian foods you can include: TVP such as Protoveg, soya flour, peanut butter, hummus, pumpkin and sesame seeds, milk, yogurt and cheese – but watch out for too much fat.

PLANNING VEGETARIAN MEALS

You can, of course, follow the traditional 'meat and two veg' model, using a vegetarian dish instead of the meat, but there are many possibilities for vegetarian meals. Try a meal consisting of just pizza or pasta – both available in many vegetarian versions – or perhaps just vegetables, in the form of a stir-fry or a platter of grilled peppers, courgettes and aubergines. Some concentrated protein such as beans, tofu or nuts could be included in the stir-fry, or you could melt some mozzarella over the grilled vegetables. Either way, the vegetables could be served with a grain – rice with the stir-fry, say, or couscous

with the grilled vegetables. Either version would constitute a nutritious meal. There are many ideas for complete meals in this book: fast, one-course meals for everyday, relaxed family lunches and suppers, or more elaborate menus for high days and holidays. I've also given serving suggestions and ideas which I hope will be useful.

HELP, I'M SHORT OF TIME!

This seems to apply to just about all of us. There seems to be less and less time for cooking. Yet preparing your own food is so rewarding in terms of pleasure and general satisfaction, economy and quality. Good vegetarian cooking need not take all day; indeed, it need not take any more than 30 minutes, as the recipes in the Really Fast Food chapter of this book show. There are also some very quick recipes in the other chapters, so I hope I can entice you into the kitchen one way or another.

EQUIPMENT

You don't need lots of fancy equipment but a few efficient tools make all the difference to the speed and pleasure of cooking. Top of the list come good sharp knives, and for these you get what you pay for. It's worth going to a kitchen store and holding some, to find one that feels right for you. My favourite is a classic Sabatier knife with a medium-length (11cm/4¹/₂ inch) blade. A longer one is useful, too, as is a small, inexpensive, lightweight stainless steel serrated knife for cutting delicate fruit such as peaches. You also need a strong chopping board that won't warp. A thick, heavy one isn't cheap but will last for ever; lighter, but well made and practical are the dishwasher-proof wooden boards available from Lakeland Limited (tel: 015394 88100; fax 015394 88300). Other small tools I find indispensable are a swivel potato peeler with a long handle that's easy to hold, and a citrus zester, which is a surprisingly useful gadget. I find a garlic press more bother than it's worth – you can do the job much more quickly and effectively with a knife and a board.

A food processor isn't essential, and many of the recipes in this book can be made without one, but it does open up many more possibilities – lovely creamy soups, pâtés and dips, for instance. As with so many things, it pays to buy a larger model than you think you'll need; go for something simple in design that doesn't try to do too many jobs. Make room for it on your work surface if possible, so that it's always there at the ready. An electric hand whisk is also very useful and is reasonably priced. I find a pressure cooker handy because I love making soups and it cooks them very quickly. Some people are wary of pressure cookers because of all the hissing, but modern ones are safe and easy to use. A large saucepan with a steamer on top is another piece of equipment that I wouldn't be without. Steamed vegetables are healthy and delicious, and you can also save space on the stove by cooking one type of vegetable in the steamer and another in the saucepan.

THE STORECUPBOARD

Most of the recipes in this book are based on a combination of fresh ingredients and ones that keep well in a storecupboard, such as pasta, rice, beans, lentils, nuts and spices. A well-stocked storecupboard saves time; after the initial stocking-up it's just a matter of replenishing it when required. One big advantage with vegetarian ingredients is that the staples keep very well, so if you're moderately organized you really only need to shop for these every four weeks or so. Most fresh ingredients will keep for several days in the fridge, which means you can cut shopping time to a quick blitz once a week.

CHOOSE ORGANIC

One very good reason for cooking your own food is that you have control over what ingredients you use. Of particular concern at the time of writing is the number of manufactured foods that contain genetically modified organisms (GMOs), thought to be at least 60 per cent. Many people, myself included, feel that these have been introduced far too fast and too secretively, in a manner that overrules our freedom of choice. There is a feeling that we are being forced to accept something we don't want, and which may prove to have far-reaching effects on both our own health and that of the environment. Fortunately, several supermarket chains have now decided to phase out GMOs from their own-label products; many large manufacturers are following suit. If you want to know more about this, I recommend you read *How to Avoid GM Food* by Joanna Blythman (Fourth Estate Ltd).

One way of avoiding GMOs, and probably a whole cocktail of chemicals as well, is to buy organic food. I am very pleased that this is becoming much more widely available and that the range and quality are improving all the time. I am very much in favour of using organic produce whenever possible and look forward to the day when organic will be the norm, not the exception. Look for the Soil Association logo on foods to make sure they are genuinely organic. For more about organic foods and where to find them, contact the Soil Association, Bristol House, 40–56 Victoria Street, Bristol BS1 6BY; Tel: 0117 929 0661.

Dry goods

For quick meals, I like to keep in stock several varieties of pasta and also split red lentils, which cook more quickly than other pulses and don't need soaking. If you have time, do experiment with other dried beans such as red kidney beans and chick peas. They need soaking in plenty of cold water for eight hours or overnight. After that, rinse them, put them into a saucepan with plenty of fresh water and boil for 10 minutes, then turn the heat down and leave them to simmer until tender – about $1\frac{1}{2}$ hours, or sometimes longer for chick peas, which can be a bit obstinate. A 500g/1lb 2oz pack of beans makes the equivalent of five 425g/15oz cans. I generally divide the cooked batch into five portions, put them into polythene bags and freeze until needed. You can cook brown, green or Puy lentils without pre-soaking; the little ones take about 40 minutes, the larger ones about 50 minutes.

Various types of rice are indispensable. I particularly like brown basmati rice, both for flavour and speed of cooking, and I also like to keep a packet of risotto rice such as arborio in the cupboard. I always keep rolled oats in stock, plus couscous, bulgur wheat, instant polenta, chick pea (gram) flour, cornflour and dried breadcrumbs for occasional use. Flour – both white and wholemeal – and baking powder are good storecupboard staples.

Wheatmeal and amaretti biscuits keep fairly well and make a good base for various puddings. Dried fruits are useful for both sweet and savoury dishes, as are nuts and seeds: I try to keep several types in stock, such as walnuts, hazelnuts, cashews, pine nuts, sunflower seeds and sesame seeds; also desiccated coconut, coconut milk powder and creamed coconut. It's best to buy nuts and seeds in small quantities and store them in the fridge or freezer to prevent them going rancid.

Canned and frozen food

A few cans are useful, particularly for quick cooking. I always keep canned tomatoes in stock – preferably in juice, preferably organic – also cans of chick peas, green lentils and beans; canned sweetcorn (without added sugar) and artichoke hearts, which I like. Canned chestnuts and unsweetened chestnut purée come in handy, whether it's to make a hearty winter stew or Christmas sausage rolls. I like the vacuum-packed peeled whole chestnuts that are now available and it's also possible to buy frozen peeled chestnuts. Other frozen foods that I like to keep in stock are petits pois, sweetcorn and leaf spinach. Sticks of frozen double or whipping cream are useful, too, for when you need just a small quantity.

Flavouring ingredients

It's worth spending a little time and money building up a collection of herbs and spices, sweet and savoury flavourings, and good oils and vinegars. At the most basic level, you need good salt – I like flaky Maldon sea salt, which you can crush in your fingers – and a grinder for black peppercorns. Other basics are light olive oil for shallow-frying and extra-virgin olive oil for salads. Rapeseed, soya and groundnut oil are most suitable for deep-frying and stir-frying; I also like dark sesame oil for adding flavour to stir-fries and oriental dishes. Vinegars to keep in stock are red wine vinegar, balsamic vinegar and brown rice vinegar, all of which have their own individual character. Tabasco sauce and soy sauce pep up food instantly – choose soy sauce that is naturally brewed and contains only soya beans and salt. Then there's mustard, preferably smooth Dijon as well as wholegrain Meaux mustard; good bought mayonnaise such as Hellman's; and jars of capers, black olive pâté (the type made only with black olives and olive oil is best), sun-dried tomatoes, pesto sauce and black olives – my favourites are the Greek Kalamata or the little Niçoise olives – all these are best kept in the fridge.

For sweet flavourings, I use both clear and thick honey and stem ginger preserved in syrup; I also find ginger preserve, a kind of ginger jam, useful. Rose and orange flower waters are versatile flavourings, and perhaps even better are liqueurs such as cointreau or Amaretto, and eau de vie. I'm fond of the high-fruit-content, no-added-sugar spreads that you can now buy – apricot, black cherry and raspberry are all useful for adding to fruit compotes, stirring into yogurt or making other quick puddings.

The spices I use most are cinnamon (in sticks and ground), cloves, cardamom, cayenne, chilli powder, whole and ground coriander, whole and ground cumin, ground turmeric, paprika, dried red chillies, and whole nutmegs for grating when needed. Mustard seeds and curry powder are good for occasional use. As far as herbs are concerned, thyme, sage, rosemary and oregano seem to survive the drying process well, and bay is actually better and more concentrated in flavour when dried. Fresh herbs make a tremendous difference to the flavour and appearance of dishes – in particular, mint, basil, dill, coriander, chives, chervil, tarragon and parsley (particularly the flavoursome flat-leaf type). I find they keep well in their little pots or in jars of water. Lemon grass, green chillies and fresh ginger root are also widely available: keep them in the fridge.

Fresh produce

Basic dairy produce such as eggs – always free range and preferably organic – milk, cream and yogurt need, of course, to be kept in the fridge, along with soft and hard cheeses, including a piece of fresh Parmesan for grating as required. Fresh vegetables such as tomatoes, salad leaves, carrots and cabbage will keep well in the fridge, too. Other basic standbys are onions, garlic, potatoes, oranges and lemons, which I keep in a cool, dark cupboard, and bread, which goes into a bread crock, with a back-up supply in the freezer.

So, enough of the preliminaries: let's get into the kitchen.

As the pace of life gets faster and faster there seems to be less and less time to cook. The range of fresh ingredients available, however, has never been greater, so the best way to cope is to make the most of these in order to produce decent meals quickly without resorting to convenience foods. If you use really good ingredients that are naturally full of flavour, you don't have to do much to them in order to make a great meal. You just need a bit of know-how and a few simple recipes, which is what this chapter is all about. It's a collection of my favourite fast-food recipes, all taking about 30 minutes or less – some a lot less – to make, and they're all prepared from wholesome ingredients in as near-natural a state as possible. Many of the recipes are as quick to make as heating up a cook/chill meal or going to the takeaway, and they certainly taste better and do you more good. So good vegetarian food can be fast food – in fact it's what I make nearly all the time.

I've kept the recipes as simple as possible and arranged them under 'storecupboard' sections, so you check what you've got in or what looks good in the shops and then choose a recipe accordingly. Most of the recipes can be varied and you can often substitute one ingredient for another, so don't feel too restricted when you're following them.

I've also kept the range of equipment quite minimal, and all the recipes can be made on top of the stove or under the grill – you don't need to use the oven so you won't have to wait for it to heat up. Many of the recipes serve just one or two people because this seems to be most appropriate for this kind of cooking, but you can always multiply the amounts if necessary. However many you're cooking for – one, two or a crowd – I hope you'll find this chapter helpful and inspiring and will enjoy making the recipes and eating good vegetarian fast food.

REALLY

FAST

FOOD

BREAD

There's a huge range of delicious breads around now, and it's fun to try different types. In this section I've included some of my favourites – not just breads and rolls but also more unusual products such as poppadums and tortillas, as well as croissants, bagels, panettone and brioche. Plenty of other interesting baked goods are worth experimenting with, and they all make an ideal basis for fast food. For a long time bread was unfairly dismissed as 'stodge', but now it is recognized as a healthy food which contributes valuable minerals and vitamins, as well as protein and energy, to our diet.

CROSTINI & BRUSCHETTA

---- ✳ ----

These Italian toasts are really very similar: crostini are delicate rounds of light, crisp bread whereas bruschetta is made from coarse country bread and rubbed with garlic to flavour it. They can be served plain to accompany soup, salads or dips, or topped with all kinds of delicious things to make canapés, quick snacks or light meals. If you are making a meal of them they are good served with some salad. You can use either a small or large baguette for crostini, depending on how big you want the rounds to be, and since one baguette yields about 50 slices, you only need a small piece to make a snack or meal for two people.

BASIC RECIPE

4 slices from a large baguette or 8 slices from a small one, cut 6 mm / ¼ inch thick, for crostini
2 slices from a country-style loaf for bruschetta

olive oil
1 garlic clove, peeled and cut in half, for bruschetta

1   Lay the slices of bread on a grill pan and grill until they are dried out and slightly golden on one side, then turn them over and grill the second side.
2   For crostini, brush the slices lightly with olive oil if you wish; I prefer them without. For bruschetta, rub the cut clove of garlic lightly over the surface and brush or drizzle with some olive oil. Serve plain, or with any of the toppings suggested below.
SERVES 2

TOPPINGS

All these toppings make enough for 8 small or 4 large crostini, or 2 bruschetta. Serve the crostini or bruschetta as soon as possible after adding the toppings.

— 1 —

CHERRY TOMATOES, FETA AND THYME

6–8 cherry tomatoes crostini or bruschetta (see above)
50g / 2oz feta cheese

sprigs of thyme
freshly ground black pepper

1   Slice the cherry tomatoes and arrange them over the crostini or bruschetta then crumble the feta cheese over them.
2   Snip a little fresh thyme over that and add a grinding of black pepper.

— 2 —

BLACK OLIVE PATE, RED PEPPER AND CAPERS

1 red pepper
black olive pâté
crostini or bruschetta (see above)

2–3 tsp capers
a few leaves of flat-leaf parsley

1   Cut the pepper into quarters then grill it for about 10 minutes or until the skin has blistered and charred in places.

2. Cool slightly, then remove the skin and seeds and slice or chop the flesh.

3. Spread black olive pâté over the crostini or bruschetta then top with the red pepper, capers and a few leaves of flat-leaf parsley.

— 3 —

AUBERGINE AND MINT

1 medium aubergine	salt and freshly
olive oil	ground black pepper
4 sprigs of mint	crostini or bruschetta
balsamic vinegar	(see page 18)

1. Slice the aubergine into rounds about 3 mm/⅛ inch thick and lay them on the grill pan.

2. Brush with olive oil on both sides then grill on high for 5–10 minutes, until golden brown and tender.

3. Tear the mint sprigs and mix with the aubergine. Add a few drops of balsamic vinegar and salt and pepper to taste then divide between the crostini or bruschetta.

— 4 —

LENTILS WITH CRANBERRIES

This Christmassy variation can be made very quickly with canned lentils.

1 small onion, peeled	crostini or bruschetta
and chopped	(see page 18)
1 tbls olive oil	2 tbls cranberry sauce,
1 × 425g / 15oz can of	preferably containing
lentils	whole cranberries
	sprigs of flat-leaf
	parsley

1. Fry the onion in the olive oil for 7–10 minutes, until soft and lightly browned.

2. Drain the lentils and add to the onion, mashing them a bit so that they hold together.

3. Spread this mixture on top of the crostini or bruschetta, piling it up well.

4. Dot the cranberry sauce over the top and decorate with sprigs of flat-leaf parsley.

— 5 —

BLUE CHEESE WITH GRAPES, PINE NUTS AND CHICORY

crostini or bruschetta	125g / 4oz blue cheese
(see page 18)	6 black grapes
a few leaves of chicory	a few pine nuts

1. Cover the crostini or bruschetta with chicory leaves, breaking or shredding them as necessary.

2. Thinly slice the blue cheese and arrange on top.

3. Halve and pip the grapes and lay these on top, then scatter over a few pine nuts.

— 6 —

GOAT'S CHEESE, ROCKET AND SUN-DRIED TOMATO

125g / 4oz soft white	several rocket leaves
goat's cheese	freshly ground black
crostini or bruschetta	pepper
(see page 18)	
8 sun-dried tomatoes	
in oil, drained	

1. Spread the soft white goat's cheese thickly on the crostini or bruschetta.

2. Chop the sun-dried tomatoes and arrange them on top of the goat's cheese, together with a few leaves of rocket, then grind some black pepper coarsely over the top.

— 7 —

HUMMUS, OLIVE AND PAPRIKA

125g / 4oz hummus	olive oil
crostini or bruschetta	8 black olives
(see page 18)	a few sprigs of
paprika pepper	flat-leaf parsley

1. Spread the hummus thickly on top of the crostini or bruschetta. Sprinkle some paprika pepper over the top, then drizzle a little olive oil on top of that.

2. Decorate with the black olives and a sprig or two of flat-leaf parsley.

You can buy very good hummus at most of the big supermarkets and it makes an excellent topping for crostini.

— 8 —

MUSHROOM PATE

225g / 8oz mushrooms	salt and freshly
25g / 1 oz butter	ground black pepper
1 garlic clove, crushed	crostini or bruschetta
2 eggs or 4 quail's eggs	(see page 18)
	black olive pâté

1 Wash and dry the mushrooms then chop them finely (use a food processor for this if you have one). Melt the butter in a saucepan, put in the mushrooms and garlic and cook them over a fairly high heat until the mushrooms are tender and any liquid they produce has evaporated – this may take 10 minutes.

2 Meanwhile, boil the eggs for 10 minutes or the quail's eggs for 2½ minutes. Shell them and slice them fairly thinly, or cut the quail's eggs in half. Season with salt and pepper.

3 Season the mushroom mixture then either leave it to cool slightly or spread it on the crostini or bruschetta while still hot. Top with the egg slices and a little black olive pâté.

— 9 —

PLUM TOMATO, MOZZARELLA AND BASIL

Plum tomatoes usually have a good flavour and nice firm texture, but you could use other well-flavoured tomatoes.

4 fresh plum tomatoes	crostini or bruschetta
salt and freshly	(see page 18)
ground black pepper	8 fresh basil leaves
olive oil	
50g / 2oz Mozzarella	
cheese (packed in	
water)	

1 Slice the tomatoes into rounds, put them on a plate and sprinkle them with salt, pepper and a few drops of olive oil. Cut the Mozzarella cheese into small pieces.

2 Arrange the tomatoes on top of the crostini or bruschetta then dot the cheese over the tomatoes.

3 Tear the basil leaves over the top of the tomatoes and cheese and grind over some more black pepper to taste.

— 10 —

GOLDY GREENY SPREAD

A strange and interesting recipe, adapted from New Food For All Palates *by Sally and Lucian Berg (Gollancz, 1967). Frozen beans are fine for this.*

1 onion, peeled and	salt and freshly
thinly sliced	ground black pepper
2 tbls olive oil	crostini or bruschetta
125g / 4oz green beans	(see page 18)
1 egg, hard-boiled	

1 Fry the onion in the oil until golden brown and crisp (this is very important for the flavour).

2 Cook the green beans in a little boiling water for 3–4 minutes, until tender, then drain.

3 Shell and roughly chop the hard-boiled egg. Put the beans, egg and half the onion into a food processor and whizz to a purée. Season to taste.

4 Spread on top of the crostini or bruschetta and top with the remaining onion.

— 11 —

PECORINO AND PEAR ON WATERCRESS

125g / 4oz soft pecorino	1 ripe dessert pear
cheese	50g / 2oz hard pecorino
crostini or bruschetta	or Parmesan cheese,
(see page 18)	grated
a little milk (optional)	freshly ground black
a few watercress leaves	pepper

1 Spread the soft pecorino cheese over the crostini or bruschetta (mix the cheese with a little milk first if necessary).

2 Press the watercress into the cheese. Peel, core and thinly slice the pear and arrange on top.

3 Sprinkle generously with the grated cheese and grind some pepper over, then serve straight away or flash under a hot grill to melt the cheese.

OPPOSITE: *A selection of Crostini, topped with* **Mushroom Pâté, Plum Tomato, Mozzarella and Basil, and Goldy Greeny Spread**

QUICK PIZZAS

—— ✳ ——

*It's unrealistic to try and make a pizza from scratch in 30 minutes but you can make a
good quick tomato sauce, spread it over a ready-made base, add a topping
and flash it under a hot grill. Although you can buy pizza bases, I like to use a range of different
breads, such as granary, ciabatta and muffins. The bases and toppings in the following recipes
can be mixed and matched, if you prefer, to suit whatever ingredients you have to hand.*

TOMATO SAUCE

1 tbls olive oil
1 onion, peeled and
   chopped
2 garlic cloves, crushed
1 × 400g / 14oz can
   tomatoes

8 sun-dried tomatoes
   in oil, drained
   (optional)
salt and freshly
   ground black pepper

1️⃣ Heat the oil in a saucepan, add the onion then cover and cook gently for 10 minutes, until tender but not brown.

2️⃣ Stir the garlic into the onion, cook for 1–2 minutes longer, then stir in the tomatoes, together with their juice, breaking them up with a wooden spoon. Chop the sun-dried tomatoes roughly, if you are using them, and add these to the pan too.

3️⃣ Let the mixture simmer away for about 10–15 minutes until the liquid has evaporated. Season with salt and pepper to taste.

MAKES ENOUGH FOR 2 MUFFINS, OR 1 GRANARY
OR CIABATTA PIZZA

MUSHROOM PIZZA

225g / 8oz button
   mushrooms
2 tbls olive oil
salt and freshly
   ground black pepper
2 muffins

125g / 4oz Cheddar or
   other cheese
tomato sauce (see
   above)

*To make a quick
lettuce salad, cut
1 or 2 little gem
lettuces across into
thick slices; wash
and drain in a
colander, then put
into a bowl, sprinkle
with 1 tablespoon
of lemon juice,
2 tablespoons of
olive oil, some
sea salt and freshly
ground black pepper,
and toss lightly.*

1️⃣ Wash and slice the mushrooms then fry them in the olive oil for 1–2 minutes until they are tender. Season with salt and pepper.

2️⃣ Cut the muffins in half and toast on both sides under the grill. Thinly slice the cheese.

3️⃣ Heat the tomato sauce then spread it over the muffins. Top with the mushrooms and cheese and heat under the grill for a few minutes, until the pizzas are piping hot and the cheese is golden brown and bubbling.
SERVES 2

RED AND YELLOW
PEPPER PIZZA

1 red pepper
1 yellow pepper
1 oval or round
   granary loaf
   (400g / 14oz)
olive oil
tomato sauce (see
   above)

salt and freshly
   ground black pepper
50g / 2oz Parmesan
   cheese
a few fresh basil
   leaves

1️⃣ Cut the peppers into quarters, put them cut-side down on a grill pan and grill for about 10 minutes or until the skin has blistered and charred in places. Remove from the grill and, when cool enough to handle, peel off the skin, remove the seeds and stem, and slice the peppers.

2️⃣ Cut the loaf horizontally in half, scoop out a

little of the crumb, then brush the inside with olive oil and toast it under the grill. Toast both sides if you want a crisp pizza base.

3 Heat the tomato sauce then spread this evenly over the bread and top with the peppers, mixing up the colours. Season the peppers lightly, then grate the cheese and sprinkle it over the pizzas.

4 Heat the pizzas under the grill for a few minutes until they are piping hot and the cheese is melted and lightly browned. Tear a little basil over the top and serve.

SERVES 2–4

CIABATTA PIZZA WITH ARTICHOKES

The nicest artichoke hearts to use for this are the ones that you can buy preserved in oil. Any that are left over keep well in the fridge. Alternatively, drained canned artichoke hearts make a good substitute.

1 red onion, peeled and sliced
olive oil
1 ciabatta loaf
tomato sauce (see opposite)

125g / 4oz Mozzarella cheese
125g / 4oz artichoke hearts, sliced

1 Fry the onion in 1 tablespoon of olive oil until softened, about 5–7 minutes.

2 Meanwhile, cut the loaf horizontally in half, brush each cut surface with olive oil and toast it under the grill. Toast both sides if you want a crisp pizza base.

3 Heat the tomato sauce then spread it evenly over the bread. Slice the cheese and arrange it on top of the sauce, then top with the artichoke hearts and fried onion.

4 Heat the pizzas under the grill for a few minutes until they are piping hot and the cheese is melted and lightly browned.

SERVES 2–4

GORGONZOLA AND WALNUT PIZZA

1 oval or round granary loaf (400g / 14oz)
olive oil
tomato sauce (see opposite)

125g / 4oz Gorgonzola cheese
50g / 2oz walnut pieces

1 Cut the granary loaf horizontally in half, scoop out a little of the crumb, then brush the inside with olive oil and and toast it under the grill. Toast both sides if you want a crisp pizza base.

2 Heat the tomato sauce then spread this evenly over the bread. Slice the cheese and arrange it on top of the sauce, then top with the walnuts.

3 Heat the pizzas under the grill for a few minutes until they are piping hot and the cheese is melted and lightly browned.

SERVES 2–4

PESTO PIZZA

1 ciabatta loaf
olive oil
tomato sauce (see opposite)
75g / 3oz Parmesan cheese

2–4 tbls pesto sauce
a few black olives (optional)

1 Cut the loaf horizontally in half, brush each cut surface with olive oil and toast it under the grill. Toast both sides if you want a crisp pizza base.

2 Heat the tomato sauce then spread it over the bread. Slice the cheese into thin slivers and arrange on top of the sauce, then drizzle the pesto over everything and add the olives if you're using these.

3 Heat the pizzas under the grill for a few minutes until they are piping hot and the cheese is melted and lightly browned.

SERVES 2–4

Bottled pesto is readily available nowadays, and some Italian delicatessens and large supermarkets stock fresh pesto sauce. If you have time, you might like to make your own (see page 65).

TWO-CHEESE PIZZA

2 muffins
125g / 4oz Mozzarella
  cheese
50g / 2oz Parmesan
  cheese

12 black olives
tomato sauce (see
  page 22)

Light rolls or baps, or pieces of French stick or ciabatta bread, split in half, also make good bases for these toppings.

1. Cut the muffins in half and toast them on both sides under the grill.
2. Meanwhile, thinly slice the cheeses and halve and stone the olives.
3. Heat the tomato sauce and spread it over the muffins, then top with the slices of cheese and the olives.
4. Heat the pizzas under the grill for a few minutes until they are piping hot and the cheese is golden brown and bubbling.

SERVES 2

SWEETCORN AND CHERRY TOMATO PIZZA

2 muffins
125g / 4oz Cheddar
  cheese
6 cherry tomatoes
tomato sauce (see
  page 22)

50g / 2oz canned or
  frozen sweetcorn
  kernels
salt and freshly
  ground black pepper

1. Cut the muffins in half and toast them on both sides under the grill.
2. Meanwhile, grate the cheese and slice the cherry tomatoes.
3. Heat the tomato sauce and spread it evenly over the muffins, then top with the grated cheese, sweetcorn and cherry tomatoes. Season with salt and pepper.
4. Heat the pizzas under the grill for a few minutes until they are piping hot and the cheese is golden brown and bubbling.

SERVES 2

RED PEPPER, AUBERGINE AND GOAT'S CHEESE PIZZA

1 small red pepper
1 medium aubergine
olive oil
2 muffins
tomato sauce (see
  page 22)

salt and freshly
  ground black pepper
50g / 2oz goat's cheese
  log

1. Cut the pepper into quarters then put it cut-side down on a grill pan. Cut the aubergine into slices about 3 mm / ⅛ inch thick and lay these on the grill pan too. Brush the aubergine slices on both sides with olive oil then grill on high for 5–10 minutes, until the skin on the pepper is blistered and charred in places and the aubergine is golden brown and tender. Remove from the grill but leave it on. Cover the pepper with a damp cloth.
2. Cut the muffins in half and toast them on both sides under the grill.
3. Heat the tomato sauce then spread it over the muffins and top with the aubergine slices. Remove the loose skin and seeds from the pepper, cut it into long, thin strips and arrange on top of the aubergine. Season with salt and pepper.
4. Break off small pieces of goat's cheese and dot them over the top of the pizzas. Grind a little black pepper coarsely over the goat's cheese then heat the pizzas under the grill for a few minutes until they are piping hot.

SERVES 2

OPPOSITE: *Two-Cheese Pizza, Sweetcorn and Cherry Tomato Pizza, Red Pepper, Aubergine and Goat's Cheese Pizza*

SNACKS ON TOAST

TOASTED CHEESE

This simple version of cheese on toast is quick and easy to make and you can vary it by using different types of bread and cheese, substituting beer, wine or cider for the milk, and adding extra ingredients such as tomatoes, onion, herbs, mushrooms, chutney or pickle – whatever takes your fancy.

1–2 slices of bread
75–125g / 3–4oz
* Cheddar cheese,*
* grated*

1–2 tbls milk
freshly ground black
* pepper*

1 Preheat the grill and toast the bread on one side.

2 Mix the cheese with the milk to make a paste then season with freshly ground black pepper.

3 Spread the cheese mixture on the untoasted side of the bread, grill until puffed up and golden brown then serve at once.
SERVES 1

VARIATIONS

1 WITH ASPARAGUS

This is an extremely nice variation if you are making toasted cheese for more than one person and want something that is extra special. Allow about 3–4 asparagus spears per person, trim them then cut them into 2.5 cm/1 inch lengths and cook in boiling water for 2–4 minutes, until just tender. Drain and serve heaped on top of the toasted cheese.

2 WITH CIDER AND APPLES

Use cider instead of the milk. Peel and core a small, mellow eating apple such as Cox's, then cut it into thin rings or slices and arrange it on the toast. Cover with the cheese mixture and grill until the cheese is puffed up and golden brown and the apple is tender.

3 WITH OLIVES

I like this best made with feta cheese, which you can crumble rather than grate. Add 6–8 black or green olives, or a mixture of both, to the cheese.

4 WITH ONION AND MUSTARD

Mix the cheese with beer instead of milk and add ½–1 teaspoon of made mustard and 1 finely chopped small onion.

5 WITH CHILLI

De-seed and finely chop 1 small green chilli and add it to the grated cheese.

MOZZARELLA IN CARROZZA

Use the best Mozzarella you can find – certainly one packed in water – for this delicious mixture of hot melting cheese and crisp fried bread.

125g / 4oz Mozzarella
* cheese*
4 slices of bread, crusts
* removed*

2 eggs
olive oil

1 Drain and slice the cheese and sandwich it between the slices of bread, pressing them firmly together.

2 Lightly beat the eggs, then strain them into a shallow dish. Put the sandwiches in the egg and leave them for a few minutes to soak it up, turning them over once.

3 Heat a little olive oil in a frying pan and fry the sandwiches on both sides until they are golden brown and crisp. Drain them quickly on kitchen paper and serve at once.
SERVES 2

Mozzarella in Carrozza means 'Mozzarella in a carriage', a poetic and apt description.

BUTTERY SCRAMBLED EGGS ON TOAST

2 slices of bread
butter
4 eggs

salt and freshly
* ground black pepper*

1. Toast the bread, butter it and keep it warm.
2. Lightly beat the eggs and season with salt and pepper.
3. Melt a knob of butter in a saucepan. When it sizzles, add the eggs and cook over a low heat for a few minutes, stirring.
4. Just before the eggs set, move the pan from the heat and, to make the scrambled eggs extra delicious, stir in a few slivers of butter. The eggs will continue to cook in the heat of the pan.
5. Pile the scrambled eggs on to the toast and serve at once on warmed plates.

SERVES 2

VARIATIONS

1 WITH FRESH HERBS

Add 1–2 tablespoons of chopped fresh herbs at the end of the cooking time, along with the extra butter.

2 PIPERADE

Piperade takes longer to cook than plain scrambled eggs but it is nice when you want something a bit more substantial.

Melt 25g/1oz butter in a pan then add 1 large onion, peeled and chopped, and 1 green pepper, de-seeded and chopped. Cover and cook for 10 minutes, until soft but not browned, then add 450g/1lb tomatoes, skinned and chopped, and 1 clove of garlic, crushed. Cook gently, uncovered, for about 10 minutes, until the vegetables are soft but not mushy. Meanwhile, toast and butter 4 slices of granary or wholewheat bread, cut it into fingers and keep it warm. Lightly beat 4 eggs then pour them into the pan with the vegetables and stir gently until they begin to set. Remove from the heat (the eggs will continue to cook in the heat of the pan), season and serve immediately with the toast fingers.

CLUB SANDWICH

3 slices of wholewheat
* bread*
butter
2 lettuce leaves
1 small tomato, sliced
mayonnaise or
* mustard*

½ small avocado
salt and freshly
* ground black pepper*
4 cocktail sticks
4 stuffed olives

1. Toast the bread, butter one piece and arrange the lettuce, tomato and a little mayonnaise or mustard on top.
2. Cover with another piece of toast, buttered on both sides. Peel, stone and slice the avocado, arrange on top of the toast and season with salt and pepper.
3. Butter the third piece of toast and place, butter-side down, on top of the avocado. Press down on the sandwich, cut it into quarters then spear each quarter with a cocktail stick and decorate with a stuffed olive.

SERVES 1

CAMEMBERT TOAST WITH APRICOT JAM

I love the combination of Camembert cheese and something sweet. If you find the jam too sweet, however, mango chutney is also very good.

1 slice of wholewheat
* bread*
2 portions of
* Camembert cheese*

2–3 tsp good-quality
* apricot jam*
2–3 tsp chopped
* hazelnuts*

1. Heat the grill and toast the bread on both sides.
2. Mash the Camembert roughly on the toast then put some dollops of apricot jam on top of that.
3. Grill until the cheese has melted then sprinkle with the nuts and grill again until lightly browned.

SERVES 1

A good way of using up the other half of the avocado is to make guacamole; mash the avocado with 1 skinned, chopped tomato and some finely chopped chilli; then add plenty of chopped fresh coriander and season to taste.

27

OPEN SANDWICHES & PAN BAGNAT

✶

RADICCHIO AND CREAM CHEESE

75g / 3oz cream cheese or curd cheese
2 slices of dark rye bread
a few radicchio leaves

2 dill-pickled cucumbers, sliced
sprigs of fresh dill (optional)

1　Spread about half of the cream or curd cheese on the bread, then press the radicchio leaves on top of that.

2　Spoon the remaining cheese on top, then arrange slices of dill-pickled cucumber on top of that and finish with a sprig of fresh dill, if you like.
SERVES 2

BRIE AND RED ONION

mayonnaise
2 slices of wholewheat bread
2–4 little gem lettuce leaves

50g / 2oz Brie
3–4 slices of red onion
a few walnuts

1　Spread a thin layer of mayonnaise on the bread then arrange the lettuce on top, pressing it down into the mayonnaise to make it stick.

2　Slice the Brie thinly then arrange it on top of the lettuce with the red onion slices and sprinkle with a few walnuts.
SERVES 2

EGG AND OLIVE

2 slices of white poppyseed bread
mayonnaise
4 frisée lettuce leaves

1 hard-boiled egg
6 black olives
paprika pepper

1　Spread the bread with a thin layer of mayonnaise then arrange the lettuce on top.

2　Chop the hard-boiled egg into chunks and mix with a little mayonnaise to moisten. Divide this mixture between the bread slices and garnish with the olives and a little paprika.
SERVES 2

PAN BAGNAT

1 long French stick
450g / 1lb tomatoes
salt and freshly ground black pepper
1 lettuce

225g / 8oz Mozzarella cheese
1 large avocado
lemon juice
fresh basil leaves

1　Cut the French stick into quarters. Slice each piece open and scoop out most of the crumb.

2　Slice the tomatoes and sprinkle with salt. Wash the lettuce and spin or pat dry; slice the Mozzarella cheese; stone, peel and slice the avocado and sprinkle the slices with lemon juice, salt and pepper.

3　Fill the bread with layers of the ingredients, adding torn basil leaves and seasoning to each layer. If you are eating the sandwiches later, wrap them tightly and keep in the fridge until needed.
SERVES 4

OPPOSITE: *(top) Pan Bagnat and (bottom) Open Sandwiches*

You can vary the filling for pan bagnat according to your taste and what is available: try adding slices of cheese, or cream cheese, hummus with some olives, or any of the fillings for pitta pockets (see pages 30–31). The main thing is to be generous with the filling.

PITTA POCKETS

✶

Pitta breads make very convenient containers for all kinds of delicious ingredients that would be too moist or bulky to put in a sandwich. Salads and stir-fries can be piled into warmed pitta pockets; grilled vegetables, too, freshly cooked and still sizzling; and simple mixtures of beans, vegetables, cheese and hummus. Here is a selection of fillings.

You can sprinkle the aubergine with salt, leave it for 30 minutes, then rinse it if you wish; this isn't usually necessary as a precaution against bitterness, but it can reduce the amount of oil the aubergine absorbs.

SPICED CHICK PEAS

A tomato, sliced into quarters or eighths, is nice added to this for a change.

1 onion, peeled and
   finely chopped
2 tbls olive oil
2 garlic cloves, crushed
1 tsp cumin seeds
1 × 425g / 15oz can
   chick peas, drained
2 pitta breads

4–6 lettuce leaves
4 tbls thick Greek
   yogurt, or a mixture
   of yogurt and good-
   quality mayonnaise
salt and freshly ground
   black pepper
paprika pepper

1 Fry the onion in the oil, with a lid on the pan, for 5 minutes. Stir in the garlic and cumin seeds, cover again and cook for a further 2–3 minutes until the onion is tender.

2 Add the chick peas to the onion and cook for 4–5 minutes, until heated through and perhaps lightly browned in places.

3 Warm the pitta breads under the grill then cut them lengthwise in half. Gently open up each half and put in the lettuce, tearing it as necessary, then spoon in the chick pea mixture. Season the yogurt or yogurt and mayonnaise, spoon on top of the chick peas and sprinkle with a little paprika pepper. Serve at once.

SERVES 2

AUBERGINE WITH PESTO

1 large aubergine
olive oil
2 pitta breads
1–2 tbls good-quality
   bought pesto sauce,
   or home-made (see
   page 65)

salt and freshly ground
   black pepper

1 Heat the grill. Cut the aubergine lengthwise into slices about 3 mm/⅛ inch thick and lay these on a grill pan. Brush the slices on both sides with olive oil then grill on high for 5–10 minutes, turning them over as necessary, until golden brown and tender.

2 Warm the pitta breads under the grill, then cut them lengthwise in half and gently open up each half. Mix the aubergine slices with pesto to taste, season, then spoon them into the pitta breads and serve at once.

SERVES 2

GREEK SALAD

4–6 lettuce leaves
small piece of
   cucumber
2 small tomatoes
4 spring onions
a few black olives,
   stoned
2 tbls olive oil

2 tsp wine vinegar
salt and freshly
   ground black pepper
125g / 4oz feta cheese
chopped fresh mint or
   oregano
2 pitta breads

1 Wash the salad ingredients then tear the lettuce, dice the cucumber, slice the tomatoes, chop the spring onions and put them into a bowl. Add the olives, oil, vinegar and a grinding of pepper.

2 Cut the feta into cubes and mix it with the other ingredients, then add the fresh mint or oregano and a little salt if necessary.

3 Warm the pitta breads through under the grill, then cut them lengthwise in half, gently open up each half and fill with the feta mixture.

SERVES 2

COUSCOUS, TOMATO AND MINT

125g / 4oz couscous	juice of 1 lemon
50g / 2oz raisins (optional)	4 tbls chopped fresh mint
2 spring onions	salt and freshly ground black pepper
4 tomatoes	
2 pitta breads	

1 Put the couscous and the raisins, if you are using them, into a bowl and cover with boiling water. Leave on one side for 10 minutes.

2 Meanwhile, trim and chop the spring onions, chop the tomatoes and warm the pitta breads under the grill.

3 Drain the couscous and mix with the spring onions, tomatoes, lemon juice, mint and salt and pepper to taste.

4 Split the pitta breads lengthwise in half, gently open each half and fill with the couscous mixture.

SERVES 2

RED BEAN AND SWEETCORN

2 tbls olive oil	1 × 200g / 7oz can sweetcorn, drained
1 small onion, peeled and chopped	1 × 225g / 8oz can red kidney beans, drained
1 small green pepper, chopped	salt and freshly ground black pepper
1 × 200g / 7oz can tomatoes	2 pitta breads

1 Heat the oil in a pan, put in the onion and pepper, cover and cook gently for 10 minutes, or until they are getting tender.

2 Mash in the tomatoes with their juice, cover and cook for a further 10 minutes, then add the sweetcorn and kidney beans. Cook gently for a few more minutes until hot. Season with salt and pepper.

3 Warm the pitta breads under the grill, then cut them lengthwise in half, gently open up each half, fill with the red bean mixture and serve at once.

SERVES 2

You could use bulgur wheat instead of couscous for a change: prepare it in the same way.

CHEESE AND CARROT VINAIGRETTE

2 carrots (about 225g / 8oz)	2 tbls olive oil
125g / 4oz Cheddar cheese	2 tsp wine vinegar
4 spring onions	salt and freshly ground black pepper
	2 pitta breads

1 Scrape or peel the carrots then coarsely grate the carrots and cheese into a bowl. Trim and slice the spring onions and add them to the bowl, together with the oil, vinegar and a seasoning of salt and pepper. Mix well.

2 Warm the pitta breads under the grill, then cut them lengthwise in half, gently open up each half, fill with the carrot mixture and serve at once.

SERVES 2

TORTILLAS & POPPADUMS

TORTILLA SALAD ROLLS

2 tortillas
6–8 iceberg lettuce
  leaves
2 tomatoes
small piece of
  cucumber
2 spring onions

4 tbls mayonnaise,
  soured cream, yogurt
  or a mixture
hot chilli sauce such
  as Tabasco
salt and freshly
  ground black pepper

1 Put the tortillas into a frying pan over a moderate heat, one at a time, to warm through, or heat them under the grill.

2 Shred the lettuce leaves and chop the tomatoes, cucumber and spring onions. Mix with the mayonnaise, soured cream or yogurt then add a dash of hot chilli sauce and some salt and pepper to taste.

3 Spread the salad mixture on to the warm tortillas, roll them up firmly and serve at once.

SERVES 2

POPPADUMS WITH AVOCADO AND CURRIED MAYONNAISE

2 tsp curry powder
2 tbls mayonnaise
2 tbls plain yogurt
1 tsp mango chutney
salt and freshly
  ground black pepper

1 avocado
2 tomatoes
squeeze of lemon juice
2–3 poppadums
paprika pepper or
  fresh coriander

OPPOSITE: (top) *Poppadums with Avocado and Curried Mayonnaise and (bottom) Pitta Pockets with (left) Cheese and Carrot Vinaigrette and (right) Red Bean and Sweetcorn, page 31*

1 Put the curry powder into a dry saucepan and heat for 1–2 minutes until it smells aromatic. Remove from the heat and mix with the mayonnaise, yogurt, chutney and salt and pepper to taste.

2 Peel, stone and chop the avocado then put it in a bowl. Dice the tomatoes and add to the avocado with the lemon juice and salt and pepper to taste.

3 Put the poppadums on a plate, spoon the avocado mixture on the side and trickle the curried mayonnaise over it. Finish with a sprinkling of paprika pepper or a little chopped fresh coriander.

SERVES 1

RED BEAN BURRITOS

2 onions, peeled and
  chopped
2 tbls olive oil
2 garlic cloves, crushed
1 chilli, de-seeded and
  chopped
1 tsp cumin seeds
2 tomatoes

1 × 425g / 15oz can red
  kidney beans, drained
2 tbls chopped fresh
  coriander
salt and freshly ground
  black pepper
2 tortillas
soured cream to serve

1 Fry the onions in the oil, with a lid on the pan, for 5 minutes. Add the garlic, chilli and cumin and cook for 1–2 minutes.

2 Cover the tomatoes with boiling water for a few seconds, then drain and slip off the skins. Chop and add to the pan with the kidney beans. Cook gently for 5 minutes or until heated through, mashing the beans to make a rough purée. Add the coriander and season with salt and pepper.

3 Warm the tortillas one at a time in a frying pan over a moderate heat, or heat them under the grill. Spread the bean mixture on the warm tortillas, roll them up and serve with soured cream.

SERVES 2

The tortillas that you can now buy make a good fast-food snack, warmed through, filled with tasty ingredients and then rolled up. They can be eaten immediately or topped with grated cheese and put under a hot grill to melt the cheese. The remaining tortillas will keep well in a polythene bag in the freezer.

CROISSANTS, ROLLS & SWEET IDEAS

✳

SPEEDY GARLIC BREAD

Although garlic bread is usually made in the oven, you can speed things up by using the grill instead.

½ *French stick or 2*   50g / 2oz butter,
  crusty rolls, white or   *softened*
  wholewheat
2 *garlic cloves, crushed*

1   Heat the grill. Cut the French stick on the diagonal into slices about 2.5 cm/1 inch thick, or cut the rolls in half.

2   Mix together the garlic and butter then spread this over the cut surfaces of the bread.

3   Grill the bread until hot and sizzling on one side, then turn it over to heat the other side. Serve immediately, or cover with foil and keep warm.
SERVES 2

CREAMY ASPARAGUS CROISSANTS

This delicious snack for one is rather like a cheat's version of feuilleté of asparagus in cream.

125–225g / 4–8oz   *salt and freshly ground*
  asparagus spears   *black pepper*
15g / ½ oz butter   *freshly grated nutmeg*
1½ tsp cornflour   2 croissants
150ml / 5fl oz single
  cream

1   Trim the asparagus as necessary and cut it into 2.5 cm/1 inch lengths. Keep the tips separate from the stems.

2   Cook the chopped stems in 2.5 cm/1 inch of boiling water for 2 minutes, then add the tips and cook for a further 2 minutes, until they are beginning to get tender but are still crunchy. Drain.

3   Melt the butter in a pan and stir in the cornflour. Add the cream and stir over a moderate heat until it comes to the boil and thickens. Cook for 1–2 minutes then remove from the heat and stir in the asparagus. Season with salt, pepper and nutmeg.

4   Slice the croissant horizontally in half. Grill on both sides until crisp and lightly browned.

5   Serve the croissant halves with the asparagus, sandwiching them together with the mixture if you like, and letting the excess run on to the plate.
SERVES 2

GARLIC MUSHROOM ROLL

175g / 6oz button   *salt and freshly*
  mushrooms   *ground black pepper*
15g / ½ oz butter   1 *high, rounded, crusty*
1 tsp olive oil   *roll, white or granary*
1–2 *garlic cloves,*
  crushed

1   Wash and roughly chop the mushrooms, then fry them in the butter and olive oil for 5 minutes or until they are tender. If they give off a lot of liquid, go on cooking them until this has evaporated; this may take as long as 10 minutes.

2   Add the garlic and cook for 1–2 minutes longer. Season with salt and pepper.

3   Meanwhile, heat the grill. Slice the top off the roll to make a lid; scoop out and discard most of the crumb. Warm through the roll and lid under the grill, turning it.

4   Spoon the mushrooms into the roll and replace the lid. Serve at once.
SERVES 1

Cheese and Garlic Bread makes a nice variation: simply put slivers of cheese (such as Gruyère) on the garlic bread before grilling it; or try herb bread, using 1 tablespoon of chopped fresh parsley and chives instead of, or as well as, the garlic.

CHUTNEY BEAN BURGER

Use whatever chutney or pickle you like in this; you could also add extras such as grated cheese, mustard, mayonnaise, sliced tomato and lettuce to make a kind of burger with everything.

1 onion, peeled and
   chopped
1 tbls olive oil
1 garlic clove, crushed
1 × 225g / 8oz can
   butter beans, drained

1–2 tbls chutney or
   pickle
salt and freshly
   ground black pepper
1 soft burger roll

[1]   Fry the onion in the olive oil, with a lid on the pan, for 5 minutes. Add the garlic to the pan and cook for 1–2 minutes longer.

[2]   Add the beans to the pan and cook gently for about 5 minutes, until heated through, mashing the beans to make a rough purée. Stir in the chutney or pickle and season with salt and pepper.

[3]   Heat the grill. Cut the burger roll in half and warm it through under the grill, then pile the bean mixture on one half, top with the other half, press down and serve immediately.
SERVES 1

BRIOCHE WITH VACHERIN AND APRICOT CONSERVE

An indulgent breakfast, brunch or pudding.

1 individual brioche
125g / 4oz Vacherin
   cheese

1–2 tbls best-quality
   apricot conserve

[1]   Warm the brioche in the oven or under the grill, then serve with the Vacherin cheese and apricot conserve.
SERVES 1

GINGER AND CREAM CHEESE BAGELS

125g / 4oz cream
   cheese, full fat or
   low fat
2 pieces of preserved
   stem ginger

6 walnut halves
a little milk (optional)
2 bagels

[1]   Put the cream cheese into a bowl. Chop the ginger and walnuts and beat into the cream cheese, adding a little milk if necessary to soften it.

[2]   Cut the bagels in half, spread with the filling and sandwich together.
SERVES 2

BAGELS WITH CHOPPED-HERRING-WITHOUT-HERRING

This filling is a piquant and intriguing relish from New Food For All Palates *by Sally and Lucian Berg. It also makes a good topping for crostini or bruschetta.*

25g / 1oz white bread,
   crusts removed
7 tsp white wine
   vinegar
2 eggs, hard-boiled
40g / 1½ oz mild onion
25g / 1oz green pepper

25g / 1oz peeled sharp
   apple
1 rounded tsp sea salt
4 tsp olive oil
white pepper
2 bagels

[1]   Tear the bread into pieces, put these into a bowl and sprinkle with the vinegar.

[2]   Shell the eggs, chop them roughly and put them into a food processor with the onion, green pepper and apple, also in rough chunks. Add the bread, salt and oil and whizz to a chunky purée. Season, adding some white pepper to taste.

[3]   Cut the bagels in half, spread the filling over them and sandwich together.
SERVES 2

PANETTONE WITH FRESH FIGS

This makes a good quick festive pudding. Other fruits such as clementines, peeled and sliced, could be substituted for the figs, or instead of the fresh fruit you could use fruits preserved in alcohol.

6–8 fresh figs	**a few flaked almonds**
4 slices of panettone	
1 tub of thick Greek	
yogurt	

1 Wash and slice the figs, then arrange them on individual plates with a slice of panettone, a good dollop of Greek yogurt and a few flaked almonds.
SERVES 4

CINNAMON TOAST WITH HONEYED APPLES

Rather like an apple charlotte, this is a pleasant combination of crisp, sugary cinnamon toast and buttery apple slices. The recipe also works well with pears instead of apples, and white bread rather than brown. Some chilled thick yogurt or pouring cream makes a good accompaniment.

2 sweet, mellow eating	**2–4 tbls demerara**
apples, such as Cox's	**sugar**
butter	**ground cinnamon**
2 tbls honey	
2–4 slices of white	
bread	

1 Peel the apples, cut them into quarters, remove the cores, then cut each quarter into thin slices.
2 Heat a little butter in a saucepan and add the apples and honey. Cook, uncovered, over a gentle heat, until the apple slices have softened, about 3–4 minutes, stirring gently from time to time.

3 Meanwhile, make the cinnamon toast: toast the bread on both sides – don't get it too brown and crisp. Remove the crusts if you like, then butter the toast. Cover each slice evenly with demerara sugar and sprinkle with cinnamon.
4 Put the toast under the grill for 1–2 minutes until the sugar has melted a bit to make a crisp coating. Cut into fingers or triangles.
5 Spoon the apple slices on to a small plate and arrange the cinnamon toast around them.
SERVES 2

CROISSANT WITH CREAM AND BLACK CHERRY CONSERVE

Unless a croissant is superb in flavour and texture, I think that halving and grilling it is by far the nicest way to serve it – either with butter or with a sweet or savoury filling. Here, a combination of three of my favourite foods makes an indulgent occasional treat.

1 croissant	**a little icing sugar**
1–2 tbls black cherry	**(optional)**
conserve	
1–2 tbls thick double	
cream, crème fraîche	
or soured cream	

1 Slice the croissant in half horizontally. Grill on both sides until crisp and lightly browned.
2 Spread the bottom half with black cherry conserve, cover with the cream, then replace the top half of the croissant.
3 Sift a little icing sugar over, if you like.
SERVES 1

OPPOSITE: *(left) Panettone with Fresh Figs, (top) Croissant with Cream and Black Cherry Conserve, (right) Cinnamon Toast with Honeyed Apples*

EGGS, CHEESE & DAIRY FOODS

These foods are easy to turn into a quick feast, with dishes such as Tortilla, Spinach and Stilton Crêpes, Haloumi with Spiced Leeks or Chocolate Amaretti Pudding. Cheese is perfect for simple instant meals – see No-Cook Cheese Feasts for ideas – and yogurt, soft cheeses and cream form the basis of quick and easy desserts. Dairy products do contain fat, but used in moderation and balanced with vegetables, fruit and cereals they definitely have a place in a healthy, fast-food diet.

OMELETTES
✳

SUN-DRIED TOMATO AND HERB OMELETTE

2 eggs
4 sun-dried tomatoes
in oil, drained
2 tbls chopped fresh
herbs, such as chervil,
chives and parsley

salt and freshly
ground black pepper
15g / ½ oz butter

If you are making a sweet soufflé omelette, for a flashy finish fill the omelette with your chosen mixture, fold it in half, then sift 2 tablespoons of icing sugar over the top and caramelize the sugar by laying a red-hot skewer on top for a moment or two in a criss-cross pattern.

1 Break the eggs into a bowl and beat them lightly until just combined. Chop the sun-dried tomatoes and add to the eggs, together with the herbs. Season with salt and pepper.

2 Put a 15 cm/6 inch frying pan over a medium heat. When it is hot add the butter, turn the heat up and swirl the butter around – don't let it brown.

3 Pour in the eggs, tilting the pan to distribute them evenly, then, using a fork, draw the set edges towards the centre and let the liquid egg run to the edges. Repeat until the omelette is almost set.

4 Tilt the pan over a warmed plate, then fold the edge of the omelette over to the centre and let it fold over again on to the plate. Serve immediately.
SERVES 1

VARIATIONS

1 CHEESE AND HERB

Grate 40g/1½ oz Gruyère cheese and add half to the beaten eggs instead of the tomatoes. When the omelette is almost set, sprinkle the remaining cheese over the centre.

2 FRESH TOMATO

Skin, de-seed and chop 1 large tomato, warm it through in a little butter in a small pan and season. When the omelette is almost set, spoon the tomato over the centre. You could add some slivers of spring onion, or some fresh basil or other herbs, too, if you like. Turn out the omelette and serve dusted with finely grated fresh Parmesan cheese.

SOUFFLE OMELETTE

Halfway between a soufflé and an omelette (though far quicker to cook than a soufflé) a soufflé omelette makes a pleasant change and can be served with sweet or savoury fillings.

2 eggs, separated
salt and freshly
ground black pepper
(for a savoury
omelette)

15g / ½ oz butter

1 Heat the grill. Put the egg yolks into a bowl, add 2 tablespoons of water, and some seasoning if you're making a savoury omelette, and mix well.

2 Whisk the egg whites until they stand in stiff peaks, but don't let them get too dry. Stir a spoonful of beaten egg white into the yolks, then gently fold in the rest with a metal spoon.

3 Heat a 15 cm/6 inch frying pan over a moderate heat then put in the butter and tilt the pan so that the butter coats the sides. Pour the egg mixture into the pan and cook over a moderate heat for 1–2 minutes, until golden brown underneath. Put the pan under the grill for 1–2 minutes to brown the top of the omelette.

4 Cut across the centre of the omelette (don't cut right through it), spoon your chosen filling (see below) over one half, then fold over the other half. Lift the omelette out of the pan and serve.
SERVES 1

SAVOURY FILLINGS

1 ASPARAGUS

Boil or steam 2–4 asparagus spears until just tender then cut them into 2.5 cm/1 inch lengths.

2 PEPPER

Grill ½ red or yellow pepper, or a combination, until charred then peel off the skin and slice thinly.

3 MUSHROOM

Wash, dry and slice 50g/2oz mushrooms – any type, or a mixture – then sauté them in 15g/½ oz butter until they are tender and any liquid they produce has boiled away (this may take up to 15 minutes). Season with salt and pepper.

4 CHEESE

Mix 2 tablespoons of grated cheese with the egg yolks, then sprinkle another 2 tablespoons on top of the omelette just before you fold it. Gruyère or Parmesan, or a mixture, are good.

5 RATATOUILLE

Leftover ratatouille (see page 46) makes a very good filling; reheat gently, allowing 2 heaped tablespoons per omelette.

6 TRUFFLE

For a luxurious treat, put a few truffle shavings on top of the omelette before folding it.

7 PETITS POIS AND MINT

Cook 50g/2oz fresh or frozen petits pois in a little boiling water for 2 minutes. Drain, add a knob of butter and 2 teaspoons of chopped fresh mint.

SWEET FILLINGS

1 FRESH FRUIT

Any sweet, soft-textured fruit is good, such as blackberries or blueberries, sliced sweet ripe mango, or sliced banana with a sprinkling of cinnamon. Or use 50g/2oz strawberries or other red berries, sliced and sprinkled with sugar and 1 tablespoon of liqueur: try Cointreau with strawberries or kirsch with cherries.

2 JAM

Melt 1 tablespoon of jam in a small pan over a gentle heat – apricot or black cherry are especially good. You could also add a dash of liqueur.

3 PRESERVED FRUIT

Use 2 tablespoons of fruits preserved in liqueur, or coarsely chopped stem ginger.

TORTILLA

This simple Spanish omelette is wonderfully tasty and filling, and like all flat omelettes it can be eaten hot, warm or cold. Any that's left over is delicious the next day, reheated and served with a fresh tomato sauce or served hot or cold with salad.

900g / 2lb potatoes	*3 tbls olive oil*
1 large onion or 1	*salt and freshly ground*
bunch of spring	*black pepper*
onions	*6 eggs*

1 Half fill a saucepan with water and put it on the stove to heat up. Peel the potatoes, cut them into chunks about 1 cm/½ inch square then add them to the pan and boil for 6–8 minutes or until just tender. Drain and set aside.

2 Meanwhile, peel and chop the onion or trim and chop the spring onions. Heat 2 tablespoons of the olive oil in a 20 cm/8 inch frying pan then put in the onion. Cover and cook until tender: 7–8 minutes for the onion, 2–3 minutes for the spring onions.

3 Add the potatoes to the frying pan, stirring to mix all the ingredients together and adding some salt and pepper to taste. Leave the vegetables to cook gently while you beat the eggs with a little salt and pepper.

4 Pour the eggs into the frying pan. Cook the tortilla gently until it is lightly browned underneath and looks set on top, about 5–10 minutes.

5 Invert a large plate over the frying pan and turn the tortilla out on to it. Heat the remaining oil in the pan then slide the tortilla back in to cook the other side: this will take about 3–4 minutes. Serve cut into wedges.
SERVES 4

VARIATION

MIXED VEGETABLE TORTILLA

De-seed and chop 1 green pepper and fry it with the onion. Boil 125g/4oz frozen peas with the potatoes, adding them a couple of minutes before the end of the cooking time.

Tortilla makes a good appetizer, cut into small squares and accompanied by a spicy dipping sauce.

SWISS CHARD TORTILLA

6 eggs	salt and freshly
125g / 4oz cheese,	ground black pepper
grated (Parmesan,	3 tbls olive oil
Gruyère or a mixture)	225g / 8oz Swiss chard,
3–4 tbls chopped fresh	without stalks
basil or parsley	

1 Beat the eggs and stir in three quarters of the cheese, plus the herbs and some salt and pepper.

2 Heat 2 tablespoons of the olive oil in a large saucepan, put in the chard and stir-fry for 1–2 minutes until wilted. Be careful not to let it burn.

3 Heat the remaining oil in a 20 cm/8 inch frying pan and tip in the chard, spreading it over the pan – it will still be very springy and leafy. Then pour the eggs on top of the leaves. Check that the mixture isn't sticking to the bottom of the pan then cover and cook over the lowest possible heat for about 15 minutes, until set.

4 Heat the grill. Sprinkle the remaining cheese over the tortilla and place under the grill for 1–2 minutes to cook the top. Serve cut into wedges.
SERVES 4

SUMMER FRITTATA

225g / 8oz tender	2 tbls chopped fresh
asparagus spears	parsley
225g / 8oz courgettes	salt and freshly
8 sun-dried tomatoes	ground black pepper
in oil, drained	2 tbls olive oil
4 eggs	
25g / 1oz Parmesan	
cheese, grated	

OPPOSITE: (left) Cheese and Herb Omelette, page 40, (top) Mushroom Soufflé Omelette, page 41, (right) Vegetable Frittata with Mint Sauce

1 Trim the asparagus and cut the courgettes into 6 mm/¼ inch slices. Cook the vegetables in a little boiling water for a few minutes until tender but slightly crunchy. Drain immediately.

2 Heat the grill. Chop the sun-dried tomatoes. Whisk the eggs lightly, add the cheese, tomatoes and parsley and season with a little salt and pepper.

3 Heat the oil in a 20 cm/8 inch frying pan, add the vegetables then pour in the egg mixture. Cook for 4–5 minutes, until the bottom of the frittata is set and golden brown, then put the frying pan under the grill and leave for a further minute or two to set the top. Serve cut in half or in thick wedges.
SERVES 2

VEGETABLE FRITTATA WITH MINT SAUCE

225g / 8oz cauliflower	15g / ½ oz butter
1 carrot	
125g / 4oz petits pois	FOR THE MINT SAUCE
4 eggs	25g / 1oz mint
salt and freshly	1 tbls honey
ground black pepper	1 tbls wine vinegar

1 First make the mint sauce: wash the mint and remove any tough stems, then chop the leaves in a food processor or by hand and add the honey and vinegar. Put into a bowl to serve with the frittata.

2 Wash the cauliflower and cut it into florets then scrape and slice the carrot. Cook the vegetables in 5 cm/2 inches of boiling water for about 4 minutes, until just tender, then drain and return to the still-warm pan. Stir in the peas.

3 Heat the grill. Whisk the eggs lightly and season with salt and pepper.

4 Melt the butter in a 20 cm/8 inch frying pan, add the vegetables then pour in the eggs. Cook for 4–5 minutes, until set and golden brown underneath, then put under the grill for 1–2 minutes to set the top. Serve cut into wedges, with the mint sauce.
SERVES 2

You won't need the thick, juicy stalks from the chard for this recipe: these are excellent cooked in boiling water until just tender then served with butter and/or shavings of Parmesan, or in a light cheese sauce. If you can't get Swiss chard you can make the tortilla with spinach.

CREPES

✳

Any leftover crêpes freeze well: interleave them with non-stick paper and wrap in foil so that you can take them out singly. A stack of crêpes in the freezer makes any of these recipes practical for one person.

BASIC CREPE RECIPE

125g / 4oz plain flour – white or half white and half wholewheat
2 eggs
2 tbls oil or melted butter, plus extra for frying
300ml / ½ pint skimmed milk or milk and water

1 If you've got a liquidizer or food processor, put in the flour, eggs, oil or melted butter and milk and whizz to a batter. If not, put the flour into a bowl and beat in the eggs, oil or butter and about a third of the milk. Mix until smooth, then gradually beat in the rest of the milk. The batter should be the consistency of single cream.

2 Put a 15 cm/6 inch frying pan over a low heat and brush it with a little oil or melted butter: a good way to do this is with a pad of kitchen paper.

3 When the pan is hot enough to sizzle if a drop of water is flicked into it, pour in 2 tablespoons of batter and tilt the pan until the base is thinly coated.

4 Fry for 1–2 minutes until the top is set then, using a palette knife and your fingers, flip the crêpe over and cook the other side for a few seconds. Cook the remaining crêpes in the same way, brushing the pan with oil or butter between every couple of crêpes. As the crêpes are done, stack them up on a plate, cover them with another plate and keep them warm over a pan of steaming water.

SERVES 4

VARIATIONS

1 HERB CREPES

Add 2 tablespoons of chopped fresh herbs to the batter.

2 ORANGE OR LEMON CREPES

Add the grated rind of 1 orange or lemon and 1 tablespoon of caster sugar to the batter.

3 CHOCOLATE CREPES

Mix 1 tablespoon of cocoa powder and 1 tablespoon of caster sugar in with the batter ingredients.

SPINACH AND STILTON CREPES

crêpe batter (see above)
900g / 2lb fresh spinach
225g / 8oz Stilton cheese
salt and freshly ground black pepper

1 Make the crêpes as described above.

2 Wash the spinach, then cook it in a dry pan for about 7–10 minutes, until it is tender. Drain well.

3 Heat the grill. Crumble or grate the cheese and add half to the spinach, then season with salt and pepper. Spread a little of this mixture on to each crêpe and roll it up. Put the crêpes side by side in a shallow heatproof dish then sprinkle with the rest of the cheese.

4 Put the crêpes under the grill for a few minutes until the cheese on top has melted and everything is bubbling hot. Serve at once.

SERVES 4

VARIATION

CREPES WITH GARLIC AND HERB CREAM CHEESE

Mash 450g/1lb garlic and herb cream cheese with a little milk then spread this on the crêpes and roll them up loosely. Sprinkle with 50g/2oz finely grated Parmesan cheese and brown under the grill.

Crêpes are delicious wrapped around a tasty filling then sprinkled with cheese and browned quickly under the grill. If you have more time you could make a thin cheese sauce (see page 73) and pour this over the crêpes before grilling. Serve with a simple salad and a cooked vegetable for a satisfying meal.

OPPOSITE: *Crêpes Suzette with Mixed Berries, page 47*

RED CABBAGE, APPLE AND RAISIN CREPES

crêpe batter (see
   page 44)
450g / 1lb red cabbage
1 apple
2 tbls olive oil
1 onion, peeled and
   chopped

salt and freshly
   ground black pepper
50g / 2oz raisins
50g / 2oz Cheddar
   cheese, grated
soured cream
   (optional)

The red cabbage mixture can cook for longer than 15 minutes, if you've got time, and will just go on improving as long as it doesn't stick. If there's any over, it's lovely with baked potatoes and soured cream : in fact, it's almost worth making extra for this!

1   Make the crêpes as described on page 44.
2   Wash the red cabbage and shred it as finely as you can. Chop the apple. Heat the oil in a pan and put in the cabbage, apple and onion. Add a sprinkling of salt and the raisins, cover and cook for 10–15 minutes, until tender. Stir occasionally and add 1–2 tablespoons of water if the mixture starts to stick.
3   Season the cabbage mixture well, then spoon it on to the crêpes and roll them up. Put the crêpes side by side in a shallow heatproof dish then sprinkle over the grated cheese.
4   Put the crêpes under a hot grill for a few minutes until the cheese has melted and everything is bubbling hot. Serve at once, topped with a spoonful of soured cream, if you are using this.
SERVES 4

RATATOUILLE CREPES

herb crêpe batter (see
   page 44)
1 tbls olive oil
1 onion, peeled and
   chopped
1 red pepper
1 aubergine, about
   225–350g / 8–12oz

225g / 8oz courgettes
1 × 400g / 14oz can
   tomatoes
1 garlic clove, crushed
salt and freshly
   ground black pepper
50g / 2oz Parmesan
   cheese, finely grated

1   Make the crêpes as described on page 44.
2   Heat the oil in a pan, add the onion and start to cook this over a moderate heat.
3   Meanwhile, halve, de-seed and chop the red pepper and add this to the onion. Chop the aubergine and the courgettes, and add these to the pan. Finally add the garlic. Cover the pan and cook gently for 5 minutes.
4   Add the tomatoes and their juice, breaking them up with a spoon. Simmer for 15–20 minutes until all the vegetables are tender and the liquid has reduced. Season with salt and pepper then spoon this mixture on to the crêpes and roll them up. Put the crêpes side by side in a shallow heatproof dish then sprinkle over the Parmesan cheese.
5   Put the crêpes under a hot grill for a few minutes until the cheese has melted and everything is bubbling hot. Serve at once.
SERVES 4

VARIATION

CHILLI CREPES

These are nice served with some guacamole and soured cream, or a chopped avocado salad. Increase the amount of tomatoes to 450g/1lb and use a 425g/15oz can of red kidney beans, drained, instead of the courgettes. Cook as above, seasoning the mixture with a good pinch of chilli powder. Substitute Cheddar cheese for the Parmesan.

CHOCOLATE AND CHERRY CREPES

These are best made with fresh, ripe black cherries, which you need to stone. Wear rubber gloves so your nails don't get stained and use a cherry stoner or a sharp knife.

450g / 1lb ripe black
  cherries
caster sugar
dash of kirsch

chocolate crêpe batter
  (see page 44)
150ml / 5fl oz soured
  cream

1 Stone the cherries then put them into a bowl and sprinkle with a little sugar and a dash of kirsch.
2 Make the crêpes as described on page 44.
3 Spread the crêpes with the soured cream and top with the cherries. Roll them up, sprinkle with sugar and serve.
SERVES 4

CREPES SUZETTE WITH MIXED BERRIES

These are wonderful for a quick special pudding but I also like them as an unconventional light meal.

orange crêpe batter
  (see page 44)
125g / 4oz unsalted
  butter
150ml / 5fl oz freshly
  squeezed orange juice
grated rind of 1 orange
125g / 4oz caster sugar

4 tbls orange-
  flavoured liqueur
  such as Cointreau or
  Grand Marnier, or
  brandy
50g / 2oz redcurrants
  and blueberries

1 Make the crêpes as described on page 44, using melted butter to grease the frying pan.
2 Gently melt the unsalted butter in a large frying pan then add the orange juice and rind, sugar and half the liqueur or brandy. Heat this mixture gently.

3 Place one crêpe in the pan and cook for a few seconds to heat it through. Fold it in half then in half again to make a triangle and push it to the far side of the pan. Repeat this process with the remaining crêpes. Sprinkle the redcurrants and blueberries into the pan.
4 Put the remaining liqueur or brandy into a metal ladle or a small saucepan and warm it over the gas flame or hot plate. When it is tepid, set it alight with a match, standing well back and averting your face. Pour it over the crêpes and serve immediately.
SERVES 4

APPLE CREPES

Although sweet crêpes are usually served as a pudding, I rather like to have them occasionally as a light main course, instead of at the end of a meal when I feel too full to enjoy them. A pudding and a pot of black coffee make a pleasant meal occasionally!

orange crêpe batter
  (see page 44)
450g / 1lb sweet,
  mellow eating
  apples such as Cox's
15g / ½oz butter

2–3 tsp granulated
  sugar
50g / 2oz sultanas or
  raisins (optional)
a little caster sugar

1 Make the crêpes as described on page 44.
2 Peel and core the apples and slice them thinly. Melt the butter in a saucepan, add the apples and sugar, and the sultanas or raisins if you are using them, and stir to mix together. Cook, uncovered, over a low heat, stirring gently from time to time, for about 3–4 minutes or until the apples slices have softened.
3 Spoon this mixture on to the crêpes and roll them up. Sprinkle with a little caster sugar and serve immediately, perhaps with some crème fraîche.
SERVES 4

These crêpes are particularly delicious if you add to the apple mixture a good pinch of cinnamon and / or ground cloves or a splash of Calvados.

CHEESE SALADS

ROQUEFORT SALAD

1 oak-leaf lettuce
1 tbls rice vinegar
1 tbls olive oil
salt and freshly
  ground black pepper

1–2 tbls chopped fresh
  chives
100g / 3½ oz Roquefort
  cheese

1 Wash the lettuce and put the leaves in a salad spinner or colander to drain.
2 Put the rice vinegar, oil and some seasoning into a salad bowl and mix. Then put in the chives. Tear the lettuce roughly on top.
3 Cut or break the Roquefort into pieces and add to the bowl, then gently toss the salad to coat the leaves with dressing and distribute the ingredients.
SERVES 2

BROCCOLI, CHERRY TOMATO AND FETA SALAD

1 tbls olive oil
1 tbls rice vinegar
salt and freshly
  ground black pepper
225g / 8oz cherry
  tomatoes

4 spring onions
100g / 3½ oz feta cheese
450g / 1lb broccoli
a few sprigs of
  oregano

1 Put the oil, vinegar and some seasoning into a salad bowl. Halve the tomatoes, trim and chop the spring onions and put them in the bowl. Break the feta into rough chunks and add to the bowl, too.

OPPOSITE: *(left) Broccoli, Cherry Tomato and Feta Salad, (top) Warm Carrot and Goat's Cheese Salad, (right) Roquefort Salad*

2 Wash the broccoli and separate it into small florets. Peel and slice the stems. Cook, covered, in 2.5 cm/1 inch of boiling water for 4 minutes, then drain immediately into a sieve, pat dry with kitchen paper and add to the other ingredients in the bowl.
3 Tear the oregano over the top, mix gently and serve the salad at once, while it is still warm.
SERVES 2

WARM CARROT AND GOAT'S CHEESE SALAD

The idea for this came from an excellent quiche I ate at Stephen Bull's restaurant in London. I loved the combination of ingredients, which I have recreated as this salad, adding a thyme and honey vinaigrette.

200g / 7oz firm goat's
  cheese log
8 sun-dried tomatoes
  in oil, drained
450g / 1lb carrots
2 tbls oil from the sun-
  dried tomatoes
4 tsp clear honey

2 tbls balsamic
  vinegar
½ tsp dried thyme or
  1 tsp chopped fresh
  thyme
salt and freshly
  ground black pepper
sprigs of fresh thyme

1 Cut the goat's cheese into 6 mm/¼ inch dice and put it into a bowl. Chop the sun-dried tomatoes and add these to the bowl, too.
2 Scrape the carrots and slice them very thinly – the side of a grater or a mandolin is good for this. Cook in a little boiling water for 1 minute; drain, pat dry with kitchen paper and add to the bowl.
3 Add the oil, honey, vinegar, thyme, a little salt and a grinding or two of pepper and mix well. Garnish with the sprigs of thyme then serve at once, while the carrots are still warm.
SERVES 2–4

I like rice vinegar because it's light and sweet, so you can use less oil in the dressing and thus reduce the dreaded calories.

49

CHEESE DIP
WITH CRUDITES

In my experience this is very popular with children and teenagers – and a good way of encouraging them to eat more vegetables, since they can choose their favourite raw vegetables and salad ingredients to eat with it.

*about 350g / 12oz raw
    vegetables: sticks of
    cucumber, carrot and
    celery; small florets
    of cauliflower; cherry
    tomatoes, radishes,
    spring onions; crisp
    lettuce, etc.*
*50g / 2oz Cheddar or
    other hard cheese*

*25g / 1oz low-fat soft
    cheese or plain
    yogurt, or 2 tbls milk
    and 15g / ½ oz soft
    butter*
*freshly ground black
    pepper*

☐1 Prepare the vegetables, cutting them into pieces suitable for dipping.

☐2 Finely grate the cheese. Put it into a bowl with the soft cheese, yogurt, or milk and butter and beat them together until creamy.

☐3 Season with pepper, then spoon into a small dish and put this on a plate or into a shallow basket, surrounded by the vegetables. Or you can spoon the dip straight on to a plate and arrange the vegetables around it.
SERVES 1

A REALLY GOOD
PLOUGHMAN'S

A ploughman's lunch can be delicious, although in my experience the ones you get in pubs often aren't: hunks of boring bread and cheese, syrupy brown pickle, some tired lettuce and tomato, and a spoonful of synthetic-tasting coleslaw. But choose the cheese with care and serve it with good, warm bread, fresh, crisp salad and interesting pickles, and it's a feast.

*fresh, crusty bread,
    white, wholewheat
    or granary*
butter (optional)
*50–100g / 2–3½oz
    mature farmhouse
    Cheddar or Stilton
    cheese*

*crisp lettuce leaves
1 firm tomato, sliced
pickled onions or other
    pickle to taste*

☐1 Warm the bread, then cut or break it into thick slices and arrange it on a platter with the remaining ingredients. Serve with a glass of beer or cider.
SERVES 1

VARIATIONS

1 FRENCH PLOUGHMAN'S

Use good crusty French bread – either a baguette or French country bread – and a French cheese of your choice: Brie or a firm goat's cheese would be fine. Add a handful of black olives, some salad leaves such as lamb's lettuce or chicory, and plum tomatoes. Serve with French red country wine.

2 GREEK PLOUGHMAN'S

The basis of this variation is some crumbly, salty feta cheese and some Kalamata olives. Serve with soft, country-style bread and a tomato and onion salad, and drink some chilled white wine with it.

3 GERMAN PLOUGHMAN'S

Choose a dark rye bread, such as pumpernickel, and cheese flavoured with caraway or cumin seeds or paprika. Serve with pickled cucumbers.

GRILLED GOAT'S CHEESE SALAD

In fashionable circles this is now regarded as a bit of a has-been, but really it's a classic and so quick, as well as being one of my personal favourites. It's best if the goat's cheese log is the same width as the baguette.

125g / 4oz mixed salad leaves	125g / 4oz goat's cheese log
fresh herbs, if available; chervil is especially good	1 tsp balsamic vinegar
	1 tbls olive oil
2–4 thin slices of baguette	salt and freshly ground black pepper

1 Wash the salad leaves, shake them dry and put them into a bowl with some torn-up herbs, if you have them.

2 Lightly toast the baguette slices on one side under the grill.

3 Cut the goat's cheese into 2 or 4 slices and place on the untoasted side of the baguette, then put them under the grill until brown and bubbling.

4 Meanwhile, sprinkle the vinegar and oil over the salad with a little salt and pepper and toss the leaves. Cut the pieces of baguette in half, put them on top of the salad, and serve at once.

SERVES 1

NO-COOK CHEESE FEASTS

With the excellent cheeses, breads, fruit and vegetables that are now widely available, you can put together a wonderful feast that requires no cooking and hardly any preparation – just a bit of careful shopping. Here are some good combinations: you could serve one or several at a time, depending on the number of people. Some red or white wine (or fruit juice spritzers) would complete the spread. You need to allow about 125g/4oz cheese per person.

1 APPLES AND CHEDDAR

Choose really good apples with melting, sweet flesh – mature Cox's or Russets, for instance – and a good, mature farmhouse Cheddar. Some whole-wheat bread, especially the home-made, rather heavy, moist type, goes well with this.

2 VIGNOTTE OR CAMEMBERT AND GRAPES

This is a gorgeous combination, more like a pudding than a main course. Choose the best grapes available – perhaps a mixture of two colours – and some crumbly oatcakes.

3 PEAR WITH GORGONZOLA OR PECORINO

Buttery, sweet ripe pears – preferably Comice – with either Gorgonzola or Pecorino cheese, and perhaps some peppery watercress or rocket leaves and good plain Italian bread.

4 RICOTTA, BLUE CHEESE AND CELERY

Two contrasting cheeses and crisp, clean-tasting celery stalks make a good combination. Serve either warm, crusty bread or some thin crackers to accompany them.

5 INSALATA TRICOLORE

Slice some good-quality, water-packed Mozzarella cheese – preferably buffalo Mozzarella – and arrange it on a plate with sliced plum or beefsteak tomatoes, slices of ripe avocado tossed in lemon juice, and torn leaves of fresh basil. Serve this classic salad with warm Italian bread.

6 CREAM CHEESE WITH RIPE PINEAPPLE

The success of this depends more than anything on the quality of the pineapple. If you can get a really ripe, sweet, juicy one, it can be superb. Peel the pineapple, removing all the little tufts and the inner core, then cut it into chunks or slices and arrange on a plate with the cheese. You could use mascarpone or a cream cheese from the deli: both full-fat and lighter varieties are fine.

For an even quicker cheese salad that never seems to go out of fashion, mash 50g / 2 oz blue cheese with 4 tablespoons of yogurt or soured cream, season to taste then spoon on top of little gem lettuces, cut into quarters.

Pineapples are usually ready to eat when they smell slightly syrupy and one of the inner leaves pulls out easily.

FRIED, MELTED & GRILLED CHEESE

✳

HALOUMI WITH SPICED LEEKS

Moist, tender leeks spiced up with cumin seed and the sharp tang of lime make a delicious base for crisp slices of haloumi cheese. Serve this with a salad, bread or rice. Basmati rice will cook quickly while you're preparing the haloumi mixture.

Haloumi is an unusual cheese because it is very firm and keeps its shape well when grilled or fried. Read the packet to make sure you're getting a vegetarian one. Unopened, it keeps for ages in the fridge and for even longer in the freezer.

700g / 1½ lb tender leeks, trimmed to give 450g / 1lb	*2 tbls olive oil*
	½ tsp cumin seeds
225g / 8oz haloumi cheese	*juice of 1 lime*
	salt and freshly ground black pepper

1 Slice the leeks fairly finely. Cut the cheese into slices about 8 mm/⅓ inch thick then cut each slice in half to make squarish pieces.

2 Heat the oil in a frying pan, put in the cheese and fry for 1–2 minutes until golden brown on one side, then flip the pieces over and fry the other side. This whole process only takes 2–3 minutes.

3 Drain the cheese on kitchen paper and leave on one side.

4 Put the leeks into the frying pan and stir-fry for about 5 minutes or until they are just tender. Then add the cumin seeds and stir for a moment or two longer. Add the lime juice and season with salt and pepper.

5 Put the cheese back into the pan with the leeks and heat through for a few minutes. Serve on warm plates.

SERVES 2

HALOUMI AND COURGETTES WITH TOMATO SALSA

225g / 8oz tomatoes	*350g / 12oz courgettes*
½ onion, peeled and chopped	*225g / 8oz haloumi cheese*
2 tbls chopped fresh coriander	*3 tbls olive oil*
salt and freshly ground black pepper	

1 First make the salsa: pour boiling water over the tomatoes, leave for a few seconds, then drain and cover with cold water. Slip off the skins with a sharp knife then chop the tomatoes and put them into a bowl. Add the onion, coriander and some salt and pepper to taste.

2 Wash and thinly slice the courgettes. Cut the cheese into slices about 8 mm/⅓ inch thick then cut each slice in half to make squarish pieces.

3 Heat 2 tablespoons of the oil in a frying pan, put in the courgettes and fry for 3–4 minutes or until they are tender and golden brown in patches. Then remove them from the pan and keep them warm.

4 Heat the remaining oil in the pan, put in the cheese and fry for 1–2 minutes, until it is golden brown on one side. Then flip the pieces over and fry the other side. This whole process only takes 2–3 minutes.

5 Put the courgettes back in the pan, mix with the haloumi and turn gently to make sure everything is really hot. Serve on to plates and top with the salsa.

SERVES 2

OPPOSITE: *Haloumi with Spiced Leeks*

DEEP-FRIED CAMEMBERT

If you're just making this for one or two people the cheese can be fried in a medium saucepan in a relatively small amount of oil, saving the hassle of using a deep-fryer. Serve on top of some green salad leaves, if you like; the combination of hot, melted cheese and cool, crisp leaves is particularly good. I like some sweet mango chutney or apricot jam with it, too.

1 box of Camembert cheese triangles, chilled in the fridge
1 egg, beaten with 1 tbls water

dried breadcrumbs for coating
oil for deep-frying

1. Dip the pieces of Camembert into the beaten egg, then into the crumbs to coat them. Repeat the process so that they are really well coated then chill them in the fridge while you heat the oil.

2. Half-fill a saucepan with oil and heat it. Test the temperature by dipping a wooden chopstick or the handle of a wooden spoon into it: the oil should immediately form bubbles around it.

3. Put in the pieces of Camembert and fry for 4–5 minutes, until they are crisp and golden brown. Remove them with a draining spoon and put them on crumpled kitchen paper to absorb excess oil. Serve immediately.

SERVES 2

CHEESE FONDUE

Cheese fondue is very quick to make. It can be served from the pan without using a fondue burner, or simply poured over crusty warm bread, though I think it's more fun to eat if you dip the bread into it. You can make fondue for one person but it's more enjoyable when you're sharing it.

1 French stick
1 garlic clove, halved
225g / 8oz Edam or Emmenthal cheese
150ml / 5fl oz dry white wine or cider

2 tsp cornflour
1 tsp lemon juice
salt and freshly ground black pepper
freshly grated nutmeg

1. Cut or break the bread into bite-sized pieces, spread them out on a baking sheet or heatproof dish and put them under a not-too-hot grill to warm.

2. Rub the garlic around the inside of a medium-sized saucepan, then discard it. Grate the cheese.

3. Put all but 1 tablespoon of the wine or cider into the saucepan, add the cheese and bring just to the boil – the cheese will look like a lumpy mess at this stage but don't worry.

4. Blend the cornflour with the remaining wine or cider then pour this into the cheese mixture, stirring vigorously over the heat. The mixture will thicken and become smooth.

5. Remove from the heat and add the lemon juice and some salt, pepper and grated nutmeg to taste. Serve at once with the warm bread, and have long forks available so that you can spear pieces of bread and dip them into the fondue in the pan.

SERVES 2

You can vary the fondue by using different cheeses; try Cheddar and light ale for a very British flavour, or blue cheese with cider or a fruity white wine.

GRILLED BRIE WITH ALMONDS

This is very easy and makes a good quick meal served with a crisp leafy salad or a tomato salad.

225–350g / 8–12oz Brie
25g / 1oz flaked
  almonds

1 Slice the Brie, including the rind, and arrange it in a shallow layer in a heatproof dish.
2 Place the dish under a hot grill for about 5–7 minutes, until the Brie has begun to melt, then sprinkle the almonds evenly on top and grill for a few more minutes, until the nuts have toasted. Watch it carefully because they will burn quickly. Serve at once.
SERVES 2

GRILLED FETA WITH OLIVES

This quick supper dish needs to be served with plenty of soft, plain bread – no butter – and some salad leaves.

225g / 8oz feta cheese   50g / 2oz large green
50g / 2oz black olives,   olives
  preferably Kalamata

1 Heat the grill. Cut the feta cheese into cubes and put them into a shallow heatproof dish. Add the olives, distributing them amongst the cheese.
2 Heat under the grill for about 5 minutes, or until the feta is melting and has become golden brown in places. Serve at once.
SERVES 2

CHEESY TOMATO GRILL

A good recipe for when you're on a diet or watching your fat intake. You can leave the Parmesan out if you want to reduce the fat and calories even further, but it is only a very small amount and it does add a lot of flavour. Peppery salad ingredients such as watercress or rocket go well with this, or some quickly steamed broccoli or French beans.

1 beefsteak tomato   15g / ½ oz fresh
salt and freshly   Parmesan cheese, cut
  ground black pepper   into slivers or grated
a few fresh basil
  leaves
125g / 4oz very-low-
  fat cottage cheese,
  plain or with chives
  and/or onion

1 Heat the grill. Slice the tomato into thick rounds. Place these in a shallow ovenproof dish in a single layer, season with salt and pepper and tear over some basil leaves.
2 Spoon the cottage cheese evenly over the tomato, then sprinkle with the Parmesan cheese.
3 Grill for about 10 minutes, or until everything is heated through and the top is golden brown.
SERVES 1

PUDDINGS WITH CHEESE, CREAM & YOGURT

✳

This is a very quick chocolate pudding, consisting of a biscuity base with a light, creamy chocolate topping. You can eat it almost immediately or leave it overnight – it just gets better all the time! It's a useful emergency pudding because the ingredients are so simple, but it is essential that you use good-quality plain chocolate.

CHOCOLATE AMARETTI PUDDING

300g / 10oz plain chocolate, at least 50% cocoa solids
25g / 1oz butter
125g / 4oz amaretti biscuits
200ml / 7fl oz single cream
½ tsp finely grated orange rind
strands of orange rind to decorate

1 First make a start on the topping: break 200g/7oz of the chocolate into pieces and put them into a deep bowl set over a pan of steaming water. Leave until the chocolate has melted then remove the bowl from the pan and stand it in a bowl of cold water to cool it down quickly.

2 While the chocolate is melting, make the base, but first draw a potato peeler down the length of the remaining chocolate to make a few chocolate curls for decorating the pudding: keep these on one side. Break the rest of the chocolate into pieces, put them into a medium saucepan with the butter and melt over a very low heat.

3 Crush the amaretti biscuits then remove the chocolate mixture from the heat and stir in the biscuit crumbs until they are well coated.

4 Put a 17.5–20 cm/7–8 inch plain flan ring on a plate and spoon the crumb mixture into it, pressing it down firmly with the back of a spoon. Put it in a cool place (I put mine in the freezer).

5 Now pour the cream into the bowl of melted chocolate, add the grated orange rind and whisk until thick and pale. This will only take a few minutes if the mixture is cold enough: if it takes longer, put it in the fridge or freezer for a few minutes.

6 Spoon the chocolate cream on to the base, taking it right to the edges and smoothing the top with the back of the spoon. You can serve it almost immediately or refrigerate it. Run a knife around the edges and remove the flan ring, neatening the edges with the knife – the longer you leave it the easier it will be to turn out. Decorate the top with the reserved chocolate curls and the orange strands before serving. It's nice as it is, or with some extra single cream, or with cream lightly whipped with 1 tablespoon of rum, brandy or Amaretto liqueur.
SERVES 4–6

GREEK YOGURT WITH FRESH DATES

This is my slightly adapted version of one of Prue Leith's ideas. As she says, the better the quality of the ingredients you use, the better the pudding will be.

50g / 2oz almonds
225g / 8oz fresh dates
450g / 1lb thick Greek yogurt
4 tbls thick cream
4 tbls clear honey such as acacia

1 First skin the almonds: put them into a small saucepan, cover with water and boil for 1 minute. Then remove from the heat, drain, and pop the nuts out of their skins. Chop them roughly.

2 Stone the dates and chop them roughly.

3 Put a few dates in the bottom of four glass bowls. Put 2 good heaped tablespoons of yogurt into each bowl then put the rest of the dates on top. Spoon the cream on top, then drizzle the honey over that and finally sprinkle over the chopped almonds.
SERVES 4

OPPOSITE: *(left) Chocolate Amaretti Pudding, (centre) Ricotta Cream with Crystallized Fruit, page 58, (right) Greek Yogurt with Fresh Dates*

RICOTTA CREAM WITH CRYSTALLIZED FRUIT

This is a nice pudding to make when there is some colourful crystallized fruit available. Vanilla sugar is easy to make, but if you haven't got any, use ordinary caster sugar and a few drops of real vanilla extract.

175g / 6oz mixed crystallized fruit	175g / 6oz ricotta cheese
2 tbls Marsala wine	1 tbls single cream
50g / 2oz almonds	1 tbls vanilla sugar

1 Cut the crystallized fruit into fairly small pieces. Put them into a bowl and add the Marsala.

2 Put the almonds into a small saucepan, cover with water and boil for 1 minute. Then remove from the heat, drain, and pop the nuts out of their skins. Stir them into the fruit mixture.

3 Put the ricotta into a bowl and mix in the cream and vanilla sugar. Leave in a cool place until you want to serve the pudding. Stir the fruit again.

4 To serve, divide the ricotta mixture between two plates then spoon the fruit on to the plates.
SERVES 2

MASCARPONE LEMON CREAM

The lemon cuts the richness of the mascarpone in this delectable and easy pudding.

225g / 8oz mascarpone cheese	25–50g / 1–2oz sugar slivers of lemon rind to decorate
rind and juice of ½ lemon	

1 Put the mascarpone cheese into a bowl with the lemon rind and juice and mix until smooth.

2 Mix in sugar to taste then spoon into dishes and decorate with slivers of lemon rind.
SERVES 2–3

A zester, which is inexpensive to buy, is invaluable for producing long strands of citrus rind quickly and easily.

COFFEE RICOTTA PUDDING

Ricotta is a medium-fat cheese, so this isn't very calorific; you could make it even less so by using a low-fat soft cheese, if you wish. A really good-quality instant espresso coffee will give this the best flavour.

225g / 8oz ricotta cheese	chocolate-covered coffee beans, flakes of chocolate or toasted flaked almonds to decorate
1 tsp instant espresso coffee	
25–50g / 1–2oz sugar	

1 Put the ricotta cheese into a bowl and break it up with a spoon.

2 Dissolve the coffee in 1 tablespoon of hot water and add it to the ricotta, then add sugar to taste.

3 Mix until everything is well blended, then spoon into individual dishes and decorate with chocolate-covered coffee beans, a few flakes of chocolate or some toasted flaked almonds.
SERVES 2

YOGURT BRULEE

This can be as rich or as low in fat as you wish, depending on the type of yogurt you use and whether you add any cream. In any case, the crisp topping, which you have to smash with your spoon before eating the yogurt, makes it special.

300ml / ½ pint plain yogurt, or 150ml / 5fl oz plain yogurt and 150ml / 5fl oz double or whipping cream	75g / 3oz caster sugar, plus extra to sweeten if desired

1 If you are using cream, whisk this until thick then fold in the yogurt. Sweeten to taste with a little sugar if you wish, remembering that the topping will add sweetness.

2   Spoon the yogurt or yogurt and cream into two ramekins, leaving some space at the top.

3   Put the caster sugar into a small saucepan and heat gently until it has turned to syrup and become golden brown – don't let it get too dark. Then immediately pour it over the yogurt. It will set hard within a few minutes; chill until needed.

SERVES 2

LIME CHEESECAKE

This is astonishingly quick to make, though it won't come to any harm if you keep it, well covered, in the fridge for several hours or even overnight. Some single cream and/or fresh fruit go well with it.

50g / 2oz butter	50g / 2oz caster sugar
175g / 6oz digestive biscuits	150ml / 5fl oz double cream
225g / 8oz low-fat soft white cheese	thin slices of lime or slivers of rind and a few crushed pistachio nuts to decorate
grated rind and juice of ½ lime	

1   First make the cheesecake base: melt the butter in a saucepan over a gentle heat; crush the biscuits into crumbs. Stir the biscuit crumbs into the butter, off the heat, until they are well coated.

2   Put a 20 cm/8 inch plain flan ring on a plate and spoon in the crumbs, pressing down with the back of the spoon. Put it in a cold place while you make the topping (I put mine in the freezer).

3   Put the soft cheese into a bowl with the lime rind and juice, sugar and double cream. Stir vigorously for 1–2 minutes, until very thick.

4   Spoon the filling on top of the base, taking it right to the edges. Decorate with lime slices or rind and pistachio nuts. You can serve it almost immediately, as it sets quickly, or leave it in the fridge. Run a knife around the edges and remove the flan ring, neatening the edges with the knife.

SERVES 4

QUICK CHOCOLATE WHIP

This can be whipped together in a few minutes and is a real treat, served in small glasses with some light, crisp biscuits.

300g / 10oz plain chocolate, at least 50% cocoa solids	flakes of plain chocolate
300 ml / ½ pint single cream	

1   Break the chocolate into pieces and put it into a deep bowl set over a pan of steaming water. Leave until the chocolate has melted then remove the bowl from the pan and put it in a cool place or in a bowl of cold water to cool it down quickly.

2   When the chocolate has cooled a little, pour in the single cream, which will cool it down further. Then whisk until the mixture gets thick and pale. This will only take a few minutes if the mixture is cold enough; if it takes longer, put it in the fridge or freezer for a few minutes.

3   Spoon the thick chocolate whip into glasses, decorate with the chocolate flakes and keep in the fridge or a cool place until required.

SERVES 4

VARIATION

1   RUM AND RAISIN CHOCOLATE WHIP

Before you start making the whip, put 50g/2 oz raisins into a small bowl, cover with 2 tablespoons of rum and leave to plump up. Divide the raisins and any liquid that hasn't been absorbed between 4 glasses, then spoon the chocolate mixture on top.

To clean a pan in which sugar syrup has been made, leave the pan to cool then fill it with water and bring to the boil: this will dissolve the hard, sticky coating, making the pan easy to clean.

To crush biscuits, put them into a large polythene bag and roll with a rolling pin.

PASTA

As long as you have a packet of pasta in the
cupboard you can always rustle up a quick meal:
pasta is good even when served simply with just
olive oil or butter. If you add a few more
ingredients and make sure you have plenty of
different pasta shapes in your storecupboard, the
scope is enormous. Dishes such as Quick
Mediterranean Pasta, Fusilli with Fennel and
Mangetout, Spinach Tagliatelle with Walnuts and
Fettuccine with Asparagus Sauce can all be made
within 30 minutes, and they need little
accompaniment – perhaps a simple salad or some
bread – to make a satisfying meal.

TOMATO SAUCES
✳

QUICK MEDITERRANEAN PASTA

I like this with some full-bodied red wine and a leafy salad containing rocket – some supermarket salad mixes include it. Dress the salad with 2 teaspoons of red wine vinegar, 2 tablespoons of olive oil and some seasoning, and serve with the pasta.

1 tbls oil from the sun-dried tomatoes
1 onion, peeled and chopped
2 garlic cloves, crushed
1 × 400g / 14oz can tomatoes
8 sun-dried tomatoes in oil, drained
½ × 400g / 14oz can artichoke hearts
50g / 2oz black olives
salt and freshly ground black pepper
225g / 8oz penne rigate or rigatoni
6 fresh basil leaves
fresh Parmesan cheese, cut into slivers (optional)

Fresh Parmesan cheese (Parmigiano Reggiano) sold in a piece has the best flavour and can be found in specialist Italian shops and supermarkets. Vegetarian Parmesan is available : ask at the cheese counter.

1 First fill a saucepan with 2 litres/3½ pints of water and bring to the boil for the pasta.

2 Meanwhile, heat the oil in a saucepan then add the onion, cover and cook gently for 10 minutes, until tender but not brown. Stir in the garlic and cook for 1–2 minutes longer.

3 Add the tomatoes, together with their juice, breaking them up with a wooden spoon. Chop the sun-dried tomatoes and add these to the pan too. Simmer for about 10–15 minutes, until the liquid has evaporated. Meanwhile, drain and slice the artichoke hearts and add these to the sauce along with the olives and plenty of salt and pepper.

4 When the water boils, add the pasta and let it bubble away, uncovered, for about 8 minutes or until it is *al dente*. Drain the pasta, return it to the pan and season with some salt; then add the sauce and stir so that all the pasta gets coated.

5 Tear the basil over the pasta, then serve topped with slivers of Parmesan cheese, if you like.
SERVES 2

Al dente means tender but still firm, with some 'bite' to it.

SPAGHETTI WITH ROASTED PEPPER AND TOMATO SAUCE

Roasted red pepper and sun-dried tomatoes give this a mellow, slightly sweet flavour; a leafy salad and some shavings of fresh Parmesan go perfectly with it.

1 red pepper
225g / 8oz spaghetti
1 onion, peeled and chopped
1 tbls oil from the sun-dried tomatoes
1–2 garlic cloves, crushed
1 × 400g / 14oz can tomatoes
4 sun-dried tomatoes in oil, drained
salt and freshly ground black pepper
fresh Parmesan cheese, cut into slivers

1 Cut the pepper into quarters, put it on a grill pan cut-side down and grill under a high heat for about 10 minutes, until charred and blistered in places. Remove from the heat, cool slightly then peel off the skin and discard the stem and seeds.

2 Fill a saucepan with 2 litres/3½ pints of water and bring to the boil, then add the spaghetti and cook, uncovered, for about 8 minutes, until *al dente*.

3 Meanwhile, cook the onion gently in the oil for 10 minutes, until tender but not brown. Add the garlic and cook for 1–2 minutes longer, then stir in the canned tomatoes and their juice, breaking them up with a wooden spoon. Chop the sun-dried tomatoes and add these to the pan too. Simmer for about 10–15 minutes, until the liquid has evaporated.

4 Either put the sauce into a food processor with the red pepper and whizz to a purée, or chop the pepper and stir it into the sauce. Season well. Drain the pasta, return it to the saucepan and add some salt, then stir in the sauce so that all the pasta gets coated. Serve topped with slivers of Parmesan.
SERVES 2

OPPOSITE: *Quick Mediterranean Pasta*

PENNE WITH CHILLI, TOMATO AND MUSHROOM SAUCE

The chilli gives this sauce a kick while a splash of cream cools it down a bit, making a nice balance – though you could leave out either of them and the sauce would still be good.

225g / 8oz button mushrooms	225g / 8oz penne
1 green chilli	4 tbls cream
1 tbls oil	salt and freshly ground black pepper
1 onion, peeled and chopped	fresh Parmesan cheese, grated
1 garlic clove, crushed	
1 × 400g / 14oz can tomatoes	

1 First fill a saucepan with 2 litres/3½ pints of water and bring to the boil for the pasta.

2 Meanwhile, slice the mushrooms and halve, de-seed and chop the chilli. Fry them in the oil in a large saucepan, along with the onion and garlic, for about 10 minutes, until softened but not brown.

3 Stir in the tomatoes and their juice, breaking them up with a wooden spoon, then simmer for 10–15 minutes, until the liquid has evaporated.

4 When the water boils, add the pasta and let it bubble away, uncovered, for about 8 minutes or until it is *al dente*. Meanwhile, stir the cream into the sauce and season it with salt and pepper.

5 Drain the pasta, return it to the still-warm saucepan and season with some salt. Then add the sauce and stir so that all the pasta gets coated. Serve out on to warm plates and hand round fresh Parmesan cheese separately.

SERVES 2

VARIATION

PENNE WITH PIQUANT SAUCE

This is a lively dish, particularly good on a chilly night. Cook the pasta and make the tomato sauce as above, but omit the mushrooms, chilli and cream. Instead, when the sauce is cooked, add 50g/2oz black olives, stoned and chopped, 1 tablespoon of capers, and a good pinch each of chilli powder and cayenne pepper. Season with salt and pepper and add more chilli or cayenne, if necessary. Serve with grated Parmesan.

FETTUCCINE WITH FRESH TOMATO SAUCE

This is at its best in the summer when made from flavourful fresh tomatoes.

1 tbls olive oil	salt and freshly ground black pepper
1 onion, peeled and chopped	6–8 fresh basil leaves
450g / 1lb fresh tomatoes	fresh Parmesan cheese, grated (optional)
1 garlic clove, crushed	
225g / 8oz fettuccine or other delicate pasta	

1 First fill a saucepan with 2 litres/3½ pints of water and bring to the boil for the pasta.

2 Next start making the sauce: heat the oil in a large saucepan then add the onion, cover and cook gently for 10 minutes, until tender but not brown.

3 Meanwhile, put the tomatoes in a bowl, cover with boiling water and leave for a few seconds until the skins loosen. Drain, cover with cold water and slip off the skins. Chop the tomatoes roughly, removing any hard bits of core.

4 Stir the garlic into the onion and cook for 1–2 minutes longer, then stir in the tomatoes and leave to cook, uncovered, for about 10–15 minutes, until the sauce is thick with no trace of wateriness.

5 When the water boils, add the fettuccine and let it bubble away, uncovered, for about 8 minutes or until it is *al dente*. Drain the pasta, return it to the pan and add the sauce. Season very well then mix together and tear the basil leaves over. Serve at once, with fresh Parmesan cheese if you like.

SERVES 2

Some supermarkets now sell tomatoes that are 'grown for flavour' – why can't this apply to them all? – and these are worth trying. Shiny red plum tomatoes are usually a good bet too.

LIGHT PASTA DISHES

PENNE WITH GRILLED PEPPERS AND ROCKET

Grilled peppers, so moist and tender and sweet, make an excellent contrast to firm pasta, and the peppery rocket adds the final touch. If you can't get rocket, use some fresh basil leaves instead but add them straight to the cooked pasta; don't wilt them in the hot oil first.

1 large red pepper	salt and freshly
1 large yellow pepper	ground black pepper
small handful of	1 garlic clove, crushed
rocket	fresh Parmesan cheese,
175g / 6oz penne, or	cut into slivers
similar-shaped pasta	(optional)
2 tbls olive oil	

1. First prepare the peppers: cut them into quarters, put them on a grill pan cut-side down and grill under a high heat until the skin has charred and blistered in places – this will take about 10 minutes and the pieces may need turning to make sure they grill evenly. When they are done, remove them from the heat and cover with a damp tea towel to cool them down and help loosen the skin.
2. Next fill a saucepan with 2 litres/3½ pints of water and bring to the boil for the pasta.
3. Wash the rocket but don't chop it. Strip the skin off the peppers with a sharp knife, discard the stems and seeds and cut the flesh into long, thin pieces.
4. When the water boils, add the pasta to the pan then let it bubble away, uncovered, for about 8 minutes or until it is *al dente*. Drain the pasta, return it to the still-warm saucepan and gently mix in 1 tablespoon of the oil and some salt to taste. Cover and keep warm.
5. Heat the remaining oil in another pan and put in the garlic, rocket and peppers; stir-fry for 1–2 minutes until everything is heated through, then tip the whole lot in with the pasta and toss well to combine. Check the seasoning and add some coarsely ground black pepper, then serve out on to warm plates and top with some slivers of Parmesan cheese if you wish.

SERVES 2

PASTA WITH PESTO

Pasta with pesto is delicious, and very quick to prepare using ready-made pesto. However, if you have a food processor you can easily whizz up your own. I like to use a long pasta such as spaghetti or tagliatelle and to serve it with a simple tomato and lettuce salad with a vinaigrette dressing.

225g / 8oz pasta	4 tbls olive oil
50g / 2oz fresh basil	salt and freshly
25g / 1oz fresh	ground black pepper
Parmesan cheese,	fresh Parmesan cheese,
grated	grated, to serve
25g / 1oz pine nuts	

1. Fill a saucepan with 2 litres/3½ pints of water and put it on the stove to heat up for the pasta. When the water boils, add the pasta to the pan then let it bubble away, uncovered, for about 8 minutes or until it is *al dente*.
2. While the pasta is cooking, make the pesto: wash the basil and remove any large stems then put the leaves into a food processor or liquidizer along with the grated Parmesan cheese, pine nuts and olive oil. Whizz together briefly to make a bright green sauce.
3. Drain the pasta then put it back into the still-warm pan. Add the pesto, season well, then serve out on to warmed plates and hand round extra Parmesan cheese.

SERVES 2

PAPPARDELLE WITH PORCINI

Pappardelle is a particularly satisfying pasta – thick ribbons that you can really get your teeth into – and in this recipe it picks up the delicious flavour of the porcini mushrooms. Some extra shavings of fresh Parmesan make a nice finishing touch.

Dried porcini mushrooms – or ceps if you get the French ones – can be bought in tiny packets and are now stocked by some large supermarkets. They can be used on their own or added to mushroom mixtures to intensify the flavour.

1 × 10–15g / ¼ –½ oz packet of dried porcini mushrooms	salt and freshly ground black pepper fresh Parmesan cheese, cut into slivers
225g / 8oz pappardelle	
25g / 1oz butter	

1 Put the porcini into a small bowl and cover with boiling water. Leave on one side to soak.

2 Next fill a saucepan with 2 litres/3½ pints of water and bring it to the boil. Add the pasta to the pan, then let it bubble away, uncovered, for about 8 minutes or until it is *al dente*.

3 Just before the pasta is ready, drain the porcini through a sieve lined with a piece of kitchen paper or muslin and placed over a bowl. Chop the porcini finely, then put them into a small saucepan with their soaking liquid and boil for a few minutes until almost all the liquid has gone.

4 Drain the pasta then put it back into the still-warm pan with the butter, the porcini and some salt and pepper to taste. Mix gently, then serve out on to warmed plates and top with slivers of fresh Parmesan cheese.

SERVES 2

PASTA WITH FRESH HERBS

There are some excitingly flavoured pastas around and these are fun to try for a change, although I must say they often look much more exotic than they taste. They are most effective when served simply. A flavoured pasta – or a combination of two or three – is ideal in this recipe, although it is also delicious with plain pasta. Choose the herbs to complement the flavour of the pasta: basil for tomato; parsley and/or chives for mushroom; basil, parsley or chives for spinach; dill for beetroot; mixed herbs or perhaps something assertive like tarragon for plain pasta.

225g / 8oz pasta – perhaps a flavoured one, or two or three different colours	25g / 1oz butter salt and freshly ground black pepper fresh Parmesan cheese, grated (optional)
bunch of fresh herbs	

1 First fill a saucepan with 2 litres/3½ pints of water and bring to the boil. Add the pasta to the pan then let it bubble away, uncovered, for about 8 minutes or until it is *al dente*.

2 While the pasta is cooking, wash and chop the herbs – you need about 4 tablespoons.

3 Drain the pasta then put it back into the still-warm pan with the butter, herbs and some salt and pepper to taste. Mix gently, then serve out on to warmed plates, with fresh Parmesan if you wish.

SERVES 2

SUMMER SPAGHETTI WITH AVOCADO

This is good served with some hot garlic bread and a leafy summer salad.

450g / 1lb tomatoes	1 avocado
175g / 6oz spaghetti	lemon juice
2 tbls olive oil	6–8 large basil leaves
1 garlic clove, crushed	freshly grated
salt and freshly ground black pepper	Parmesan cheese (optional)

1 First fill a saucepan with 2 litres/3½ pints of water and bring it to the boil for the pasta.

2 Put the tomatoes into a bowl, cover with boiling water and leave for a few seconds until the skins split. Drain, cover with cold water and slip off the skins with a sharp knife. Chop the tomatoes roughly, removing any hard bits of core.

3 When the water boils, add the spaghetti and cook, uncovered, for about 8 minutes, until *al dente*.

4 Heat the oil in a large saucepan, add the garlic and cook over a moderate heat for 1–2 minutes. Add the chopped tomatoes and salt and pepper to taste and heat gently, just to warm through. Peel, stone and chop the avocado and toss it in a little lemon juice.

5 Drain the pasta and return it to the still-warm saucepan. Add the tomato mixture and the avocado and toss well to mix, then tear in the basil, check the seasoning, and serve. Hand round Parmesan cheese separately, if you like.

SERVES 2

PASTA WITH GARLIC AND HERB MAYONNAISE

You can make this less rich by replacing some of the mayonnaise with plain yogurt, if you like. Summery and easy to prepare, it can be served either hot or cold. A simple salad goes well with it, and/or some warm bread.

225g / 8oz pasta, such as conchiglie	**1 garlic clove, crushed**
bunch of fresh herbs	**salt and freshly**
4 tbls mayonnaise, a	**ground black pepper**
good bought one such	**fresh Parmesan cheese,**
as Hellman's, or	**grated (optional)**
mayonnaise and	
plain yogurt mixed	

1 First fill a saucepan with 2 litres/3½ pints of water and bring to the boil. Add the pasta to the pan, then cook, uncovered, for about 8 minutes or until it is *al dente*.

2 While the pasta is cooking, wash and chop the herbs – you need about 4 tablespoons.

3 Drain the pasta then put it back into the still-warm pan. Add the mayonnaise, or mayonnaise and yogurt, and the herbs and garlic. Mix gently, season with salt and pepper, then serve out on to warmed plates, with fresh Parmesan if you wish.

SERVES 2

FUSILLI WITH FENNEL AND MANGETOUT

225g / 8oz fennel bulb	**salt and freshly**
125g / 4oz mangetout	**ground black pepper**
or sugar-snap peas	**fresh Parmesan cheese,**
15g / ½oz butter	**grated (optional)**
175g / 6oz fusilli	

1 First fill a saucepan with 2 litres/3½ pints of water and bring to the boil for the pasta.

2 Next prepare the vegetables: trim off any tough outer leaves and stems from the fennel, reserving any green leafy bits for garnish. Wash and slice the fennel; wash, top and tail the mangetout or peas.

3 Cook the fennel in 5 cm/2 inches of boiling water for about 7 minutes, until it is almost tender, then put in the mangetout or sugar-snap peas and cook for a further 2 minutes. Drain, add the butter and leave on one side.

4 When the water boils, add the pasta to the pan, then let it bubble away, uncovered, for about 8 minutes or until it is *al dente*.

5 Just before the pasta is ready, gently reheat the vegetables, then drain the pasta and return it to the still-warm saucepan. Add the vegetables and snip in any reserved leafy bits of fennel. Check the seasoning and serve, with Parmesan cheese if you like.

SERVES 2

CAVATAPPI WITH SPINACH, RAISINS AND PINE NUTS

I love this mixture of contrasting flavours and textures; the sweetness of the raisins and the crunchiness of the toasted pine nuts complement the spinach and pasta perfectly. Cavatappi is a corkscrew-shaped pasta, but if you can't find it you can use fusilli instead.

450g / 1lb tender fresh spinach or frozen leaf spinach	*25g / 1oz pine nuts*
25g / 1oz raisins	*salt and freshly ground black pepper*
40g / 1½oz butter	*freshly grated nutmeg*
175g / 6oz cavatappi or similar pasta	*fresh Parmesan cheese, grated*

1. First fill a saucepan with 2 litres/3½ pints of water and bring to the boil for the pasta.
2. Next prepare the spinach: if you are using fresh spinach, wash it in two or three changes of water and remove any tough stems. Put the fresh or frozen spinach into a saucepan and cook over a high heat until the spinach has wilted and is tender. If the frozen spinach is very solid you may need to add a few tablespoons of water to the pan to prevent it sticking. Drain the spinach, add the raisins and half the butter and leave on one side until the pasta is done.
3. When the water boils, add the pasta to the pan, then let it bubble away, uncovered, for about 8 minutes or until it is *al dente*. While the pasta is cooking, toast the pine nuts under a hot grill; keep your eye on them as they only take 1–2 minutes and can quickly burn. When they are golden brown, remove them from the grill and keep on one side.
4. Just before the pasta is ready, gently reheat the spinach. Drain the pasta, return it to the still-warm saucepan with the rest of the butter and add the spinach mixture and the toasted pine nuts. Season with salt, pepper and freshly grated nutmeg and serve at once on to warmed plates. Hand round the Parmesan cheese separately.

SERVES 2

FUSILLI WITH COURGETTES AND TOMATOES

225g / 8oz courgettes	*salt and freshly ground black pepper*
225g / 8oz tomatoes	*6 large basil leaves*
175g / 6oz fusilli	*fresh Parmesan cheese*
2 tbls olive oil	
1 garlic clove, crushed	

1. First fill a saucepan with 2 litres/3½ pints of water and bring to the boil for the pasta.
2. Next prepare the vegetables: wash the courgettes and cut them into rounds or matchsticks. Put the tomatoes into a bowl, cover with boiling water and leave for a few seconds until the skins split. Drain, cover with cold water and slip off the skins with a sharp knife. Chop the tomatoes into chunky pieces, removing any tough pieces around the stem.
3. When the water boils, add the pasta to the pan, then let it bubble away, uncovered, for about 8 minutes or until it is *al dente*.
4. While the pasta is cooking, heat the oil in a large saucepan and add the courgettes and garlic. Cook over a moderate heat, stirring often, for about 4 minutes or until the courgettes are just tender, then add the tomatoes and salt and pepper to taste.
5. Just before the pasta is ready, gently reheat the courgette mixture then drain the pasta and return it to the still-warm saucepan. Stir the courgettes and tomatoes into the pasta; tear in the basil, check the seasoning, and top with some flaked or freshly grated Parmesan cheese.

SERVES 2

OPPOSITE: *(top) Spinach Tagliatelle with Walnuts, page 70, and (bottom) Fusilli with Courgettes and Tomatoes*

CHEESE & CREAM SAUCES

✳

SPINACH TAGLIATELLE WITH WALNUTS

This is a rich pasta dish which only needs a simple salad accompaniment: a fresh tomato and basil salad or a green salad, such as oak-leaf lettuce, with a very light dressing would be nice.

To make a light balsamic vinegar vinaigrette to serve two people, mix 1 tablespoon of olive oil, 1 teaspoon of balsamic vinegar and some seasoning in a salad bowl. Put the salad leaves on top and toss just before you are ready to eat.

15g / ½ oz butter	*salt and freshly*
1 onion, peeled and	*ground black pepper*
chopped	*225g / 8oz spinach*
1 garlic clove, crushed	*tagliatelle*
150ml / 5fl oz double	*25–50g / 1–2oz*
cream	*walnuts, chopped*

1 First fill a saucepan with 2 litres/3½ pints of water and bring to the boil for the pasta.

2 Next start making the sauce: melt the butter in a small saucepan then put in the onion, cover and cook gently for 10 minutes, until tender but not brown. Stir in the garlic, cook for 1–2 minutes, then stir in the cream.

3 Let the mixture simmer gently for about 10 minutes, until the cream has reduced a bit and thickened, then season well with salt and pepper. Keep on one side until the pasta is done.

4 When the water boils, add the pasta to the pan, then let it bubble away, uncovered, for about 8 minutes or until it is *al dente*.

5 Just before the pasta is ready, gently reheat the sauce. Drain the pasta, return it to the still-warm saucepan and season with some salt, then add the sauce and most of the walnuts and stir so that all the pasta gets coated. Serve out on to warm plates with the remaining nuts sprinkled on top.

SERVES 2

TAGLIATELLE AL DOLCELATTE

Very quick and easy, this can be made with other blue cheeses, such as Gorgonzola, if you prefer. You can use single or double cream, depending on how rich you want it to be. A simple green salad, perhaps with some thin rings of red onion and a light balsamic vinegar vinaigrette, goes well with this.

75g / 3oz Dolcelatte	*salt and freshly*
cheese	*ground black pepper*
150ml / 5fl oz single	*225g / 8oz tagliatelle*
cream	*fresh Parmesan cheese,*
15g / ½ oz butter	*grated*

1 First fill a saucepan with 2 litres/3½ pints of water and bring to the boil for the pasta.

2 Next start making the sauce: crumble the Dolcelatte into a saucepan and add the cream and butter. Heat gently, stirring, until the ingredients have melted together and formed a sauce. Remove from the heat and season with salt and pepper.

3 When the water boils, add the pasta to the pan, then let it bubble away, uncovered, for about 8 minutes or until it is *al dente*.

4 Just before the pasta is ready, gently reheat the sauce. Drain the pasta, return it to the still-warm saucepan and season with some salt; then add the sauce and stir so that all the pasta gets coated. Serve out on to warm plates and hand round the Parmesan separately.

SERVES 2

PAPPARDELLE WITH CREAM AND PARMESAN

This delicious and simple pasta dish is rich, but can be enjoyed as part of a healthy diet if you serve it as a main course with a simple salad of leaves or ripe plum tomatoes and keep the rest of the day's meals free from fat: balance is the key. I love this made with wide ribbon pasta – pappardelle – but you could use a lighter, finer ribbon type such as tagliatelle or fettuccine, if you prefer. Really good freshly grated Parmesan cheese makes all the difference to this recipe.

175–225g / 6–8oz
  pappardelle
25g / 1oz butter
150ml / 5fl oz double
  cream

salt and freshly
  ground black pepper
50g / 2oz fresh
  Parmesan cheese,
  grated

1 Fill a saucepan with 2 litres/3½ pints of water and bring to the boil. Add the pasta and cook uncovered, for about 8 minutes, until it is *al dente*.

2 Just before the pasta is ready, put the butter and cream into a small saucepan and heat gently until the butter has melted into the cream.

3 Drain the pasta, return it to the still-warm saucepan and season with salt. Pour in the cream mixture and add the Parmesan cheese. Check the seasoning, adding plenty of freshly ground black pepper, then serve at once on to warmed plates.

SERVES 2

FARFALLE WITH NO-COOK MASCARPONE SAUCE

Another almost-instant pasta dish, which you can flavour in any way you please – try chopped fresh herbs, crushed garlic, sun-dried tomatoes, or simply lots of coarsely ground black pepper. It's quite rich, so a refreshing salad – tomato and basil is my favourite – is all the accompaniment it needs.

225g / 8oz farfalle
125g / 4oz mascarpone
  cheese
freshly grated nutmeg

salt and freshly
  ground black pepper
fresh Parmesan cheese
  (optional)

1 Fill a saucepan with 2 litres/3½ pints of water and bring to the boil. Add the pasta then cook, uncovered, for about 8 minutes, until it is *al dente*.

2 Drain the pasta then put it back into the pan. Add the mascarpone and some nutmeg and mix gently. Season well, then serve topped with some flaked or freshly grated Parmesan if you wish.

SERVES 2

CONCHIGLIE WITH RICOTTA AND SPINACH

175g / 6oz conchiglie
225g / 8oz tender fresh
  spinach or frozen leaf
  spinach
1 tbls olive oil
1 garlic clove, crushed
125g / 4oz ricotta
  cheese

salt and freshly
  ground black pepper
freshly grated nutmeg
fresh Parmesan cheese,
  grated

1 First fill a saucepan with 2 litres/3½ pints of water and bring to the boil. Add the pasta and cook, uncovered, for about 8 minutes, or until *al dente*.

2 If you're using fresh spinach, wash it in two or three changes of water, removing any tough stems.

3 Heat the oil in a saucepan and put in the garlic. Cook for a few seconds, then add the spinach and cook over a high heat until the spinach has wilted and is tender. If the frozen spinach is very solid it will take a bit longer and you will need to watch it carefully to make sure it doesn't stick.

4 Drain the conchiglie, return it to the pan and gently stir in the spinach and the ricotta. Season with salt, pepper and freshly grated nutmeg and serve at once, with Parmesan cheese.

SERVES 2

Small pasta shapes work best for this recipe – farfalle, fusilli or lumache, for instance.

MACARONI CHEESE

Macaroni cheese is so popular with my daughter Claire and her friends that I get tired of making it, though they never seem to get tired of eating it. I try to vary it by adding different ingredients. In this version tomatoes add freshness and moisture as well as colour. I would serve it with watercress or, for the children, probably frozen peas (and tomato ketchup!).

75g / 3oz quick-
   cooking macaroni
1 or 2 medium to large
   tomatoes
breadcrumbs made
   from 1 small slice of
   stale bread
1 tbls finely grated
   Parmesan cheese

FOR THE CHEESE SAUCE
25g / 1oz butter
25g / 1oz plain flour
300ml / ½ pint semi-
   skimmed milk
½ tsp mustard powder
3 tbls finely grated
   Parmesan cheese
salt and freshly
   ground black pepper

1   Bring a large saucepan of water to the boil, add the macaroni then cook, uncovered, for about 8 minutes or until the macaroni is *al dente*.

2   Meanwhile, make the cheese sauce: melt the butter in a saucepan and stir in the flour. When it froths, stir in about a third of the milk then beat well, over the heat, until it thickens. Repeat until all the milk has been used. Don't worry if it goes lumpy; just keep beating and all will be well.

3   Let the sauce simmer gently for a few minutes. Blend the mustard powder with a little water and add to the sauce, with the cheese and seasoning.

4   Heat the grill. When the macaroni is done, drain and add to the sauce. Check the seasoning, adding more salt and pepper if necessary.

5   Slice the tomatoes. Put the macaroni cheese into a shallow heatproof dish then cover with the tomato slices. Top with a light scattering of breadcrumbs and the cheese. Grill for a few minutes until the topping is golden brown.

SERVES 2

OPPOSITE: *(top) Fettuccine with Asparagus Sauce and (bottom) Macaroni Cheese*

FETTUCCINE WITH ASPARAGUS SAUCE

This is a lovely summery pasta dish; a salad of lettuce and fresh herbs goes well with it.

15g / ½ oz butter
1 onion, peeled and
   chopped
1 garlic clove, crushed
150ml / 5fl oz double
   cream

salt and freshly
   ground black pepper
freshly grated nutmeg
125–225g / 4–8oz
   asparagus spears
225g / 8oz fettuccine

1   First fill a saucepan with 2 litres/3½ pints of water and bring to the boil for the pasta.

2   Next start making the sauce: melt the butter in a small saucepan then put in the onion, cover and cook gently for 10 minutes, until tender but not brown. Stir in the garlic, cook for 1–2 minutes, then stir in the cream. Let the mixture simmer gently for about 10 minutes, until the cream has reduced a bit and thickened. Season with salt, pepper and freshly grated nutmeg and keep on one side until the pasta is done.

3   While the sauce is cooking, trim the asparagus, removing the ends of the stems if they are tough and cutting it into 2.5 cm/1 inch lengths. Keep the tips separate from the stems.

4   Bring 2.5 cm/1 inch of water to the boil in a pan and put in the chopped asparagus stems. Boil for 2 minutes, then add the tips, cover and cook for a further 2 minutes, or until they are beginning to get tender but are still crunchy. Drain well, then stir into the cream sauce, reserving a few of the asparagus tips.

5   When the water boils, add the pasta to the pan, and let it bubble away, uncovered, for about 8 minutes or until it is *al dente*.

6   Just before the pasta is ready, gently reheat the sauce. Drain the pasta, return it to the still-warm saucepan and season with some salt; then add the sauce and stir so that all the pasta gets coated.

7   Serve out on to warm plates with the reserved asparagus tips on top, and grind on some additional coarse black pepper if liked.

SERVES 2

TAGLIATELLE WITH INSTANT GARLIC AND CHEESE SAUCE

225g / 8oz tagliatelle
1 × 125g / 4oz packet
  of garlic and herb
  cream cheese

salt and freshly
  ground black pepper

1. Fill a saucepan with 2 litres/3½ pints of water and bring to the boil then add the pasta and cook, uncovered, for about 8 minutes, until it is *al dente*.
2. Drain the pasta then put it back in the pan. Gently mix in the garlic and herb cream cheese, season well, then serve out on to warmed plates.
SERVES 2

FUSILLI WITH LEMON, CREAM AND PEAS

I think of this as a summer recipe, but it's also lovely in the winter, bringing a feeling of sunshine with it.

15g / ½oz butter
1 onion, peeled and
  chopped
1 garlic clove, crushed
150ml / 5fl oz double
  or single cream
grated rind of ½ lemon

salt and freshly
  ground black pepper
175g / 6oz fusilli
125g / 4oz fresh
  podded peas, or fresh
  or frozen petits pois
6 basil leaves

1. First fill a saucepan with 2 litres/3½ pints of water and bring to the boil for the pasta.
2. Meanwhile, melt the butter in a pan then put in the onion, cover and cook for 10 minutes, until tender but not brown. Stir in the garlic and cook for 1–2 minutes longer, then stir in the cream and simmer gently for 10 minutes, until it has reduced a bit and thickened. Add the lemon rind and seasoning.
3. When the water boils, add the pasta to the pan, and cook, uncovered, for 8 minutes, until *al dente*.

4. Cook the peas in a little boiling water for 2–3 minutes or until they are just tender, then drain.
5. Just before the pasta is ready, gently reheat the sauce and add the peas. Drain the pasta, return it to the pan and add some salt, then stir in the sauce. Tear in the basil leaves, stir again, then serve.
SERVES 2

CONCHIGLIE WITH COURGETTES AND CREAM

15g / ½oz butter
1 onion, peeled and
  chopped
1 garlic clove, crushed
150 ml / 5fl oz double
  or single cream
salt and freshly
  ground black pepper

175g / 6oz conchiglie
225g / 8oz courgettes
small bunch of chervil
  or parsley
lemon juice

1. First fill a saucepan with 2 litres/3½ pints of water and bring to the boil for the pasta.
2. Meanwhile, melt the butter in a pan then put in the onion, cover and cook gently for 10 minutes, until tender but not brown. Add the garlic and cook for 1–2 minutes longer, then stir in the cream and simmer gently for about 10 minutes, until it has reduced a bit and thickened. Season to taste.
3. When the water boils, add the pasta to the pan and cook, uncovered, for 8 minutes, until *al dente*.
4. Slice the courgettes, then cook them in a little boiling water for about 2 minutes, until just tender but still slightly crisp. Drain and add to the sauce.
5. Wash and chop the chervil or parsley – you need about 2 tablespoons.
6. Just before the pasta is ready, gently reheat the sauce. Drain the pasta, return it to the pan and add some salt; then stir in the sauce and the herbs. Add a little lemon juice to sharpen the sauce then serve out on to warmed plates.
SERVES 2

FARFALLE WITH CREAMY BROCCOLI SAUCE

The cream sauce in this case is a Béchamel. For a lighter version, leave out the cream and use semi-skimmed milk.

25g / 1oz butter	175g / 6oz farfalle
20g / ¾ oz plain flour	225g / 8oz broccoli
300ml / ½ pint milk	salt and freshly
1 bay leaf	ground black pepper
a few stalks of	4 tbls cream (optional)
parsley, if available	freshly grated nutmeg
slice of onion, if	
available	

1 First fill a saucepan with 2 litres/3½ pints of water and bring to the boil for the pasta.

2 Meanwhile, make the sauce: melt the butter in a saucepan and stir in the flour. When it froths, stir in half the milk and beat well, over the heat, until it thickens, then stir in the rest of the milk and keep stirring vigorously over the heat until the sauce is thick and smooth. Add the bay leaf, along with the parsley stalks and slice of onion if you have them, then contine to cook the sauce over a very low heat.

3 When the water boils, add the pasta then let it bubble away, uncovered, for about 8 minutes, until it is *al dente*.

4 Wash the broccoli then break or chop the florets into bite-sized pieces and peel and slice into matchsticks any of the stem that is tender enough to use. Cook the broccoli in 5 cm/2 inches of boiling water for 3–4 minutes, until it is just tender. Drain and keep it warm.

5 Drain the pasta and return it to the saucepan. Add the broccoli and season with some salt. Remove the bay leaf, onion and parsley from the sauce, scraping as much sauce off them as you can, then discard them. If you're using the cream, stir this into the sauce over the heat, and season with salt, pepper and freshly grated nutmeg to taste.

6 Pour the sauce in with the pasta and broccoli, stir gently to mix, then serve.
SERVES 2

FETTUCCINE WITH CREAM AND HERB SAUCE

This sauce can be made with either single or double cream, depending on how rich you want it to be. (It's most delicious with double cream, I have to say, but it does work with single cream.) You can use almost any fresh herbs: I like chervil, parsley and chives, or tarragon for a more assertive flavour.

15g / ½ oz butter	salt and freshly
1 onion, peeled and	ground black pepper
chopped	freshly grated nutmeg
1 garlic clove, crushed	bunch of mixed fresh
150ml / 5fl oz double	herbs
or single cream	225g / 8oz fettuccine

1 First fill a saucepan with 2 litres/3½ pints of water and bring to the boil for the pasta.

2 Next start making the sauce: melt the butter in a small saucepan then put in the onion, cover and cook gently for 10 minutes, until tender but not brown. Add the garlic and cook for 1–2 minutes longer, then stir in the cream and leave the mixture to simmer gently for about 10 minutes, until the cream has reduced a bit and thickened. Season with salt, pepper and freshly grated nutmeg and keep on one side until the pasta is done.

3 While the sauce is cooking, wash and chop the herbs – you need about 2–4 tablespoons.

4 When the water boils, add the fettuccine to the pan and let it bubble away, uncovered, for about 8 minutes or until it is *al dente*.

5 Just before the pasta is ready, gently reheat the sauce. Drain the fettuccine, return it to the still-warm saucepan and season with some salt; then add the sauce and most of the herbs and stir so that all the pasta gets coated. Serve out on to warm plates with the remaining herbs scattered on top.
SERVES 2

Freshly grated nutmeg is a useful flavouring: buy a nutmeg grater and some whole nutmegs – they can be grated in moments.

PULSES, GRAINS & NUTS

These are packed full of nutrients. Nuts are a very concentrated source of energy, and small quantities go a long way. They make a wonderful fast food – great for putting into lunchboxes with some salad or fruit for a nourishing, fastest-ever meal. Most pulses need soaking and long cooking, so all the recipes in this book rely on canned ones to save time, except for split red lentils which cook quickly without soaking. Grains are invaluable, too, and are much richer in protein, minerals and vitamins than many people realize.

BEANS & LENTILS

✳

CHICK PEA BROTH WITH PARSLEY DUMPLINGS

This is cheap, comforting, tasty and quick to make: what more can one ask of a simple recipe? The dumplings are based on one of Nigel Slater's recipes.

2 onions
4 garlic cloves
4 carrots
4 celery stalks
2 tbls oil
2 × 425g / 15oz cans
  chick peas
salt and freshly
  ground black pepper

FOR THE DUMPLINGS
200g / 7oz plain flour
2 tsp baking powder
1 tsp salt
50g / 2oz Cheddar
  cheese, grated
4–6 tbls chopped fresh
  parsley
1 egg
about 100ml / 4fl oz
  milk

1 Peel and chop the onions; peel and crush the garlic; scrape the carrots and cut them into thin rounds; trim and dice the celery. The vegetables need to be cut up small so that they will cook quickly.

2 Heat the oil in a large saucepan and cook the vegetables, with a lid on the pan, for 5 minutes. Then add the chick peas, together with their liquid, 1.7 litres/3 pints of water and some salt and pepper. Cover and leave to simmer for 15–20 minutes.

3 Meanwhile, make the dumplings: sift the flour and baking powder into a bowl and add the salt, grated cheese and parsley. Whisk the egg and stir that in, along with enough milk to make a soft but not sticky dough. Form the dough into eight balls and drop these into the soup.

4 Cover the pan and leave to cook for 10–12 minutes, until the dumplings are puffed up, light and cooked through, and all the vegetables are tender.
SERVES 4

TUSCAN BEAN SOUP

This soup makes a good light meal on its own with some bread, or serve it with some crostini (see pages 18–20) and a chunky little gem lettuce salad for a more substantial meal.

1 tbls olive oil
1 onion, peeled and
  chopped
2 garlic cloves,
  crushed
1 × 425g / 15oz can
  cannellini beans

salt and freshly
  ground black pepper
lemon juice
extra virgin olive oil
  (optional)
roughly chopped flat-
  leaf parsley

1 Heat the oil in a large saucepan, add the onion then cover and cook gently for 10 minutes, until tender but not brown. Stir in the garlic and cook for 1–2 minutes longer.

2 Add the cannellini beans, together with their liquid, then purée in a food processor or blender until fairly smooth and creamy.

3 Return the mixture to the pan and add some water to adjust the consistency to your liking: about 300ml/½ pint makes a medium-thick soup. Bring to the boil then season with salt and pepper and a squeeze or two of lemon juice.

4 Serve the soup in warmed bowls, topped with some extra virgin olive oil, if you like, some flat-leaf parsley and coarsely ground black pepper.
SERVES 2

SPICY LENTIL SOUP

1 tbls oil	pinch of chilli powder
1 onion, peeled and chopped	1 bay leaf
8–10 cardamom pods	175g / 6oz split red lentils
2 garlic cloves, crushed	juice of ½–1 lemon
1½ tsp turmeric	salt and freshly ground black pepper

1 Heat the oil in a large saucepan, then add the onion, cover and cook gently for 5–7 minutes.

2 Meanwhile, bruise the cardamom pods in a pestle and mortar or with a wooden spoon. Add them to the onion, along with the garlic, turmeric, chilli powder and bay leaf, and cook over a gentle heat for a further 2–3 minutes.

3 Stir in the lentils, then pour in 750ml/ 1½ pints of water. Bring to the boil and simmer, uncovered, for 20–25 minutes, until the lentils are very tender and pale coloured.

4 Sharpen the flavour with lemon juice to taste, season with salt and pepper, then serve accompanied by poppadums if you like.

SERVES 2

BUTTERBEAN AND TOMATO SOUP

Butterbean and tomato is a combination I remember from my vegetarian childhood and I still think it's good. Cheesy garlic bread or bruschetta (see pages 18–20) go well with it.

1 tbls olive oil or oil from a jar of sun-dried tomatoes	1 × 425g / 15oz can butterbeans
1 onion, peeled and chopped	3–4 sun-dried tomatoes
1 garlic clove, crushed	salt and freshly ground black pepper
1 × 400g / 14oz can tomatoes	

1 Heat the oil in a large saucepan then add the onion, cover and cook gently for 5 minutes, until softened. Stir in the garlic and cook for 2 minutes, then pour in the canned tomatoes and the butterbeans, together with their liquid.

2 Chop the sun-dried tomatoes and add these to the pan. Simmer, uncovered, for about 10 minutes.

3 You can serve the soup as it is, but I think it's nicest if you purée half of it in a food processor or blender then stir it back in, because this gives a slightly thickened, creamy consistency. Season with salt and pepper and serve.

SERVES 2

PROVENCAL FLAGEOLET BEAN SOUP

This is light yet filling, and the pesto gives it a sunny Mediterranean flavour. It's good with some warm granary bread or hot garlic bread.

125g / 4oz carrot	1 garlic clove, crushed
1 tbls olive oil	1 × 425g / 15oz can flageolet beans
1 onion, peeled and chopped	1–2 tbls pesto
125g / 4oz leek	salt and freshly ground black pepper
125g / 4oz courgettes	

1 Scrape the carrot then cut it into tiny dice (about 6 mm/¼ inch) so that it will cook quickly. Heat the oil in a large saucepan and fry the onion and carrot, with a lid on the pan, for 5 minutes, until beginning to soften. Wash, trim and finely slice the leek; wash, trim and dice the courgettes.

2 Add the leek and the garlic to the pan; cover and cook for a further 5 minutes, then add the courgettes, flageolet beans and 600ml/1 pint of water. Bring to the boil and simmer for about 10 minutes until the vegetables are tender.

3 Stir in pesto to taste and season with salt and pepper, then serve.

SERVES 2

LENTIL CHILLI BURGERS WITH DILL SAUCE

This is a pleasant combination of hot and cool, crisp and creamy. Serve with a simple salad or a steamed vegetable such as broccoli. The burgers are nicest if they are deep-fried, which you can do quickly in a medium saucepan rather than going through all the rigmarole of getting out a deep-fryer – or they can be shallow-fried.

1 onion, peeled and
  chopped
1 tbls olive oil
1 garlic clove, crushed
1 fresh green chilli,
  de-seeded and
  chopped, or chilli
  powder to taste
2 tsp ground coriander
1 × 425g / 15oz can
  green lentils, drained
oil for deep- or
  shallow-frying
1 slice white or whole-
  wheat bread, crusts
  removed

1 packet fresh
  coriander, chopped
salt and freshly
  ground black pepper
1 egg, beaten
4 tbls dried
  breadcrumbs

FOR THE SAUCE
2–3 tbls chopped fresh
  dill
150ml / 5fl oz creamy
  yogurt

1 Fry the onion in the oil, with a lid on the pan, for 5 minutes. Add the garlic, chilli and ground coriander then cover and cook for 2–3 minutes. Remove from the heat and stir in the lentils.

2 If you are going to deep-fry the burgers, put the oil on to heat, but keep your eye on it. Cover the bread with water, drain immediately, then squeeze out all the water and crumble the bread – this is a quick way of making breadcrumbs. Add to the lentil mixture along with the fresh coriander and seasoning, mashing the mixture with the spoon or a potato masher so that it holds together.

3 Divide the mixture into four and form into sphere shapes if you are going to deep-fry them, or flattish burger shapes for shallow-frying.

4 Dip the burgers first in the beaten egg, then in the dried breadcrumbs, making sure they are well coated. Then fry them until crisp and brown: they will need about 3–4 minutes on each side if shallow-frying and 4–5 minutes in total if deep-frying. Drain them well on kitchen paper.

5 Serve with a sauce made by stirring the chopped dill into the creamy yogurt and seasoning with salt and pepper.

SERVES 2

LENTILS WITH GRILLED PEPPERS

This is a very pleasant combination of flavours, textures and colours: so simple, but so good. I like a green salad with it and some good light bread, such as ciabatta.

1 large red pepper
1 large yellow pepper
1 × 425g / 15oz can
  green or brown
  lentils

2 tbls balsamic
  vinegar
salt and freshly
  ground black pepper
sprigs of basil

1 Cut the peppers into quarters, place them cut-side down on a grill pan and grill them on high for 10 minutes or until the skins have blistered and charred in places. Remove from the grill and cover with a damp cloth.

2 Meanwhile, gently heat the lentils, in their liquid, in a saucepan.

3 When the peppers are cool enough to handle, pull off the skin with a sharp knife, discard the seeds and stalks, cut the flesh into strips and put into a serving dish.

4 Drain the lentils and add to the peppers with the balsamic vinegar, salt and pepper to taste, and some torn basil leaves.

SERVES 2

OPPOSITE: (*left*) *Lentil Chilli Burgers with Dill Sauce,* (*above*) *Provençal Flageolet Bean Soup, page 79,* (*right*) *Lentils with Grilled Peppers*

LENTILS WITH CORIANDER AND HARD-BOILED EGGS

Hard-boiled eggs and lentils are one of those classic combinations, like tomato and basil or bread and cheese – and a colourful and nutritious pair they are too. Serve this on its own or with some rice, bread or chutney – it's very versatile, so please yourself!

If you can get the little Puy lentils, which cook in 40 minutes, you can use them for this recipe instead of canned green lentils. 100g / 3½ oz dried lentils is equivalent to a 425g /15 oz can. Cook the lentils in plenty of boiling water until tender.

2 eggs
1 tbls olive oil
1 onion, peeled and sliced
1 garlic clove, crushed
2 tsp ground coriander

1 × 425g / 15oz can green lentils, drained
2 tbls chopped fresh coriander
salt and freshly ground black pepper

1 Hard-boil the eggs by simmering them in a pan of boiling water for 7–10 minutes. Then drain them, cover with cold water and leave to cool.

2 Heat the olive oil in a pan, add the onion and garlic then cover and cook gently for 5 minutes, until softened.

3 Add the ground coriander to the onion and garlic, stirring for 1–2 minutes, then put in the lentils and leave to cook very gently until the lentils are thoroughly heated. Meanwhile, shell the hard-boiled eggs, rinse them under cold water, then slice them.

4 Add the chopped fresh coriander to the lentil mixture, taste and season with salt and pepper. Serve the lentils and the eggs together: you could stir the eggs into the lentil mixture if you wish, or just arrange them around it attractively.

SERVES 2

CHICK PEA CROQUETTES WITH CORIANDER RAITA

These are crisp on the outside, moist and spicy within, lovely with a yogurt raita and a fresh salad – perhaps diced cucumber and chopped spring onion. You really do need a food processor to purée the chick peas for this recipe.

1 onion, peeled and chopped
1 tbls olive oil
1 garlic clove, crushed
1 tsp cumin seeds
1 × 425g / 15oz can chick peas, drained
salt and freshly ground black pepper
1 egg, beaten

4 tbls dried breadcrumbs
oil for shallow-frying

FOR THE RAITA
2 tbls chopped fresh coriander
150ml / 5fl oz creamy yogurt

1 Fry the onion in the oil, with a lid on the pan, for 5 minutes, until beginning to soften, then add the garlic and cumin seeds and fry for a further 2–3 minutes. Remove from the heat.

2 Put the onion mixture into a food processor. Drain the chick peas, reserving the liquid, then add them to the food processor and whizz to form a thick purée that holds together. If necessary, add a little of the reserved chick pea liquid to obtain the right consistency, but be careful not to let the mixture get too moist.

3 Season with salt and pepper, then divide the mixture into four and form into flattish croquettes; don't make them too thick or the inside won't heat through properly.

4 Dip the croquettes first in the beaten egg then in the dried breadcrumbs, making sure they are well coated. Then heat the oil in a frying pan and shallow-fry the croquettes for 3–4 minutes on each side, until crisp and brown. Drain them well on kitchen paper.

5 Serve with a raita made by stirring the chopped coriander into the creamy yogurt and seasoning with salt and pepper.

SERVES 2

CHICK PEA PUREE WITH SPICED ONION TOPPING

This is so simple to make, and good with some warm bread and perhaps a cucumber and tomato salad with some chopped fresh coriander and slices of lemon.

2 onions, peeled and chopped	1 tsp ground cumin
2 tbls olive oil	1 × 425g / 15oz can chick peas
2 garlic cloves, crushed	salt and freshly ground black pepper
2 tsp ground coriander	

1 Fry the onions in the oil, with a lid on the pan, for 5 minutes or until beginning to soften, then add the garlic, coriander and cumin.

2 Cover and fry for a further 2–3 minutes, then take out a third of the mixture and put it into a food processor. Continue to cook the rest of the onions and spices until the onions are brown, but don't have the heat too high or the spices might burn.

3 Meanwhile, put the chick peas and about half of their liquid into the food processor with the onions. Whizz to a purée, adding more of the liquid if necessary to make a thick but creamy mixture.

4 Season with salt and pepper, then transfer the purée to a pan and heat through. Serve topped with the crisp, browned spicy onion mixture.

SERVES 2

RED BEAN BURGERS WITH SOURED CREAM SAUCE

Soured cream has the same fat content as single cream, so it's not over-rich when used in small quantities. However, for a lower-fat sauce plain yogurt is very good instead. Another option is to serve the burgers with a good dollop of guacamole (see page 27) or, of course, you could forget about a sauce altogether and serve the burgers in light rolls or with salad.

1 onion, peeled and chopped	1 egg, beaten
1 tbls olive oil	4 tbls dried breadcrumbs
1 garlic clove, crushed	oil for shallow-frying
1 tomato	
75g / 3oz bread, crusts removed	**FOR THE SAUCE**
1 × 425g / 15oz can red kidney beans, drained	2 tbls chopped fresh chives
salt and freshly ground black pepper	150ml / 5fl oz soured cream

1 Fry the onion in the oil, with a lid on the pan, for 5 minutes, until beginning to soften. Add the garlic and fry for a further 2–3 minutes.

2 Meanwhile, pour boiling water over the tomato and leave for a few seconds until the skin splits, then slip off the skin with a sharp knife. De-seed and chop the tomato, removing any hard bits of core, then add it to the onion and garlic. Stir, then cook, uncovered for 3–4 minutes, until the tomato has cooked down a bit.

3 Remove the pan from the heat. Roughly tear the bread and add to the pan, together with the beans. The mixture has to be mashed very well at this stage to blend together all the ingredients, and the easiest way to do this is to tip it into a food processor and whizz it to a thick purée. You can do it by hand, however, with patience, elbow grease and a good strong potato masher.

4 Season the mixture with salt and pepper, then divide it into four and form into flattish burger shapes; don't make them too thick or the inside won't heat through.

5 Dip the burgers first in the beaten egg then in the dried breadcrumbs, making sure they are well coated. Then heat the oil in a frying pan and shallow-fry them for 3–4 minutes on each side, until they are crisp and brown. Drain them well on kitchen paper.

6 Serve the burgers straight away with a sauce made by stirring the chopped fresh chives into the soured cream and seasoning with salt and pepper to taste.

SERVES 2

Cumin (both whole and ground) and coriander (ground is most useful) are wonderful for flavouring pulses and vegetables.

ULTIMATE RED BEAN CHILLI

This quick chilli is good with bread, mashed potatoes, plain pasta or rice, or some potato wedges, soured cream and chives (see page 112). If there is any left over, it's nice cold as a salad, or stuffed into pitta bread, or as a filling for crêpes or tortillas.

1 tbls olive oil	*1 large green chilli*
1 onion, peeled and chopped	*1 × 425g / 15oz can red kidney beans, drained*
1 red pepper	*salt and freshly ground black pepper*
125g / 4oz carrot	*chilli powder (optional)*
1 garlic clove, crushed	
1 × 400g / 14oz can tomatoes	

1   Heat the oil in a medium-large saucepan, then put in the onion, cover and cook for 5 minutes.

2   De-seed and chop the red pepper; scrape and dice the carrot. Add to the pan with the garlic. Stir, then cover and cook for 10 minutes.

3   Stir the tomatoes into the mixture, breaking them up with the spoon. De-seed the chilli, slice it into rings and add it to the saucepan. Cook gently, uncovered, for 10–15 minutes or until the carrot is tender.

4   Put in the red kidney beans and cook for a further 1–2 minutes to heat them through. Season with salt and pepper and add a pinch or so of chilli powder if it needs more of a kick, then serve.
SERVES 2

RED BEANS WITH THYME AND COCONUT CREAM

This is a quick version of a West Indian recipe. It's very warming and good with some rice. I think brown rice goes best with it, but if you're doing that you'll need to get it started first to give it time to cook.

This is a very easy salad which can be varied as much as you like by using different dressings, different types of beans and additional ingredients. Hot garlic bread goes well with it. Any leftover salad will keep well for 24 hours, covered, in the fridge.

1 × 425g / 15oz can red kidney beans	*1 tsp dried thyme or 1 tbls fresh thyme*
1 onion, peeled and chopped	*25g / 1oz creamed coconut*
1 carrot, finely sliced	*salt and freshly ground black pepper*
1 garlic clove, crushed	

1   Tip the red kidney beans and their liquid into a pan, add 300ml/½ pint of water and heat gently.

2   Add the onion, carrot, garlic and thyme and let the mixture simmer gently for about 15 minutes, until the vegetables are tender.

3   Flake the creamed coconut or chop it finely and add it to the pan, stirring gently until it has melted. Then season with salt and pepper and serve.
SERVES 2

TWO-BEAN SALAD WITH GARLIC BREAD

2 × 425g / 15oz cans beans, choose 2 contrasting types	*salt and freshly ground black pepper*
1–2 tsp balsamic vinegar	*2–4 tbls chopped fresh herbs, such as chives, parsley and chervil or tarragon*
3 tbls olive oil or plain low-fat yogurt, or a mixture	*few thin slices of red onion (optional)*
½ tsp Dijon mustard (optional)	*garlic bread (see page 34)*

1   Drain the beans. Mix 1 teaspoon of balsamic vinegar with the oil and/or yogurt in a salad bowl. Taste, and add more vinegar if necessary. Add the mustard, if you're using this, and plenty of seasoning.

2   Add the beans, herbs and onion, if you're using this; stir gently then leave on one side while you prepare the garlic bread. Stir again before serving.
SERVES 4

OPPOSITE: **Ultimate Red Bean Chilli**

MEXICAN BEAN SALAD

1 small lettuce	*salt and freshly*
4 tomatoes	*ground black pepper*
1 small red pepper	*1 avocado*
1 tbls olive oil	*2 tbls chopped fresh*
1 onion, peeled and	*chives*
chopped	*150ml / 5fl oz plain*
1 green chilli	*low-fat yogurt or*
1 garlic clove, crushed	*soured cream*
1 × 425g / 15oz can red	*a few fresh coriander*
kidney beans,	*leaves, if available*
drained	

1 Wash the lettuce and put it into a colander to drain. Put the tomatoes in a bowl, pour boiling water over them and leave for a few seconds until the skins split. Drain, cover with cold water and slip off the skins. Cut two of the tomatoes into eighths and chop the other two. Wash and slice the pepper, discarding the stem and seeds.

2 Heat the oil in a saucepan then add the onion, cover and cook over a moderate heat for 5 minutes, stirring occasionally.

3 Meanwhile, de-seed and chop the chilli, washing your hands carefully after handling it. Add the chilli, garlic and chopped tomatoes to the onion and cook for 5 minutes.

4 Add the beans to the onion mixture, mashing them roughly with a wooden spoon or a potato masher to give a chunky texture. Heat through, then season with salt and pepper and keep warm over a low heat.

5 Cover a large platter with the lettuce leaves and arrange the red pepper and tomato randomly on top.

6 Peel, stone and roughly chop the avocado. Stir the chives into the yogurt or soured cream.

7 Spoon the red bean mixture on to the centre of the salad. Sprinkle the chopped avocado over it, then drizzle some of the yogurt or soured cream mixture over everything – put the rest into a small bowl to serve with the salad. Serve the salad at once, garnished with fresh coriander leaves, if you have any.

SERVES 2

VARIATION

REFRIED BEANS WITH TORTILLA CHIPS

Omit the red pepper, 2 of the tomatoes and the avocado. Make the bean mixture as described above and stir some fresh coriander into it, if available. Transfer to a shallow heatproof dish and top with 150g/5oz tortilla chips and 125g/4oz Cheddar cheese, grated. Place under a hot grill to melt the cheese, then serve with the lettuce leaves (crisp ones are best) and the yogurt or soured cream mixture.

WHITE BEANS COOKED IN CREAM

This is rich and delicious, lovely for a treat, with fingers of toast and a green salad.

15g / ½oz butter	*squeeze of lemon juice*
1 onion, peeled and	*salt and freshly*
chopped	*ground black pepper*
1 garlic clove, crushed	*freshly grated nutmeg*
150ml / 5fl oz single	*fresh parsley*
cream	
1 × 425g / 15oz can	
white beans, such as	
haricot or cannellini	

1 Melt the butter in a medium saucepan then put in the onion, cover and cook gently for 5 minutes, until tender but not brown.

2 Stir in the garlic and cook for 1–2 minutes longer, then stir in the cream and leave the mixture to simmer gently for about 5 minutes, until the cream has reduced a bit and thickened.

3 Drain the beans and add them to the pan. Heat gently, stirring often. Add the lemon juice and then season with salt, pepper and freshly grated nutmeg. Make sure the beans are really hot, then serve them out on to heated plates and snip a little parsley over the top.

SERVES 2

QUICK BEANY BAKE

There's nothing in the slightest bit gourmet about this recipe but it's adored by all kids. I think it originally came from a children's TV programme – my daughter Kate told it to me.

1 tbls olive oil	225g / 8oz can
1 onion, peeled and	sweetcorn, drained
chopped	4–6 slices of bread
225g / 8oz can baked	125g / 4oz cheese,
beans	grated
225g / 8oz can red	
kidney beans,	
drained	

1   Heat the oil in a medium saucepan, then add the onion and cook, covered, for about 10 minutes, until it has softened.

2   Add the baked beans, kidney beans and sweetcorn to the pan. Cook the mixture gently until everything is hot.

3   Heat the grill. Transfer the beany mixture to a shallow heatproof dish that will fit under your grill. Roughly tear the slices of bread over the top (with or without the crusts) then cover with the grated cheese.

4   Grill for about 10 minutes, or until the bread is crisp and the cheese melted and golden brown. Serve at once.

SERVES 2–4

EASY VEGETABLE DAL

Soothing and colourful, this is enough for two to four people depending on what you serve with it – Indian breads and/or boiled rice make good accompaniments. Any that's left over tastes good, if not better, the next day. This recipe contains no fat and is a special favourite of mine for that reason, as well as for its flavour and comforting qualities.

200g / 7oz split red	1 onion
lentils	2 carrots
2 thin slices of fresh	1 garlic clove
ginger root	125g / 4oz frozen peas
½ tsp turmeric	juice of ½ lemon
1 tsp cumin seeds	salt and freshly
1 tsp ground coriander	ground black pepper
pinch of chilli powder	

1   Put the lentils, ginger root, turmeric, cumin seeds, ground coriander and chilli powder into a medium saucepan with 1 litre/1¾ pints of water and bring to the boil.

2   Meanwhile, peel and slice the onion, scrape or peel the carrots and slice them quite finely, and peel and crush the garlic. Add all these vegetables to the lentils as they continue to simmer away. Let the lentil mixture cook for about 25 minutes altogether. At first it will look hopelessly watery, then when it is done it will become thick and soft, like porridge, and all the vegetables should be tender, too.

3   Add the peas to the mixture and cook for a further 2–3 minutes, until they are heated through. Then stir in the lemon juice and season to taste with salt and pepper.

SERVES 2–4

SPLIT PEA AND OKRA DAL

This quick dal uses canned split peas and is good served with poppadums and some basmati rice. I sometimes add sliced tomatoes and a coriander raita (see page 82) for an easy Indian meal – much quicker than phoning the takeaway, as well as cheaper and less fatty.

1–2 tbls olive oil	½ tsp turmeric
2 onions, peeled and chopped	2 × 425g / 15oz cans yellow split peas
175g / 6oz okra	squeeze of lemon juice
1 green chilli	salt and freshly ground black pepper
1 garlic clove, crushed	chopped fresh coriander (optional)
2 tsp cumin seeds	
2 tsp ground coriander	

1 Heat the oil in a medium-large saucepan and put in the onions. Cook gently, with a lid on the pan, for 5 minutes.

2 Meanwhile, top and tail the okra and de-seed and chop the chilli. Add these to the pan, along with the garlic, cook for 2–3 minutes, then put in the cumin seeds, ground coriander and turmeric and stir over the heat for a minute or two.

3 Add the split peas to the vegetables, together with their liquid, then cook gently, uncovered, for 5–10 minutes or until the okra are tender and any wateriness has disappeared from the mixture.

4 Add the lemon juice and salt and pepper to taste and serve sprinkled with chopped fresh coriander, if you have it.

SERVES 4

OPPOSITE: *(left) Spiced Red Lentils and Potatoes with Caramelized Onions and (right) Split Pea and Okra Dal*

SPICED RED LENTILS AND POTATOES WITH CARAMELIZED ONIONS

This delicious spicy mixture evolved from the rather unpromising starting point of some potatoes and dried red lentils. It's good served with fresh chutney and a side salad.

125g / 4oz split red lentils	½ tsp grated fresh ginger root
225g / 8oz potatoes	15g / ½oz creamed coconut, flaked or chopped
2 onions, peeled and chopped	
1–2 tbls oil	squeeze of lemon juice
1 garlic clove, crushed	½ packet fresh coriander, chopped
½ tsp turmeric	salt and freshly ground black pepper
½ tsp black mustard seeds	paprika pepper

1 Put the lentils into a medium saucepan with 450ml/¾ pint of water. Bring to the boil, then leave to simmer, uncovered, for about 20 minutes.

2 Meanwhile, peel the potatoes and cut them into 2.5 cm/1 inch dice. Add these to the lentils after they have been cooking for 10 minutes. When the lentils are done – soft and pale-coloured – the potatoes should be just tender. Remove from the heat.

3 Fry the onions in 1 tablespoon of oil, with a lid on the pan, for 5 minutes, then remove half the onion and put on one side for the moment. Stir the garlic, turmeric, mustard seeds and ginger into the remaining onion in the pan, cover and cook for a further 4–5 minutes.

4 Add the onion and spice mixture and the creamed coconut to the lentils and stir gently until everything is combined and the coconut has melted. Then add the lemon juice, fresh coriander and a good seasoning of salt and pepper, and keep warm.

5 Put the remaining onion back in the pan, with more oil if necessary, and fry it over a moderate to high heat for 3–5 minutes, until golden brown and crisp. Serve the lentil mixture topped with the crisp onion and a sprinkling of paprika pepper.

SERVES 2

To make fresh chutney to serve with this, mix together some chopped tomato, chopped red onion and plenty of chopped fresh mint; add a squeeze of lemon juice, a dash of balsamic vinegar and seasoning to taste.

RICE

— ✳ —

SPICED VEGETABLE AND CASHEW NUT PILAU

Although the ingredients list is quite long, this is actually very quick and easy to make. My favourite accompaniments are fresh chutney, mango chutney and poppadums. I've given quantities to serve two, but for four just double everything except the oil. You can use brown or white basmati rice – white cooks more quickly.

2 tbls oil	200g / 7oz basmati rice
1 onion, peeled and	small piece of
chopped	cinnamon stick
1 carrot, finely sliced	¼ tsp turmeric
1 leek, cleaned and	1 bay leaf
sliced	50g / 2oz cashew nuts
1 garlic clove, crushed	salt and freshly
6 cardamom pods	ground black pepper
1 tsp cumin seeds	

1. Heat the oil in a saucepan, then put in the onion and carrot, cover and cook for 5 minutes. Stir in the leek, garlic, cardamom and cumin, crushing the cardomom pods against the pan with a wooden spoon. Cover and cook for another 5–10 minutes, stirring occasionally, until the vegetables are tender.

2. Meanwhile, wash the rice in a sieve under the cold tap then put it into a saucepan with the cinnamon stick, turmeric, bay leaf and 450ml/¾ pint of water. Bring to the boil, then cover, turn the heat right down and leave it to cook very gently for 10–12 minutes.

3. Heat the grill. Spread out the cashew nuts on a grill pan and grill for 1–2 minutes, until they are golden brown, turning them to brown both sides. Remove from the grill and leave on one side.

4. Fork the rice gently, then combine it with the vegetable mixture, stirring gently with the fork and adding some salt and pepper. Stir the cashew nuts into the mixture just before you serve it.

SERVES 2

RICE WITH TOMATOES, SWEETCORN AND CHILLI

The best rice to use for this is either ordinary white long grain rice or brown basmati, although you could use quick-cook brown long grain rice instead.

1 tbls oil	1 bay leaf
1 onion, peeled and	125g / 4oz frozen
chopped	sweetcorn
1 fresh chilli	125g / 4oz frozen peas
1 garlic clove, crushed	salt and freshly ground
200g / 7oz rice	black pepper
1 × 225g / 8oz can	2 tbls chopped fresh
tomatoes	parsley

1. Heat the oil in a large saucepan, then put in the onion, cover and cook for 5 minutes.

2. Halve, de-seed and chop the chilli, being careful not to get the juice anywhere near your face, and washing your hands well afterwards. Add the chilli and the garlic to the pan and stir well.

3. Add the rice, tomatoes, bay leaf and 450ml/¾ pint of water to the pan. Bring to the boil, then turn down the heat, cover and leave to cook very gently for 20 minutes for brown basmati rice, 15–20 minutes for long grain white rice or 25 minutes for quick-cook brown rice.

4. Cook the frozen sweetcorn and peas together in a little boiling water for 2 minutes then drain and add them to the rice mixture, along with some salt, pepper and the parsley. Stir gently with a fork and serve as soon as possible.

SERVES 2

WARM RICE SALAD

This looks fresh and pretty and is made with a delicious honey and garlic dressing; you can leave out the oil if you want a lighter result.

200g / 7oz basmati rice	225g / 8oz cherry
1 garlic clove, crushed	tomatoes
1 tbls honey	4 tbls chopped fresh
1 tbls vinegar	chives
1 tbls olive oil	4 tbls chopped fresh
salt and freshly	mint
ground black pepper	

1 Wash the rice in a sieve under the cold tap then put it into a saucepan with 450ml/¾ pint of water. Bring to the boil, then cover, turn the heat right down and leave it to cook gently for 10–12 minutes. Turn off the heat and let the rice stand, covered, for a further 10 minutes, if there is time.

2 While the rice is cooking, make the dressing: put the garlic, honey, vinegar, olive oil and some salt and pepper into a large bowl and mix well.

3 Wash and slice the cherry tomatoes. Put the rice into the bowl with the dressing, add the cherry tomatoes and herbs then stir gently with a fork. Check the seasoning, then serve while still warm.

SERVES 2–3

EGG AND COCONUT CURRY

75g / 3oz desiccated	25g / 1oz butter
coconut	1 onion, peeled and
2 eggs	chopped
175g / 6oz brown or	1 garlic clove, crushed
white basmati rice	2 tsp medium curry
½ cinnamon stick	powder
4 cloves	25g / 1oz plain flour
4 cardamom pods	25g / 1oz sultanas
salt and freshly	1 tbls lemon juice
ground black pepper	

1 Put the coconut in a bowl and cover with 450ml/¾ pint of boiling water. Leave to infuse.

2 Hard-boil the eggs by simmering them in a pan of boiling water for 7–10 minutes. Then drain them, cover with cold water and leave to cool.

3 Wash the rice in a sieve under the cold tap. Put it in a saucepan with 350ml/12fl oz of water, the cinnamon stick, cloves and cardamom, crushing the cardamom pods against the side of the pan with a wooden spoon. Add a good pinch of salt and bring to the boil.

4 Turn the heat down very low and leave the rice to cook until it is tender and all the water has been absorbed, 20 minutes for brown rice, 10–12 minutes for white rice. Then turn off the heat and leave it to stand, still covered, for 10 minutes.

5 Meanwhile, melt the butter in a pan and gently cook the onion and garlic for 5 minutes. Strain the coconut through a sieve, pressing it against the sieve to extract as much liquid as possible. Discard the coconut but keep the liquid.

6 Stir the curry powder into the onion mixture, then add the flour and stir for 1–2 minutes until it froths. Pour in the strained coconut water, stirring until it thickens. Add the sultanas, then let it simmer very gently for 7–10 minutes.

7 Make sure the rice is still hot and check the seasoning; reheat it gently if necessary. Shell and slice the hard-boiled eggs and then add them to the sauce with the lemon juice and salt and pepper to taste. Fluff up the rice with a fork and serve with the curry.

SERVES 2

VARIATIONS

1 CHEESE CURRY

Cut 125g/4oz cheese – haloumi if you want one that keeps its shape, or good old Cheddar for a 'melting' result – into smallish cubes and stir them into the sauce instead of the eggs. Heat gently until the cheese has warmed through, then serve.

2 BUTTERBEAN OR SOYA BEAN CURRY

Add 225g/8oz canned beans to the sauce instead of the eggs and cook gently until heated through.

This is a simple English-style curry rather than an authentically spiced Indian one, and I think it makes a pleasant change. Using a medium curry powder will produce a mild curry here; you can adjust the heat according to the type and amount of curry powder you use.

ALL-SEASONS MUSHROOM RISOTTO

My favourite risotto is this rich-tasting mushroom one, with extra flavour coming from the porcini. Chestnut mushrooms are good if you can get them, because they retain their firm texture and don't produce much liquid.

Although if pushed you can use an ordinary long grain rice, Arborio or risotto rice (which is now quite widely available) is best because it cooks to exactly the right creamy consistency, with the grains tender but slightly chewy.

1 × 10g / ¼oz packet
  porcini mushrooms
1 bay leaf
3 tbls olive oil
50g / 2oz butter
1 onion, peeled and
  chopped
350g / 12oz chestnut
  mushrooms or
  button mushrooms
2 garlic cloves,
  crushed

350g / 12oz Arborio or
  other risotto rice
salt and freshly
  ground black pepper
chopped fresh parsley,
  preferably flat-leaf
50g / 2oz fresh
  Parmesan cheese, cut
  into thin slivers

1 Put the porcini into a saucepan with the bay leaf and 1.5 litres/2½ pints of boiling water. Let it simmer while you prepare the other ingredients.

2 Heat the olive oil and half the butter in a large saucepan, then put in the onion, cover and cook for about 5 minutes, until soft but not browned.

3 Slice the fresh mushrooms and add to the onion with the garlic and rice. Stir for 2–3 minutes, until the rice is coated with the buttery juices.

4 Add a ladleful of the simmering water from the pan containing the porcini and stir well; once it has been absorbed, add another. Keep the water in the porcini pan simmering away and continue to add it to the risotto a ladleful at a time as each addition is absorbed, stirring the risotto constantly.

5 Fish out the porcini from the pan, chop them up and add them to the risotto. Stop adding water once the rice is tender but not soggy – *al dente*, in fact. This will be after about 20 minutes and you will probably have used all the water.

6 Stir in the rest of the butter and season to taste with salt and pepper. Serve immediately, scattered with the parsley and slivers of Parmesan.
SERVES 4

QUICK MICROWAVE RISOTTO

It's blissfully easy to make a risotto in the microwave and the results are wonderful. This method was developed by the American cookery writer Barbara Kafka, and works like a dream.

25g / 1oz butter
1 tbls olive oil
1 onion, peeled and
  chopped
3 garlic cloves,
  crushed

175g / 6oz Arborio or
  other risotto rice
50g / 2oz fresh
  Parmesan cheese
salt and freshly
  ground black pepper

1 Put the butter and oil into a deep, microwave-proof casserole, put into the microwave and cook, uncovered, on high for 2 minutes.

2 Add the onion and garlic and stir to coat them in the butter and oil. Cook, uncovered, on high, for 4 minutes.

3 Add the rice, stir, then cook, uncovered, on high for 4 minutes.

4 Pour in 750ml/1¼ pints of boiling water. Cook, uncovered, on high for 9 minutes. Stir well, then cook for 9 minutes more.

5 Remove from the microwave. Leave the risotto to stand, uncovered, for 5 minutes, so the rice absorbs the rest of the liquid; stir it several times. Flake the Parmesan with a potato peeler or a sharp knife then stir this in, together with salt and pepper to taste. Serve immediately.
SERVES 2

OPPOSITE: *All-Seasons Mushroom Risotto*

BULGUR, COUSCOUS & POLENTA
✳

BULGUR AND CHEESE PILAU

Bulgur wheat is crushed and pre-cooked so it is quick to prepare. You can serve it as an accompaniment, like rice, or you can stir in some extra ingredients and turn it into a main course, as in this recipe.

1 tbls olive oil
15g / ½ oz butter
1 onion, peeled and chopped
1 red pepper, de-seeded and chopped
2 garlic cloves, crushed
225g / 8oz bulgur wheat

50g / 2oz raisins
salt and freshly ground black pepper
50g / 2oz almonds
100g / 3½ oz Gruyère cheese
2 tbls chopped fresh parsley

Serve this pilau with a salad of green leaves, herbs, a little finely sliced onion, and a light lemon and olive oil dressing. A soured cream sauce is a luxurious finishing touch (see page 83).

1 Heat the oil and butter in a large saucepan and put in the onion and red pepper; stir, then cover and leave to cook gently for 5–10 minutes. Add the garlic, then boil some water in a kettle.

2 Add the bulgur wheat and raisins to the onion and pepper mixture, stirring well so that the wheat gets coated with the butter and oil, then pour in 600ml/1 pint of boiling water and add a good teaspoonful of salt. Bring to the boil, then cover and leave to cook gently for 15 minutes.

3 Meanwhile put the almonds into a small saucepan, cover with water and bring to the boil. Boil for 1–2 minutes, then drain and slip off the skins with your fingers.

4 Heat the grill. Cut the almonds lengthwise with a sharp knife to make long slivers. Spread these out on a grill pan and grill them for 1–2 minutes, until golden brown.

5 Cut the Gruyère cheese into 6 mm/½ inch dice. Add them to the bulgur wheat, together with cheese and parsley, forking them through gently. Check the seasoning, then serve.

SERVES 4

BRIGHTLY COLOURED TABBOULEH

Here's a deliciously inauthentic version of this famous salad: it isn't left to stand for hours and it's a riot of colour. It tastes wonderful and doesn't need any accompaniments.

175g / 6oz bulgur wheat
1 red pepper
1 yellow pepper
1 garlic clove, crushed
juice of ½ lemon
1–2 tbls olive oil
salt and freshly ground black pepper

2–3 tomatoes
4 spring onions
1 small avocado
1 small head of radicchio
8 sprigs of flat-leaf parsley

1 Boil some water in a kettle and set the grill on high. Put the bulgur wheat into a large bowl then cover with 350ml/12fl oz of boiling water. Leave on one side to swell.

2 Cut the peppers into quarters, place them cutside down on a grill pan and grill for 10 minutes or until the skins have blistered and charred in places. Remove from the grill and cover with a damp cloth.

3 Meanwhile, put the garlic into a bowl with the lemon juice, olive oil and some salt and pepper.

4 Wash and chop the tomatoes and trim and chop the spring onions. Peel, stone and chop the avocado. Wash and roughly tear the radicchio and parsley. Add all these to the garlic.

5 Peel the peppers, pulling off the skin with a sharp knife; discard the seeds and stalks, then cut the flesh into strips and add to the other salad ingredients in the bowl.

6 Fork through the bulgur wheat then add this to the salad and mix gently to distribute all the ingredients well, adding some salt and pepper to taste as you do so.

SERVES 2 AS A MAIN COURSE, 4–6 AS AN ACCOMPANIMENT

VEGETABLE COUSCOUS

This is a quick way with couscous that may not result in every grain being immaculate separate, but who cares? It tastes good, and it doesn't need any accompaniment except perhaps a glass of spicy wine.

1 fennel bulb	225g / 8oz tomatoes
225g / 8oz carrots	225g / 8oz courgettes
2 tbls olive oil	225g / 8oz couscous
1 onion, peeled and chopped	15g / ½oz butter
1 tbls coriander seeds	1–2 tbls chopped fresh parsley
1 garlic clove, crushed	

1   Trim off any green leafy bits from the fennel, then pare away any tough outer layers using a potato peeler or sharp knife. Slice the fennel; scrape and slice the carrots.

2   Heat the oil in a large pan and put in the fennel, carrots and onion. Cover and leave to cook gently, with a lid on the pan, for 10 minutes.

3   Meanwhile, crush the coriander seeds in a pestle and mortar or with a wooden spoon. Then add these to the vegetables, along with the garlic.

4   Put the tomatoes into a bowl, cover with boiling water and leave for a few seconds until the skins split. Drain, cover with cold water and slip off the skins with a sharp knife. De-seed and chop the tomatoes and add them to the pan.

5   Wash, trim and slice the courgettes and add these to the pan, too. If the vegetables show any signs of sticking, add 1–2 tablespoons of water. Cover and cook for 5 minutes or until the courgettes are tender.

6   Meanwhile, prepare the couscous. Put 300ml/½ pint of water into a saucepan and bring to the boil. Sprinkle in the couscous, then remove the pan from the heat and leave for 2 minutes. Add the butter and a little seasoning, put the pan back on the stove and heat gently, stirring with a fork, for 3 minutes.

7   By this time the vegetables should all be tender. Check the seasoning, sprinkle with the parsley and serve with the couscous.

SERVES 2–3

SWEET COUSCOUS WITH APRICOTS

This is a very adaptable dish. While I really created it as a pudding it also makes a delicious brunch recipe, and can even be served as a salad if you put it on a base of lettuce. If you try it, you'll see what I mean. Some thick Greek yogurt goes particularly well with it, however you serve it.

50g / 2oz ready-to-eat dried apricots	½ tsp cinnamon
50g / 2oz raisins	1 tbls clear honey
25g / 1oz creamed coconut	125g / 4oz couscous
	25g / 1oz flaked almonds

1   Chop the apricots roughly then put them into a saucepan with the raisins and enough water just to cover. Bring to the boil then cover and leave to simmer gently while you prepare the couscous.

2   Cut the creamed coconut into flakes or tiny cubes then put it into a saucepan with the cinnamon, honey and 300ml/½ pint of water. Heat gently until the water comes to the boil and the coconut cream has melted, then pour in the couscous. Cover and remove from the heat.

3   Heat the grill. Spread the almonds out on a grill pan and grill for 1–2 minutes, until they are golden brown.

4   Stir the couscous gently with a fork to separate the grains. Drain the apricots and raisins, or boil rapidly to evaporate the water, if you prefer. Add the apricots and raisins to the couscous, along with the toasted flaked almonds.

SERVES 2–4

Creamed coconut can be bought in a block and will keep for ages in the fridge after opening.

INSTANT POLENTA WITH GRILLED VEGETABLES

1 tsp salt	*225g / 8oz large flat*
75g / 3oz instant	*mushrooms*
polenta	*olive oil*
1 large red onion	*1 or 2 sprigs of*
1 large fennel bulb	*rosemary*
2 beefsteak tomatoes	

1 Put 300ml/½ pint of water and the salt into a medium non-stick saucepan and bring to the boil, then sprinkle the polenta in and stir until smooth. Let the mixture cook gently for 4–5 minutes, until it has thickened, then tip it on to a large flat plate and quickly spread it out so that it is about 1 cm/½ inch thick. Leave to cool while you prepare the vegetables. Set the grill to high.

2 Bring 5 cm/2 inches of water to the boil in another pan for the onion and fennel. Peel the onion. Trim the fennel by removing any tough leaves or pieces of stem but leaving enough stem to hold the leaves together at the base. Cut the fennel and the onion down first into halves, then into quarters and eighths.

3 Cook the onion and fennel in the boiling water for about 6–8 minutes or until they are just tender without being at all soggy. Drain well and dry on kitchen paper.

4 Thickly slice the tomatoes; wash and trim the mushrooms.

5 Brush all the vegetables with olive oil, then arrange them on a grill pan, sprinkle with the leaves from the rosemary sprigs and grill for about 15 minutes or until lightly charred on both sides, turning as necessary.

6 Meanwhile, cut the polenta into triangles and fry them in olive oil in a frying pan for about 4–5 minutes per side, until crisp and lightly browned. Drain the polenta on kitchen paper and serve with the vegetables.

SERVES 2

OPPOSITE: *Instant Polenta with Grilled Vegetables*

VARIATION

POLENTA WITH GARLIC MAYONNAISE AND SALAD

Make the polenta as described above. Serve the fried polenta with a lettuce, tomato and spring onion salad and some garlic mayonnaise made by stirring 1 garlic clove, crushed, into 4 tablespoons of mayonnaise, or a mixture of mayonnaise and yogurt.

OLIVE POLENTA WITH TOMATO SAUCE

1 tsp salt	*1 garlic clove, crushed*
75g / 3oz instant	*1 × 400g / 14oz can*
polenta	*tomatoes*
50g / 2oz olives, green	*salt and freshly*
or black or a mixture	*ground black pepper*
olive oil	
1 onion, peeled and	
chopped	

1 Put 300ml/½ pint of water and the salt into a medium non-stick saucepan and bring to the boil, then sprinkle the polenta in and stir until smooth. Cook gently for 4–5 minutes, until it has thickened.

2 Stone the olives and stir them into the cooked polenta then tip it on to a large flat plate and quickly spread it out so that it is about 1 cm/½ inch thick. Leave to cool while you prepare the sauce.

3 Heat 1 tablespoon of oil in a pan then add the onion, cover and cook gently for 10 minutes. Add the garlic and cook for 1–2 minutes, then stir in the tomatoes together with their juice, breaking them up with a wooden spoon. Simmer for 10–15 minutes until the excess liquid has evaporated.

4 Meanwhile, cut the polenta into pieces and fry in olive oil for about 4–5 minutes per side until crisp and lightly browned. Drain on kitchen paper.

5 Season the sauce with salt and pepper and serve with the polenta.

SERVES 2

I have recently discovered instant polenta, which I find excellent – it brings polenta into the fast-food category and I prefer the flavour to that of traditional slow-cooking polenta. Serve it with grilled vegetables for a meal that really brings the Mediterranean sunshine with it.

The olives give this a pleasant salty tang. Serve with a refreshing side salad.

NUTS
✳

LITTLE NUT CROQUETTES WITH CAPER SAUCE

Serve these crunchy nut croquettes with a quick-cooking vegetable such as mangetout or green beans, or with a crisp green salad or a tomato, avocado and basil salad. Some mashed potatoes go well with them, too, for a more substantial meal.

50g / 2oz butter
4 tbls plain flour
1 bay leaf
600ml / 1 pint milk
1 large onion, peeled and finely chopped
1 tbls olive oil
100g / 3½oz bread
100g / 3½oz cashew nuts

100g / 3½oz pecan nuts
salt and freshly ground black pepper
3 tbls capers
2 tsp wine vinegar
2 tbls chopped fresh chives
oil for deep-frying

1 Melt the butter in a medium saucepan and stir in the flour. Cook for 1–2 minutes, stirring, then add the bay leaf and half the milk; bring to a simmer and stir until very thick. Put half the mixture in a bowl and set aside. Then stir the remaining milk into the pan, beating hard until smooth. Leave the sauce to simmer very gently for a few minutes.

2 Meanwhile, gently fry the onion in the oil for 5–10 minutes, until lightly browned.

3 Break the bread into chunks and put it into a food processor with the cashew nuts and pecans; whizz until they are all finely chopped.

4 Add the reserved thick sauce to the onion, along with the nuts and breadcrumbs and some salt and pepper to taste. Add a little water, if necessary, for a firm but soft and pliable consistency. Form the mixture into 20 balls roughly the size of walnuts.

5 Add the capers, vinegar, chives and some salt and pepper to the sauce, then keep warm.

6 Heat some oil for deep-frying in a saucepan, wok or deep-fryer. Test the temperature by dipping a wooden chopstick or the handle of a wooden spoon into it: the oil should immediately form bubbles around it. Put in the croquettes and fry for 4–5 minutes, until brown and crisp. Drain on kitchen paper and serve at once, in a pool of the sauce.
SERVES 4

CHESTNUT AND MUSHROOM CASSEROLE

This goes well with mashed potatoes or, better still, baked potatoes – the timing of these will fit in if you allow the longer cooking time for the casserole.

5 outer stems from 1 head of celery
2 large carrots
2 large leeks
2 tbls olive oil
1 large onion, peeled and chopped
225g / 8oz field or button mushrooms
2 garlic cloves, crushed

1 × 250g / 9oz can whole chestnuts
2 tbls plain flour
good sprig of thyme
150ml / 5fl oz red wine
1 tsp vegetable stock concentrate
2 tbls soy sauce
salt and freshly ground black pepper
chopped fresh parsley

1 Wash, trim and slice the celery. Put it into a saucepan with 600ml/1 pint of water and bring to the boil. Scrape and slice the carrots; wash, trim and slice the leeks. Add all these to the pan.

2 While the vegetables simmer away, heat the oil in another pan and fry the onion for 5 minutes. Slice the mushrooms and add to the onion, along with the garlic. Stir and cook for 5 minutes.

3 Add the chestnuts to the onion mixture, then stir in the flour and cook for 2 minutes. Tip in the vegetables from the other pan, with their water.

4 Add the thyme, wine, stock concentrate, soy sauce and seasoning. Simmer gently until all the vegetables are tender. This may take only 10 minutes, but if you have time to cook it for longer – up to 45 minutes – the flavours will improve. Serve sprinkled with chopped parsley.
SERVES 4

OPPOSITE: *(top) Chestnut and Mushroom Casserole and (bottom) Little Nut Croquettes with Caper Sauce*

CHESTNUTS WITH SAVOY CABBAGE AND SAGE

This is a particularly warming and delicious dish for the autumn and winter. Do use Savoy cabbage if you can get it because its flavour is the best, although other types of cabbage can be used as well. I like this as a main course, served with some light, creamy mashed potatoes.

25g / 1oz butter
1 onion, peeled and
   sliced
1 garlic clove, crushed
½ Savoy cabbage,
   about 225g / 8oz after
   trimming

1 × 250g / 9oz can
   whole chestnuts
2–3 sprigs of sage
salt and freshly
   ground black pepper

1. Melt the butter in a medium saucepan and put in the onion; stir, then cover and cook gently for 5 minutes. Add the garlic, then cover and cook for 1–2 minutes longer.

2. Meanwhile, wash and coarsely shred the cabbage, then cook it in 1 cm/½ inch of boiling water for about 7 minutes or until just tender.

3. Add the chestnuts to the onion mixture in the pan, mashing them a bit to break them up. Heat gently until the chestnuts are warmed through.

4. Drain the cabbage thoroughly and add it to the chestnut mixture. Tear in the sage leaves, then season everything well with salt and pepper and serve immediately.

SERVES 2

Different types of nuts can be used in the pâté, but they are best if they are roasted first. This can be done under the grill or in the oven at 180°C/350°F/ Gas Mark 4 for about 20 minutes, until golden brown. In the case of hazelnuts, rub off the skins in a soft cloth. For speed, use ready-roasted nuts.

NUT PATE WITH DATE AND MINT CHUTNEY

This is one of the nicest nut pâté mixtures I know. It's equally good hot or cold, with a cooked vegetable such as green beans or a salad. The chutney makes a delicious accompaniment, but if you don't have time to prepare it the pâté is equally good without it.

150g / 5oz low-fat
   garlic and herb soft
   cheese
150g / 5oz roasted
   cashew nuts
dash of Tabasco or
   hot pepper sauce
   (optional)
50g / 2oz dried
   breadcrumbs
   (optional)

FOR THE CHUTNEY
125g / 4oz dates
1 small onion, peeled
   and chopped
1 tbls wine vinegar
2 tbls chopped fresh
   mint
pinch of cayenne
   pepper
salt and freshly
   ground black pepper

1. Make the chutney first to allow time for the flavours to develop: chop the dates then put them into a saucepan with the onion, vinegar and 3 tablespoons of water. Cover and cook gently for about 5 minutes, until both have softened and the mixture is no longer liquid.

2. Remove from the heat and add the chopped mint, cayenne pepper and some salt and pepper to taste. Transfer to a bowl and leave on one side.

3. Next make the pâté: put the cheese into a bowl and mash until soft and creamy. Grind the nuts in a food processor or with a rotary hand grater.

4. Stir the nuts into the cheese to form a mixture that is soft but will hold its shape. Add the Tabasco, if you wish, and season with salt and pepper.

5. Form the pâté into a log shape then coat it all over with the breadcrumbs, if you are using these.

6. Serve the pâté as it is (it can be chilled until needed, in which case it will firm up a bit more), or put it under a moderate grill and grill for about 3 minutes each on the top, bottom and sides, until crisp and brown and heated right through. Cut into 6 slices and serve with the date and mint chutney, if you're having this.

SERVES 2

CELERY ALMONDINE

This simple dish consists of celery in a creamy sauce with a base and topping of flaked almonds. Serve as a starter or an accompaniment, or with some boiled new potatoes for a light and unusual main course.

1 head of celery or 2 celery hearts	100g / 3½ oz flaked almonds
1 bay leaf	a little milk (optional)
25g / 1oz butter	25g / 1oz plain flour
1 onion, peeled and chopped	2 tbls cream
	salt and freshly ground black pepper

1. Wash and trim the celery, removing any damaged or tough stems, then chop it quite finely: do this by cutting down the length of each stem several times to produce long, thin strips then cutting across to produce little dice.

2. Put the celery into a saucepan with the bay leaf and water just to cover, then bring to the boil, cover and simmer for about 15 minutes or until the celery is very tender.

3. Meanwhile, melt the butter in a saucepan, add the onion and cook gently, covered, for about 5 minutes or until softened.

4. Heat the grill. Spread half the almonds out on a grill pan and grill for 1–2 minutes, until golden brown. Remove from the grill, leaving the grill on.

5. Drain the celery, reserving the liquid and making it up to 300ml/½ pint if necessary with some water or a little milk.

6. Stir the flour into the onion and cook for 1–2 minutes. Then add the celery liquid, stirring all the time. Simmer gently over a very low heat for about 5 minutes. Add the celery and continue to cook gently until the celery is heated through.

7. Scatter the toasted almonds evenly over the base of a shallow gratin dish. Stir the cream into the celery mixture, season with salt and pepper, then spoon it into the dish on top of the almonds. Sprinkle the remaining, untoasted, almonds on top and put it under the grill until the almonds are golden brown and everything is piping hot.

SERVES 2 AS A MAIN COURSE

CHESTNUT FOOL

1 × 250g / 9oz can unsweetened chestnut purée	300ml / ½ pint whipping cream
50g / 2oz icing sugar	marrons glacés and/or grated chocolate to decorate
2 tbls brandy or Armagnac	

1. Put the chestnut purée into a large bowl with the icing sugar and brandy or Armagnac and beat it until it is smooth.

2. Whisk the cream until it is thick but not standing in peaks, then fold it into the chestnut mixture.

3. Spoon the mixture into small glasses and decorate with *marrons glacés* or grated chocolate (or both). Chill until needed.

SERVES 6

ALMOND AND CHOCOLATE SLICES

200g / 7oz good-quality milk chocolate	100g / 3½ oz flaked almonds
	100g / 3½ oz raisins
	75g / 3oz cornflakes

1. Break the chocolate into pieces and put it into a large bowl set over a pan of steaming water. Leave until the chocolate has melted. Meanwhile, line a 20 cm/8 inch square cake tin with non-stick paper.

2. Remove the bowl of chocolate from the pan. Add the flaked almonds and raisins then add the cornflakes, crushing them with your hands as you do so; they need to be slightly powdery.

3. Mix thoroughly, then spoon the mixture into the tin, spreading it right into the corners and pressing it down well. Put the tin in the fridge or even the freezer if you are very rushed. It will set in about 10–15 minutes and can then be turned out, stripped of the paper, and cut into pieces.

MAKES 9

This pudding can be whizzed up at a moment's notice. Stand the can of chestnut purée on a radiator or in a pan of very hot water for a few minutes before using it, if there's time, because then it will be soft and easy to mix.

This is a variation on the well-known cornflakes-and-chocolate crunchies adored by children. It's a useful recipe if you need to produce home-made biscuits in a hurry.

VEGETABLES

Vegetables are excellent fast foods and make the basis of hundreds of speedy dishes. Most are quick to cook or can be served raw, and now that you can buy many of them ready washed the preparation time is even quicker. They can be made into wonderful main courses such as Provençal Potatoes, Broccoli with Cashew Sauce or Grilled Mediterranean Vegetables with Mozzarella; comforting soups, including Green Pea and Mint and Creamy Onion; or salads such as Thai Cabbage Salad or Italian Country Salad; vegetables are so versatile that there's plenty of scope for experiment.

SOUPS & TOP-OF-THE-STOVE DISHES

GREEN PEA AND MINT SOUP

If you're looking for a quick soup this one is hard to beat. Although it can be made all year round, it has a refreshing summery flavour.

15g / ½ oz butter	4–5 sprigs of mint
1 onion, peeled and chopped	salt and freshly ground black pepper
125g / 4oz potato, diced	1–2 tbls lemon juice
450g / 1lb frozen petits pois	

1. Melt the butter in a large saucepan and gently fry the onion and potato for about 10 minutes.
2. Add the petit pois, the leaves from the mint sprigs, and 1 litre/1¾ pints of water. Bring to the boil, then simmer gently for 10–15 minutes or until the potato and onion are tender.
3. Liquidize the soup, then pour it through a sieve back into the pan. Thin with a little water if you like, then reheat gently. Season well with salt and pepper and a good squeeze of lemon juice.
SERVES 4

QUICK VEGETABLE SOUP

Although this soup is very quick to make, the vegetables are cooked slowly in oil initially, which really helps them to release their flavour.

225g / 8oz carrots	2 tbls chopped fresh parsley
225g / 8oz parsnips	salt and freshly ground black pepper
225g / 8oz leeks	
1 tbls light olive oil	
1 × 400g / 14oz can tomatoes	

This is a very adaptable vegetable soup : throw in a handful of small pasta and add a little extra liquid 10 minutes before serving to make it more substantial; and/or add a can of haricot or cannellini beans. For a Mediterranean flavour, stir in a couple of spoonfuls of pesto just before you serve it. Eat it as it is, or with grated cheese on top. Some country-style bread goes well with it, too.

1. Scrape the carrots and cut them into tiny dice. Peel the parsnips and dice them in the same way then trim the leeks and slice them finely.
2. Heat the oil in a large saucepan and put in the vegetables. Cover and cook gently for 10 minutes, then add the tomatoes with their juice and 600ml/ 1 pint of water. Bring to the boil then reduce the heat and simmer for about 15 minutes, until tender.
3. Add the parsley, season with salt and pepper, then serve in warmed bowls.
SERVES 2–3

CREAMY ONION SOUP

700g / 1½ lb potatoes	salt and freshly ground black pepper
700g / 1½ lb onions	freshly grated nutmeg
25g / 1oz butter	
3–4 tbls single cream (optional)	

1. Peel and dice the potatoes and put them into a saucepan with 450 ml/¾ pint of water. Bring to the boil, then cover and simmer for 15–20 minutes, until very tender. Meanwhile, peel the onions and slice them into half-circles.
2. Melt the butter in another saucepan and put in the onions. Cover and cook over a gentle heat until tender. This will take about 15 minutes and they'll need stirring from time to time to prevent sticking.
3. When the potatoes are done, either mash them very thoroughly in their water or, which is easier, whizz them to a purée in a food processor then return them to the pan.
4. Tip the onions and their liquid into the potato purée and add the cream, if you're using this. Thin the soup with a little more water, reheat gently, then season with salt, pepper and freshly grated nutmeg.
SERVES 4

ROOT VEGETABLES STEWED IN OIL AND BUTTER

A warming dish for winter and one of my favourite ways of cooking root vegetables. You can use any combination you like: celeriac, Jerusalem artichokes, turnips and kohlrabi are all good. Serve this as a main course, with some coarse country-style bread.

225g / 8oz onions
225g / 8oz carrots
225g / 8oz parsnips
225g / 8oz sweet
  potatoes
2 tbls olive oil
25g / 1oz butter
salt and freshly
  ground black pepper
a little chopped fresh
  parsley, if available

1 Peel and chop the onions; scrape the carrots and slice them thinly. Peel and slice the parsnips and sweet potatoes – these can be in slightly bigger pieces.
2 Heat the oil and butter in a large saucepan and put in the vegetables. Cook very gently, with a lid on the pan, for 15–20 minutes or until tender.
3 Season with salt and pepper and scatter with a little chopped parsley, if available.
SERVES 2

VARIATION

LEEKS AND POTATOES
STEWED IN OIL AND BUTTER

Substitute 450g/1lb potatoes and 450g/1lb leeks for the root vegetables. Peel the potatoes and cut them into quite chunky slices; wash the leeks and slice them fairly thickly. Then proceed as above.

BROCCOLI WITH CASHEW SAUCE

Creamy and lightly spiced, this is delicious served with plain rice and some Indian bread.

1 tbls oil
1 onion, peeled and
  chopped
1 cinnamon stick,
  broken
small knob of fresh
  ginger root
1 garlic clove, crushed
6–8 cardamom pods
½ tsp turmeric
100g / 3½ oz cashew
  nuts
salt and freshly
  ground black pepper
1–2 tbls lemon juice
  (optional)
450g / 1lb broccoli

1 Heat the oil in a medium saucepan, add the onion and the cinnamon stick then cover and cook gently for 5 minutes, until the onion has softened. Grate the ginger on the fine side of a grater, add the ginger and the garlic to the onion, cover again and cook for 2–3 minutes.
2 Crush the cardamom so that the seeds come out of the pods; discard the pods and crush the seeds a bit. Stir these into the onion along with the turmeric and cook for 1–2 minutes longer.
3 Take the cinnamon out of the pan but don't throw it away. Tip the onion mixture into a food processor and add the cashew nuts and 300ml/ ½ pint of water. Whizz thoroughly until creamy.
4 Tip the mixture back into the pan and add the cinnamon stick again. Season with salt and pepper, sharpen with a little lemon juice if necessary, then reheat the sauce gently and keep it warm while you prepare the broccoli.
5 Wash the broccoli and divide it into florets. Peel the stems thickly to remove any tough skin, then slice them into rounds or matchsticks. Cook the broccoli in 2.5 cm/1 inch of boiling water for about 3–4 minutes, until tender; don't let it get soggy. Drain immediately and season lightly.
6 You can mix the broccoli into the cashew sauce or pour a little of the sauce on to warmed serving plates, top with the broccoli and pour the remaining sauce on top – this looks more attractive.
SERVES 2

Many other vegetables can be substituted for the broccoli: try carrots, green beans, cauliflower, pumpkin, okra, or a mixture.

LEMONY SPRING VEGETABLES

Tender spring vegetables and early herbs are so delicious and welcome when they arrive that I like to serve them on their own as a main course. You can use whatever vegetables are available, choosing contrasting colours and flavours.

225g / 8oz tiny new
  potatoes
225g / 8oz baby carrots
225g / 8oz young green
  beans, or broad beans
  still in their pods
225g / 8oz baby
  turnips or fennel

15–25g / ½–1oz butter
chopped fresh herbs,
  such as mint, parsley,
  chives, tarragon or
  chervil
squeeze of lemon juice
salt and freshly
  ground black pepper

1 Bring 5 cm/2 inches of water to the boil in a large pan. Meanwhile, clean and trim the vegetables as necessary.

2 Put the vegetables into the boiling water, adding them according to the time they will take to cook: about 10 minutes for the potatoes and carrots; 6–8 minutes for the turnips and fennel; and 2 minutes for the beans. Cook until just tender.

3 Drain the vegetables, add the butter, herbs, lemon juice and seasoning, then serve at once.
SERVES 2

PROVENCAL POTATOES

This is good served with green salad or some baby spinach – for speed, buy spinach ready washed and microwave it in the packet, or cook it without water in a pan for a few minutes until just wilted.

1 onion, peeled and
  chopped
1 tbls olive oil
1 garlic clove, crushed
1 × 400g / 14oz can
  tomatoes
350g / 12oz potatoes
2 sun-dried tomatoes
  in oil, drained

50g / 2oz Kalamata
  olives
salt and freshly
  ground black pepper
shavings of fresh
  Parmesan cheese
  (optional)

1 Fry the onion in the oil for 5 minutes, then add the garlic and the canned tomatoes, breaking the tomatoes up with a wooden spoon. Bring to the boil and simmer for 10–15 minutes, until very thick.

2 Meanwhile, bring 5 cm/2 inches of water to the boil for the potatoes. Peel the potatoes then cut them into 6 mm/¼ inch thick slices. Add to the pan, cover and simmer for 7–10 minutes, until tender but not breaking up, then drain.

3 Chop the sun-dried tomatoes and add to the sauce along with half the olives. Season, then mix together the sauce and the potatoes, top with the remaining olives and serve immediately. Or top with Parmesan cheese, brown under the grill, then garnish with the remaining olives and serve.
SERVES 2

COLCANNON

700g / 1½ lb potatoes
700g / 1½ lb kale or
  dark cabbage
2 leeks

125ml / 4fl oz milk or
  single cream
50g / 2oz butter
salt and freshly
  ground black pepper

1 Peel and dice the potatoes then boil for 15–20 minutes, until tender.

2 Meanwhile, wash the kale or cabbage, remove any tough stems and shred the rest coarsely. Cook, covered, in 1 cm/½ inch of boiling water for 15–20 minutes: it needs cooking for longer than usual.

3 Clean and trim the leeks then slice them quite finely. Put them into a saucepan with the milk or cream and simmer gently for 5–6 minutes, until tender. Put the butter into a small bowl and set it on top of the pan of leeks to melt the butter.

4 Drain the kale or cabbage and quickly chop it. Put it back in the pan to keep warm.

5 Drain the potatoes and mash with the leeks and milk or cream. Mix in the kale and season well. Transfer the mixture to heated plates, make a well in the centre and pour the melted butter into it.
SERVES 4

OPPOSITE: *(left) Quick Vegetable Soup, page 104, (right) Lemony Spring Vegetables, (bottom) Provençal Potatoes*

GRATINS & GRILLS

✳

CHEESY VEGETABLE GRATIN

This works best if you use a big shallow gratin dish so that you end up with quite a thin layer of vegetables and lots of lovely, golden cheesy topping. You can use a variety of different vegetables; choose ones that take about the same time to cook, or add them to the boiling water in succession, according to their cooking time.

225g / 8oz carrots
225g / 8oz fennel
225g / 8oz courgettes
125–175g / 4–6oz
  Gruyère or Cheddar
  cheese

salt and freshly
  ground black pepper

1 Put the kettle on. Scrape the carrots and slice them thinly then put them into a saucepan, pour over boiling water to cover, and simmer for 5 minutes while you prepare the fennel.

2 Trim the fennel, paring away any tough parts on the outer leaves, then slice it into slightly bigger pieces than the carrots. Add to the pan and cook for 5 more minutes.

3 Meanwhile, wash and trim the courgettes, then slice them thinly and add to the pan. Cook for 2–3 minutes, until all the vegetables are tender.

4 Heat the grill. Drain the vegetables (keep the water, if you like; it makes excellent stock). Put the vegetables into a shallow gratin dish and season them lightly with salt and pepper. Then grate or slice the cheese, arrange it on top of the vegetables and put the dish under the grill for 7–10 minutes, until the cheese is golden brown and bubbling.

SERVES 2

Balsamic vinegar has a wonderful sweet, mellow flavour and comes in a wide price range, depending on how long it has been aged. A few drops of even a modestly priced one (which is what I use most of the time) will do wonders for many foods.

GRILLED FENNEL PLATTER

Tender, slightly sweet grilled fennel is combined here with peppery leaves, tangy red peppers and creamy hummus or soft cheese. Serve this platter with some good warm bread.

2 red peppers
2 large fennel bulbs
1 tbls olive oil
dash of balsamic
  vinegar
salt and freshly
  ground black pepper

75g / 3oz rocket or
  watercress
125g / 4oz hummus or
  soft cheese, such as
  white goat's cheese,
  curd cheese or ricotta

1 Heat the grill. Cut the peppers into quarters, place them cut-side down on a grill pan and grill on high for 10–15 minutes, until the skins have blistered and charred in places. Remove from the grill and cover with a damp cloth.

2 Meanwhile, bring 2.5 cm / 1 inch of water to the boil in a saucepan. Trim the fennel, paring away any tough parts on the outer leaves and cutting off the feathery top, then cut it into either six or eight pieces that still hold together at the base. Add to the boiling water, cook for about 8 minutes, until almost completely tender, then drain (keep the water, if you like; it makes excellent stock).

3 Toss the fennel in the oil so that the pieces are completely coated, then spread them out on a grill pan and grill under a high heat for 5–10 minutes or until they are lightly browned, turning them halfway through.

4 Meanwhile, skin and de-seed the red peppers and cut them into strips.

5 Season the fennel and peppers with the balsamic vinegar and salt and pepper to taste. Mix them together if you like, and arrange them on a platter with the rocket or watercress and the hummus or soft cheese.

SERVES 2

BUTTERNUT SQUASH AND GOAT'S CHEESE GRATIN

This unusual gratin is excellent served with a chicory and walnut salad.

*1 butternut squash,
    about 1.1kg / 2½ lb*
15g / ½oz butter
*1 onion, peeled and
    chopped*
1 garlic clove, crushed
*salt and freshly
    ground black pepper*
*200g / 7oz goat's
    cheese log*

1 Put the kettle on. Peel and de-seed the butternut squash, then cut the flesh into slices about 6 mm/¼ inch thick. Put them into a saucepan and cover with boiling water, then simmer for about 7 minutes, until tender.

2 Meanwhile, melt the butter in a saucepan, add the onion and garlic, cover and cook gently for about 5 minutes, until the onion is tender.

3 Heat the grill. Drain the butternut squash, reserving the liquid, then return the squash to the pan and add the onion and garlic. You can mash the butternut squash, adding a little of the reserved liquid, if you wish, or leave it as it is. In any case, season with salt and pepper.

4 Put the mixture into a shallow gratin dish. Then slice the cheese thinly, including the rind, and arrange it on top in overlapping slices, like roof tiles. Put it under the grill for 7–10 minutes, until the cheese is golden brown.

SERVES 4

CAULIFLOWER TOMATO CHEESE

This tasty and colourful variation of an old favourite, is good served with a crisp green salad, a quickly cooked green vegetable or something easy such as frozen peas or beans.

1 tbls olive oil
*1 onion, peeled and
    chopped*
1 garlic clove, crushed
*1 × 400g / 14oz can
    tomatoes*
*1 small to medium
    cauliflower*
*salt and freshly
    ground black pepper*
*125g / 4oz Cheddar or
    Gruyère cheese,
    grated*

1 First make the tomato sauce: heat the olive oil in a medium pan then fry the onion in it for 5 minutes, until beginning to soften. Add the garlic and tomatoes, breaking the tomatoes up roughly with a wooden spoon.

2 Bring to the boil and let the mixture simmer away for 10–15 minutes, until it is very thick and any excess liquid has evaporated.

3 Meanwhile, wash and trim the cauliflower, breaking it up into even-sized florets. Cook it in 5 cm/2 inches of boiling water for about 5 minutes, until tender, then drain.

4 Heat the grill. Mix the cauliflower florets with the tomato sauce and season well with salt and pepper. Spoon it into a shallow gratin dish, sprinkle with the grated cheese and grill until the cheese is golden brown.

SERVES 2–3

Various types of cheese can be used for this: try blue cheese or feta for a tangy flavour, or one of the flavoured cheeses, such as sage Derby or Cotswold with chives and onion.

MUSHROOMS STUFFED WITH FETA AND RED ONION

These are good served on a base of shredded crisp lettuce, though you could serve them on rounds of toast or fried bread, if you prefer.

1 red onion	6 large flat mushrooms
olive oil	125g / 4oz feta cheese

1 Peel the onion then slice it into thin rings. Heat 1 tablespoon of oil in a pan, add the onion, cover and cook gently for 5–10 minutes, until tender.

2 Heat the grill to high. Wipe the mushrooms and remove the stalks. Brush the caps lightly with olive oil, then place them on a grill pan and grill for 5–10 minutes, until tender and lightly browned. To check if they are done, turn them over and look underneath – it should be moist and tender.

3 Cut the feta cheese into 6 mm/¼ inch cubes. Mix these with the onion in the pan (off the heat).

4 Turn all the mushrooms so that the gills are uppermost, then divide the cheese mixture between them. Put them back under the grill for 5–10 minutes, until the cheese has melted and browned and the mushrooms are piping hot. Serve at once.

SERVES 2

GRILLED MEDITERRANEAN VEGETABLES WITH MOZZARELLA

1 large aubergine, about 350g / 12oz	350g / 12oz tomatoes, preferably cherry tomatoes
350g / 12oz courgettes	
2 tbls olive oil	225g / 8oz Mozzarella cheese
salt and freshly ground black pepper	sprigs of basil

1 Set the grill to high. Cut the aubergine into pieces about 6 mm/¼ inch thick, 5 cm/2 inches long and 2.5 cm/1 inch wide; slice the courgettes into 6 mm/¼ inch rounds. Put them on a grill pan then sprinkle with the olive oil and some salt and

This only needs some good bread – perhaps a crusty Italian-style loaf – to accompany it.

pepper and, using your hands, mix the vegetables so that they all get coated with oil.

2 Put the vegetables under the grill for about 10 minutes, turning them as necessary. Then add the tomatoes – cherry tomatoes whole, others quartered – and grill for a further 5 minutes.

3 Meanwhile, cut the Mozzarella cheese into smallish chunks and add these to the vegetables. Grill for about 5 minutes longer, until the cheese has melted and browned lightly, then tear the basil over the top and serve at once.

SERVES 2

PARSNIP AND HAZELNUT GRATIN

This goes well with some peppery watercress for a quick light lunch or evening meal.

700g / 1½ lb parsnips	salt and freshly ground black pepper
15g / ½ oz butter	
150ml / 5fl oz soured cream	100g / 3½ oz hazelnuts

1 Put the kettle on. Peel the parsnips and cut them into even-sized pieces. Put them in a saucepan, pour over boiling water to cover and simmer for about 10 minutes, until tender.

2 Heat the grill. Drain the parsnips, add the butter and mash well, then stir in the soured cream and season with salt and pepper to taste.

3 Spoon the mixture into a shallow gratin dish. Crush the hazelnuts with a rolling pin or whizz them briefly in a food processor. Scatter them on top of the parsnip mixture.

4 Put the dish under the grill for 5 minutes or so, until the hazelnuts are golden brown.

SERVES 2

OPPOSITE: *Grilled Mediterranean Vegetables with Mozzarella*

POTATO WEDGES

✳

Jacket potatoes are a wonderful convenience food because they are so quick to prepare, but the drawback is the long cooking time. Here is a version that is both fast to prepare and fast to cook. This is achieved by cutting and parboiling the potatoes first, then brushing them with olive oil and grilling them to cook them through. They're best served with moist toppings and dips, and a simple crisp salad such as little gem lettuce or chicory and watercress.

BASIC RECIPE

I generally buy a bag of potatoes which are good all-rounders (such as Desiree, King Edward or Maris Piper) and use the larger ones for this recipe; the large ones which supermarkets label 'baking potatoes' often cost much more than the ones you pick out yourself!

2 × 225–350g / 8–12oz	*olive oil*
potatoes	*sea salt*

1. Put the kettle on. Scrub the potatoes, cut each one in half lengthways and then in half again, to make four long wedges.
2. Put the potato wedges into a saucepan, cover with boiling water and bring back to the boil. Cook for 5 minutes from the time the water boils, then drain thoroughly.
3. Meanwhile, heat the grill. Brush the drained potato wedges all over with olive oil, then put them on a baking sheet or a grill pan and place them under the grill.
4. Grill on high for 10–15 minutes, until the potatoes are tender right through and golden brown, turning them as necessary. Remove from the grill, sprinkle with sea salt, then serve with any of the toppings below.

SERVES 2

VARIATIONS

1 POTATO WEDGES WITH HERBS

Sprinkle the potatoes with fresh rosemary or thyme before grilling; caraway seeds are good, too, if you like the flavour.

2 POTATO STEAKS

These are made in the same way, except that this time you cut the potatoes into slices about 1 cm/ ½ inch thick – like steaks – instead of into wedges.

TOPPINGS

All these toppings make enough for two large potatoes. As well as the recipes below, you could try the following suggestions: soured cream mixed with horseradish sauce or chopped fresh chives; guacamole (see page 27); good-quality bought pesto or homemade (see page 65); soft goat's cheese, cream cheese or cottage cheese; hummus; garlic butter; or, of course, plenty of butter and grated cheese.

— 1 —

MUSHROOMS IN SOURED CREAM

225g / 8oz chestnut	*salt and freshly*
mushrooms	*ground black pepper*
25g / 1oz butter	*chopped fresh chives*
1 garlic clove, crushed	
150ml / 5fl oz soured	
cream	

1. Wipe and slice the mushrooms. Melt the butter in a saucepan and add the mushrooms then cook, uncovered, for about 5 minutes, until tender.
2. Add the garlic and cook for a further 1–2 minutes, then remove from the heat.
3. Just before you are ready to serve, put the pan back on the heat and get the mushrooms sizzling again. Then add the soured cream and stir until it has heated through; don't let it boil or it will curdle. Remove from the heat, season, and serve with some chopped chives on top.

— 2 —
RED AND YELLOW PEPPER SALSA

Start making this before you prepare the potato wedges, so the peppers can be grilling while you scrub and boil the potatoes.

1 red pepper	*salt and freshly*
1 yellow pepper	*ground black pepper*
2 large tomatoes	

[1] Heat the grill. Cut the peppers in half and put them cut-side down on a grill pan, then grill them under a fierce heat until they are blistered and charred in places. Remove them from the grill and cover with a damp tea towel.

[2] Pour boiling water over the tomatoes, leave for a few seconds until the skins loosen, then drain them and cover with cold water. Remove the skins with a sharp knife. Chop the tomatoes and put them into a bowl.

[3] Remove the skin from the pepper halves – it will peel off easily – and also remove any seeds. Thinly slice the peppers and add to the tomatoes. Mix well and season with salt and pepper.

— 3 —
CHILLI-TOMATO SAUCE

1 tbls olive oil	*chilli powder*
1 onion, peeled and	*salt, freshly ground*
chopped	*black pepper and*
1 garlic clove, crushed	*sugar*
1 × 400g / 14oz can	
tomatoes	

[1] Heat the oil in a saucepan, then put in the onion, cover and cook for 10 minutes.

[2] Stir in the garlic and cook for 1–2 minutes, then pour in the tomatoes, breaking them up with the spoon. Add a pinch or so of chilli powder to taste. Cook for 10–15 minutes, uncovered, until the mixture is thick.

[3] Season with salt and pepper then add extra chilli powder if the sauce needs more of a kick, and a dash of sugar if necessary.

— 4 —
HERB CREAM CHEESE

Put a packet of garlic and herb cream cheese into a bowl and add 2 tablespoons of hot water, then beat it until it is smooth and creamy, adding more water if necessary to achieve this consistency.

— 5 —
ROMESCO SAUCE

1 red pepper	*piece of dried red chilli*
olive oil	*or a pinch of chilli*
25g / 1oz white bread	*powder*
25g / 1oz flaked	*1 tomato, skinned and*
almonds	*quartered*
1 small garlic clove,	*salt and freshly*
peeled	*ground black pepper*
	balsamic vinegar

[1] Heat the grill. Cut the pepper in half, put the halves cut-side down on a grill pan and grill under a fierce heat for about 10 minutes, until they are blistered and charred in places. Remove from the grill and cover with a damp tea towel.

[2] Meanwhile, heat a little olive oil in a frying pan and fry the bread until it is crisp and golden brown on both sides. Then remove it from the pan and put in the almonds, frying them until they are golden brown.

[3] When the pepper is cool enough to handle, peel off the skin, remove the seeds and stem, and cut the pepper into rough chunks. Put it into a food processor with the bread, roughly torn, and the almonds, garlic, chilli and tomato. Whizz to a creamy purée.

[4] Season with salt and coarsely ground black pepper then mix in a few drops of balsamic vinegar to taste.

— 6 —
CREAMY SWEETCORN

25g / 1oz butter	225g / 8oz frozen
2 tbls plain flour	sweetcorn
300ml / ½ pint milk	salt and freshly
½–1 red pepper,	ground black pepper
chopped (optional)	

1 Melt the butter in a saucepan, then stir in the flour. Let it cook for a minute or two, then stir in the milk. Bring it to the boil, stirring, to make a smooth sauce. If you are using the red pepper, add this now, then leave the sauce to simmer over a low heat for 5 minutes.

2 Add the frozen sweetcorn and cook for a further 3–4 minutes, then season to taste with salt and pepper.

— 7 —
CHEDDAR CHEESE AND SPRING ONION DIP

15g / ½oz soft butter	2 spring onions
125g / 4oz Cheddar	salt and freshly
cheese, grated	ground black pepper
4 tbls single cream or	
milk	

1 Put the butter into a bowl and add the cheese and cream or milk. Beat to make a creamy mixture.

2 Trim and chop the spring onions then stir them into the dip and season to taste.

— 8 —
GREEN HERB MAYONNAISE

Put 4 tablespoons of good-quality mayonnaise, or 2 tablespoons of mayonnaise and 2 tablespoons of yogurt, into a small bowl and stir in 4 tablespoons of finely chopped fresh herbs, such as parsley, chives, tarragon, chervil.

OPPOSITE: *Baked Potato Wedges and Steaks topped with Pesto, Romesco Sauce and herbs*

— 9 —
VERY MINTY TZATZIKI

½ cucumber	½ garlic clove, crushed
salt and freshly	4 tbls chopped fresh
ground black pepper	mint
150ml / 5fl oz thick	
Greek yogurt	

1 Peel the cucumber and cut it into small dice. Put these into a sieve, sprinkle with salt, cover with a plate and a weight and leave on one side to draw out excess moisture.

2 Put the yogurt into a bowl and mix in the garlic and most of the fresh mint.

3 Just before you are ready to serve, pat the cucumber dry on kitchen paper then stir it into the yogurt mixture. Check the seasoning, then sprinkle the rest of the mint on top.

— 10 —
COLESLAW

Home-made coleslaw is so much nicer than the bought variety and it's dead simple to make.

125g / 4oz cabbage	2 spring onions
2 small carrots	(optional)
8 tbls good-quality	salt and freshly
mayonnaise, or a	ground black pepper
mixture of	
mayonnaise and	
plain yogurt	

1 Wash the cabbage, then shred it finely and put it into a bowl.

2 Scrub or scrape the carrots then grate them into the bowl.

3 Stir in the mayonnaise or mayonnaise and yogurt. Trim and chop the spring onions, if you're using them, and add them to the bowl, too. Season with salt and pepper to taste.

SPICED VEGETABLE DISHES

SPICED MIXED VEGETABLES IN CREAMY SAUCE

This is a very simple spiced vegetable dish and I think it's nicest served with some plain basmati rice. You can use all kinds of different vegetables, and if you don't like the idea of the soured cream (which has the same fat content as single cream) you could substitute single cream or even milk.

There's no need to peel fresh ginger if you're grating it: just use a fairly fine grater.

175g / 6oz carrots	½ tsp garam masala
175g / 6oz potatoes	150ml / 5fl oz soured
175g / 6oz courgettes	cream
125g / 4oz frozen peas	salt and freshly
2 tbls oil	ground black pepper
knob of fresh ginger	chopped fresh
root	coriander
2 tbls ground	
coriander	

1 Put the kettle on. Scrape the carrots and slice them thinly; peel the potatoes and cut them into bigger pieces. Put them into a saucepan, pour over boiling water to cover, then simmer for about 10 minutes, until they are nearly tender.

2 Meanwhile, wash, trim and slice the courgettes. Add them to the pan, along with the frozen peas, and cook for 2–3 minutes, until just tender. Drain the vegetables (keep the water, if you like; it makes excellent stock).

3 Heat the oil in a large saucepan, grate the ginger and add it to the pan. Cook for a few seconds, then stir in the ground coriander and garam masala and cook for a few seconds more.

4 Add the cooked vegetables and stir over the heat until they are coated with the spices, then stir in the soured cream and continue to cook for a few minutes more until the cream is heated through. Season with salt and pepper and serve sprinkled with chopped coriander.

SERVES 2

MIXED VEGETABLE CURRY

This makes quite a large quantity and tastes very good the next day, reheated.

1 onion	2 tbls ground
1 large carrot	coriander
2 tbls olive oil	6 curry leaves or ¼ tsp
1 potato, about	curry powder
225g / 8oz	salt and freshly
knob of fresh ginger	ground black pepper
root	½ medium cauliflower
1 garlic clove	125g / 4oz green beans
1 green chilli	fresh coriander, if
½ tsp turmeric powder	available

1 Peel and chop the onion; scrape and thinly slice the carrot. Heat the oil in a large saucepan, put in the onion and carrot, then cover and cook gently. Peel the potato, cut it into even-sized pieces and add these to the pan.

2 Grate the ginger and crush the garlic; halve, de-seed and chop the chilli. Add these to the pan along with the turmeric, ground coriander and curry leaves or powder and stir well for 1–2 minutes so that everything gets coated with the spices.

3 Add 450ml/¾ pint of water, 2 teaspoons of salt and a grinding of pepper to the pan. Bring to the boil, then leave to simmer, covered, for 5 minutes.

4 Meanwhile, wash the cauliflower and remove the leaves, saving any that are tender; chop these up. Break the cauliflower into florets of roughly equal size. Wash and trim the green beans.

5 Stir the cauliflower and beans into the pan then cover and cook for 7–10 minutes or until all the vegetables are just tender. If the mixture looks too liquid, turn up the heat and let it bubble away for a minute or two. Then check the seasoning and serve. It's nice with some fresh coriander snipped over the top, if you have some.

SERVES 2–4

SPICED SPINACH AND POTATOES

I love the combination of potatoes and dark green leafy vegetables. It's found in a number of peasant dishes around the world. From Ireland there's the soothing Colcannon (see page 106), while India offers this spicy mixture, very different in character yet equally appealing. It's good with some dal (see page 87), if you've time to make that too, otherwise just serve with plain rice or Indian breads.

225g / 8oz potatoes	1 garlic clove, crushed
2 tbls oil	450g / 1lb tender fresh
1 red chilli, fresh or	or frozen leaf spinach
dried	salt and freshly
2 tsp cumin seeds	ground black pepper
½ tsp turmeric	
1 onion, peeled and	
chopped	

1 Peel the potatoes and cut them into 1 cm/ ½ inch cubes. Heat the oil in a large saucepan, then put in the whole chilli, the cumin seeds and turmeric; stir over the heat for a few seconds, letting the spices fry but not burn.

2 Add the potatoes, onion and garlic then cover and leave them to cook gently for about 15 minutes, or until the potatoes are tender. Stir from time to time and add 1–2 tablespoons of water if the vegetables start to stick.

3 Meanwhile, cook the spinach: if you are using fresh spinach, wash it and put the leaves, still damp, into a large saucepan without any extra water. Cover and cook for 5–8 minutes until tender. If you are using frozen spinach, cook it in 6 mm/¼ inch of boiling water for about 3 minutes. Drain the spinach well.

4 Add the spinach to the potato mixture and remove the chilli. Season with salt and pepper and then serve.

SERVES 2

THAI-FLAVOURED AUBERGINE IN COCONUT MILK

Aubergine cooked like this is rich and full of flavour. I like it best served with some plain boiled basmati rice. The aubergine won't spoil if it's cooked ahead of time and reheated – in fact this gives the flavours a chance to develop. Don't leave out the fresh coriander; it really is essential for this dish.

1 tbls dark sesame oil	salt, freshly ground
1 onion, peeled and	black pepper, and
chopped	sugar
1 garlic clove, crushed	1 packet of fresh
1 green or red chilli	coriander
1 large aubergine	
1 tbls coconut milk	
powder	

1 Heat the oil in a medium saucepan, add the onion and garlic, then cover and cook gently for 5 minutes, until softened.

2 Meanwhile, halve, de-seed and chop the chilli; wash the aubergine and remove the stem. Cut the aubergine into chunky pieces roughly 1 cm/½ inch square. Add the chilli and aubergine to the pan, then cover and cook for a further 5 minutes. There won't be enough oil for the aubergine to soak up, but that's all right.

3 Put the coconut milk powder into a jug and stir in 300ml/½ pint of water, then pour this into the pan and bring to the boil. Cover and leave to simmer for about 20 minutes, or until the aubergine is tender and the liquid has reduced to a shiny sauce. If there is too much liquid at this stage, just turn up the heat and let it boil, uncovered, for a few more minutes.

4 Season with plenty of salt and freshly ground black pepper, and some sugar – I find it needs about half a teaspoonful for the right balance of flavours. Then snip in a generous amount of fresh coriander. You can serve the aubergine straight away, if you like, but it is also extremely good eaten at room temperature.

SERVES 2

You can buy coconut milk powder at Chinese shops and some large supermarkets. If you can't get it you can substitute canned coconut milk, or use desiccated coconut as described on page 91.

FRITTERS & FRIED VEGETABLES

✳

*Although most health-conscious people are cutting down on their fat intake, fritters can still have
their place in a healthy diet as a delicious occasional treat – and they're quick and easy to make.
Serve them with low-fat accompaniments such as salad, steamed vegetables or plain rice.*

ONION BHAJEES

*These are often served as a nibble, but they make a
filling meal served with some plainly cooked rice,
chutney and perhaps a raita.*

125g / 4oz chick pea (gram) flour	1 tsp salt
2 tsp ground coriander	oil for deep-frying
1 tsp ground cumin	1 onion, peeled and finely chopped
pinch of cayenne pepper	1 tbls chopped fresh coriander (optional)

1 Sift the chick pea flour into a bowl with the
ground coriander, cumin and cayenne. Add the
salt, then pour in 150ml/5fl oz of tepid water and
stir to make a batter.

2 Heat some oil in a deep-fryer or large
saucepan. Stir the chopped onion, and the fresh
coriander if you are using this, into the batter, then,
when the oil is hot, drop teaspoonfuls of the mixture into the pan and fry, in batches, for about 5
minutes, until they are really crisp and the onion is
cooked through.

3 Drain the bhajees on kitchen paper and keep
the first batch warm, uncovered, while you cook
the rest. Then serve immediately.

SERVES 2

VEGETABLES IN CHICK PEA BATTER

*This is more of a snack than a main meal. Serve with
mango chutney and a raita made by stirring fresh
coriander, mint or crushed garlic into plain yogurt.*

75g / 3oz chick pea (gram) flour	1 tsp oil
½ tsp cumin seeds	oil for deep-frying
½ tsp ground coriander	175–225g / 6–8oz mixed vegetables:
good pinch of cayenne pepper	onions, cauliflower and courgettes
½ tsp salt	

1 Make the batter: sift the chick pea flour into a
bowl then stir in the spices and salt. Add the oil and
about 125–150ml/4–5fl oz warm water to make a
fairly thick batter.

2 Heat some oil in a deep-fryer, wok or large
saucepan. Meanwhile, prepare the vegetables. They
need to be in fairly small pieces so that they will
have cooked by the time the batter is crisp. Peel
onions and slice them into rings; cut cauliflower
into fairly small florets and courgettes into batons
or rounds.

3 Dip the vegetables in the batter and shake off
the excess. Fry them in the oil, in batches, for a few
minutes, until they are crisp and golden brown on
the outside, tender within. Drain on kitchen paper
and serve at once, before they lose their crispness.

SERVES 2

*A wok is excellent
for deep-frying
because it has a
large surface area
but does not require
a great deal of oil.
Groundnut and corn
are two of the most
suitable oils for
deep-frying; but
try not to re-use
the oil too many
times.*

OPPOSITE: *Vegetables in Chick Pea Batter*

MUSHROOMS IN BATTER WITH GARLIC MAYONNAISE

The batter for these is taken from Elizabeth David's French Provincial Cooking, *except that I don't usually let it stand for two hours and certainly not if I'm in a hurry. As Elizabeth David says, it always comes out light and crisp. The mushrooms make a good main course if you serve them with watercress or some other salad.*

125g / 4oz plain flour
3 tbls olive oil
salt and freshly ground black pepper
oil for deep-frying
225g / 8oz baby button mushrooms, really tiny ones are best
1 garlic clove, crushed
4 tbls good bought mayonnaise, or a mixture of mayonnaise and yogurt
1 egg white

1. Sift the flour into a bowl, then add the olive oil, 1 teaspoon of salt, a grinding of pepper and 150ml/5fl oz of tepid water. Beat well until it becomes a smooth cream.
2. Heat some oil in a deep-fryer or a large saucepan. Wipe the mushrooms with damp kitchen paper, then put them on a plate and sprinkle them with salt and a grinding of pepper. Mix the garlic with the mayonnaise or mayonnaise and yogurt.
3. Whisk the egg white until it is stiff then fold it gently into the batter. When the oil is hot, dip the mushrooms into the batter to coat them, then drop them, a few at a time, into the hot oil. Let them fry for about 3–4 minutes, until golden brown and crisp. It's important that they are in the oil long enough to cook through.
4. Drain the mushrooms on kitchen paper and keep the first lot warm, uncovered, while you cook the rest. Then serve immediately, while they're still really crisp, with the garlic mayonnaise.
SERVES 2–3

Test the temperature of oil for deep-frying by dipping a wooden chopstick or the handle of a wooden spoon into it: if the oil is hot enough it should immediately form bubbles around it.

CHILLI AND ONION CORN CAKES

These crisp golden-brown savoury cakes make an excellent main course served with a lettuce or tomato salad and some cooked rice. They are also good with chutney, or a sauce made by stirring chopped fresh herbs into plain yogurt.

1 × 350g / 12oz can sweetcorn, drained
125g / 4oz instant polenta
2 eggs
50g / 2oz fresh Parmesan cheese, grated
4 tbls milk
4 spring onions
1 green chilli
salt and freshly ground black pepper
oil for shallow-frying
a little extra grated Parmesan to serve (optional)

1. Put the sweetcorn into a bowl with the polenta. Add the eggs, grated Parmesan and milk, and mix together well.
2. Trim and finely chop the spring onions; halve, de-seed and finely chop the chilli, washing your hands well afterwards. Add the spring onions and chilli to the sweetcorn mixture and season with salt and pepper.
3. Pour enough oil into a frying pan to cover the base thinly. When it is hot, drop heaped table-spoonfuls of the mixture into the pan to make flat 'cakes'. Fry them for about 2 minutes, until crisp and brown underneath, then flip them over and fry the other side for the same amount of time.
4. Drain the cakes on kitchen paper and keep them warm while you fry the remaining mixture. Serve immediately, sprinkled with some more grated Parmesan, if you like.
SERVES 4

QUICK POTATO PANCAKES

2 large potatoes, about   *butter*
  450g / 1lb altogether   *oil*
1 tsp salt

☐1 Peel the potatoes, then grate them on the coarse side of a grater. Mix the grated potatoes with the salt (don't rinse the potatoes; the starch is necessary to hold the pancakes together).

☐2 Heat a knob of butter and 1 tablespoon of oil in a frying pan and put in spoonfuls of the potato mixture, flattening them with the back of the spoon. After about 3 minutes, when the underneath is crisp and brown, turn the pancakes over and cook the other side for about 3 minutes, until brown.

☐3 Drain on kitchen paper, then cook the remaining mixture in the same way, adding more butter and oil if necessary. Serve immediately.

SERVES 2

POTATO KOFTAS WITH SPICY BEAN SAUCE

This consists of crisp potato balls served with a spiced bean mixture. It was inspired by a recipe in The Flavours of Gujerati, *published by Virani Food Products, from which I've adapted the koftas.*

450g / 1lb potatoes
1 tbls olive oil
1 onion, peeled and
  chopped
1 garlic clove, crushed
1 × 400g / 14oz can
  tomatoes
oil for deep-frying
2 tbls lemon juice
3 tbls cornflour
chilli powder

1 tbls chopped fresh
  coriander
salt, freshly ground
  black pepper, and
  sugar
50g / 2oz dried
  breadcrumbs
1 × 425g / 15oz can red
  kidney beans,
  drained
1 × 350g / 12oz can
  sweetcorn, drained

☐1 Half-fill a medium-sized pan with water and bring to the boil for the potatoes. Peel the potatoes and cut them into 1 cm/½ inch cubes. Add them to the water and cook for about 10 minutes, until tender. Drain and mash the potatoes.

☐2 Start making the sauce: heat the olive oil in a medium pan then fry the onion in it for 5 minutes, until beginning to soften. Stir in the garlic and tomatoes, breaking the tomatoes up roughly with the spoon. Bring to the boil and simmer for 10–15 minutes, until the sauce is very thick with no excess liquid.

☐3 Start heating some oil for deep-frying, but keep your eye on it. Then finish making the potato koftas: add the lemon juice, cornflour, a pinch of chilli powder, and the chopped coriander to the potatoes, then season with some salt, pepper and perhaps a pinch of sugar, if necessary.

☐4 Form the potato mixture into balls about the size of walnuts and roll them in the dried breadcrumbs to coat them lightly.

☐5 When the oil is hot enough, put in a batch of the koftas and fry for 3–4 minutes, until crisp and golden brown. Drain them on kitchen paper and keep them warm while you fry the rest.

☐6 Meanwhile, add the kidney beans and sweetcorn to the tomato sauce, then season with salt, pepper, chilli powder to taste, and a pinch of sugar, if necessary. Warm over a gentle heat until the beans and sweetcorn are heated through. Spoon the bean mixture on to warmed plates, top with the koftas and serve at once.

SERVES 4

The simplest of potato pancakes, quickly made and delicious. Try serving them with soured cream, or apple or cranberry sauce, plus a salad or green vegetable. They are also surprisingly good with hummus.

ROSTI WITH SPRING ONIONS

Rösti is very quick and simple to prepare and makes a wonderful snack. This version includes spring onions but you can vary it by adding different ingredients such as herbs, onion, grated fresh ginger and spices. It's good served with a juicy salad such as tomato and basil, and perhaps some yogurt with fresh herbs stirred into it. Alternatively, serve the crisp rösti with mushrooms in soured cream (see page 112).

450g / 1lb potatoes	*salt*
small bunch of spring onions	*4 tbls oil*

1 Scrub the potatoes then put them into a saucepan, cover with cold water and bring to the boil. Boil them for about 5 minutes, until they are just beginning to get tender on the outside. Meanwhile, trim and chop the spring onions then cut them into long, thin pieces.

2 Drain the potatoes and leave them until they are cool enough to handle, then slip off the skins using a small sharp knife and your fingers. Grate the potatoes coarsely and season with a little salt, then mix in the spring onions.

3 Heat the oil in a frying pan, then add the potato mixture and press it down with a spatula to make one large round. Fry over a moderate heat for about 7 minutes, until crisp and brown underneath. Turn the rösti over by turning it out on to a plate then sliding it back into the frying pan.

4 Continue to cook the rösti until the second side is browned and crisp, then drain on kitchen paper, sprinkle with salt and serve at once, cut into wedges.

SERVES 2

OPPOSITE: *(left) Rösti with Spring Onions, (right)* **Crisp Fried Aubergine with Parsley Sauce**

CRISP FRIED AUBERGINE WITH PARSLEY SAUCE

I love these crisp slices of aubergine with their creamy sauce. You can serve them just as they are or make more of a meal of them by adding a cooked green vegetable or salad – and even some chips if you've got time to do them!

1 medium aubergine, about 225g / 8oz	FOR THE PARSLEY SAUCE
50g / 2oz ground almonds	*25g / 1oz butter*
1 tsp chopped fresh dill	*20g / ¾ oz plain flour*
1 egg, beaten	*300 ml / ½ pint milk*
light olive oil for frying	*4 tbls cream (optional)*
fresh dill to garnish	*2–3 tbls chopped fresh parsley*
	salt and freshly ground black pepper

1 First make the parsley sauce: melt the butter in a saucepan and stir in the flour; when it froths, stir in half the milk, then beat well until it thickens. Stir in the rest of the milk and keep stirring vigorously over the heat, until the sauce is thick and smooth.

2 Let the sauce simmer over a very low heat for about 7 minutes, checking to make sure it doesn't stick or burn. Then stir in the cream, if you're using this, the parsley and plenty of salt and pepper.

3 Wash the aubergine and remove the stem. Cut the aubergine lengthwise into slices about 6 mm/ ¼ inch thick then season with salt and pepper.

4 Mix the ground almonds with the dill and some salt and pepper and put them on a flat plate. Dip the aubergine slices first in beaten egg and then into the ground almond mixture, making sure they are well-coated with almonds on both sides.

5 Heat a little oil in a large frying pan then put in the aubergine slices. You'll probably have to cook them in two batches; turn on the grill so that you can keep the first batch warm. Fry the aubergine over a moderate heat for about 4 minutes per side, until crisp and golden on both sides and tender inside when pierced with a knife. Drain on kitchen paper, garnish with dill and serve with the sauce.

SERVES 2

STIR-FRIES

—— ✳ ——

THAI STIR-FRY

This stir-fry is delicately flavoured with coconut milk but has the added kick of hot red chilli and the tang of lemon grass and fresh coriander. It's delicious with some plain boiled rice; put this on to cook first of all.

If you can't find fresh lemon grass, substitute the grated rind of half a lemon.

40g / 1½oz creamed coconut	2 tbls groundnut oil
1 dried red chilli	50g / 2oz raw peanuts
1 large carrot	1 lemon grass stalk
125g / 4oz mangetout	1 garlic clove, crushed
125g / 4oz baby sweetcorn	25g / 1oz fresh coriander leaves, roughly chopped
1 bunch of spring onions	salt and freshly ground black pepper
1 red pepper	

1 First prepare the coconut milk: either grate the coconut or cut it into thin flakes, then put it into a small saucepan with 150ml/5fl oz of water and bring to the boil. Stir until the coconut has melted, then remove from the heat and leave on one side.

2 Halve the chilli and scrape away and discard the seeds if you prefer less heat. Then chop the chilli finely and add it to the coconut cream.

3 Scrape the carrot and slice it thinly; top and tail the mangetout; halve the baby sweetcorn if they are large; trim and chop the spring onions; halve, de-seed and slice the red pepper.

4 Heat the oil in a wok or very large saucepan. When it is smoking, put in the peanuts and fry them for a few minutes until they smell and look roasted, then add all the vegetables and stir-fry for 1–2 minutes.

5 Finely chop the lemon grass and add it with the garlic to the vegetables; continue to stir-fry for 1–2 minutes until the vegetables are hot but still quite crisp, then pour in the coconut cream and stir-fry for a few seconds until this is hot. Add the coriander, season with salt and pepper and serve.

SERVES 2

CHINESE VEGETABLE STIR-FRY

The vegetables suggested here provide a good mixture of colours and textures but you can use different ones if you prefer. Some plain basmati rice goes well with this – put it on to cook before you start preparing the stir-fry.

To cook plain basmati rice, allow 50g/2oz rice and 300ml/½ pint of water per person. Wash the rice in a sieve under the cold tap, then bring the water to the boil, pour in the rice and boil fast for about 10 minutes, or until it is tender but still firm. Drain in a sieve and rinse with hot water, then put it back in the pan and keep warm until needed.

1 red onion	knob of fresh ginger root, grated
2 carrots	1 tbls cornflour
½ head of Chinese leaves	2 tbls good-quality soy sauce, such as Kikkoman
125g / 4oz broccoli	1 tsp sugar
125g / 4oz baby sweetcorn	good pinch of Chinese five-spice powder
125g / 4oz button mushrooms	salt and freshly ground black pepper
1 tbls groundnut oil	
1 garlic clove, crushed	

1 Peel, halve and slice the onion; scrape the carrots and cut them diagonally into fairly thin slices; wash the Chinese leaves and cut them into fairly chunky slices; separate the broccoli into small florets, removing any tough stem; halve the baby sweetcorn if they are large; wash and slice the mushrooms.

2 Heat the oil in a wok or very large saucepan. When it is smoking, put in all the vegetables and the garlic and ginger and stir-fry for 2–3 minutes, until they are wilting but still crunchy.

3 Put the cornflour into a small bowl or cup and mix with the soy sauce and sugar. Add this to the pan and stir-fry for 1–2 minutes longer, until the mixture has thickened and clings to the vegetables.

4 Add the five-spice powder and some salt and pepper and serve at once.

SERVES 2

OPPOSITE: *Thai Stir-fry*

MANGETOUT AND MUSHROOM STIR-FRY

This is good served simply with some rice, and it also goes extremely well with the red pepper and cashew nut stir-fry, if you want to serve two different dishes for four people.

2 tbls oil
1 large onion, peeled
  and chopped
knob of fresh ginger
  root
1 garlic clove, crushed
225g / 8oz mangetout
225g / 8oz button
  mushrooms

1 tbls cornflour
1 tsp sugar
1 tbls sherry
1 tbls soy sauce
salt and freshly
  ground black pepper

1   Heat the oil in a large frying pan or wok, put in the onion then cover and cook gently. Grate the ginger and add it to the pan, along with the garlic.

2   Wash and trim the mangetout and mushrooms as necessary, slicing or halving the mushrooms if they are large.

3   In a cup or small bowl, mix together the cornflour, sugar, sherry and soy sauce. Leave this on one side for the moment.

4   When the onion is almost done, add the mangetout and mushrooms and stir-fry for 2–3 minutes, until just tender. Then give the soy sauce mixture a quick stir and pour it in; stir until the mixture has thickened and coats the vegetables thinly. Season with salt and pepper, then serve.

SERVES 2

RED PEPPER AND CASHEW NUT STIR-FRY

This is my recreation of a dish I enjoyed in a Chinese restaurant – the combination of soft, sweet peppers and chewy cashews is very good. Serve it with some plain boiled rice.

2 large red peppers
2 tbls oil
1 hot red chilli, fresh
  or dried
100g / 3½oz cashew
  nuts

1 tbls cornflour
1 tbls soy sauce
salt and sugar

1   Halve, de-seed and slice the red peppers. Heat the oil in a wok or large saucepan and put in the whole chilli; let it sizzle away for a few seconds.

2   Add the peppers and cashew nuts to the pan, cover and cook gently for about 5 minutes, stirring occasionally. Add 300 ml / ½ pint of water and cook for a further 10 minutes, until the peppers are very tender.

3   Meanwhile, blend the cornflour to a paste with the soy sauce, adding a little water if necessary. Pour this into the pepper mixture, stirring until it thickens.

4   Taste, and season with salt and a pinch of sugar if necessary, then serve.

SERVES 2

MAIN-COURSE SALADS

✳

WARM JERUSALEM ARTICHOKE SALAD

This is very filling and makes a good meal for the end of winter or very early spring. The hard-boiled eggs add colour, but they can be swapped with Brazil (or other) nuts for a vegan dish.

2 eggs
450g / 1lb Jerusalem
  artichokes
1 tbls olive oil
1 tbls balsamic
  vinegar

salt and freshly
  ground black pepper
a few lettuce leaves
2 tbls chopped fresh
  chives

1. Hard-boil the eggs by simmering them in a pan of boiling water for 7–10 minutes. Then drain them, cover with cold water and leave to cool.
2. Meanwhile, peel the Jerusalem artichokes, dropping them straight into cold water when they're done to keep them white. Then cut them into 6 mm/¼ inch slices.
3. Heat the oil in a medium saucepan and put in the artichoke slices; shake the pan to coat them with the oil, then cover and leave to cook very gently for about 20 minutes, until they are completely tender.
4. Meanwhile, shell the eggs, rinse them under cold water and cut them into quarters or sixths.
5. Remove the artichokes from the heat, stir in the balsamic vinegar and season with salt and pepper. Arrange the lettuce leaves on a serving plate or two individual plates. Spoon the artichokes on top and sprinkle the chives over them, then arrange the hard-boiled eggs around the edges. Serve at once.

SERVES 2

ITALIAN COUNTRY SALAD

This is a pleasant mixture of flavours and textures. Serve it simply with some country-style bread.

4 eggs
225g / 8oz fine green
  beans
225g / 8oz courgettes
1 garlic clove, crushed
1 tbls red wine vinegar

3 tbls olive oil
salt and freshly
  ground black pepper
125g / 4oz black olives
50–125g / 2–4oz
  Parmesan cheese

1. Hard-boil the eggs by simmering them in a pan of boiling water for 7–10 minutes. Then drain them, cover with cold water and leave to cool.
2. Meanwhile, bring 2.5 cm/1 inch of water to the boil in a large saucepan. Wash and trim the beans; wash and slice the courgettes. When the water boils, put in the beans and boil for 1–2 minutes, then add the courgettes and cook for a further 1–2 minutes, until just tender. Drain the vegetables.
3. Put the garlic into a salad bowl with the vinegar, olive oil and some salt and pepper. Mix well, then add the vegetables (which can still be hot). Stir gently.
4. Shell the hard-boiled eggs and rinse them under cold water, then slice them and add them to the bowl, along with the olives.
5. Cut the Parmesan cheese into thin flakes with a sharp knife or a swivel-bladed potato peeler and add these to the salad. Toss all the ingredients gently and serve.

SERVES 4

Jerusalem artichokes have such a delicious, almost nutty flavour that it's a pity many people avoid them because of their anti-social effects on the digestive system... I think their reputation in this respect is a bit exaggerated; anyway, they're certainly worth trying, and enjoying on the right occasions.

GREEN BEAN, AVOCADO AND CASHEW NUT SALAD

This is a rich and filling salad which just needs some good bread to go with it.

175g / 6oz thin green
  beans
1 medium avocado
juice of ½ lemon
1 tbls olive oil

50g / 2oz roasted
  cashew nuts
salt and freshly
  ground black pepper

1 Bring 1 cm/½ inch of water to the boil in a large pan for the green beans. Trim the beans then add them to the boiling water, cover and cook for 2–4 minutes or until just tender. Drain, and put them into a bowl.

2 Halve the avocado, remove the stone and skin, then cut it into long, thin slices.

3 Put the avocado slices into the bowl with the beans and add the lemon juice, olive oil, cashew nuts and a seasoning of salt and pepper. Go easy on the salt if the cashew nuts are already salted. Serve the salad at once.

SERVES 2

WALDORF SALAD IN RADICCHIO

This is a light version of the classic Waldorf salad and it includes grapes as well as apples, for a change. It's nicest made with freshly shelled walnuts, if you have time to crack them, and it makes a good lunch or light supper dish, perhaps served with a slice of malt bread or fruit loaf spread with cream cheese or curd cheese.

OPPOSITE: *(top) Green Bean, Avocado and Cashew Nut Salad, (right) Thai Cabbage Salad, (bottom) Waldorf Salad in Radicchio*

1 celery heart
225g / 8oz Cox's apples
125g / 4oz purple or
  red grapes
2 tbls good-quality
  mayonnaise

2 tbls plain yogurt
salt and freshly
  ground black pepper
25g / 1oz walnuts
few leaves of radicchio

1 Wash and slice the celery; peel, core and slice the apples; wash, halve and pip the grapes. Put all these ingredients into a bowl with the mayonnaise, yogurt and some salt and pepper to taste and mix gently until combined.

2 Stir in half the walnuts, then spoon the mixture into the radicchio leaves and sprinkle the remaining nuts on top. Serve at once.

SERVES 2

THAI CABBAGE SALAD

1 hot red chilli
1 lemon grass stalk
225g / 8oz white
  cabbage
125g / 4oz baby
  sweetcorn
25g / 1oz fresh
  coriander

1 tbls sesame oil
1 tbls soy sauce
juice of ½ lime
salt and freshly
  ground black pepper
sugar (optional)

1 Finely chop the chilli, scraping out and discarding the seeds if you prefer. Finely slice the lemon grass, removing any tough stem, then finely shred the cabbage, slice the baby sweetcorn into rounds and chop the coriander.

2 Heat the oil in a pan and put in the chilli and lemon grass; fry for a few seconds, then add the cabbage and baby sweetcorn; stir-fry for 1–2 minutes, until wilted, then remove from the heat, and add the soy sauce and lime juice. Mix well, then lightly stir in the coriander leaves. Season with salt, pepper and perhaps a pinch of sugar. Serve the salad while still warm.

SERVES 2–4

The Thai flavourings in this salad make it quite unusual. Serve it as a side salad with a main dish or with something simple – and most unoriental! – such as grilled cheese on toast.

FRUIT

If you're looking for something to give you a quick burst of energy, fruit beats sugary convenience foods any day: it's easy to carry, sweet and delicious to eat, and doesn't make you fat or rot your teeth. But fruit isn't just for snacking. It can also be the basis of starters, such as Three-Pear Salad, and light main courses, such as Apricots with Ricotta and Mint or Tarragon Pear with Cream Cheese. And, of course, fruit is perfect for quick nutritious desserts, from light, refreshing Peaches in Wine or Rhubarb and Ginger Compote to more substantial puddings such as Blueberry Crumble.

FRUIT SALADS & SAVOURY FRUIT DISHES

✳

MELON WITH STRAWBERRIES AND MINT

Although most often served as a starter, melon makes a pleasant dessert or even a light, refreshing snack. Small round melons with green flesh, such as baby Ogen or Galia, are ideal for this, if you can get them; otherwise use one large melon, cut it into quarters and pile the strawberries on top.

To blanch almonds, put them into a small saucepan, cover with water and boil for 2 minutes, then drain them and pop off the skins with your fingers.

225g / 8oz ripe strawberries	16 blanched almonds
caster sugar	2 baby green-fleshed melons, or 1 larger
4 sprigs of mint	melon

[1] Wash and hull the strawberries then cut them into halves or quarters. Put them in a bowl and sprinkle with a little caster sugar.
[2] Roughly tear some mint leaves to release the flavour, and add them to the strawberries, along with the almonds.
[3] Cut the baby melons in half or, if you're using one large melon, cut it into quarters. Scoop out and discard the seeds and fill the cavities with the strawberry mixture.
SERVES 4

THREE-PEAR SALAD

Although pawpaws aren't pears, their shape qualifies them for inclusion in this pretty, refreshing salad, and their flavour combines extremely well with avocado and dessert pears. This is a good starter or light lunch dish. Having the fruits perfectly ripe makes all the difference, and it's worth buying them a few days in advance, if necessary, and letting them ripen in a fruit bowl.

1 large ripe dessert pear, preferably Comice	1 large ripe avocado pear
juice of 1 lime	sprigs of fresh chervil and slices of lime to
1 large ripe pawpaw	decorate

[1] Cut the pear into quarters then peel and core it. Cut it into long thin slices and sprinkle with a little of the lime juice.
[2] Peel and quarter the pawpaw, scooping out and discarding the seeds, then cut it in the same way as the pear and sprinkle with lime juice.
[3] Prepare the avocado similarly, tossing it in the remaining lime juice.
[4] Arrange slices of the three 'pears' on individual plates, decorate with the chervil and lime slices and serve as soon as possible.
SERVES 2 AS A LIGHT MEAL, 4 AS A STARTER

OPPOSITE: *(left) Three-Pear Salad, (top) Melon with Strawberries and Mint, (right) Festive Fruit Salad, page 134*

FESTIVE FRUIT SALAD

Fruit with contrasting and toning colours, textures and flavours makes a quick and easy winter dessert with a festive air. Choose whatever fruits you fancy from what is available.

4 clementines	*1 star fruit*
2 sharon fruit	*1 pomegranate*
12 lychees	*8–12 physalis*

1 Peel the clementines then slice them into rounds and put them into a bowl. Wash the sharon fruit, remove the stems and cut the fruit into eighths or smaller segments; add to the bowl.

2 Peel and stone the lychees; wash the star fruit and cut it into thin slices to reveal the starry shapes. Add to the bowl, along with the lychees.

3 Halve the pomegranate then, holding a half over the bowl, scoop out the scarlet seeds with a pointed teaspoon, discarding any tough membranes. Repeat the process with the other half. Stir the seeds gently into the fruit.

4 Gently pull back the outer dry sepals on each physalis to form 'petals'. Arrange the physalis on top of the fruit salad.

SERVES 4

TARRAGON PEAR WITH CREAM CHEESE

This combination is simple but superb, and makes a good light meal or snack. You can control the fat content by your choice of cheese – full-fat cream cheese, medium-fat curd cheese, or even cottage cheese are all suitable.

2–3 lettuce leaves	*salt and freshly*
1 perfectly ripe pear,	*ground black pepper*
preferably Comice or	*125g / 4oz soft white*
Conference	*cheese*
½ tsp red wine vinegar	*sprig of tarragon*

1 Arrange the lettuce leaves on a serving plate. Cut the pear into quarters, then peel and core it. Cut the quarters into long, thin slices and arrange these on top of the lettuce leaves.

2 Sprinkle the vinegar over the pear, then top with plenty of coarsely ground black pepper and a less generous scattering of salt – preferably the type you can scrunch up with your fingers.

3 Put the cheese on the plate next to the pear slices, then tear some of the lower leaves from the tarragon over the top and decorate with the tender top part of the tarragon sprig.

SERVES 1

APRICOTS WITH RICOTTA AND MINT

This is only worth doing if you can get really ripe, well-flavoured apricots. It makes a lovely light dish, somewhere between a starter, salad and a dessert! I like it as a summery lunch or supper when I'm not feeling very hungry.

3–4 ripe apricots	*a little milk or single*
2–3 tsp clear honey	*cream*
75–125g / 3–4oz	*4–6 fresh mint leaves*
ricotta cheese	

1 Halve, stone and slice the apricots then put them into a bowl with the honey and mix gently.

2 Put the ricotta cheese into another bowl and mix in enough milk or cream to make a soft, creamy consistency. Then spoon it on top of the apricots but do not cover them completely.

3 Tear the mint leaves roughly and scatter on top. Serve as soon as possible.

SERVES 1

FRESH FRUIT PLATTER

Choose fruits that contrast well in colour and texture – figs, kiwi fruit, redcurrants, raspberries, strawberries, apricots, blueberries and cherries all look good. The more people you are making this for, the more varieties of fruit you can use.

175g–225g / 6–8oz fresh fruit per person

sprigs of mint, edible flowers, flaked almonds or crushed pistachios to decorate (optional)

1. Wash and prepare the fruit and cut some in halves or quarters if you like. Figs look especially attractive when quartered.
2. Arrange the fruit on a platter. Decorate, if you wish, with mint sprigs, edible flowers such as borage or nasturtium, or almonds or pistachios.

ORANGE AND KIWI FRUIT SALAD

This is a very fresh-looking and fresh-tasting fruit salad, perfect after a rich main course.

2 kiwi fruit
1 large orange
1 tbls orange blossom honey

½ tsp orange flower water

1. Peel the kiwi fruit then slice them thinly into rounds and put them into a bowl.
2. Holding the orange over the bowl, cut off the peel with a sawing motion, removing all the white pith with the rind. Then cut the segments out from between the membranes and add to the bowl.
3. Add the honey and orange flower water to the fruit and mix gently. Leave in a cool place until ready to serve.

SERVES 1–2

Orange flower water is available from good kitchen shops, Middle Eastern shops and supermarkets, but you can leave it out if you can't get it.

COLD PUDDINGS
———— ✳ ————

BANANAS WITH CREAM AND SESAME CRISP

You can vary the richness of this, using just Greek yogurt or, at the other extreme, just cream. If you don't want to go to the trouble of making the sesame crisp – although it couldn't be easier – buy some sesame crisp bars and use them instead.

2 tbls sesame seeds
6 tbls caster sugar
150ml / 5fl oz
  whipping cream

150ml / 5fl oz Greek
  yogurt
4 large bananas

1 First make the sesame crisp: have ready a square of non-stick paper. Put the sesame seeds into a small heavy-based saucepan with the sugar and place over the heat. After a minute or so the sugar will melt and then within a few seconds it will turn golden. At this point, remove it from the stove and pour it in a thin layer over the non-stick paper. Leave on one side to harden.
2 Whip the cream then fold it carefully into the Greek yogurt.
3 Peel and slice the bananas, then put them into one large or four individual bowls. Spoon the yogurt cream on top.
4 Peel the paper off the sesame crisp, then crush it into pieces by banging it with a rolling pin; scatter the pieces on top of the bananas and cream.
SERVES 4

HONEYED PEARS WITH ALMOND HALVA

Almond halva, a delicious Middle Eastern confection, can be bought in large supermarkets, delicatessens or Middle Eastern grocery shops. If you can't get it, you could use good-quality nougat instead. Chopped up and sprinkled over ripe fresh fruit, halva makes a good topping, and turns a simple fruit dish into a more substantial dessert. It works best with delicately flavoured, sweet fruit such as pears or bananas.

4 large ripe pears,
  preferably Comice
juice of ½ lemon
3–4 tbls mild honey,
  clear or thick

75–125g / 3–4oz
  almond halva

1 Cut the pears into quarters then peel and core them. Cut the quarters into long, thin slices, put them into a mixing bowl and toss them in the lemon juice to preserve their colour.
2 Put the honey into a pan, judging the amount according to the sweetness of the pears and your own preference. Heat gently until it is liquid, then pour it over the pears. Stir the pears gently and leave on one side until you are ready to serve them.
3 Chop the halva into small pieces. Transfer the pears to one large serving bowl or four individual ones, top with the halva, then serve.
SERVES 4

OPPOSITE: *(left) Fresh Fruit Platter, page 135, (centre) Orange and Kiwi Fruit Salad, page 135, (right) Bananas with Cream and Sesame Crisp*

RASPBERRIES WITH LEMON SYLLABUB

In this recipe, a tangy syllabub is layered with sweet fresh raspberries. It looks good served in tall glasses – wine glasses are ideal – and other fruit could be used instead of the raspberries. Try it with strawberries, substituting orange for the lemon in the syllabub.

200ml / 7fl oz whipping cream	25–50g / 1–2oz caster sugar
grated rind and juice of ½ lemon	225g / 8oz raspberries

1 Put the cream into a bowl with the lemon rind and juice and 25g/1oz caster sugar, then whisk until the mixture forms soft peaks. Taste and add more sugar if necessary, remembering that the raspberries will be slightly sharp.

2 Starting with raspberries, layer the raspberries and the lemon syllabub into two tall glasses. Chill until needed.

SERVES 2

STRAWBERRY FOOL

This is a simple recipe, with the fruit just crushed then folded into a mixture of yogurt and cream. For a lower-fat version, use all yogurt or a larger proportion of yogurt to cream. Other fruits can be used: ripe peaches or apricots, for instance.

225g / 8oz strawberries	150ml / 5fl oz plain yogurt
25–40g / 1–1½oz caster sugar	
150ml / 5fl oz whipping cream	

1 Wash the strawberries, remove the stems and slice the fruit roughly. Put it into a large bowl and sprinkle with sugar to taste.

2 Whisk the cream until it stands in soft peaks.

3 Add the yogurt to the strawberries, then mash them into the yogurt with a fork, but don't make the mixture smooth.

4 Fold the whipped cream into the yogurt and strawberries. Taste, and gently stir in a little more sugar if necessary.

SERVES 2–3

FRESH PINEAPPLE FOOL

You really need a sweet, well-flavoured pineapple for this recipe – choose a ripe, strongly scented one. It is tempting to make a lower-fat version using half cream and half yogurt, but I don't find that it works as well – yogurt is fairly acidic, whereas the richness of double cream balances the natural sharpness of the pineapple.

1 ripe pineapple	300ml / ½ pint double cream
juice of 1 orange	
25g / 1oz caster sugar, or to taste	chopped pistachio nuts or fresh mint leaves to decorate (optional)
2 tbls orange liqueur, such as Cointreau or Grand Marnier	

1 Peel the pineapple, removing all the tufts and the hard inner core, then chop it fairly finely or purée it in a food processor.

2 Add the orange juice to the pineapple and sprinkle with the sugar and the liqueur.

3 Whip the cream until it forms soft peaks – the acidity of the pineapple will firm it up a bit, so don't make it too stiff. Then fold the pineapple gently into the cream. Taste, and sweeten with a little more sugar if necessary.

4 Spoon the mixture into tall glasses or individual bowls and chill well before serving. Decorate with chopped pistachio nuts or fresh mint leaves, if you like.

SERVES 4

FRUIT AND ICE-CREAM

Good-quality bought ice-cream, mixed with fresh fruit and other extras such as nuts, alcohol, chocolate or coffee, makes an almost instant dessert that is popular with most people. Decent vanilla ice-cream goes with almost any fruit, and good fruit sorbets are also useful. More strongly flavoured ice-creams, such as chocolate or ginger, can be very effective if you pair them with the right fruit. Here are some ideas.

1 VANILLA ICE-CREAM WITH MELON AND GINGER

If you can get ripe, sweet baby melons, serve them cut in half and topped with a scoop of vanilla ice-cream, some chopped preserved ginger and some of its syrup. Or you could use a larger melon cut into pieces.

2 VANILLA ICE-CREAM WITH RUM RAISINS AND HOT CHOCOLATE SAUCE

For each person, put 1 tablespoon of raisins and 1 tablespoon of rum into a small pan and heat gently, then leave on one side to steep. Make the chocolate sauce (see page 146). Let the ice-cream soften at room temperature while you eat your main course, then fold the raisins and rum into the ice-cream and pour the chocolate sauce over the top.

3 VANILLA ICE-CREAM WITH BANANAS AND COFFEE

Make some espresso coffee – good-quality instant espresso will do. Slice a banana into a bowl, top with a scoop of vanilla ice-cream then pour the hot coffee over the top. Some whipped cream is good with this, too, if you really want to go to town.

4 VANILLA ICE-CREAM WITH ARMAGNAC PRUNES

Allow about 4 prunes for each serving – they should be the plump, ready-to-eat type. Put them into a shallow dish and sprinkle with 1 tablespoon of Armagnac, then leave them to steep – the longer you can leave them the better. Serve with a scoop of vanilla ice-cream and some toasted flaked almonds, if you like.

5 LEMON SORBET WITH RASPBERRY SAUCE

Make the raspberry sauce (see page 142). Pour a pool of sauce on to each plate and top with some good-quality lemon sorbet.

6 MANGO SORBET WITH EXOTIC FRUITS

Make bought mango sorbet into a festive dessert by serving it in scoops surrounded by pieces of exotic fruit: mango, lychee, pawpaw, sharon fruit, physalis – whatever is available. Passion fruit sorbet is also good served like this.

7 CHOCOLATE ICE-CREAM WITH PEARS, CHERRIES OR ORANGES

Serve scoops of rich chocolate ice-cream with any of these fruits, perhaps tossed with a little liqueur or eau de vie: poire William for pears, kirsch for cherries (they should be juicy dark ones, with the stones removed), Grand Marnier or Cointreau for oranges. Strawberries are also good: marinate these in an orange-flavoured liqueur.

8 COFFEE ICE-CREAM WITH PEARS AND MAPLE SYRUP

Peel and slice a ripe pear for each person; top with scoops of softened coffee ice-cream, drizzle over some maple syrup, and sprinkle with chopped pecan nuts.

9 STRAWBERRY ICE-CREAM WITH PEACHES AND AMARETTI

Skin and slice a large ripe peach for each person; top with a scoop of strawberry ice-cream and some softly whipped cream, then sprinkle over 2–3 crushed amaretti biscuits.

When you buy maple syrup, read the label to make sure it's the real stuff and not 'maple-flavoured' syrup. It's expensive but a little goes a long way and it keeps very well in the fridge.

RHUBARB AND GINGER COMPOTE

Fresh-tasting and succulent, this is good with almond- or orange-flavoured biscuits and some thick yogurt or cream. It can be served either cold or hot.

2 pieces of stem ginger preserved in syrup	*50g / 2oz sugar*
1kg / 2lb rhubarb	*4 tbls ginger syrup from the jar*

1 Finely chop the ginger. Trim the rhubarb and remove any stringy bits then cut it into 2.5 cm / 1 inch lengths. Wash these, then put them into a pan with the sugar, ginger syrup and chopped ginger, reserving some ginger for decoration.

2 Cover and leave to cook very gently for 2–3 minutes. Stir gently, then cook for a further 2–3 minutes, until the rhubarb is tender. Decorate with the reserved chopped ginger before serving.
SERVES 4

FRESH FRUIT MUESLI

We usually think of muesli as a cereal-based breakfast dish, but the original version was served for supper and was prepared mostly of fruit, usually grated apple. Made like this, with the addition of honey, nuts and plain yogurt, muesli makes a good pudding or, as I sometimes like to eat it, a complete lunch or supper dish.

2 tbls raisins	*1 large sweet eating apple or pear*
150ml / 5fl oz plain yogurt	*2 tbls toasted flaked almonds or hazelnuts*
1–1 ½ tbls clear honey	*single cream (optional)*
1 tbls rolled oats	

1 Put the raisins into a small bowl, cover with a little boiling water and leave to plump up.

2 Put the yogurt into a bowl and add 1 tablespoon of the honey and the oats.

3 Wash the apple or pear then grate it quite coarsely into the bowl on top of the yogurt. Drain the raisins and add them to the bowl, then gently stir everything together.

4 Top with the almonds or hazelnuts. You can drizzle a little more honey over the top if you want to make it sweeter, and serve with some single cream for a richer version.
SERVES 1

MARINATED NECTARINES AND RASPBERRIES

A quick but good summer dessert. Unless the fruit is particularly sweet, I think it needs a little help – you could use either sugar or a mild, clear honey, whichever you prefer.

2 ripe nectarines	*1–2 tbls kirsch, eau de framboise or eau de vie (optional)*
450g / 1lb fresh raspberries	
25–50g / 1–2oz sugar, or a little clear honey	

1 Halve, stone and slice the nectarines then put them into a bowl. Wash the raspberries gently, then add them to the bowl.

2 Add sugar or honey to taste, and the alcohol, if you're using this. Stir gently, then leave to marinate for 15–30 minutes.
SERVES 2–3

OPPOSITE: *Rhubarb and Ginger Compote*

PEACHES IN WINE

Ideally this should be made in advance to give the flavours time to develop, so prepare it before you start making the rest of the meal. Light biscuits and some thick creamy yogurt, lightly whipped cream or good-quality vanilla ice-cream go well with it.

*4–6 large ripe peaches
300ml / ½ pint sweet
  white wine*   *sugar*

1   Put the peaches into a bowl, cover them with boiling water for 2 minutes, until the skins loosen, then slip off the skins with a sharp knife.

2   Halve, stone and thinly slice the peaches. Put them into a bowl – a pretty glass one looks good – and pour over the wine.

3   Sweeten the mixture with a little sugar to taste, then cover the bowl and chill for as long as possible before serving.

SERVES 4

STRAWBERRIES IN RASPBERRY SAUCE

This is an ideal pudding to make in the early summer, when strawberries are at their best. You can use frozen raspberries for the sauce if fresh ones aren't available.

*450g / 1lb raspberries
2 tbls caster sugar, or
  to taste*   *450g / 1lb strawberries*

1   Purée the raspberries in a food processor then pass them through a nylon sieve to remove the seeds. Stir in the sugar.

2   Wash and hull the strawberries, then slice them. Mix the strawberries with the raspberry sauce; taste, and add more sugar if necessary.

SERVES 4

Strawberries in raspberry sauce are good on their own or with a dollop of thick Greek-style yogurt or crème fraîche and some crisp, delicate biscuits.

FRUITS IN LIQUEUR OR BRANDY

Marinating ripe fresh fruits in liqueur, brandy or eau de vie is a great way to turn them into a dessert. The longer you leave them to soak the better; if you prepare them before you start making the rest of the meal the flavours will have a chance to emerge. Choose really ripe, sweet fruit.

TRY THE FOLLOWING COMBINATIONS:
*Pineapple (make sure
  it is really ripe) or
  black cherries with
  kirsch
Satsumas, clementines
  or tangerines, peeled
  and sliced into thin
  rings, with an orange
  liqueur such as
  Grand Marnier*

*Strawberries with
  orange liqueur
Peaches with brandy
Plums with Amaretto
  (the plums must be
  very sweet and ripe)
Pear (my favourite)
  preferably a perfectly
  ripe Comice, peeled,
  sliced and sprinkled
  with poire William
  liqueur*

1   Peel, trim, core and slice the fruit as necessary – the smaller the pieces, the more they'll absorb the flavours.

2   Put the fruit into a bowl, sweeten with a little sugar to taste and pour over a few tablespoons of your chosen alcohol.

3   You can add extras just before serving, such as a sprinkling of pistachio nuts, flaked almonds or some flakes of plain chocolate. Serve accompanied by yogurt, cream and/or biscuits, if you like.

GRAPES IN BEAUMES DE VENISE

This is good served in large wine glasses – so you can drink the last drops of delicious juice! It doesn't really need any accompaniment, although you could consider a delicate, almondy biscuit to go with it.

225–350g / 8–12oz
  sweet grapes, white
  or a mixture of white,
  red and black

about 150ml / 5fl oz
  Beaumes de Venise

1 Wash and halve the grapes and remove the pips. Put the grapes into two glasses or a glass serving bowl.

2 Pour the Beaumes de Venise over the grapes and leave until you are ready to serve – but don't chill them as this dulls the flavour.

SERVES 2

MELON, GINGER AND KIWI COMPOTE

This is a very good way of improving the flavour of a melon that isn't as good as it might be. Ginger preserve is used for flavouring and sweetening – or you could use chopped preserved ginger from a jar, with some of the syrup.

1 medium-sized melon
4 tbls ginger preserve
4 kiwi fruit

1 Halve the melon and remove the seeds, then chop the flesh into pieces and put them into a bowl with the ginger preserve.

2 Peel the kiwi fruit and cut them into fairly thin slices; add these to the bowl. Stir, then leave until you are ready to serve the pudding – the longer you can leave it, the more the flavours will develop.

SERVES 4

SATSUMAS IN CARAMEL SAUCE

This is a quick and easy way of dressing up satsumas for an elegant dessert. You can, of course, use other members of the satsuma family, such as tangerines or clementines – if they are small you'll need more than four. Very small ones look pretty peeled and served whole on top of the sauce.

175g / 6oz caster sugar   **4 large satsumas**

1 Put half the sugar into a small saucepan and heat gently until it melts and becomes caramel coloured – this will take several minutes.

2 Standing well back and covering your hand with a cloth, pour in 2 tablespoons of water; the mixture will erupt and turn lumpy.

3 Add the remaining sugar and continue to cook over a gentle heat until the sauce has become smooth again.

4 Leave the sauce on one side to cool slightly while you peel the satsumas and slice them into thin rounds, if they are large. Then pour the sauce on to four plates, top with the satsumas, and serve.

SERVES 4

HOT PUDDINGS

—— ✳ ——

HOT HONEY PEACHES WITH AMARETTI

This is a good way of cheering up peaches – or indeed other fruits, such as apricots or pears – that are not as sweet and juicy as they might be. They are good with some thick Greek yogurt.

1–2 peaches
2–3 tsp mild honey,
   clear or thick

2–3 amaretti biscuits

1. Slice the peaches finely, skinning them first if you prefer, then put them into a small pan, add honey to taste and heat gently.
2. Let the peach slices cook over a low heat for a few more minutes until they are sweet and tender, then serve them straight away with the amaretti biscuits: either leave them whole or crush them and sprinkle them over the peaches.
SERVES 1

BUTTERED APPLES

Mellow eating apples such as Cox's or really tasty Golden Delicious, if you can get them, work best in this recipe – and sweet, ripe pears are also good. It's best served hot, with thick creamy Greek yogurt and perhaps an almond- or orange-flavoured biscuit or shortbread.

450g / 1lb eating
   apples
15g / ½oz butter

2 tsp sugar
50g / 2oz sultanas

1. Peel and quarter the apples, remove the cores, then cut each quarter into thin slices.
2. Melt the butter in a saucepan and add the apples, sugar and sultanas. Stir, then cook, uncovered, over a gentle heat for about 3–4 minutes, stirring gently from time to time, until the apples have heated through and softened. Serve at once.
SERVES 2

QUICK BLUEBERRY CRUMBLE

A crumble is the most popular of puddings and also one of the quickest to prepare. To speed up the cooking, this one is grilled instead of baked, producing a really good crisp topping. You can use many other types of fruit instead of blueberries. Choose soft fruit that doesn't need pre-cooking.

225g / 8oz blueberries
150g / 5oz plain flour
125g / 4oz caster sugar

125g / 4oz butter
15g / ½oz flaked
   almonds

1. Wash the blueberries then put them into a shallow heatproof dish. Heat the grill to medium.
2. To make the crumble, put the flour and sugar into a bowl and rub in the butter with your fingertips. Or whizz all these ingredients together in a food processor fitted with a plastic blade.
3. Arrange the crumble evenly on top of the blueberries and grill for 10–15 minutes or until the crumble is brown and the blueberries bubbling. If the crumble seems to be browning too quickly, cover the dish with foil. Scatter the almonds over the crumble 2–3 minutes before it is ready, removing the foil, if you are using it, so that they brown.
SERVES 2–3

OPPOSITE: *(top) Buttered Apples, (bottom) Quick Blueberry Crumble*

BANANAS OR PEARS WITH HOT CHOCOLATE SAUCE

Chocolate sauce is quick to make and turns bananas or pears into a hot pudding when you want something simple and easy but a bit special.

100g / 3½ oz plain chocolate
15g / ½ oz unsalted butter
4 medium bananas or sweet ripe pears

a few flaked almonds
whipped cream (optional)

The better the chocolate, the better the sauce... one with at least 50 percent cocoa solids is best (read the packet) though you don't want too bitter a chocolate for this recipe.

1 First make the chocolate sauce: break up the chocolate and put it into a small saucepan with the butter and 75ml/3fl oz of water. Heat gently until the chocolate has melted.
2 Peel and slice the bananas, or peel, core and slice the pears. Arrange in four individual dishes.
3 Give the chocolate sauce a stir then pour it over the fruit just before you want to serve it. Top with a few flaked almonds, and a little whipped cream if you are using this.
SERVES 4

FLAMBEED FRUIT

This is good made with tropical fruits: bananas and pineapple work particularly well. It's quite dramatic when the flames go up, so stand well back.

1 small ripe pineapple
2 large bananas
25g / 1oz unsalted butter
25g / 1oz brown sugar

juice of 1 orange
4 tbls dark rum
toasted flaked coconut or toasted flaked almonds (optional)

1 Peel the pineapple, removing the tufts and hard core, then cut it into medium-sized chunks. Peel and slice the bananas.

2 Melt the butter and sugar in a saucepan then add the fruit and orange juice. Cook, stirring, for 3–4 minutes, until the fruit is heated through.
3 Put the rum into a small saucepan or metal ladle and warm it over the gas flame or hot plate. When it is tepid, set it alight with a match, standing well back and averting your face. Tip it into the fruit and let it burn, then serve immediately, sprinkled with the flaked coconut or almonds.
SERVES 4

INDIVIDUAL BANANA AND ALMOND CRUMBLES

4 large bananas
125g / 4oz plain flour
50g / 2oz ground almonds
25g / 1oz softened butter

50g / 2oz light brown sugar
25g / 1oz flaked almonds

1 Heat the grill to medium. Peel the bananas and slice each one fairly thinly into a ramekin dish.
2 Sift the flour into a bowl. Add the ground almonds, butter and sugar and mix them to a crumbly consistency with a fork. Then mix in the flaked almonds.
3 Spoon the crumble evenly on top of the bananas then grill for 10–15 minutes, until the topping is crisp and golden brown and the bananas are heated through. If the crumble is getting too brown before the bananas are hot, cover with some foil.
SERVES 4

ORANGE ZABAGLIONE WITH STRAWBERRIES

You can whizz this luxurious pudding up in no time at all with an electric hand whisk; without one it takes a little longer. Sponge fingers or delicate thin almond biscuits go well with it.

175–225g / 6–8oz strawberries	1 tbls orange liqueur, such as Cointreau
3 tbls caster sugar	shreds of orange rind
2 egg yolks	to decorate
grated rind of ½ orange	

1. Set a heatproof bowl over a pan of water and heat until the water is steaming. Make sure the bowl is not touching the water in the pan.
2. Wash and hull the strawberries then halve or slice them. Divide them between two bowls, sprinkle with 1 tablespoon of the caster sugar and leave on one side.
3. Put the egg yolks into the bowl and add the remaining sugar and the grated orange rind. Keeping the bowl over the pan of steaming water, whisk until pale and thick: about 5 minutes with an electric whisk, 10–15 minutes by hand.
4. Stir in the orange liqueur, then spoon the zabaglione over the strawberries, decorate with a few strands of orange rind, and serve at once.
SERVES 2

BANANA FRITTERS WITH LIME

oil for deep-frying	3 bananas
125g / 4oz plain flour	caster sugar
1 tbls melted butter	1 lime, sliced
1 egg white	crème fraîche

1. Set the oven to 150°C/300°F/Gas Mark 2. Heat some oil for deep-frying in a saucepan.
2. Next make the batter: sift the flour into a bowl, make a well in the centre and add the butter and 150ml/5fl oz of water. Mix until smooth. Whisk the egg white until it is standing in stiff peaks, then fold it into the batter.
3. Peel the bananas and cut them into chunks. Dip them into the batter, drain off the excess and fry in the hot oil, a few at a time, for 2–3 minutes, turning them over half way through.
4. Drain the fritters on kitchen paper and keep them warm in the oven while you fry the rest. As soon as they are all done, serve the fritters sprinkled with caster sugar and decorated with slices of lime. Serve the crème fraîche separately in a small bowl.
SERVES 4

PLUMS WITH CINNAMON CRUNCH

This quick, unconventional topping goes well with many types of cooked fresh fruit.

900g / 2lb red plums	125g / 4oz porridge oats
175g / 6oz demerara sugar	1 tsp cinnamon
40g / 1½oz butter	pinch of ground cloves

1. Halve and stone the plums, then cut them into chunky slices. Put them into a saucepan with 2 tablespoons of water and two thirds of the sugar and cook gently until the sugar has melted and the plums are just tender.
2. Preheat the grill. Melt the butter in a separate pan, then stir in the oats and the remaining sugar. Mix well, then spread the mixture on a grill pan or baking sheet and grill for about 10 minutes, stirring often, until the mixture is brown and crisp. Stir in the cinnamon and cloves.
3. Reheat the plums, then transfer them to a pie dish that will fit under your grill, spread the oat mixture on top, and keep warm under the grill until you are ready to serve.
SERVES 4

As I worked on this chapter I realised more and more how much the seasons still affect us, even though, thanks to modern transportation and refrigeration, our cooking and eating are no longer tied to them in the way they once were. And I realised too how much the foods which are naturally available at a given time of year are in tune with the demands of that season and harmonise with our needs.

In winter, for instance, just when we feel like eating warming, substantial foods to keep out the cold, we have a wonderful range of root vegetables, designed by nature to be suitable for storing for many weeks. As spring approaches cleansing, astringent foods like fresh green leafy vegetables come into season, preparing us for the lighter meals and greater physical activity which comes with the return of the longer, warmer days. Then juicy fruits and vegetables refresh us in the warmth of summer. In autumn the seasonal produce becomes more substantial and filling as we move towards winter once again.

I've discovered how much pleasure and satisfaction there is in using seasonal produce and how it is often associated with traditional festivals and celebrations throughout the year, making these more special and enjoyable. Carl Jung said that fully experiencing every chapter of our lives, from childhood to old age, is vital for our complete well-being. In a similar way I think the same can be said of the seasons, each of which has its particualr pleasures and qualities as well as its challenges. Being attuned to each season means enjoying it to the full whilst at the same time accepting that, as in the whole of life, nothing is permanent. We have to enjoy what we have now, then let go, move on and enjoy the next moment.

So, there are a number of good reasons for using foods in season, and it can certainly make sense from an economic point of view. But, having said that, I would not like to think that anyone will feel they have to use the suggestions in this chapter rigidly. Do by all means enjoy out-of-season recipes if they take your fancy or you fall for something unseasonable but enticing in the supermarket – this kind of inspiration is all part of the pleasure of cooking. Happy cooking and eating.

COOK'S
YEAR

SPRING

During spring the days get longer, the sun climbs higher in the sky each day, the sap rises and there's a feeling of new life and energy everywhere. Where I live, although spring does not officially begin until March we see the first promises in February, as the early crocuses and snowdrops push their way up through the hard earth and the early cherry delights us with its pink blossom – a resurgence of life that culminates in the celebration of Easter, with its focus on re-birth and resurrection. I love this time of year; the buds on the trees are bursting into leaf and the air is heady with blossom – so much external activity, yet underlying it there is a great stillness.

Spring is a time of transition. We are aware of this in the kitchen in the early spring as we use up the last of the stored fruits and vegetables and prepare for the arrival of the first of the new ones. The weather, too, at least where I live, is often unsettled. So spring cookery demands flexibility; a readiness to produce meals which protect us from the still-chilly winds and rainy days, or allow us to make the most of warm days with al fresco eating, picnics and lunches in the garden. And also to introduce new flavours as the substantial foods of winter give way to the lighter, fresher ones of the new season, as the precious early crops arrive.

It's interesting that many of these are quite astringent and even slightly bitter – rhubarb, for instance, and vegetables such as turnips, radishes, spring onions and even tender young dandelion leaves and nettles – which used to be eaten to cleanse and tone the system, country lore with which modern herbalists would agree. Even the first herbs – mint, chives and rocket – are ones which seem made for waking up our tastebuds and getting us ready for the new flavours of the incoming season.

The new spring root vegetables – carrots, turnips, spring onions, potatoes – are light and juicy, needing very short cooking times, different in nature from their mature, stored counterparts which have nourished us so well during the cold winter months. Another early home-grown crop is broad beans, which perfectly bridge the gap between the dried pulses of winter and the light vegetables of summer. Apart from rhubarb, which although technically not a fruit is used as such, and is pleasant for a change, spring is a sparse time for fruit and one during which we can justifiably enjoy the occasional treat of exotic fruits such as pineapple, mango and kiwi.

Spring is a natural time for eggs, which can be enjoyed in a variety of sweet and savoury dishes such as Frittata with Baby Carrots and Spring Onions (page 166), Savoury Spinach Gâteau (page 167) and Hot Lemon Soufflé (page 172). From a moral point of view, although I do not wish to eat animals that have been killed, I do not object to eating eggs because in a natural environment, unless fertilized and then incubated, eggs would simply lie around until they rotted and were reabsorbed into the earth. So why not eat them? It goes without saying, though, that they should be truly free-range, from a reliable, salmonella-free source, and eaten in moderation as part of an all-round balanced diet.

SPRING STARTERS

NEW VEGETABLES WITH AIOLI

You need a blender or food processor for this quick version of aioli, although you can adapt the recipe for making it by hand if you use two egg yolks instead of a whole egg, and add the oil drop by drop, as you whisk the mixture. The amount of garlic is very much a question of taste and can be reduced – or increased. The vegetables, too, can of course be varied. They can be served raw or, as in this version, cooked just to take the rawness off, then served warm. Although most people serve this as a starter, and a very good one it makes, my favourite way of eating this dish is as a main course, with my fingers rather than a knife and fork. It would serve four as a main course.

For a vegan version of aioli, use the special mayonnaise recipe on page 180, using soya milk instead of single cream and 2–3 garlic cloves.

FOR THE AIOLI

2-3 garlic cloves
1 egg
¼ tsp salt
¼ tsp mustard powder
2-3 grindings of black
  pepper
2 tsp wine vinegar
2 tsp lemon juice
200ml / 7fl oz light
  olive oil or
  grapeseed oil

FOR THE VEGETABLES

2 fennel
8 baby turnips
450g / 1lb baby carrots
1 small cauliflower or
  2-4 miniature ones
450g / 1lb baby
  courgettes

First make the aioli. Put the garlic in a food processor or blender and purée it as smoothly as you can, then add the egg, salt, mustard, pepper, vinegar and lemon juice. Blend for a minute at medium speed until the ingredients are well mixed, then turn the speed up to high and gradually add the oil, drop by drop, through the top of the goblet. When you have added about half the oil, you will hear the sound change to a 'glug-glug' noise and you can add the rest of the oil more quickly, in a thin stream. Taste the aioli and adjust the seasoning if necessary. If it seems a bit on the thick side, you can thin it by beating in a teaspoonful or two of boiling water.

Next, prepare the vegetables. If they are young and tender, they will only need trimming and washing. Remove any tough layers from the fennel, then cut each bulb down first into quarters then into eighths. Trim and scrub the turnips and carrots. Cut the cauliflower or miniature cauliflowers as necessary, to produce chunky pieces for dipping in the aioli; halve or quarter the courgettes to make long slim batons if they are thick; if they are really slender, leave them whole.

Cook the fennel for about 8 minutes in fast-boiling water; remove the fennel, rinse under the cold tap to cool it quickly, then put it into a colander to drain thoroughly. Boil the turnips in the same water; as soon as they are just tender, drain and refresh them and put them in the colander with the fennel; repeat the process with the carrots and then the cauliflower. The vegetables will only take a minute or two to cook; keep testing them with the point of a knife, and remove them from the water as soon as they are just tender. Finally, cook the courgettes which will only take about 60 seconds.

Put the aioli into a shallow bowl on a large platter. Arrange the vegetables around it, patting them dry on kitchen paper as necessary before serving.
SERVES 6-8

OPPOSITE: *(top) Mediterranean Cooked Green Salad, page 155, and (bottom) New Vegetables with Aioli*

JAPANESE-STYLE SALAD WITH DIPPING SAUCE AND GOMASIO

This is a light, refreshing first course. If you can't get rice vinegar, ordinary wine vinegar will do but it hasn't got quite the same sweetness and delicacy as rice vinegar (which you can get at some health shops or Chinese shops).

packet or bunch of
   radishes
bunch of spring onions
225g / 8oz mooli or
   turnip

FOR THE DIP
1 tbls grated fresh
   ginger

2 tbls soy sauce
2 tbls rice vinegar

FOR THE GOMASIO
4 tbls sesame seeds
1 tsp salt

Wash and trim all the vegetables. Cut the radishes into lotus flowers, if you are feeling enthusiastic, and pop them into a bowl of icy cold water for the petals to open. Cut the green part off each spring onion to leave about 5 cm/2 inch of the white part. Make cuts in the white part in from both ends towards the centre, then put them into the water, too, to curl. Peel the mooli or turnip and cut into thin sticks; make five equal cuts down each stick almost to the base and fold in the second and fourth sections, as shown in the photograph, to make a flower. All this can be done 2 hours or so before you want to serve the salad.

While the flowers are opening, make the dip by mixing together all the ingredients and then putting it into four tiny bowls, or one larger one if you prefer. Make the gomasio by putting the sesame seeds and salt into a dry frying pan set over a moderate heat. Stir for a couple of minutes or so as the sesame seeds toast and smell nutty and delicious, then remove from the heat. When the mixture has cooled, pulverize it in a coffee grinder, or with a

OPPOSITE: *Japanese-style Salad with Dipping Sauce and Gomasio*

pestle and mortar, or in a bowl, with the end of a wooden rolling pin. Put a small quantity into four tiny bowls, or one larger one.

Drain the flowers and arrange them on four plates. If you're using tiny bowls for the dip and gomasio, you might put these on the plates, too, as part of the arrangement; or serve them separately.
SERVES 4

MEDITERRANEAN COOKED GREEN SALAD

The frequent, often daily, use of dark green leafy vegetables is one of the characteristics of the Mediterranean diet, and a typical and popular way of serving them is as a cooked salad, served warm or cold. Other ingredients, such as whole lentils or chopped hard-boiled eggs can be added, turning this simple dish into a complete light meal.

450g / 1lb spinach or
   other dark green
   leafy vegetables
4 spring onions
1 garlic clove, crushed
   (optional)

1-2 tbls lemon juice
2-3 tbls olive oil
salt and freshly ground
   black pepper
lemon wedges to
   garnish

Wash the spinach thoroughly. Put it into a dry saucepan, cover, and cook for 7-10 minutes, until it is tender, pressing down with a fish slice as it cooks. Drain the spinach in a colander, pressing out the water with the fish slice. Put into a bowl.

Wash, trim and chop the spring onions and add most of them to the spinach, saving some for a garnish. Mix the garlic with the lemon juice and olive oil and add to the spinach, stirring to make sure it is well distributed. Season with salt and pepper. Turn the mixture into a shallow dish and garnish with the remaining spring onions and some lemon slices. Serve warm or cold, with more olive oil for people to help themselves.
SERVES 4

Use a good quality soy sauce for the dipping sauce, one that's been naturally fermented, without the addition of caramel (read the label).

VEGETABLE TERRINE

This is a pretty starter – a loaf-shaped terrine of white curd cheese flecked with vegetable pieces of different colours, with a green coat of spinach and a vinaigrette sauce.

*250g / 9oz spinach
   leaves
50g / 2oz French beans
50g / 2oz spring onions
50g / 2oz red pepper
olive oil
225g / 8oz curd cheese
2 tbls chopped fresh
   chives*

*2 eggs
salt and freshly ground
   black pepper*

FOR THE VINAIGRETTE

*2 tbls red wine vinegar
6 tbls olive oil*

First set the oven to 160°C/325°F/Gas Mark 3, then line a 450 g/1lb loaf tin with a strip of non-stick paper to cover the base and extend up the narrow ends. The deep type of loaf tin is best if you have one.

Next, half-fill a fairly large saucepan with water and bring it to the boil. Meanwhile, wash the spinach; trim and wash the beans and spring onions; wash the red pepper and cut it into strips just less than 1 cm/½ inch wide. When the water boils, put in the spinach and boil it for 1-2 minutes, until it is just soft, then drain it into a colander, saving the hot water, and refresh under the cold tap. Put the hot water drained from the spinach back into the pan, bring it to the boil, and put in the beans, spring onions and red pepper. Boil them for 2 minutes, then drain and refresh them under the cold tap. (You won't need the cooking water any more, but it now makes good stock.)

Brush the loaf tin with a little olive oil, then press a thin layer of spinach into the base and up the sides, so that they are all covered and there is enough spinach over to cover the top later. Pat the other vegetables dry on kitchen paper and cut them into 1 cm/½ inch lengths.

Put the curd cheese into a bowl with the chives and beat in the eggs, then add the pieces of vegetable and some salt and pepper to taste. Spoon the mixture into the spinach-lined tin and cover the top

with the rest of the spinach. Stand the tin in a roasting tin and pour boiling water round it so that it comes half-way up the sides; bake for 1 hour. Let the terrine cool completely in the tin, then chill it.

Meanwhile, make the vinaigrette by putting the vinegar and oil into a small jar with some salt and pepper and shaking until combined. When you're ready to serve the terrine, cut it into slices about 1 cm/½ inch wide; put each slice on a plate and pour some vinaigrette beside it.
SERVES 6-8

NETTLE SOUP

In an age when you can buy strawberries in the middle of winter and leeks in midsummer, at least weeds are still seasonal, and this soup is a great way to celebrate the coming of spring!

*1 tbls olive oil
1 onion, peeled and
   chopped
450g / 1lb tender nettles*

*150ml / 5fl oz single
   cream
salt and freshly ground
   black pepper
grated nutmeg*

Heat the oil in a large saucepan, put in the onion and cook gently, covered, for 10 minutes.

Meanwhile, wash and roughly chop the nettles. Add them to the pan, along with 1.4 L/3 pints of water. Bring to the boil, then simmer for about 15 minutes, until the nettles are very tender. Whizz to a purée in a food processor and pour back into the pan through a sieve, pushing through as much of the nettles as you can.

Stir in the cream, adjust the consistency with a little more water if necessary to make a thin, light soup, then season with salt, pepper and freshly grated nutmeg. Serve in warmed bowls.
SERVES 4

For the nettle soup, opposite, pick tender nettles from a pollution-free spot and wash them well before use.

PINK GRAPEFRUIT, RUBY ORANGES AND MINT

This pretty and refreshing mixture is good as a break-fast or brunch dish as well as a starter.

2 pink grapefruit   4 sprigs of fresh mint
4 ruby oranges

Holding a grapefruit over a bowl to catch the juice, cut off the skin and pith with a sharp knife, like peeling an apple when you want to make a long piece of peel; cut between the transparent membranes to release the juicy segments of fruit. Repeat the process with the other grapefruit and the oranges, which are a bit more fiddly to do. Add some fresh mint leaves to the mixture, and serve.
SERVES 2-4

WATERCRESS CREAM

Make this light and refreshing starter just before you want to serve it, so that the colour and flavour is fresh. Serve with some good bread.

packet or bunch of   salt and freshly ground
  watercress   black pepper
225g / 8oz fromage
  frais

Wash the watercress, removing any tough stems or damaged leaves. Reserve 4 good sprigs for garnishing; put the rest into a food processor with the fromage frais and whizz to a smooth purée, or chop the watercress finely by hand then stir it into the fromage frais. Either way, season with salt and freshly ground black pepper. Divide the purée between four plates and garnish each with a sprig of watercress.
SERVES 4

PIQUANT CUCUMBER SALAD

This is a refreshing starter, given a pleasant kick by the mustard seeds.

1 cucumber   3 tbls rice vinegar or
2 tsp white mustard   white wine vinegar
  seeds   fresh chives or young
salt and freshly ground   dill, if available
  black pepper

Peel the cucumber then cut it into quite thin slices. Layer these into a shallow dish, sprinkling the mustard seeds, some salt and a grinding of pepper between the layers. Pour the vinegar over the top. Cover the salad and leave for at least an hour, preferably longer – even overnight – for the flavours to blend. Snip over some fresh chives or dill before serving.
SERVES 4-6

KOHLRABI AND RADISH SALAD

Kohlrabi has a delicate flavour which I find pleasant, but the thing which I like about it most is its very crisp yet tender, juicy texture. It makes it perfect for early spring salads.

3 tbls olive oil   2 kohlrabi, about
1 tbls wine vinegar   225g / 8oz together
salt and freshly ground   packet or bunch of
  black pepper   radishes

Put the oil and vinegar into a bowl with salt and pepper to taste and mix to make a simple dressing. Peel the kohlrabi quite thinly, then cut it into julienne matchsticks; wash and slice the radishes. Add the kohlrabi and radishes to the bowl and stir gently to coat everything with the dressing.
SERVES 4

If you can't get kohlrabi, use turnip.

NEW VEGETABLES AND HERBS

Dandelion leaves make a delightful, slightly bitter addition to a green salad. Pick a small handful of leaves in a place free from pollution, and wash them well. Add them to a base of other salad greens — I find ordinary floppy lettuce a good neutral base for this kind of salad — tearing them up as you do so and dress with vinaigrette.

LITTLE BROAD BEAN AND MINT PATTIES

I like the crisp coating which chick-pea flour gives to these patties, although you could use ordinary flour, or even fry or bake them without flour, as they'll still get crisp. Some lightly seasoned yogurt is good with them, as well as a sauce made by stirring chopped chives into plain yogurt. Sliced tomatoes or a tomato salad, or Dandelion Leaf Salad, left, also go well with them.

900g / 2lb shelled   **salt and freshly ground**
  broad beans   **black pepper**
2 tbls chick-pea flour   **olive oil**
  plus extra for coating   **lemon slices**
6-8 sprigs of fresh mint

Cook the beans in boiling water for a few minutes until they are tender, then remove from the heat, drain, and leave until they are cool enough to handle. With your finger and thumb, pop the beans out of their grey jackets. Put the beans into a food processor with the 2 tablespoons of chick-pea flour, the mint and some salt and pepper, and whizz until a thick purée is formed. Divide this into eight portions, dip them in a little chick-pea flour and shape them into flat round patties.

Either shallow-fry the patties, turning them over so that they get crisp and brown on both sides, or bake them in the oven. To do this, set the oven to 200°C/400°F/Gas Mark 6 and put a baking sheet in the oven to heat. Brush this with oil, then put the patties on it, turning them so that their tops are lightly coated with oil. Bake them for 12-15 minutes, turn them over and bake for about 10 minutes more to brown the other side. Serve the patties with lemon slices.
SERVES 4

LEMONY RICE WITH BEANS AND SPRING ONIONS

The lemon grass gives this dish a particularly good flavour but if you can't get it, some grated lemon rind does the job pretty well. The colours – primrose yellow rice and green vegetables – are very springlike. A watercress salad goes well with it, and some crunchy roasted cashewnuts or almonds, served from a small bowl so that people can help themselves. Any rice that's over makes a good salad, served cold.

225g / 8oz brown rice   **3-4 lemon grass**
1 tsp turmeric   **225g / 8oz French beans**
salt and freshly ground   **4-6 spring onions**
  black pepper   **2 tbls fresh lemon juice**

Put the rice into a medium-large heavy-based saucepan, along with the turmeric, a teaspoonful of salt and 700 ml/1¼ pints of water. Bash the lemon grass with a rolling pin to release the flavour, and add that, too, to the pan. Bring to the boil, cover and leave to cook for 35 minutes.

Meanwhile, top and tail the French beans and cut them into 2.5 cm/1 inch lengths; trim and chop the spring onions. Put these into the pan on top of the rice, without stirring, cover and cook for a further 10 minutes, or until the vegetables and rice are tender and all the liquid has been absorbed. Fish out the lemon grass and stir in the lemon juice, which will immediately brighten up the colour of the rice. Stir gently to distribute everything, check the seasoning, grind in a bit of pepper, and serve.
SERVES 4

OPPOSITE: *Little Broad Bean and Mint Patties*

GREEN PEPPERS STUFFED WITH CAULIFLOWER CHEESE

These peppers make a good, easy supper dish served with a leafy salad, a tomato salad, or a cooked vegetable. Sometimes, while the peppers are cooking, I make a quick fresh tomato sauce (see opposite) to serve with them.

4 medium green peppers	200g / 7oz Cheddar cheese, grated
1 medium cauliflower	salt and freshly ground black pepper

Halve the peppers, cutting through their stems. Carefully remove the white inner part and seeds, keeping the stem intact. Put the peppers on a grill pan, shiny-side up, and place them under a hot grill for about 10-15 minutes, until the skin has blistered and begun to char. Remove them from the heat, cover them with a plate to keep in the steam, and leave until they're cool enough to handle.

Meanwhile, wash the cauliflower and cut it into fairly small florets. Cook these in 2.5 cm/1 inch of boiling water, with a lid on the pan, for 4-5 minutes, or until they are just tender. Drain them immediately and put them into a bowl with half the cheese and some salt and pepper.

Slip off the blistered and charred skin from the peppers with a sharp knife – they'll come off easily – then put them back on the grill pan. Fill each pepper with the cauliflower cheese mixture, dividing it between them, then sprinkle the rest of the cheese on top of them. Put the peppers under a hot grill for about 10 minutes, or until the cheese is melting, bubbling and golden brown. If serving with the tomato sauce, pour a little on each plate and place the stuffed pepper halves on top.

SERVES 4

OPPOSITE: *Green Peppers stuffed with Cauliflower Cheese*

BRAISED SPRING VEGETABLES AND HERBS

You can use a mixture of whatever tender spring vegetables are available: new carrots, baby courgettes, baby turnips, early French beans, shallots and, nicest of all if you can get them, some of those baby artichokes about the size of large rosebuds that you can eat in their entirety. I like to serve this feast of vegetables as a main course, perhaps starting the meal with a soup, or ending with a protein-rich pudding such as Hot Lemon Soufflé (see page 172).

1.2kg / 2½lb young vegetables	salt and freshly ground black pepper
2 tbls olive oil	2 tbls chopped fresh herbs
fresh thyme and parsley sprigs	

Prepare the vegetables, scrubbing rather than scraping them if they're really tender, and cutting them as necessary, aiming for pieces of roughly similar size. Baby artichokes, if you're using these, need any tough leaves trimming off; halve or quarter them unless they're really tiny. Quick-cooking vegetables like baby courgettes can be left whole or added towards the end of the cooking time.

Heat the oil in a large, heavy-based pan with a lid, then put in the vegetables which will take the longest: baby artichokes, followed by fennel, onions, turnips and carrots. Stir them so that they get coated with the oil, add the sprigs of thyme and parsley and salt and pepper, then pour in 100 ml/3½ fl oz of water. Bring to the boil, cover and leave to cook over a gentle heat for a few minutes, until they are almost tender. Artichoke hearts may take up to 20 minutes, but the other vegetables may take as little as 4 minutes.

When they are almost tender, add quick-cooking vegetables such as courgettes, spring onions, French beans, mangetouts or cauliflower. Stir again, cover and cook for a few minutes longer until all the vegetables are just tender, and bathed in a very little liquid. Fish out the herbs, check the seasoning, sprinkle with the chopped fresh herbs and serve.

SERVES 2 AS A MAIN COURSE, 4 AS A SIDE DISH

To make a fresh tomato sauce, quarter 700g / 1½ lb of tomatoes and cook them in a dry saucepan, covered, for about 15 minutes or until they're collapsed, then liquidize and sieve them, and season with salt and pepper.

PASTA PRIMAVERA

A real celebration of spring and, to be honest, early summer, this is one of my favourite pasta dishes. It's well worth taking the trouble to pop the broad beans out of their skins – for the vibrant green colour, apart from anything else! If you're doubtful about the wholewheat noodles in this recipe, I can only urge you to try them; I don't think you'll be disappointed.

If you don't like the idea of wholewheat noodles, use long thin pasta such as fettucine, spaghettini or vermicelli.

450g / 1lb broad beans, about 175g / 6oz after podding
125g / 4oz mangetout peas
225g / 8oz asparagus
25g / 1oz butter

1 garlic clove, crushed
salt and freshly ground black pepper
175g / 6oz wholewheat noodles
a few sprigs of flat-leaf parsley

Pod the beans; top and tail the mangetouts; break any tough ends of the asparagus, wash it well and cut into 2.5 cm/1 inch lengths. Cook the broad beans in fast-boiling water to cover for 2 or 3 minutes, or until the beans are tender. Strain the beans, keeping the liquid. Rinse the beans under cold water to cool them and, with your finger and thumb, pop them out of their grey skins. Re-boil the water the broad beans were cooked in and boil the mangetouts for 30 seconds then drain them; re-boil the water and cook the asparagus for about 2 minutes, or until it is just tender. (This water makes excellent stock for soups.)

Melt the butter in a large pan and add the garlic; fry for a minute or two, but don't get it brown. Add all the vegetables, and some salt and pepper, cover and leave on one side while you cook the noodles. Bring a large panful of water to the boil, drop in the noodles and bring the water back to the boil. Then draw the pan off the heat, cover and leave for 4-5 minutes until the noodles are just tender but not soggy. Give them a stir and drain them.

While the noodles are cooking, re-heat the vegetables, then add them and their buttery juices to the noodles. Mix gently, season with salt and pepper, add the parsley sprigs, and serve immediately, on to warmed plates.

SERVES 2

DEEP-FRIED PARMESAN-COATED CAMEMBERT WITH SPRING BROCCOLI

The unusual thing about this recipe is the Parmesan coating, which makes it a suitable dish for food combiners. This is usually served as a starter, but I love it as a main course – the lightly cooked spring broccoli goes particularly well with the gooey inside of the cheese. I don't like a sweet sauce with it myself, but if you disagree, try using some delicious all-fruit apricot and peach no-added-sugar jam, gently warmed in a saucepan. I've given quantities for two people here; simply double them for four.

1 × 250g / 9oz Camembert in individual portions
2 eggs, beaten

40g / 1½oz ready-grated Parmesan cheese
450g / 1lb broccoli

First prepare the Camembert: dip each portion into the beaten eggs then into the ready-grated Parmesan, making sure each one is completely coated. This can be done in advance – chill the Camembert in the fridge until about 5 minutes before you want to serve the meal.

Get the broccoli ready in advance, too: remove any tough stems and break or cut the broccoli as necessary. Have ready a large saucepan with 5 cm/2 inches of boiling water for cooking the broccoli, and a pan of hot deep fat for the Camembert. The fat should be 180°C/350°F or hot enough for a cube of bread to rise to the surface immediately and become golden brown in 1 minute.

Put the Camembert into the fat and let it fry for about 5 minutes, or until it is golden brown and crisp all over. At the same time, put the broccoli into the pan of water and cook, covered, for 4-5 minutes, or until just tender. Remove the Camembert from the fat with a slotted spoon and put on to two warmed plates along with the cooked broccoli. Serve immediately.

SERVES 2

OPPOSITE: *Pasta Primavera*

A VARIETY OF EGGS

EGG SALAD MIMOSA

This springtime starter – or it could make a lovely light lunch dish – tastes as refreshing as it looks.

2 hard-boiled eggs
½ cucumber
2 tbls wine vinegar
2 tbls olive oil
salt
1 tbls chopped fresh
　dill

1 small lettuce, an
　ordinary one is fine
½ packet or bunch of
　watercress
sprigs of fresh dill

Halve the eggs and remove the yolks. Finely chop the yolks and the whites, keeping them separate. Peel and thinly slice the cucumber; put it into a shallow dish and sprinkle with the vinegar, the olive oil, a little salt and 1 tablespoon of chopped dill. Wash and dry the lettuce and watercress. All this can be done in advance.

Just before you want to serve the salad, put a few lettuce leaves on four plates, tearing the larger leaves as necessary, then arrange the rest of the ingredients attractively on top. Garnish with some fresh dill sprigs.
SERVES 4

STUFFED LIGHTLY CURRIED EGGS

These make quite a filling starter or, served with a spring salad, a good light lunch or supper.

4 eggs, hard-boiled
2 tbls olive oil
2 onions, peeled and
　finely chopped
2 tsp curry powder
50g / 2oz finely grated
　Cheddar cheese

1 tbls milk or cream
salt and freshly ground
　black pepper
300ml / ½ pint plain
　low-fat yogurt
dash of sugar
　(optional)
1-2 tbls snipped chives

Remove the shells from the eggs and keep the eggs on one side for the moment. Heat the oil in a medium pan and put in the onions; fry for 4-5 minutes, or until tender and very lightly browned, then stir in the curry powder and cook for a further minute. Remove from the heat and put half the mixture into a medium bowl.

Cut the eggs in half and scoop out the yolks without damaging the whites. Add the yolks to the onion mixture in the bowl, together with the grated cheese, milk or cream and salt and pepper to taste; mix to a thick, soft consistency. Spoon a little of this mixture into the egg whites.

Add the yogurt to the rest of the onion mixture in the bowl, mix well, then season with salt, pepper and perhaps a tiny dash of sugar. Pour a little of the yogurt sauce mixture on to four small serving dishes, put two of the stuffed eggs on each plate beside or just on top of the sauce, and sprinkle each egg with snipped chives.
SERVES 4

OPPOSITE: *(left) Savoury Spinach Gâteau, page 167, and (right) Egg Salad Mimosa*

FRITTATA WITH BABY CARROTS AND SPRING ONIONS

You can use any tender spring vegetables for this easy and filling dish. When they come into season, asparagus or baby artichokes are particularly good. This frittata is also very good cold – a picnic food which you can eat with your fingers.

225g / 8oz spring onions	*4 tbls freshly grated Pecorino or Parmesan cheese*
225g / 8oz baby carrots	
4 eggs	*2 tbls olive oil*

Trim the spring onions and chop them into quite small pieces; scrub the carrots and cut them as necessary – if they are very tiny, they can be left whole. Steam or boil the carrots until they are just tender; the time will vary according to how young they are, but it could be as little as 4 minutes. Don't let them get soggy. A minute or two before they're done, put in the spring onions and cook them very briefly, until they, too, are just tender. Drain immediately – the water will make good stock.

Whisk the eggs and add the grated cheese. Have the grill heating up in case you need it. Heat the oil in a large frying pan and put in the drained vegetables; stir-fry them for a minute, then pour in the beaten eggs, moving the vegetables around gently to make sure the egg mixture gets right through them, and that the grated cheese is well distributed. Let the frittata cook over a moderate heat for a few minutes until the underside is cooked and lightly browned. Then, if the top is set, turn the frittata out on to a large plate and back into the frying pan, so that the other side gets cooked. If the top isn't set by the time the underside is done, pop the frying pan under the grill for about half a minute, then turn the frittata out and put it back into the frying pan as described. Cook for a minute or two longer, until the second side is set and lightly browned, cut the frittata into wedges and serve from the pan.
SERVES 2

The Swiss chard quiche, opposite, is most delicious made with cream, but for a less rich version use milk or a mixture of milk and cream.

ROCKET SALAD

Rocket is one of those herbs which really wakes up your taste buds, and I wish it were more widely available, in good-sized bunches. Anyway, once you've procured some, wash it, tear it into pieces and put into a salad bowl with 1 tablespoon good wine vinegar, 3 tablespoons olive oil, salt and pepper, and some other salad leaves, depending on how much rocket you've been able to get. A fairly neutral leaf, like floppy lettuce, is best, providing a neutral base for the flavour of the rocket.

SWISS CHARD QUICHE

Swiss chard, with its juicy stems, tender leaves and delicate flavour, makes an excellent quiche, but if you can't get it you could substitute ordinary spinach, using both the leaves and stems.

FOR THE PASTRY	FOR THE FILLING
125g / 4 oz plain fine wholewheat flour	*225g / 8oz Swiss chard*
salt	*25g / 1oz butter*
70g / 2½ oz butter	*200ml / 7 fl oz cream*
1 egg yolk	*3 egg yolks*
	salt and freshly ground black pepper
	grated nutmeg

First set the oven to 200°C/400°F/Gas Mark 6, then make the pastry. Sift the flour into a bowl or food processor and add a good pinch of salt. Put in the butter and either rub it in with your fingers, or whizz in the food processor for a few seconds; add the egg yolk and a teaspoonful of water and mix to a dough. Roll this out on a lightly floured board, then slide it from the board on to a 20 cm/8 inch flan tin, pressing it lightly into the tin to form a case; trim the edges. Prick the base very lightly and bake for 15 minutes, or until the pastry is crisp. Remove from the oven and turn the heat down to 160°C/325°F/Gas Mark 3.

Meanwhile, make the filling. Wash the Swiss chard, separate the stalks from the leaves, and chop both. Melt the butter in a saucepan, put in the stalks, cover and cook for about 4 minutes, or until they are almost tender. Put in the leaves, cover and cook for a further 2-3 minutes, or until everything is tender. Remove from the heat and mix in the cream, add the egg yolks, salt, pepper and nutmeg to taste, stirring well. Pour the mixture into the flan case and bake for 25-30 minutes, or until the filling is set. Serve hot, warm or cold.

SERVES 4-6

SAVOURY SPINACH GATEAU

I invented this for a special meal and it brought gasps of delight when it appeared. It's not difficult to make although you do need a food processor.

FOR THE GATEAU	FOR THE FILLING
1.4kg / 3lb fresh spinach or 700g / 1½ lb frozen	*1 medium cauliflower, yielding 450g / 1lb florets*
25g / 1oz butter	*225g / 8oz butter*
4 egg yolks	*4 egg yolks*
salt and freshly ground black pepper	*2 tbls lemon juice*
8 egg whites	*salt*
6 tbls ready-grated Parmesan cheese	*chervil sprigs to garnish*

Set the oven to 200°C/400°F/Gas Mark 6. Line the base of three 20 cm/8 inch sandwich tins with non-stick paper, and grease the sides. If you only have two such tins, cut a circle of paper for the third, bake two of the gâteaux, then turn one out, re-line and grease the tin, and bake the third.

If you're using fresh spinach, wash it well, then put it into a large saucepan and cook over a high heat for 7-10 minutes, or until very tender. Cook frozen spinach in a little boiling water, also for about 7 minutes. In either case, drain the spinach into a colander and press it very well to extract as much water as possible. Then put it into a food processor, along with the butter, egg yolks, salt and freshly ground black pepper, and whizz it to a smooth, creamy purée.

Whisk the egg whites until they stand in stiff peaks, then gently fold into the spinach mixture. Tip a third of the mixture into each of the tins, level the tops, then sprinkle each with 2 tablespoons of the grated Parmesan. Bake for 10 minutes, until they are golden brown on top and the centres feel firm. (If you are baking them in two batches, turn one of the gâteaux straight out, cheesy-side down, on to a large round ovenproof serving plate, re-line the tin and bake the remaining gâteau.) When they are all done, reduce the oven setting to 160°C/325°F/Gas Mark 3.

While the gâteaux are cooking, wash and trim the cauliflower, cutting it into quite small florets. Steam the cauliflower, or boil it in 2 cm/1 inch of water until tender and drain well.

Next make the sauce. Cut up the butter roughly, put it into a small saucepan and heat until it has melted and is boiling. Put the egg yolks and lemon juice into a food processor or blender with a good pinch of salt and whizz for 1 minute. With the machine running, pour the melted butter in a steady stream into the food processor or blender through the top of the goblet, and whizz for 1 minute.

Put one layer of the gâteau on an ovenproof serving plate, spread the surface with half the sauce, then put half the cauliflower on top, followed by another layer of gâteau. Cover this with sauce and cauliflower as before, then put the final layer of gâteau on top, this time with the crunchy cheese side on top. Put the gâteau, uncovered, into the oven, and leave it for 30 minutes to heat through completely before serving. Garnish with sprigs of chervil, and serve in wedges, like a cake.

SERVES 6-8

FRUITS, CUSTARDS AND CREAMS

RHUBARB CRUMBLE

This, in my experience, is one of those 'spring wouldn't be the same without' kind of puddings. Fortunately, it's also one of the easiest to make. It's good with some cream or thick yogurt.

900g / 2lb rhubarb
50g / 2oz caster sugar
¼ tsp ground cloves
½ tsp ground cinnamon

125g / 4oz soft butter
  or vegetable
  margarine
125g / 4oz demerara
  sugar

FOR THE CRUMBLE
175g / 6oz self-raising
  fine wholemeal flour

Set the oven to 200°C/400°F/Gas Mark 6.

Cut the root ends and leafy tops off the rhubarb, then cut the stalks into 2.5 cm/1 inch lengths and put them into a shallow ovenproof dish. Sprinkle them with the caster sugar, ground cloves and cinnamon.

To make the crumble, sift the flour into a bowl, adding the bran from the sieve too. With your fingertips, rub the butter or margarine into the flour until the mixture resembles fine breadcrumbs. Add the sugar and rub lightly again, to form a crumbly mixture. Spoon this on top of the rhubarb in an even layer, covering it completely. Bake for about 30 minutes, or until the crumble is crisp and lightly browned and the rhubarb feels tender when tested through the crumble with the point of a knife.
SERVES 4

MANGO AND CARDAMOM PARFAIT

I love both mango and cardamom, with its eucalyptus-like flavour. Together they make an exquisite ice-cream parfait which you can freeze in a loaf tin, without stirring, and serve in slices.

1 medium ripe mango
6-8 cardamom pods
4 egg yolks
75g / 3oz caster sugar

150ml / 5fl oz double
  cream
mango slices and
  pistachio nuts to
  decorate

Peel the mango, cut the flesh into chunks and put into a food processor. Crush the cardamom and remove the pods, then crush the seeds as much as you can, preferably with a pestle and mortar. Add them to the mango, and whizz for a minute or two until you have a completely smooth purée. Pour this through a fairly coarse nylon sieve to remove any larger pieces of cardamom.

Whisk the egg yolks until they are thick. Put the sugar into a small saucepan with 2 tablespoons of water and heat gently until the sugar has dissolved. Then boil for 2-3 minutes, until the mixture reaches 110°C/225°F on a sugar thermometer or a little of the syrup forms a thread when pulled between your finger and thumb. Pour this over the egg yolks, then whisk for 4-5 minutes, until the mixture is very thick and pale. Stir the mango purée into the egg yolk mixture. Whisk the cream until it is thick but not stiff, then fold this in too. Pour the mixture into a 450g/1lb loaf tin and freeze until solid.

Remove the parfait 15 minutes before you want to serve it. Run the blade of a knife around the edges and invert the tin over a plate, giving it a firm shake; it should come out with no problems. Decorate with mango slices and chopped pistachios.
SERVES 8

To slice a mango, cut downwards about 6mm/¼ inch from one side of the stem, then slice it the same distance the other side of the stem, thus avoiding the stone. Then remove the skin, and cut as much flesh away from the stone as you can.

OPPOSITE: *Mango and Cardamom Parfait*

SPRING FRUIT SALAD WITH VIOLETS

This fruit salad makes the most of what fruit there is during spring. It's naturally sweetened with grape juice and is most refreshing: I love to eat it for breakfast, particularly a late and leisurely Sunday one. You probably won't need all the grape juice for the fruit salad, but any that's over is nice to drink with it. (The violets are an optional extra for special occasions.)

1 honeydew melon or similar, or part of one if it's huge	*225g / 8oz seedless green grapes*
4-6 kiwi fruit	*1 bottle or carton of white grape juice*
	small bunch of violets

Halve the melon, remove the seeds and cut the flesh into pieces; peel and slice the kiwi fruit; remove the grapes from their stems and wash them. Put all the fruits into a bowl – they look especially good in a glass one – and pour in enough grape juice to moisten them well. Remove some violets from their stems and float them on top of the fruit salad. Serve as soon as possible.
SERVES 4

LITTLE COFFEE CREAMS

For a vegan version of little coffee creams, use either vegan yogurt (from health shops) or silken tofu, whizzed in a food processor.

I like these best made with mascarpone, which is rich, smooth and very creamy, but thick, Greek yogurt or fromage frais with 8% fat are also good. All of these come in tubs of varying sizes so basically aim for one that's about 200-250g/7-9oz for two people. It doesn't matter whether the coffee is with or without caffeine as long as it's a good quality one.

225g / 8oz mascarpone, Greek yogurt or fromage frais	*2 heaped tsp sugar sugar coffee beans to decorate (optional)*
2 tsp good-quality strong instant coffee	

Put the mascarpone, yogurt or fromage frais into a bowl and stir a little to make it smooth. Put the coffee granules into a cup and add about a tablespoonful of almost-boiling water – just enough to dissolve them. Add the coffee to the bowl, along with the sugar, and stir until it's all well-combined.

Spoon the mixture into two bowls, and chill until you're ready to serve them. Decorate with two or three sugar coffee beans, if you have them.
SERVES 2

SPRING FRUIT COMPOTE

This delightful compôte is sweetened with all-fruit, apricot and peach soft-set spread instead of sugar. Make sure the pineapple is sweet and ripe; it should smell syrupy, a bit like canned pineapple, and one of the inner leaves should come out quite easily when you pull it. Kiwis are nicest if they give a bit when you press them. I don't think this compôte needs any accompaniments; it's good just as it is, for a pudding or as a special breakfast dish.

1 small, ripe pineapple	*spread*
285g / 10oz jar no-added-sugar, high-fruit-content apricot	*4 kiwi fruit*
	2 eating apples

Cut the leafy top off the pineapple, cut the fruit into quarters and cut the peel and inner core off each quarter. Scoop out any 'eyes' with the point of a knife, then cut the fruit into chunky pieces and put them in a bowl with the apricot and peach spread, mixing well. Peel the kiwis and slice them into thin rounds; peel, core and slice the apples. Add these to the bowl and stir gently.

Cover and leave for at least 30 minutes, preferably 1-2 hours, for the flavours to blend.
SERVES 4

OPPOSITE: *Spring Fruit Salad with Violets*

HOT LEMON SOUFFLE WITH APRICOT COULIS

Apricot coulis freezes well, so it's useful to make extra and freeze in suitably sized containers.

This makes a good springtime pudding, hot and warming for still-chilly days but at the same time light and refreshing. The base can be prepared in advance, leaving only the whisking and folding-in of the egg whites to be done before you pop it into the oven. It's good served with pouring cream and perhaps some seasonal fruits, and especially marvellous with the coulis.

25g / 1oz butter, plus a little for greasing
25g / 1oz flour
200ml / 7fl oz milk
50g / 2oz caster sugar
grated rind of 2 lemons
1 tbls lemon juice
3 egg yolks
4 egg whites
Apricot Coulis (page 296)

Use the extra butter to grease a 1 L/1¾ pint soufflé dish. Tie a piece of non-stick paper around the outside of the dish to extend by 5 cm/2 inches or so, to allow the soufflé to rise above the top of the dish.

Melt the remaining butter in a medium saucepan. When it froths, stir in the flour, cook over the heat for a moment or two and add the milk, stirring until it forms a smooth paste. Add the sugar, lemon rind and juice, then leave on one side until you are ready to finish the soufflé.

Set the oven to 160°C/325°F/Gas Mark 3. Gently reheat the flour mixture just to soften it, but don't get it too hot, then remove it from the heat and stir in the egg yolks. Whisk the egg whites until they stand in stiff peaks. Mix a heaped tablespoon of egg white into the flour mixture to loosen it, then fold in the rest of the egg white. Pour the mixture into the soufflé dish, gently level the top, then run your thumb or a knife round the top edge to remove the soufflé from the edges of the dish and help it to rise well. Bake the soufflé for 30-35 minutes, or until it has risen well and just wobbles a little in the centre when shaken. Remove the band of paper and serve immediately, with the Apricot Coulis.

SERVES 4

CHOCOLATE MOUSSE WITH ORANGE CREAM

Cold, velvety-smooth, rich chocolate with a topping of orange-flavoured whipped cream makes an irresistible finale to any meal. It needs to be made several hours before you want to eat it – even the day before.

200g / 7oz plain chocolate, at least 50% cocoa solids
25g / 1oz butter
5 eggs
1 orange
150ml / 5fl oz whipping cream
1 tbls Cointreau or other orange liqueur
caster sugar

Break up the chocolate and put it into a large bowl with the butter. Stand the bowl over a saucepan of gently simmering water and leave for about 10 minutes until the chocolate has melted. Meanwhile, separate the eggs, putting the whites into a large bowl and the yolks into a small one.

Whisk the whites until they are stiff but not breaking up. Remove the bowl of chocolate from the pan and stir in the egg yolks, followed by a good tablespoonful of the egg white. Then tip in the rest of the egg white and fold it in very gently using a metal spoon, until there is no more white to be seen and the mixture is light and fluffy. Pour the mixture into six smallish individual glass dishes or ramekins and put into the fridge to set and chill for 6 hours or more.

Just before you want to serve the chocolate mousse, prepare the orange topping. First, scrub the orange in hot water, then with a zester remove several long strands of rind for decoration; grate the rest to make about ¼ teaspoonful. Whisk the cream until it holds its shape, add the grated orange rind, Cointreau and a little caster sugar to taste and whisk again lightly. Spoon this mixture on top of the chocolate mousse and decorate with the strands of orange rind.

SERVES 6

FLORIDA FRUIT CUP

A taste of sunshine to cheer up chilly spring days, this fruit cup is made from the tropical fruits which are good at this time of the year, and you can vary the exact composition according to what's available. The pink grapefruit makes a pleasant addition, and the passion fruit permeate the whole dish with their exotic flavour. It makes a particularly wonderful brunch offering – but it's good any time.

1 large pink grapefruit	*2 apples*
2 oranges	*225g / 8oz lychees*
125g / 4oz seedless	*1 ripe mango*
grapes	*2 passion fruit*

Holding the grapefruit over a bowl, cut off the peel in one long strip using a sawing action and making sure that you cut off the white pith as well as the skin. Cut the flesh away from between the white transparent membranes and, when you've removed all the flesh, squeeze out any remaining juice. Do the same thing with the oranges, then wash the grapes and add these to the bowl; wash and slice the apples, removing their skin or not according to its condition. Remove first the skin and then the shiny brown stones from the lychees using a sharp, pointed knife, and add the lychees to the bowl. Cut right down the mango on both sides of the big flat stone, starting about 5 mm/¼ inch each side of the stalk. Peel and slice the flesh, cutting away as much as you can from around the stone and adding that too. Finally, cut the passion fruit in half and scoop out the flesh, including the pips, with a teaspoon; add this to the other fruit and stir gently. Cover until needed.

It's best made half an hour or so before you want to eat it, to give the flavours a chance to blend and the juices to run, making a natural syrup.
SERVES 4-6

SPRING MENUS

— ❧ —

MENU

DINNER
FRESH FROM THE
GARDEN FOR FOUR

Cream of Turnip Soup
Hot Herb Bread
❧

Twice-Baked Individual Soufflés
Creamy Tomato Sauce
Platter of Fresh Vegetables
❧

Spiced Rhubarb Compôte with
Brown Sugar Meringues

CREAM OF TURNIP SOUP

If the turnips really are 'fresh from the garden', some or all of the leafy green tops can be used in this soup too; if not, add some watercress, to give pungency.

450g / 1lb turnips, plus 75g / 3oz of the leaves, or watercress
1 onion, peeled and chopped
15g / ½oz butter
4 tbls double cream
salt and freshly ground black pepper
grated nutmeg
extra cream and chopped chives to garnish

Scrub the turnips and cut them into even-sized dice; wash and roughly chop the leaves or watercress. Melt the butter in a large saucepan and put in the onion; cover and cook for 5 minutes, then add the turnips and the green tops or watercress and cook, covered, for a further 5 minutes. Pour in 850 ml/1½ pints of water, bring to the boil and simmer for about 20 minutes, or until the vegetables are tender.

Liquidize the soup thoroughly, then pour it back into the saucepan and stir in the cream, salt, pepper and nutmeg to taste. To serve, garnish with cream and chopped chives

COUNTDOWN

Up to one week in advance:
Make the meringues which can be kept in an air-tight container.

Up to one day before:
The following dishes can be made in advance, covered and kept in the fridge: the soup; the herb bread, prepared ready for cooking and wrapped in foil; the Twice-Baked Soufflés, turned out into a casserole dish ready for their final baking; the Tomato Sauce; the Rhubarb Cômpote. If you are going to microwave the vegetable platter, this can also be cooked, covered and kept in the fridge.

40 minutes before the meal:
Heat the oven. Put in the herb bread 20 minutes before you want to eat; 5 minutes later put in the Soufflés. Gently reheat the soup and sauce; just before you want to serve the meal reheat the vegetables in the microwave or cook them if you haven't done so already.

OPPOSITE: *Dinner Fresh from the Garden for Four*

HOT HERB BREAD

You can use whatever herbs are available; a few fresh chives and a bit of thyme, if you can get it, otherwise just some dried thyme.

1 wholewheat or Granary stick	*1 tbls chopped fresh chives and a sprig of fresh thyme, chopped, or ½ tsp dried thyme*
75g / 3oz butter	

Make diagonal cuts in the wholewheat or Granary stick about 2.5 cm/1 inch apart, without cutting right through the bottom crust of the bread. Beat the butter until it's soft, then mix in the chives and thyme or the dried thyme. Spread the cut surfaces of the bread with the herb butter, then wrap the bread in foil – you may need to break the loaf in half so that it will fit into the oven.

Bake the bread for 15-20 minutes in a hot oven – it will bake perfectly with the soufflés – until the butter has melted and the bread is very hot. Serve at once, with the soup.

TWICE-BAKED INDIVIDUAL SOUFFLES

A good wine to accompany this menu would be an aromatic dry white such as Sancerre, or a medium-bodied red such as a Red Burgundy.

This is my food-combining version of this modern classic, using curd cheese or skim milk cheese for the base instead of the usual thick sauce, to make a completely protein dish. It's very convenient, because everything can be done in advance except for the final baking of the soufflés. They can even be made and frozen in their dish, ready to be quickly defrosted and baked.

butter for greasing	*150g / 5oz Gruyère cheese, grated*
8 tbls ready-grated Parmesan cheese	*5 egg whites*
225g / 8oz curd or skim milk cheese	*salt and freshly ground black pepper*
4 egg yolks	

Set the oven to 180°C/350°F/Gas Mark 4. Generously grease eight ramekins, dariole moulds or old cups, then sprinkle the insides with Parmesan, using 4 tablespoons. Put the curd or skim milk cheese into a bowl and mash it until it's smooth, then gradually mix in the egg yolks and half the grated Gruyère cheese. Whisk the egg whites with a clean, greasefree whisk until they are standing in peaks, and stir a heaped tablespoonful into the egg yolk mixture to loosen it. Fold in the rest of the egg whites gently. Spoon the mixture into the ramekins, moulds or cups: it can come level with the top, but don't pile it up any higher.

Stand them in a roasting tin, pour boiling water round to come halfway up the sides and bake for 15 minutes, until they are risen and set. Remove from the oven and leave to get cold – they'll sink a bit. Loosen the edges and turn them out. (It's easiest to turn them out on to your hand, then transfer them to an ovenproof serving dish.) Sprinkle each with some of the remaining Gruyère cheese then with the rest of the Parmesan cheese.

They can now wait until you are ready to bake them. Then, heat the oven to 220°C/425°F/Gas Mark 7, and bake them for 15-20 minutes, or until they are puffed up and golden brown. Serve at once.

CREAMY TOMATO SAUCE

1 tbls olive oil	*salt and freshly ground black pepper*
1 small onion, peeled and finely chopped	*4 tbls cream*
900g / 2lb tomatoes	

Heat the oil in a large saucepan and add the onion; fry for 5 minutes without browning. Meanwhile, quarter the tomatoes and add them to the pan. Cover and cook over a gentle heat for 10-15 minutes, or until the tomatoes have collapsed, then liquidize, sieve and season. Just before you want to serve the sauce, re-heat it gently and add the cream. Check the seasoning, then serve.

PLATTER OF FRESH VEGETABLES

A platter of fresh baby vegetables is one of the joys of late spring and early summer. The exact composition is up to you – and your garden or supplier – this is just a suggestion. Trim and cut the vegetables as little as possible and cook until they're just tender.

175g / 6oz baby carrots
175g / 6oz baby turnips
175g / 6oz baby French beans
175 g/ 6oz baby courgettes
175g / 6oz sugar-snap peas
2-3 baby cauliflowers, depending on the size
50g / 2oz butter
2 tbls fresh lemon juice
salt and freshly ground black pepper
chopped fresh parsley

Wash and gently scrub the carrots and turnips, leaving some of the green leaves still attached. Wash, top and tail the French beans, baby courgettes and sugar-snap peas; wash, trim and quarter the cauliflowers (or cut them as necessary, depending on the size). The easiest way to cook a variety of vegetables like this is in a steamer – or a stack of steamers – over a large saucepan of water, since you can add the vegetables in sequence according to how long they'll take. This saves having to use several saucepans. The exact timing depends on the size of the vegetables, but if they're young and tender, none of them will take more than about 4 minutes at the most. If you wish, you can cook them separately, in advance, under-cooking them slightly, then put them into a vegetable dish, cover with a plate and microwave them just before serving.

When the vegetables are cooked, quickly melt the butter in a saucepan with the lemon juice and a good seasoning of salt and pepper, then pour this over the cooked vegetables; sprinkle with some chopped parsley just before you serve them.

SPICED RHUBARB COMPOTE

This easy-to-make recipe is a particularly good way to use the new season's rhubarb, and is delicious with the crunchy Brown Sugar Meringues below.

900g / 2lb rhubarb
50g / 2oz caster sugar
8 cloves
good pinch of ground ginger

Trim the rhubarb and strip off any stringy bits then cut into 2.5 cm/1 inch lengths and put into a heavy-based saucepan with the sugar, 4 tablespoons of water, the cloves and ginger. Cover and cook over a gentle heat for about 5 minutes, or until soft. Transfer the rhubarb to a bowl, removing the cloves as you do so, cover and chill.

Serve with the brown sugar meringues, and, if wished, some softly whipped cream.

BROWN SUGAR MERINGUES

The brown sugar in these meringues gives them a pleasant caramel-like flavour.

2 egg whites
50g / 2oz caster sugar
50g / 2oz dark brown sugar

Set the oven to 70°C/150°F/Gas Mark ¼ or to your lowest setting. Line a baking sheet with non-stick paper. Whisk the egg whites until they are very stiff. Now whisk in first the caster sugar, then the dark brown sugar, a little at a time, whisking well to make a glossy mixture. Shape spoonfuls of the mixture on to the baking sheet, leaving some space around them as they spread a little. Bake them for 2-3 hours, or until they are dry and crisp. Pick one up and look at the base of it to make sure that it is dry right through. Cool on the baking sheet then store them in an airtight container.

MENU

A LATE SPRING PICNIC FOR FOUR

Light Leek Soup

Tian of Spring Vegetables with Special Mayonnaise

Salade Nicoise with New Potatoes and Spring Onions

Little Lemon Grass Creams

LIGHT LEEK SOUP

In my experience, unless you're very lucky with the weather a soup makes the most welcome starter on a late spring picnic – and on many a summer one, too. This one is made from the last of the leeks. Take it in Thermos flasks and serve it into cups or bowls, whichever are most convenient. It's helpful to have spoons, too, to get up the last dregs of the delicious mixture. If the weather does happen to be boiling hot, by the way, this soup is also good served chilled.

700g / 1½ lb leeks	*salt and freshly ground*
1 tbls olive oil	*black pepper*
1.2L / 2 pints water	*freshly grated nutmeg*
4 tbls cream	

Trim the roots and inedible leaf parts off the leeks, then slit them up one side and rinse under the running cold tap, pulling them open to make sure you get them really clean. Cut in half downwards, down again, and then across thinly, resulting in quite small pieces.

Heat the olive oil in a large saucepan and put in the leeks, stir, then cover and let them cook very gently for 10 minutes, stirring a couple of times. Add the water and let the soup simmer for about 20 minutes, or until the leeks are very tender. Liquidize about two-thirds of the soup – leave the rest as it is to add texture. Stir in the cream and season the soup well with salt, black pepper and freshly grated nutmeg. If you want to eat it hot, pour into Thermos flasks immediately; if cold, cool first then pack into flasks.

COUNTDOWN

Up to one day before:
The soup, Tian, Special Mayonnaise and Lemon Grass Creams can be made in advance, covered securely in foil and kept in the fridge if convenient. You can also cook the potatoes, beans and hardboiled eggs for the salad, ready to assemble it on the day.

On the day:
Reheat the soup gently and put into a vacuum flask; complete the salad, put into a suitable container or bowl and cover securely with foil.

OPPOSITE: *A Late Spring Picnic for Four*

TIAN OF SPRING VEGETABLES WITH SPECIAL MAYONNAISE

A light or medium-bodied dry white wine such as Frascati, Chablis or Muscadet goes well with this menu, with plenty of still or sparkling water or fruit juice as an alternative.

I'm particularly fond of this easy, economical dish which can be made from any combination of seasonal vegetables, although I prefer it when some leafy green ones are included. The fresh herbs, too, can be varied according to what is available – I particularly like the flavour of fresh dill. It's good served either hot with some cooked vegetables and perhaps a tomato or yogurt sauce or, as suggested here, cold with mayonnaise (or a yogurt sauce) and a tomato and basil salad.

bunch of spring onions	*2 eggs*
450g / 1lb courgettes	*2 tbls chopped fresh*
225g / 8oz Swiss chard	*herbs*
or spinach	*salt and freshly ground*
125g / 4oz button	*black pepper*
mushrooms	*25g / 1oz freshly grated*
2 tbls olive oil	*Parmesan cheese*

Set the oven to 180°C/350°F/Gas Mark 4. Wash and trim the spring onions and courgettes, then slice the onions and cut the courgettes into small dice. Wash the chard or spinach, removing the stems and chop both the stems and the leaves, keeping them separate. Rinse and halve the mushrooms.

Heat the oil in a large saucepan and put in the spring onions, courgettes and chard or spinach stems. Cover and cook for 5 minutes, then add the chard or spinach leaves and the button mushrooms and cook for a further 5 minutes, without a lid. Remove the pan from the heat and beat in the eggs, then add the herbs and salt and pepper to taste. Spoon the mixture into one shallow ovenproof dish or four smaller ones, spread the top level and sprinkle with the Parmesan cheese. Bake for about 30 minutes for the large dish or 20 minutes for the smaller dishes, or until set and lightly browned. Serve hot or cold.

SPECIAL MAYONNAISE

You could use a good-quality bought mayonnaise jazzed up a bit with some lemon juice and freshly ground black pepper for the Tian, left, but a home-made one is nicer if you have the time to make it. I think that this is rather a special recipe because, although it looks and tastes like a perfectly straight-forward mayonnaise, it does not contain egg yolk. The original idea came to me when I was experimenting with vegan mayonnaises (you can make this recipe vegan by using soya milk instead of the cream), and then I realized how useful it would be for anyone worried about salmonella. It's a bit easier to make than a normal mayonnaise, because you don't have to be quite so careful about adding the oil, but it's still best to do this quite slowly until the mayonnaise shows signs of thickening. It will keep, well-covered, for a week in the fridge.

4 tbls single cream	*200ml / 7fl oz light*
¼ tsp mustard powder	*olive oil, grapeseed or*
salt and freshly ground	*groundnut oil*
black pepper	*1 tbls lemon juice*
	1 tbls red wine vinegar

Put the single cream into a bowl with the mustard powder and a good seasoning of salt and pepper, and mix them together. Add the oil gradually, a drop at a time, whisking well after each addition, exactly as if you were making an egg-yolk mayonnaise. When about half the oil has been added and the mixture has emulsified, you can add the rest more quickly in a thin, steady stream, but still whisking all the time. Finally, add the lemon juice and vinegar and stir them in very gently in one direction only, which will further thicken the mixture because of the effect of the acid on the cream. Check the seasoning – this mayonnaise needs plenty of salt and pepper.

Should the mayonnaise curdle as you're making it, you can easily remedy the situation if you start again with a tablespoon of cream in a clean bowl and whisk in the curdled mixture a bit at a time. I have just done exactly this when I was testing this recipe, and it's fine!

SALADE NICOISE WITH NEW POTATOES AND SPRING ONIONS

450g / 1lb baby new
  potatoes, scrubbed
225g / 8oz young
  French beans
2 tbls red wine vinegar
6 tbls olive oil
salt and freshly ground
  black pepper
4 tomatoes

4 hard-boiled eggs,
  shelled
bunch of spring onions
50-125g / 2-4oz black
  olives

Cook the potatoes in enough boiling water to cover for 10-15 minutes, or until they are just tender; drain them. Top and tail the French beans as necessary and cook them in 2.5 cm/1 inch of boiling water for 2-4 minutes, or until they, too, are just tender then drain them. Put the vinegar, oil and some salt and pepper into a large bowl, put in the potatoes and beans, turn gently so that they are all coated with the dressing, and leave to cool.

Cut the tomatoes and eggs into quarters or eighths and chop the spring onions. Add these to the bowl, together with the olives, and stir gently. Serve cold.

LITTLE LEMON GRASS CREAMS

Every year a national supermarket holds a nation-wide contest to find the best young cooks between the ages of 9 and 15, and very inspiring it is. At one of the regional finals which I attended, one of the competitors, Caroline Godsmark, made some exquisite lemon grass creams which all the judges loved, and it is from her that I got the idea for this fragrant dessert.

3 lemon grass
150ml / 5fl oz milk
150ml / 5fl oz single
  cream

2 eggs and 2 egg yolks
40g / 1½oz caster sugar
herb flowers such as
  sage to decorate

Set the oven to 160°C/325°F/Gas Mark 3.

Put the lemon grass on a board and bash it with a rolling pin to crush it and release the flavour. Put the crushed lemon grass into a saucepan with the milk and cream and bring to the boil, then cover and leave for 15 minutes for the flavour to infuse.

Meanwhile, whisk the eggs and egg yolks with the sugar until frothy but not thick. Remove the lemon grass from the milk and cream and bring back to the boil, then pour them over the egg and sugar mixture. Strain this into four individual ramekins and put them into a roasting tin. Cover with foil, pour boiling water around them to come two-thirds up the sides of the ramekins, and bake for about 40-45 minutes until the custards are set.

Remove them from the oven, take them out of the tin and leave to cool. Decorate with herb flowers before serving.

SUMMER

With the sun moving daily towards its highest point above the horizon, the days become even longer and sunnier, and the evenings are now warm and light. There is a feeling of relaxation and conviviality as we spend more time outside, making contact with other people, enjoying the fresh air and the sights and sounds of summer. The summer solstice marks midsummer when the sun reaches its zenith, and for me there is something especially magical about this time of year; it is a time of celebration for all the benefits bestowed by the sun to life on earth, demonstrated by the burgeoning growth and fruiting of plants all around us.

Summer vegetables are mainly light and juicy; courgettes, tomatoes, delicate summer spinach, tender young peas, fennel, many varieties of salad leaf and, of course, home-grown asparagus, for me one of the peaks of the culinary calendar for its short season which, where I live, lasts from the end of May until midsummer's day, although imported asparagus continues to be available after that. Summer fruits, too, have a high water content, to quench thirst and refresh parched throats. Perhaps the watermelon, much-loved in hot countries, is the best example of this, but soft fruits such as strawberries, raspberries and red, white and blackcurrants, not to mention peaches and nectarines, are also freely available, juicy and cooling. They form the basis of some delectable summer puddings and can make a light meal in themselves – in the intense heat they may be the only thing you fancy. Strawberries, in particular, still say 'summer' to me, even though I see them in my local supermarket all the year round. And edible flowers such as roses, nasturtiums, marigolds, borage, pinks and lavender can be used for flavour and decoration, underlying the delicacy of summer foods.

For high summer, chilled or iced soups and starters make a tempting start to a meal, refreshing a hot and jaded palate. Light, vegetable-based dishes and summer pastas and grains make tempting main courses; dishes such as the Stuffed Courgettes with Fresh Tomato Sauce (page 190) and Tomatoes Stuffed with Flageolet Beans (page 197). Herbs are of course abundant and a delightful way of adding a variety of flavours to many dishes, including salads. Light, juicy fruit and vegetables mean quicker cooking, or none at all, giving more time to spend outside. We eat in the garden at every opportunity, often just carrying our plates of food outside to eat sitting on the lawn or having a barbecue, vegetarian style, which is easy, as the menu on pages 208–213 shows. It's great, too, that the habit of eating outside in restaurants, pubs and street cafés is more popular these days.

As summer advances, the foods begin to get a little more substantial; left alone, courgettes turn into vegetable marrows, runner beans grow with speed and need frequent picking, home-grown peppers, aubergines and mature artichokes become available. Blackberries weigh down the hedgerows, free for the picking, and purple bilberries can be found on the moors, bringing more delectable flavours and possibilities for menus. Whenever possible, I like to use fruits which are naturally sweet as they are, or that need only small quantities of apple or pear juice concentrate which you can get at health food shops, or real maple syrup; or, in larger quantities, some no-added-sugar high-fruit-content spread. Sometimes I like to use chocolate, partly as a sweetener and partly for the sheer pleasure of its flavour, but I like to use one with a high cocoa solids content – at least 50 per cent, 60 per cent preferably; read the label.

CHILLED SOUPS AND STARTERS

WATERMELON AND MINT

a good-sized piece of   *8 sprigs of fresh mint*
watermelon

I enjoy this for its colour as much as anything, although watermelon and mint together make a refreshing combination on a hot day.

Cut the skin off the watermelon and remove the seeds; cut the flesh into manageable-sized pieces and put them into a bowl. Tear the leaves from four of the mint sprigs and add to the bowl. Mix, then cover and chill until required. Spoon the mixture into four individual dishes – it looks pretty in glass ones – and decorate each with a sprig of mint.
SERVES 4

ICED LETTUCE SOUP

900g / 2lb outside   *4 tbls single cream*
lettuce leaves   *salt and freshly ground*
2 tbls olive oil   *black pepper*
1 onion, peeled and   *chopped mint to*
chopped   *garnish, and extra*
2 or 3 sprigs of fresh   *cream if wished*
mint

Outside leaves of lettuce which are too tough for a salad are fine for this refreshing soup.

Wash the lettuce leaves well then shred them. Heat the oil in a large saucepan and put in the onion; cover and cook for 5 minutes, add the lettuce and mint, cover again, and cook for a further 5 minutes. Pour in 850 ml/1½ pints of water, bring up to the boil and simmer for about 15 minutes, or until the vegetables are very tender.

Liquidize the soup thoroughly, then pour it through a sieve into a pan. Stir in the cream and season with salt and pepper. Cool, then chill the soup. Serve in bowls, garnished with some chopped mint and a swirl of cream if liked.
SERVES 4

TOMATO SORBET

This tomato sorbet makes a most refreshing starter on a summer's day. You do need a food processor in order to make it.

1 tbls olive oil   **TO SERVE**
1 onion, peeled and   *lettuce leaves*
chopped   *chopped fresh chives*
450g / 1lb tomatoes   *or basil*
2 strips of lemon peel
salt and freshly ground
black pepper

Heat the oil in a large saucepan, add the onion, cover and cook for 5 minutes without browning. Meanwhile, chop the tomatoes roughly (there's no need to skin them) and add them to the pan, along with the lemon peel. Cover and cook gently for a further 15-20 minutes, or until the tomatoes have collapsed to a purée. Remove from the heat, liquidize, lemon peel and all, then pass the mixture through a sieve. Season well with salt and freshly ground black pepper. Pour into a shallow container so that the tomato purée is no more than 1 cm/½ inch thick, cool and freeze.

Just before you want to serve the sorbet, put two or three tender lettuce leaves on four serving plates or glass dishes. Take the sorbet out of the fridge, turn it out on to a chopping board and, with a sharp knife, cut it into small pieces, about 1 cm/½ inch square. Put these into the food processor and whizz for a minute or two, until the mixture turns to a smooth ice and holds together. Quickly put scoops of this on to the plates, on top of the lettuce. Sprinkle the chopped chives or basil over the top of the ice and serve.
SERVES 4

OPPOSITE: *(top) Tomato Sorbet and (bottom) Iced Lettuce Soup*

STUFFED COURGETTE FLOWERS

Courgette flowers are not easy to come by unless you grow your own, though sometimes kind friends who grow courgettes will provide them or pick-your-own places will let you pick some if you ask first. If you can get hold of them, they make a delightful light starter, which can be made more substantial by the addition of some fresh tomato sauce (see page 190) if you wish.

125g / 4oz Mozzarella cheese (packed in water)	salt and freshly ground black pepper
8 courgette flowers	ready-grated Parmesan cheese
2 eggs	olive oil
	slices of lemon to serve

Cut the Mozzarella cheese into eight pieces the right size to fit into the courgette flowers. With your fingers, pinch out the stamens from inside the flowers, then put a piece of Mozzarella cheese inside each one. Fold the tips of the petals over so that the cheese is fully enclosed.

Separate the eggs; whisk the whites until they're stiff, then beat the yolks a little to break them up, and fold in the whites. Season with salt and pepper. Holding the courgette flowers by the green baby courgette part, dip the flowers first into the egg mixture, making sure they are completely coated, then into the ready-grated Parmesan cheese. Fry them in a little olive oil, turning them over after a minute or two so that the flowers get brown and crisp all over. (They will only take 3-4 minutes in all to cook.) Drain them on kitchen paper and serve immediately on warmed, individual plates. Garnish each plate with a slice of lemon.

SERVES 4

BROAD BEAN PATE WITH GRILLED FENNEL

I think that this pâté is best if you take the time to pop the beans out of their skins first, although you can make it without doing this – in which case it will have a more chewy texture. If you don't want to do the fennel, some bread would also go well with it.

450g / 1lb shelled broad beans	2 fennel bulbs
	olive oil
25g / 1oz butter	1 tbls red wine vinegar
2 tbls lemon juice	black olives
salt and freshly ground black pepper	

Cook the broad beans in boiling water for a few minutes until they are done, then drain them. With your finger and thumb, pop them out of their grey skins; discard the skins. Put the beans into a food processor with the butter, lemon juice and some salt and pepper and whizz to a thick green purée. Season the mixture, put it into a bowl and cover.

Prepare the fennel by removing any tough leaves or pieces of stem, but leaving enough of the stem to hold the leaves together at the base. Cut each down first into halves, then into quarters and eighths, so that they are still joined together at the base if possible. Steam or parboil the fennel for about 8 minutes, or until it is just tender without being at all soggy. Drain well and dry with kitchen paper. Brush both fennel with oil and sprinkle with some salt and pepper, then grill them until they are lightly charred on both sides: this will take about 15 minutes. Cover until required. Make a simple dressing by putting the vinegar into a screwtop jar with 3 tablespoons olive oil and some salt and pepper and shaking well to mix.

To assemble the dish, spoon some of the pâté on to four individual serving plates, add some black olives, put four pieces of grilled fennel on each plate, and spoon a little dressing on top of the pâté.

SERVES 4

Served with salad, both these recipes make good light meals, in which case they will serve 2-3 people.

OPPOSITE: *Broad Bean Pâté with Grilled Fennel*

ARTICHOKES STUFFED WITH LEMON CREAM

Although these are a bit fiddly to prepare, they're so good that it's worth the effort – and as they're served cold, you can get all the main preparation done well in advance.

4 globe artichokes	*1 tbls chopped fresh*
1 lemon	*chives*
125ml / 4fl oz double	*salt and freshly ground*
cream	*black pepper*

Artichokes come in various sizes : medium to large sizes are best for this recipe.

First, half-fill two large saucepans with water and put them on the stove to heat. Next, prepare the artichokes by cutting the bases level and removing any damaged lower leaves. For a restaurant-style presentation, you can trim the points off the leaves with kitchen scissors to make them neat; I don't always bother with this. Wash the artichokes well under the cold tap, pulling back the leaves as much as you can, then divide them between the pans of boiling water.

Squeeze the juice from the lemon and reserve 2 tablespoons. Add the rest to the artichokes, dividing it between the pans. Let the artichokes simmer away for about 45 minutes, or until one of the lower leaves pulls off easily. Remove the artichokes from the water and leave them upside down in a colander to drain.

When the artichokes are cool enough to handle, gently pull back all the leaves to reveal the inner, baby leaves which cover the choke; grasp these firmly and pull them out then, with a sharp knife, cut out the remaining choke, being careful to get out all the prickly bits without taking away any more of the delicious flesh than you have to. Rinse the inside of the artichokes gently under the tap, pat them dry and leave them until just before you want to serve the starter.

Just before serving make the filling. Put the reserved lemon juice into a bowl and add the cream, chives, and salt and pepper. Stir the mixture gently with a spoon until it thickens to a floppy state, but don't get it too stiff. Put each artichoke on to an individual plate, pull back the leaves and spoon some of the cream mixture into the centre. Serve at once. It's best to eat this dish by pulling off the outer leaves one by one and dipping their bases in the dressing, then eating the artichoke base and the remaining dressing with a knife and fork.
SERVES 4

CHILLED CUCUMBER SOUP

This is a light and refreshing soup to make at the height of summer when cucumbers are good and plentiful. If you haven't any home-made vegetable stock (which can simply be the water saved from cooking tasty vegetables such leeks or fennel), it's better to use water rather than a stock cube.

1 tbls olive oil	*300ml / ½ pint vegetable*
1 onion, peeled and	*stock or water*
chopped	*4-6 tbls cream*
2 cucumbers	*salt and freshly ground*
8-10 sprigs of fresh	*black pepper*
mint	*a little chopped fresh*
	mint to garnish

Heat the olive oil in a large saucepan and put in the onion; cover and cook gently for 10 minutes until tender.

Meanwhile, peel and roughly dice the cucumbers. Add these to the onion, along with the sprigs of mint, cover the pan again and leave over a gentle heat for about 20 minutes, or until the cucumber is very tender and transparent. Liquidize the mixture thoroughly, including the mint sprigs, then return it to the saucepan and stir in the stock or water and cream. Season with salt and freshly ground black pepper and leave the soup to cool, then chill it.

Check the seasoning just before you serve the soup because chilling dulls the flavour of foods, then ladle the soup into chilled bowls and sprinkle a little chopped mint on top of each.
SERVES 4

SUMMER BEAN AND FRESH HERB SALAD

The cooked beans absorb flavours well making this a fragrant salad, refreshing yet quite satisfying. If you want to cook your own beans rather than using canned ones, you'll need 200g/7oz cannellini, haricot or flageolet beans. Soak them in plenty of cold water for several hours, simmer them in fresh water for about 1 hour (a little more for the first two types, a little less for the flageolets) until the beans are tender, then drain. You can dress the salad while the beans are still hot. Some warm crusty bread or rolls go well with this.

2 × 425g / 15oz cans cannellini or flageolet beans, or a can of each
4 tbls chopped fresh mixed herbs such as chives, chervil, parsley, tarragon, mint or dill

1 tbls red wine vinegar
3 tbls olive oil
salt and freshly ground black pepper
1 small lettuce

Drain the beans and put them into a bowl along with the fresh herbs, wine vinegar, olive oil and some salt and pepper to taste. Mix well, then cover and leave until you're ready to serve the salad. (The longer you can leave it the better, because it will give the flavours a chance to develop and blend.) Meanwhile, wash the lettuce and put the leaves into a polythene bag in the fridge to chill them and make them crisp.

To serve the salad, put one or two lettuce leaves on individual serving plates, stir the bean mixture then spoon some of it on top of the lettuce.
SERVES 4-6

EASY SUMMER TOMATO SOUP

This is a soup which really makes the most of summer tomatoes, and it couldn't be easier to make.

2 tbls olive oil
1 onion, peeled and chopped
1kg / 2¼lb tomatoes

salt and freshly ground black pepper
a little milk or single cream (optional)
fresh basil

Heat the oil in a large saucepan, add the onion, and cook, covered, for 5 minutes or so. Meanwhile, wash and chop the tomatoes roughly (there's no need to skin or de-seed them) and add them to the pan, along with a sprinkling of salt. Cover and cook gently for a further 15 minutes, or until the tomatoes have collapsed. Liquidize them thoroughly and pour them through a sieve into the pan. Add 300 ml/ ½ pint of water, or milk if you prefer, and a tablespoonful or so of single cream if you're using this.

The soup is also very good without any of these embellishments; just add some water to thin it to a nice light consistency, season with salt and freshly ground black pepper, and snip some fresh basil over the top. Chill the soup before serving – or serve it hot if you prefer.
SERVES 4

SUMMER VEGETABLES AND SALADS

SUNSHINE RATATOUILLE

4 tbls olive oil
450g / 1lb onions,
    peeled and chopped
450g / 1 lb red peppers,
    de-seeded and
    chopped

2 garlic cloves
450g / 1lb aubergines
700g / 1½lb tomatoes
salt and freshly ground
    black pepper
chopped fresh parsley

This version of ratatouille always works well for me, and it is quick and easy. It's good both hot and cold, as a first course - or as a main course for a light summer meal, which is how I like to serve it, with the salad suggested here.

Heat the oil in a large saucepan and put in the onions and red peppers. Cover and cook, without browning, for 10 minutes. Meanwhile, peel and crush the garlic and cut the aubergines into 1 cm/½ inch dice. Add these to the pan, stir well, cover again and cook gently for a further 10 minutes.

Put the tomatoes into a large bowl, cover with boiling water and leave for 30-60 seconds, or until the skins will slip off; drain and skin. Quarter the tomatoes, then remove and discard the seeds. Chop the flesh and add to the saucepan. Give it another stir, cover and cook for a further 10 minutes, or until all the vegetables are tender. Check the seasoning, adding more salt and a grinding of pepper, and serve with some chopped parsley on top.
SERVES 2-4

GREEN SALAD WITH SHAVINGS OF PARMESAN

Put 1 tablespoon wine vinegar and 3 tablespoons olive oil into a bowl with a seasoning of salt and pepper. Give them a stir to make a quick dressing, then put some crisp salad greens on top. Some chopped fresh herbs are good too. Just before you want to serve the salad, stir the leaves gently to coat them lightly in the dressing, and add some thin slivers of Parmesan cheese.

STUFFED COURGETTES WITH FRESH TOMATO SAUCE

These light and summery courgettes are good served with some French beans and perhaps some buttery new potatoes.

4 plump courgettes,
    each about 125g / 4oz
2 × 150g / 5 oz Boursin
    cheese with garlic
    and herbs
sprigs of fresh dill
    to garnish

FOR THE SAUCE
1 tbls olive oil
1 small onion, peeled
    and finely chopped
900g / 2lb tomatoes
salt and freshly ground
    black pepper

First make the sauce. Heat the oil in a large saucepan, add the onion and fry for 5 minutes without browning. Meanwhile, quarter the tomatoes and add them to the pan. Cover and cook over a gentle heat for 10-15 minutes, or until the tomatoes have collapsed, then liquidize, sieve and season. Set aside.

Halve the courgettes and cook them in 2.5 cm/1 inch of boiling water in a saucepan until they are just tender: about 3 minutes. Drain them well. Scoop out the seeds with a pointed teaspoon or grapefruit spoon and discard them. Place the courgettes in a shallow casserole or grill pan. Mash the Boursin cheese to soften it a bit, then put some into the cavity of each courgette, dividing it between them and piling them up well. Put the courgettes under a hot grill until they are heated through and the cheese has just started to brown.

Meanwhile, gently reheat the tomato sauce to serve with them. Garnish with the sprigs of dill just before serving.
SERVES 4

OPPOSITE: *Stuffed Courgettes with Fresh Tomato Sauce*

ASPARAGUS WITH HOLLANDAISE SAUCE

As far as I'm concerned, this is one of the best treats of summer. I like to serve lots of asparagus with this buttery sauce as a main course, accompanied by a salad such as the Lettuce Hearts, Lamb's Lettuce and Summer Herbs one, opposite. A flinty white wine and fresh strawberries would complete the meal.

450g / 1lb asparagus
125g / 4oz butter
1 tbls lemon juice
2 egg yolks
sea salt

First prepare the asparagus by removing any tough stalk ends, then shaving down the stems a bit with a potato peeler to trim further if necessary. Wash the stems, especially the heads, well. Cook the asparagus in a steamer until it is just tender, 5-10 minutes, or in a pan of boiling water to cover: it will take a little less time. Drain well.

Meanwhile, make the sauce. Cut up the butter roughly, put it into a small saucepan and heat until it has melted and is boiling. While this is happening, put the lemon juice and egg yolks into a food processor or blender with a good pinch of salt and whizz for 1 minute, to make a pale, thick mixture. With the machine running, pour the melted butter in a steady stream into the food processor or blender through the top of the goblet, and whizz for a further 1 minute.

Let the mixture stand for a minute or two, before serving it with the asparagus.

SERVES 2-4

OPPOSITE: *(left) Asparagus with Hollandaise Sauce and (right) Salad of Lettuce Hearts, Lamb's Lettuce and Herbs*

SALAD OF LETTUCE HEARTS, LAMB'S LETTUCE AND HERBS

Pour 1 tablespoon red wine vinegar, a good pinch of salt, a few grindings of pepper and 3 tablespoons olive oil into a dish and mix together. Then put in 2 tablespoons chopped fresh herbs. Wash 2 little gem lettuces and the lamb's lettuce and pat dry, then tear into pieces and put into the bowl. Just before serving, gently turn the leaves in the dressing, and add 25-50g/1-2oz toasted pine nuts.

Lamb's lettuce, or mâche, is available at many greengrocers and supermarkets now, and it's also really easy to grow.

SUMMER SPAGHETTI WITH TOMATOES AND BASIL

225g / 8oz spaghetti or
    wholewheat noodles
2 tsp olive oil
1 onion, peeled and
    finely chopped
4 tomatoes
sprigs of fresh basil
salt and freshly ground
    black pepper
freshly grated
    Parmesan cheese
    (optional)

Bring a large saucepan two-thirds full of water to the boil. Put in the pasta, easing it down into the water and, when the water comes back to the boil, start timing the pasta: if you're using the wholewheat noodles, cover the pan, take it off the heat, then leave it for 5 minutes.

Meanwhile, heat the oil in a medium saucepan, add the onion, cover and cook for 4 minutes. While the onion is cooking, wash the tomatoes and cut them into eighths, then add them to the onion. Stir-fry them, just to heat them through really.

Drain the pasta into a colander, then put it back into the warm pan and add the tomato mixture, some torn basil leaves and some salt and freshly ground black pepper to taste. Serve at once, with the Parmesan cheese if you're using it.

SERVES 2

FENNEL, TOMATO AND BLACK OLIVE SALAD

I prefer to buy olives loose from a delicatessen or a shop specialising in mediterranean foods.

Put 3 tablespoons olive oil and 1 tablespoon red wine vinegar into a bowl or shallow serving dish, add some salt and pepper and mix together. Wash 2 fennel bulbs and cut off any leafy parts; chop these and add to the oil mixture. If any of the outer layers of the fennel look tough, remove these, then halve the fennel and slice thinly. Wash and slice 4 tomatoes and add the tomato and fennel to the oil mixture, along with 2 tablespoons black olives. Mix gently and leave for at least 30 minutes for the flavours to blend.

RICE SALAD WITH YELLOW AND GREEN COURGETTES

The combination of yellow and green courgettes – or baby custard pie squash – makes this a pretty, summery salad. It makes a good light lunch if it's served with a salad, such as Fennel, Tomato and Black Olives, above.

75g / 3oz brown rice	*1 tbls lemon juice*
25g / 1oz wild rice	*grated lemon rind*
225g / 8oz mixed green	*2 tbls snipped chives*
and yellow courgettes	*1 tbls olive oil*
or baby custard pie	*salt and freshly ground*
squash	*black pepper*

Put the brown rice and wild rice into a sieve and wash under the tap, then put them into a heavy-based saucepan with 300 ml/½ pint water and bring to the boil. Cover the pan and turn the heat down as low as possible; leave the rice to cook, undisturbed, for 40-45 minutes, until all the water has gone and it is tender.

Meanwhile, wash, trim and slice the courgettes or baby squash. Steam them for a few minutes until they are just tender, then remove them from the heat and cover them with cold water to cool them quickly and preserve the colour. Drain and pat them dry on kitchen paper.

When the rice is cooked, stir it gently with a fork, adding the courgettes or squash, the lemon juice and a little grated rind to taste, the chives, olive oil and a good seasoning of salt and pepper. Serve as soon as possible, while the salad looks bright and glossy.

SERVES 2 AS A MAIN COURSE, 4 AS A SIDE DISH

TAGLIATELLE OF SUMMER VEGETABLES

A mixture of summer cabbage, courgettes and carrots is good for this; allow about 700g/1½lb altogether for four people. Shred the cabbage so that it forms long thin strands, then shave long pieces off the sides of the carrots and courgettes and cut these down to form long, thin strips. Bring half a saucepanful of water to the boil, put in first the carrot, and cook for a minute or two until it begins to get tender, then the cabbage; cook for a further minute, then add the courgette strands and cook for just 30-60 seconds.

Drain the vegetables, return them to the pan, add a knob of butter, some salt and freshly ground black pepper and perhaps some chopped fresh summer herbs just before serving.

OPPOSITE: *(left) Rice Salad with Yellow and Green Courgettes and (right) Fennel, Tomato and Black Olive Salad*

SUMMER VEGETABLE AND HERB BURGERS

These light summery burgers are good with a crisp leafy or tomato salad; for a more substantial meal, serve them normal burger-style in a light bun. They need to be eaten as soon as they're cooked as they tend to collapse if kept hot under the grill or in the oven. You will need a firmish soft white cheese – fromage frais would be too runny; and ready-grated Parmesan cheese is best for this recipe because of its dryness.

50g / 2oz French beans
50g / 2oz courgette
225g / 8oz curd cheese
2 tbls chopped fresh
   herbs such as chives,
   dill, parsley or chervil
50g / 2oz ready-grated
   Parmesan cheese
freshly ground black
   pepper

TO COAT AND FRY
6 tbls soft white
   breadcrumbs
1 tbls ready-grated
   Parmesan cheese
olive oil

For a completely food-combining version of the summer vegetable and herb burgers, replace the white breadcrumbs in the coating with very dry ready-grated Parmesan cheese and fry the burgers carefully to maintain their shape.

Wash and trim the French beans then cut them into 1 cm/½ inch lengths; wash and trim the courgette and cut into 5 mm/¼ inch dice. Bring 2.5 cm/1 inch of water to the boil in a medium saucepan and put in the French beans; boil for 1 minute, then add the courgette and boil for 30 seconds. Drain into a sieve and refresh them under the cold tap, then pat dry on kitchen paper.

Put the curd cheese into a bowl and mix in the chopped herbs, then stir in the vegetables, Parmesan cheese and freshly ground black pepper.

To make the coating, mix together the breadcrumbs and the Parmesan cheese on a piece of greaseproof paper. Divide the curd cheese mixture into four and put them on top of the crumb mixture; form into flat round burgers, rolling them in the crumb mixture so that they are well coated. Chill until just before you want to serve them.

To finish the burgers, heat 2 tablespoons of olive oil in a frying pan – preferably non-stick – and put in the burgers. Fry them for a minute or two until they are crisp and golden brown on one side, then carefully turn them over and fry them until the other side, too, is crisp and golden brown, and the inside has heated through. Serve immediately with salad or in buns.

MAKES 4

SPINACH ROULADE WITH MOZZARELLA AND TOMATO FILLING

A spinach roulade is a classic dish which can be varied by using different fillings. I particularly like this version, which is good either hot or cold.

450g / 1lb fresh spinach
   or 175g / 6oz frozen
15g / ½oz butter
4 eggs, separated
salt and freshly ground
   black pepper
grated nutmeg
4 tbls ready-grated
   Parmesan cheese

FOR THE FILLING
2 × 150g / 5oz
   Mozzarella cheese
   (packed in water)
4 medium tomatoes
3-4 sprigs of fresh
   basil

Set the oven to 200°C/400°F/Gas Mark 6. Line a 23 × 33 cm/9 × 13 inch Swiss roll tin with non-stick paper, to extend a bit up the sides.

If you're using fresh spinach, wash it three times in sinkfuls of cold water, then put it into a large saucepan and cook over a high heat for 7-10 minutes, or until it is very tender. Keep pushing it down into the pan with a fish slice as it cooks. Cook frozen spinach in a tiny amount of boiling water, just enough to prevent it from sticking to the pan; it takes much the same length of time. In either case, drain the spinach into a colander and press it very well to extract as much water as possible. Put it into a food processor, along with the butter, egg yolks and a seasoning of salt and freshly ground black pepper and nutmeg, and whizz it all at top speed to make a smooth, creamy-looking purée.

Whisk the egg whites until they stand in stiff peaks, then gently add the spinach mixture and carefully fold it into the egg whites, incorporating it as well as you can without stirring too hard. Tip the mixture into the tin, level the top gently and sprinkle it with 2 tablespoons of the Parmesan. Bake for 10-12 minutes, until the top is springy.

While the roulade is baking, get ready a piece of non-stick paper to turn it out on to, by sprinkling it with the rest of the Parmesan. Now prepare the filling: drain the Mozzarella and slice thinly; cut the tomatoes into thin rounds and chop the basil.

Take the roulade out of the oven and turn it out on to the non-stick paper. Peel the paper off the roulade, cover with a layer of Mozzarella slices, then a layer of tomato rounds and finally chopped basil and salt and pepper to taste. Roll up the roulade, starting at one of the long ends. Serve it immediately, or put it on a plate, cover with foil and put it into the oven, turned down to 160°C/325°F/Gas Mark 3, for 15 minutes or so.
SERVES 4

First, set the oven to 200°C/400°F/Gas Mark 6, then put the rice into a medium heavy-based saucepan, add a teaspoonful of salt and 600 ml/1 pint of water. Bring to the boil, cover and leave to cook very gently for 30 minutes, or until it's tender and all the water has gone.

Next, prepare the tomatoes. Slice the tops off – the stalks can stay – and scoop out the seeds to make a good cavity for the stuffing. Sprinkle the insides of the tomatoes with salt and pepper. Mix the flageolet beans with the basil and lemon rind and spoon this mixture into the tomatoes; replace the tops. Put the tomatoes in a shallow casserole and bake them for about 20 minutes, or until they are heated right through but not collapsing.

Finish off the rice by adding the fresh herbs and forking them gently through the rice, fluffing it at the same time. Serve the tomatoes with the rice.
SERVES 4

TOMATOES STUFFED WITH FLAGEOLET BEANS, WITH RICE

Using canned flageolet beans makes this a quick and easy dish to make, although you could use dried ones. You would need 100g/3½oz if you were using dried beans; soak them in water for a few hours, then boil them in plenty of water for 45-60 minutes, or until they are tender. If you cook extra for another time, they'll freeze perfectly in a suitable container.

4 beefsteak tomatoes
salt and freshly ground
*   black pepper*
1 × 400g / 14oz can
*   flageolet beans,*
*   drained*
2 tbls chopped fresh
*   basil*
1 tsp grated lemon rind

FOR THE RICE
225g / 8oz brown rice,
*   preferably Basmati*
4 tbls chopped fresh
*   parsley and chives*

LETTUCE AND NASTURTIUM FLOWER SALAD

This is just a simple salad of lettuce, tossed in a dressing of 1 tablespoon wine vinegar and 3 tablespoons olive oil, plus some salt and pepper, some snipped chives and, added at the last minute just before serving, some bright nasturtium flowers.

FRUITS, CUPS AND ICES

SUMMER ICE-CREAM CAKE

For a completely food-combining version of the summer vegetable and herb burgers, replace the white breadcrumbs in the coating with very dry ready-grated Parmesan cheese and fry the burgers carefully to maintain their shape.

We have a number of summer birthdays in my family and this is a favourite birthday 'cake'.

9 egg yolks
225g / 8oz caster sugar
850ml / 1½ pints
  whipping cream
125g / 4oz chocolate, at
  least 50% cocoa
  solids but not a very
  bitter continental one
125g / 4oz strawberries
grated rind of 4 small
  or 2 large oranges

orange food colouring
  (optional)
1 vanilla pod

TO DECORATE
whipped cream
strawberries
chocolate curls
slivers of orange rind
  (optional)

This cake consists of three layers of ice cream, chocolate, orange and strawberry, and real vanilla. Of course you could use different flavourings – sieved raspberries, for a raspberry layer, are good. You make one batch of basic ice cream mixture, then divide it into three portions and add the different flavourings, then set it in layers in a cake tin.

To make the basic ice cream, put the egg yolks into a large bowl or the bowl of an electric beater and whisk until thick and creamy. Put all but 1 tablespoon of the sugar into a small saucepan with 6 tablespoons of water and heat very gently until the sugar has dissolved; turn up the heat and let it bubble for a minute or so until it reaches 110°C/225°F on a sugar thermometer or a drop of it on the back of the spoon forms a thread when pulled with a teaspoon. (It reaches this stage very quickly.) Immediately remove the pan from the heat and pour the syrup on to the egg yolks while you whisk them. Continue to whisk for 4-5 minutes until the mixture is cool and very thick and creamy. Whip the cream until it holds its shape, then fold it into the egg yolk mixture. Divide the mixture into three roughly equal portions in separate bowls.

For the first layer, break the chocolate into a bowl set over a pan of simmering water and heat gently until it has melted. Stir the melted chocolate into one lot of ice cream. Pour this into the base of a 20 cm/8 inch deep cake tin and put into the freezer to set, making sure it is standing level.

Hull and dice the strawberries, then put them into a saucepan with the remaining tablespoonful of sugar. Heat gently until the sugar has dissolved and the strawberries are tender: 5-10 minutes. Cool. Add the grated orange rind to the second bowl of ice cream, and intensify the colouring a bit if you like with orange food colouring. Gently fold in the strawberries. If you have room in your freezer, this can go into the freezer for the moment. For the final ice cream, split the vanilla pod and scrape the gooey black seeds out of the skin, using half or all of the pod to taste. Add this vanilla to the final bowl of ice cream and put that, too, into the freezer.

After about 30 minutes, or when the chocolate layer of ice cream has begun to set, gently spoon the orange and strawberry ice cream on top, in an even layer, and put the tin back into the freezer for another 15-30 minutes, or until the orange layer is beginning to get firm. Then scoop the final layer on top, beating it a bit if it has set round the edges. Smooth the top and leave to set completely.

To finish the cake, have ready some whipped cream in a piping bag fitted with a medium shell nozzle. Take the ice-cream cake out of the freezer and run the blade of a knife around the edges, invert the cake on to a suitable plate – give it a shake and the cake should come out. Pipe a little cream around the edges and in the centre, then put the cake back in the freezer and open-freeze it until required. Or decorate it straight away, with strawberries with their stems still attached, chocolate curls and slivers of orange rind, if using. Serve immediately.
SERVES 12

OPPOSITE: *Summer Ice-Cream Cake*

STRAWBERRIES IN CHOCOLATE CASES

You need a good quality plain chocolate for the cases, but not a bitter continental one. The cases need to be made a few hours in advance, to give them time to set, but not overnight as they gradually become dull.

FOR THE CASES

200g / 7oz plain chocolate, at least 50% cocoa solids

FOR THE FILLING

225g / 8oz strawberries about 3 tbls no-added-sugar, high-fruit-content raspberry spread or redcurrant jelly

TO SERVE (OPTIONAL)

raspberry coulis (see page 299) a few strawberry leaves, to decorate

First make the chocolate cases which need to be done a few hours in advance. Break the chocolate into a bowl set over a pan of simmering water and heat gently to melt. Have ready some paper cake cases. Using two cases together for firmness, coat the inside quite thickly with melted chocolate. Repeat with all the cases then leave them for 30-60 minutes to set. Give them all another coat of chocolate, making sure it's quite thick around the rim, as this is where it tends to break. Leave them for several hours to firm up, then peel off the paper cases and put the chocolate cases on individual plates.

Hull, wash and slice the strawberries, then put a few in each chocolate case, piling them up attractively. Gently melt the fruit spread or redcurrant jelly and spoon a little on top of the strawberries, being careful not to get the hot jam on the chocolate. Serve with the raspberry coulis if you are using this, and decorate with the strawberry leaves.
SERVES 6

ROSE PETAL CREAMS

300ml / ½ pint plain low-fat yogurt 300ml / ½ pint whipping cream 2-3 tsp rosewater

caster sugar or clear honey 350g / 12oz raspberries rose petals to decorate

Put the yogurt and cream into a bowl and whisk together until the mixture is thick. Add the rosewater and a little sugar or clear honey to taste. Wash the raspberries and pat them dry very gently with kitchen paper, then sprinkle them with a little caster sugar to sweeten them as necessary.

Spoon layers of raspberries and the rose cream into six deep glasses, starting with raspberries, then cream, followed by more raspberries, and a final layer of cream. Cover and chill until needed. Scatter some pink rose petals on top before serving.

The petals can be crystallized first by coating them with lightly beaten egg white, then sprinkling all over with caster sugar and leaving to dry and crisp up on a rack covered with non-stick paper.
SERVES 4

OPPOSITE: *(left) Rose Petal Creams and (right) Strawberries in Chocolate Cases*

THE ULTIMATE PEACH MELBA

raspberry coulis (see page 299)
6 large, perfect peaches
25–50g / 1–2oz flaked almonds

FOR THE VANILLA ICE CREAM

300ml / ½ pint milk
1 vanilla pod
1 egg yolk
100g / 3½ oz caster sugar
300ml / ½ pint whipping or double cream

Traditionally the peaches for this melba should be poached in a sugar syrup but I much prefer to use really perfect, ripe peaches which do not need cooking. It's a wonderful mixture of flavours.

First make the ice cream. Put the milk into a saucepan with the vanilla pod and bring to the boil. Meanwhile, mix the egg yolk with the sugar. Pour the boiling milk over the egg yolk mixture, stir, then return the whole lot to the saucepan. Stir over a gentle heat for a minute or two until the mixture thickens slightly and will coat the back of the spoon thinly – don't let it boil. Remove from the heat immediately and cool. (You can hasten this process by transferring the mixture to a bowl and standing it in another bowl of cold water.)

Put the cream into a large bowl and whisk until it forms soft peaks, then gradually whisk in the cooled egg yolk mixture. If you have an ice-cream maker, pour the mixture into that and freeze it according to the instructions. If not, pour it into a suitable container to freeze – or freeze it in the bowl, if your freezer is big enough. As it freezes, whisk the mixture every half hour or so if you can, to break up the ice crystals and make a very smooth ice cream. (It's helpful if you freeze the ice cream in the bowl, or in a container which you can whisk it in, to avoid having to keep transferring it from container to bowl.) Once it's frozen, keep it in a covered container in the freezer. Remove it from the freezer 45 minutes before you want to serve it, to allow it to soften up.

Next, make the raspberry coulis according to recipe instructions and set aside until you need it.

Just before you want to serve the pudding, prepare the peaches by putting them into a bowl, pouring boiling water over them and leaving them for 30-60 seconds, or until the skins will slip off.

Remove all the skins, halve the peaches and remove the stones. Put two peach halves on each plate, top with a scoop of ice cream, spoon some raspberry coulis over the top and sprinkle with some flaked almonds. Serve at once.
SERVES 6

CURD CHEESE SUMMER PUDDING

Although many people love summer pudding, it's never done much for me so I wanted to see if I could make a summer's pudding with a difference. I wanted to make an outside of curd cheese, with a luscious filling of red summer fruits but for a long time I couldn't think how to make it so that the curd cheese could drain. Then I hit on the idea of using a round sieve lined with butter muslin. It worked perfectly, resulting in an unconventional summer pudding which we found delectable.

350g / 12oz soft white skim milk cheese
200ml / 7fl oz double cream
3 tbls caster sugar
450g / 1lb mixed red summer fruit
4 tbls no-added-sugar, high-fruit-content cherry spread
a few strawberries, to decorate

First, line a 16 cm/6½ inch diameter round sieve with a piece of butter muslin and set it over a bowl so that it isn't touching the base. Next, put the soft white cheese and the double cream into a bowl with the caster sugar and whisk until the mixture is stiff but not breaking up. Spoon a good two-thirds of it into the muslin-lined sieve and press it down, so that it forms an even layer.

Wash, hull and slice the fruit as necessary, then mix it with the all-fruit spread to sweeten it. Spoon the mixture into the sieve on top of the curd cheese, then spread the rest of the white cheese mixture evenly over the top. Cover with several layers of kitchen paper, then a plate and a weight, and leave for several hours or overnight. The curd cheese will drip into the bowl and firm up.

To serve the pudding, remove the kitchen paper and invert the sieve over a serving plate. Turn out the pudding, then gently remove the butter muslin. Decorate with some strawberries with their stalks still attached.

SERVES 6

CHOCOLATE TRUFFLE CAKE WITH CHERRIES IN KIRSCH

This is a very indulgent but wonderful pudding.

225g / 8oz plain
   chocolate, at least
   50% cocoa solids
25g / 1oz butter
300ml / ½ pint double
   cream
900g / 2lb ripe sweet
   red cherries

4 tbls kirsch
sugar to taste
50g / 2oz plain
   chocolate, grated
whipping cream to
   serve

First of all, line a 20 cm/8 inch shallow tin with a circle of non-stick paper. Break the chocolate into a bowl and add the butter; set the bowl over a pan of simmering water and heat gently for a few minutes until the chocolate and butter have melted. Remove from the heat and leave to cool slightly.

Meanwhile, whisk the cream until it will hold a shape but is not too stiff, then gently fold it into the chocolate. Pour this mixture into the tin and smooth the top. Cover and leave to chill and set for several hours. While the cream is chilling, wash and stone the cherries and put them into a bowl with the kirsch and just a little sugar to taste if necessary. Cover and leave until required.

Just before you want to serve the truffle cake, turn it out on to a plate – if you first loosen the edges, then put a plate over it and give it a good

shake, it should come out all right. Cover the top with a thick layer of grated chocolate. Serve with the cherries, and some extra softly whipped cream.

SERVES 6

SUMMER BERRIES WITH SABAYON SAUCE

4 egg yolks
50g / 2oz caster sugar
2 tbls Cointreau or
   other orange liqueur

150ml / 5fl oz whipping
   cream, whipped
350g / 12oz raspberries,
   strawberries and
   a little extra sugar

A classic sabayon sauce makes a delectable accompaniment for summer berries.

Put the egg yolks into a bowl set over a pan of simmering water, making sure that the base of the bowl doesn't touch the water. Add the sugar to the yolks and whisk until the mixture is very thick and creamy: this will take at least 10 minutes so it helps if you have an electric hand whisk. Remove the bowl from the heat and leave it to cool, whisking it often. Stir in the Cointreau and gently fold in the cream. Chill until required.

To finish the pudding, wash, hull and slice the fruit as necessary; spoon a pool of the sauce on to four plates, then put the red fruits in the centre and sprinkle with a little caster sugar.

SERVES 4

SUMMER MENUS

MENU

A PERFECT SUMMER LUNCH IN THE GARDEN FOR FOUR

Little Pea and Mint Custards

Summer Salad Roulade with Fresh Herb Sauce
Little New Potatoes Baked in a Parcel
French Bean Vinaigrette

Jellied Terrine of Red Summer Fruits
Orange Ice Cream with Pistachio nuts

COUNTDOWN

Up to 1 week in advance:
Make the Orange and Pistachio Ice Cream.

Up to one day before:
Make the Little Pea and Mint Custards, the Jellied
Red Fruit Terrine, the Fresh Herb Sauce and the
French Bean Vinaigrette, cover and keep in the fridge.

1-2 hours before:
Make and fill the Roulade if you are going to serve
this warm; it can be done 3-4 hours in advance if you
are planning to serve it cold. Heat the oven so that it is
ready 35 minutes before you want to eat the meal,
then prepare and bake the potatoes in their parcel.

LITTLE PEA AND MINT CUSTARDS

*Delicate in texture, flavour and appearance, these
little custards are a real treat. I make them in dariole
moulds of 150 ml/5 fl oz capacity, but little ramekins
or old cups would be an alternative.*

225g / 8oz shelled fresh peas	2 egg yolks
butter and ready-grated Parmesan cheese for preparing the moulds	150ml / 5fl oz single cream
	50ml / 2fl oz double cream
sprigs of fresh mint	salt and freshly ground black pepper
2 eggs	

Set the oven to 160°C/325°F/Gas Mark 3.

Cook the peas in boiling water for a few minutes
until they are tender, then drain. While the peas are
cooking, grease four moulds well with butter and
sprinkle with the Parmesan cheese.

Put the drained peas into a food processor with
3 good sprigs of mint and whizz to a purée then
push the mixture through a sieve into a bowl. Add
the eggs, yolks and creams and whisk well. Season
with salt and freshly ground black pepper. Pour
into the moulds, put them into a small roasting tin
and pour boiling water around them to come at
least halfway up their sides. Bake for about 35 minutes, or until they feel set, and a cocktail stick inserted into the centre of one comes out clean.

Turn them out on to warmed plates, if you want
to serve them hot; otherwise let them cool in their
moulds. I think they're best just warm. They should
come out of the moulds all right if you loosen the
edges with a knife then, holding them over a plate,
give them a shake. Garnish with mint.

OPPOSITE: *Dishes from a Perfect Summer Lunch
in the Garden for Four*

SUMMER SALAD ROULADE WITH FRESH HERB SAUCE

This light roulade can be served warm or cold; it's good either way.

butter for greasing and
  ready-grated
  Parmesan cheese for
  coating
50g / 2oz curd cheese
4 eggs, separated
150ml / 5fl oz single
  cream
200g / 7oz Gruyère
  cheese, grated

salt and freshly ground
  black pepper

FOR THE FILLING
2 heaped tbls
  mayonnaise
3 floppy lettuce leaves
2 tomatoes, skinned
2 spring onions, finely
  chopped

Accompany this lunch with an aromatic or medium-bodied dry white wine such as a Sancerre or Frascati; or try a dry rosé.

Set the oven to 200°C/400°F/Gas Mark 6. Line a 32 × 23 cm/13 × 9 inch Swiss roll tin with a piece of non-stick paper – it needn't be too tidy. Grease the paper and sprinkle with the grated Parmesan cheese. Put the curd cheese and egg yolks into a large bowl and mix together until smooth, then gradually mix in the cream; finally, stir in the grated Gruyère cheese. In another bowl, whisk the egg whites until they're stiff, then fold these into the Gruyère mixture. Season as necessary with salt and pepper.

Pour the mixture into the lined tin, smoothing it gently to the edges and making sure it's even. Bake for 12-15 minutes, until risen and just firm in the centre. Remove from the oven. Have ready a piece of non-stick paper spread out on the work surface and sprinkled with ready-grated Parmesan cheese. Turn the roulade straight out, face-down, on to the non-stick paper. Cover with a clean, slightly damp tea towel and leave to cool. (It needs to be cool enough not to wilt the salad filling.)

Spread the cooled roulade with the mayonnaise, then put the lettuce leaves on top. Slice the tomatoes very thinly and put these on top of the lettuce, and finally the spring onions and some salt and pepper. Roll up the roulade, starting from one of the long edges – it's easiest to do this if you first make an incision about 1 cm/½ inch from the edge

(but don't cut right through) then bend this down to start the rolling process. Use the paper to help you to roll it firmly. Transfer the roulade to a long serving dish and serve with the herb sauce, potatoes and green beans suggested below.

FRESH HERB SAUCE

For the herb sauce, stir 300 ml/½ pint plain low-fat yogurt until it's smooth, then mix in 2 tablespoons each of snipped chives and parsley; add salt and freshly ground black pepper to taste.

LITTLE NEW POTATOES BAKED IN A PARCEL

Based on Elizabeth David's recipe in *French Country Cooking*, this is one of the easiest and most delicious ways to prepare new potatoes. Scrub or scrape 24 very small new potatoes, then put them on to a piece of greaseproof paper with 2 mint leaves, 50g/2oz butter and 2 pinches of salt. Fold the paper over, then fold down the edges so that potatoes are securely sealed. Bake at 190°C/375°F/Gas Mark 5 for 35 minutes.

FRENCH BEAN VINAIGRETTE

Top and tail 450-700g/1-1½lb French beans, the thinner the better. Boil them in 2.5 cm/1 inch of water for 3-4 minutes, or steam them for perhaps a minute or two longer, until they have cooked a little but are still quite crisp. Drain them immediately and put them into a bowl with 1 tablespoon wine vinegar, 2 tablespoons olive oil and some salt and pepper. Leave to cool, stirring them from time to time. Serve warm or cold.

JELLIED TERRINE OF RED SUMMER FRUITS

This glistening red terrine can be made a few hours in advance and kept very cold until needed, but only turn it out a moment or two before serving. Thick cream, crème fraîche or creamy Greek yogurt go well with it.

450g / 1lb strawberries	blackcurrant juice drink
25g / 1oz caster sugar	2 sachets Vege Gel
300ml / 10fl oz raspberry juice, or raspberry and	redcurrant leaves and summer fruits, to decorate (optional)

Hull the strawberries, then wash them and pat dry with a clean cloth. Cut them into slices about 3mm / ¼ inch thick and put them into a bowl. Sprinkle with the caster sugar and mix well to make sure all the strawberries are coated. Then put them into a large sieve and leave for 15–30 minutes to drain.

Put the juice or juice drink into a saucepan and bring to the boil. Sprinkle the Vege Gel over the top, whisking to dissolve. Cook for 1 minute add the strawberries, stir, and remove from the heat.

Pour the mixture into a 450g/1lb loaf tin. Press the top strawberry slices down and ease the liquid up over them so that they are lightly covered. Leave to cool, then cover with foil or clingfilm and keep in the fridge until needed. To turn out, slip a knife round the edges to loosen, then invert a plate over the tin, turn it over, give it a little shake and you will hear it come out. Lift off the tin, decorate with a few redcurrant leaves and summer fruits, if using, and serve immediately.

ORANGE ICE CREAM WITH PISTACHIO NUTS

The flavour of orange goes well with red summer fruits, and this ice cream makes a good accompaniment for the Jellied Terrine of Red Summer Fruits. Pistachio nuts add a pleasant touch of colour and texture to the ice cream, although you could leave them out if you prefer.

2 medium oranges	50g / 2oz shelled
125g / 4oz caster sugar	pistachio nuts, quite
4 egg yolks	coarsely chopped
300ml / ½ pint whipping cream	

You can get shelled Pistachio nuts at some supermarkets and these are fine for this recipe.

Scrub one of the oranges in hot water, then dry it and grate off the rind finely. Squeeze the juice from both the oranges: you should have about 150 ml/ 5 fl oz. Put the orange juice into a small saucepan with the sugar and heat gently until the sugar has dissolved; then let it boil for about 4 minutes, until the mixture reaches 110°C/225°F on a sugar thermometer or a little of the syrup forms a thread when pulled between your finger and thumb.

Meanwhile, whisk the egg yolks until they are beginning to thicken: it's easiest to do this with an electric whisk if you have one. Pour the orange syrup on top of the egg yolks, whisking at the same time, and continue to whisk for about 5 minutes, until the mixture is thick and pale. Whip the cream until it holds its shape then fold this into the orange mixture, along with the pistachio nuts.

Transfer the mixture to a suitable container and freeze until firm. This ice cream doesn't need stirring as it freezes, but let it stand at room temperature for 30 minutes before you want to eat it to give it a chance to soften up, and give it a stir before serving. Alternatively, do this beforehand and put scoops of ice cream on to a plate, then refreeze so that you can serve it quickly and easily later.

COUNTDOWN

Up to several hours in advance:
Prepare the Polenta ready for grilling (this can be done a day ahead if convenient). Make the Tomato Sauce, Garlic Cream, Onion Salsa and Fruit and Flower Compôte. Cover them all tightly and keep in the fridge. Wash the salad and put that in a polythene bag in the fridge, too.

1 hour ahead:
Prepare the radicchio, aubergine and Haloumi cheese ready for grilling. Light the barbecue about 40 minutes before you want to start cooking. Dress and toss the salad at the last minute; reheat the Tomato Sauce. Grill the aubergine, Haloumi cheese, polenta, fennel and radicchio on the barbecue.

GRILLED AUBERGINE WITH HALOUMI CHEESE, AND TOMATO SAUCE

You can get Haloumi cheese at large supermarkets. You need to read the packets, because some batches are made with animal rennet and some are not. Haloumi cheese keeps for months in the fridge and it also freezes. Its unusual, firm texture makes it excellent for frying, grilling and barbecuing.

2 large aubergines
450g / 1lb Haloumi cheese
olive oil
cherry tomatoes to garnish

FOR THE SAUCE
2 tbls olive oil

2 onions, peeled and sliced
2-4 garlic cloves, crushed
4 thin slices of lemon
2 × 400g / 14oz can tomatoes
chilli powder
salt and freshly ground black pepper

First make the sauce, which can be done well in advance. Heat the oil in a large saucepan and put in the onions; cover and cook gently for 5 minutes, add the garlic and lemon slices, cover and cook for a further 5 minutes. Put in the tomatoes, together with their liquid, and a good pinch of chilli powder, and cook uncovered for about 10 minutes, until much of the liquid has disappeared. Liquidize the mixture, including the lemon. Taste and add salt and pepper, and more chilli powder, as necessary.

Cut the aubergines into slices just less than 1 cm/½ inch thick, aiming for 16 decent ones. If you like, sprinkle them with salt in a colander and leave for 30 minutes, then rinse under the tap to remove any bitterness, though I have never come across a bitter aubergine. Cut the Haloumi cheese into similar slices.

Oil a baking sheet and heat under a grill, then put slices of aubergine on to this or straight on to a hot oiled barbecue grid and turn them over, so that both surfaces get oiled. Then grill, first on one side

OPPOSITE: *A Family Barbecue for Eight to Ten*

and then on the other, until the aubergine is lightly browned. Put the slices on to a warm plate and quickly grill the cheese in the same way (or do the aubergine slices and the cheese slices at the same time if your baking sheet or grid is large). When both sides of the cheese are flecked with brown and the cheese is crisping at the edges, lift the slices off the baking sheet or barbecue grid with a palette knife and put one on each slice of aubergine. Garnish with the cherry tomatoes and serve with the sauce.

CHICK-PEA POLENTA WITH TOMATO AND ONION SALSA

Chick-pea flour can be cooked and made into slices in exactly the same way as polenta flour, but I prefer the chick-pea version. These slices can be fried, deep-fried or grilled, and (possibly without the cumin seeds) are enormously popular with kids and teenagers. They make ideal vegetarian barbecue food and I think they're enhanced by a bit of charring and wood-smoke flavours. The kids tend to smother them with tomato ketchup, but I think a simple salsa, made from tomatoes and fresh coriander, goes best with them. You can get chick-pea flour at health shops, Middle Eastern and Indian shops. It may be called Besan or Gram flour.

175g / 6oz chick-pea flour	*olive oil*
2 tsp salt	*1 tbls cumin seeds*
	slices of lemon

Sieve the chick-pea flour and salt into a medium saucepan and mix to a smooth paste with 600 ml/ 1 pint of cold water. Put the pan on the heat and stir gently until the mixture comes to the boil and is thick and smooth. Let it cook gently, heaving and bubbling a bit, for about 10 minutes, until it's very thick, and any raw flavour has gone. Turn the mixture out on to a piece of non-stick paper, spreading

it to a depth of about 7 mm/⅓ inch or a bit less. Leave it to get cold – or for several hours if you wish – then cut it into rectangles or other shapes. (The shapes can be open-frozen at this point and can later be grilled from frozen.)

Put the shapes on a grill pan or on a barbecue grid that has been greased with olive oil, then turn them, so that they are oiled all over. Sprinkle the cumin seeds on top, then grill the polenta for a few minutes on each side, until they are bubbling, flecked with brown and crisp at the edges. They may seem a bit soft when you turn them, but they'll crisp up as the second side cooks and should prove quite manageable as long as you have a good fish slice to turn them with. Serve with slices of lemon and tomato and onion salsa.

TOMATO AND ONION SALSA

Fry 1 mild onion, peeled and sliced, gently in a little oil for 7 minutes, until almost tender. Halve, seed and finely chop a green chilli, being careful not to get the juice anywhere near your eyes and to wash your hands afterwards. Add the chilli to the onion and fry for a further 2–3 minutes, then remove from the heat and put the mixture into a bowl.

Skin 900g/2lb tomatoes by covering them with boiling water, leaving for 60 seconds, then draining and slipping off the skins with a sharp knife. Chop the tomatoes coarsely, discarding any tough bits of stem, and add the tomatoes to the bowl. Pare off one or two strips of skin from a lime and snip them into shreds; squeeze the juice from the lime. Add to the tomatoes, with about 4-6 tablespoons chopped coriander leaves and some salt and pepper.

Pimms, for a summery touch, goes well with this menu, or lager, beer or cider for those who prefer these. My personal choice would be a chilled light fruity red such as a Beaujolais.

GRILLED FENNEL AND RADICCHIO WITH GARLIC CREAM

4 fennel bulbs
2 radicchio
olive oil
salt and freshly ground
  black pepper
lemon slices or fresh
  herb sprigs to garnish

FOR THE GARLIC CREAM
2 × 150g / 5oz Boursin
  garlic and herb
  cream cheese

The garlic cream can be made in advance and kept in a covered dish in the fridge. To make it, simply mash the garlic cream cheese to break it up and beat in 125 ml/4 fl oz hot water to make a smooth, creamy mixture.

To prepare the vegetables, trim the fennel and radicchio, removing any tough leaves and pieces of stem but leaving enough of the stem to hold the leaves together at the base. Cut each down first into halves, then into quarters and eighths, so that they are still joined together at the base if possible. Steam or parboil the fennel for about 8 minutes, or until it is just tender without being at all soggy. Drain well and dry with kitchen paper.

Brush both the fennel and the radicchio with oil and sprinkle with some salt and pepper, then grill them over hot coals until they are lightly charred on both sides: this will take about 5-8 minutes on a barbecue and slightly longer, about 15 minutes, on a conventional grill. They can be served warm, like a salad, so can be done ahead of the other barbecue items if more convenient. Garnish them with lemon slices and serve them with the garlic cream sauce.

SUMMER LEAF SALAD

This salad is never the same twice, because you can put in whatever leaves and herbs happen to be available. Sometimes I've made it with just garden lettuce and as many different herbs as I could add, but it's more interesting when you can use a good variety of leaves. When they're available, I like to put in tender dandelion and nasturtium leaves, baby spinach leaves, rocket, lamb's lettuce and any red, frilly or fancy-leaf lettuce, as well as the basic type.

1 ordinary lettuce or 2
  little gem
1 frisée or oak-leaf
  lettuce
rocket, nasturtium,
  dandelion, spinach
  and lamb's lettuce
  leaves, as available

FOR THE DRESSING
2 tbls red wine vinegar
6 tbls olive oil
salt and freshly ground
  black pepper
4 tbls chopped fresh
  herbs such as chives,
  mint, parsley, basil,
  dill, as available

Wash the lettuces and other leaves and shake or spin them dry. Make the dressing straight into the bowl from which you want to serve the salad. Put the vinegar and oil into the bowl with a good seasoning of salt and freshly ground black pepper and mix them until they emulsify; then stir in the chopped herbs.

Put the salad leaves in on top of the dressing, tearing them into manageable sizes as you do so. Toss the salad at the last minute, just before you want to serve it, so that the leaves are all crisp and lightly coated with the herb vinaigrette.

FRUIT AND FLOWER COMPOTE IN ROSE HIP TEA

The tea gives this compôte an intriguing flavour. Look for tea bags which contain both rosehip and hibiscus; the ones I particularly like are flavoured with raspberry, too; they're called Raspberry Rendezvous, made by the London Herb and Spice Company.

2 x 285g / 10oz jars no-added-sugar, high-fruit-content raspberry spread
6 rosehip, hibiscus and raspberry tea bags

8 ripe nectarines
rose petals and a few small summer flowers such as borage, lavender, pinks

Put the all-fruit spread into a saucepan with 225 ml/8 fl oz water and the tea bags, and heat gently until the spread has melted. Remove from the heat and tip the mixture into a large bowl.

Wash the nectarines, then cut them into thin slices, discarding the stone. Add the slices to the bowl and mix well. Cover and leave for at least an hour for all the flavours to develop.

Just before serving the fruit salad, remove the tea bags, squeezing all the liquid out of them and adding this to the fruit salad. Serve the compôte in a shallow glass bowl with the petals and flowers scattered on top.

BLACKBERRY FOOL

The sweeter the blackberries are the better, because you'll need to add less sugar.

450g / 1lb blackberries
1–2 tbls no-added-sugar, high-fruit-content black cherry spread
150ml / 5fl oz plain yogurt

150ml / 5fl oz whipping cream
sugar to taste

Wash the blackberries, then put them into a saucepan with the fruit spread and cook over a gentle heat for a few minutes until the juices run and the blackberries are very tender. Pureé the blackberries in a food processor, then push this pureé through a nylon sieve to remove the seeds.

When the mixture is cool, reserve about two tablespoons of the blackberry mixture and stir the yogurt into the rest, then whisk the cream and fold that into the mixture. Taste and add a little sugar if necessary. Divide the fool between four bowls and spoon the reserved blackberry mixture on top.
SERVES 4

OPPOSITE: *Fruit and Flower Compôte in Rose Hip Tea*

AUTUMN

The heat of summer gives way to the mellowness of autumn. The days become shorter and the path of the sun gets lower in the sky, crossing the equator at the time of the autumn equinox. The harvest, the precious fruits and vegetables, grains and seeds which will sustain us throughout the darkest months of the year, is gathered in. The life-processes begin to wane, the sap flows less strongly, the leaves become vibrant shades of yellow, gold and red, then drop to the ground as the earth moves to a state of peace and rest. In the country there's the smell of wood smoke in the air, the mornings are misty and cobwebs sparkle in the dew.

During autumn, for me there are three festivals which stand out. First of all, the gathering in of the harvest with thanksgiving and celebration; then, later on, Hallowe'en, All Souls and Remembrance Day which to me are linked in that they remind us that there are other dimensions to life apart from the physical. This is a time of year I particularly like, because the world of spirit seems much closer than usual. There is a good astrological reason for this since they all happen during the time when the sun is in Scorpio, the sign which is associated with death, the after-life and the world of spirit. Scorpio is the opposite sign to Taurus, and both signs belong to the fixed element, which accounts for the feeling of underlying peace and stability during this season when in one instance there is the resurgence of life and on the other, the waning: opposite sides of the perpetual cycle of life.

Autumn, like spring, is a time of change, a transition from the heat and sunshine of summer to the cold of winter. Some autumn days can be surprisingly hot, and an Indian summer has its special joy and poignancy; but the breeze has an increasingly cool edge to it. Late summer/early autumn vegetables such as peppers, aubergines, artichokes and fennel bridge the gap between summer and winter admirably, being substantial yet not stodgy; pumpkin, leeks, mushrooms and celeriac also have this quality. All these vegetables are welcome as far as I am concerned, although I have a special affection for pumpkin, with its glorious colour, light texture, delicate flavour and its association with Hallowe'en. As the season advances and we experience the first frosts, heavier, more sustaining foods become available: the first of the autumn root vegetables, the new-season pulses; nuts, with their concentrated nutrients, their warming and protective oils.

As the nights draw in, it seems a natural time to have informal get-togethers, parties and harvest suppers, and welcoming bakes and gratins made from autumn vegetables are an easy and popular way to cater for them; dishes like Aubergine, Tomato and Mozzarella Bake (page 238), Pumpkin and Goat's Cheese Gratin (page 220) and Spaghetti Marrow with Gorgonzola, Cream and Walnuts (page 225). And autumn fruits, especially apples, pears, plums and damsons, plus glowing golden quinces, with their delicate fragrance and flavour, make wonderful seasonal puddings.

Autumn is also the time to hunt for edible treasures in the fields and woods: blackberries, chestnuts, hazel or cob nuts and walnuts on the trees; bilberries and funghi on or near the ground. A mushroom hunt with a couple of reliable guidebooks can be well rewarded, although you need a certain amount of courage to try the results unless you have an expert with you, or can have them expertly identified. Anyway, whether you manage to find any wild mushrooms or just buy them from a shop, having a feast of funghi is one of the delights of the season.

SEASONAL STARTERS

——————— ❧ ———————

PEARS IN TARRAGON VINAIGRETTE

The success of this simple, refreshing starter depends on using perfect pears, ripe enough to slice with a spoon. I find it best to buy them several days before I need them and let them ripen to the right point. Comice pears give the best result.

3 ripe comice pears
2 tbls tarragon vinegar
2 tbls light olive oil
salt and freshly ground
  black pepper

several sprigs of fresh
  tarragon
lollo rosso or red frisée
  lettuce

Quarter and peel the pears, removing the core, cut them into pieces and put them into a shallow dish.

Put the vinegar, oil and some salt into a jar and shake together until blended, then pour over the pears. Chop the tarragon – there should be 2-3 tablespoonfuls – and add to the pears. Coarsely grind plenty of pepper on top, and stir the mixture gently; if possible leave it for at least 30 minutes for the flavours to develop and blend.

To serve, arrange a few torn leaves of lollo rosso or red frisée lettuce on four plates and spoon the pieces of pear and their juice on top.
SERVES 4

Buy walnuts from a shop which has a quick turnover so that they will be really fresh with no hint of bitterness.

HOT CELERIAC PUREE ON A BED OF WATERCRESS

This was one of those mixtures which happened almost by accident, because of the ingredients I happened to have in, and which turned out to be really good. The combination of hot creamy celeriac purée, cool, crisp, peppery watercress and walnuts is extremely good.

700g / 1½lb celeriac
15g / ½oz butter
2-3 tbls cream
salt and freshly ground
  black pepper

50g / 2oz fresh shelled
  walnuts
packet or bunch of
  watercress
3 tbls walnut oil
1 tbls red wine vinegar

Peel the celeriac, then cut it into even-sized chunks. Put them into a saucepan, cover with water, and boil for about 15 minutes, or until the chunks are tender when pierced with a knife. Drain – the water makes a superb stock, I always save it – then mash the celeriac with the butter, cream and salt and pepper to taste.

While the celeriac is cooking, chop the walnuts roughly, then wash the watercress and remove any tough stems. Mix the oil, vinegar and some salt and pepper in a bowl, add the watercress and mix.

To serve, divide the watercress between four plates, put a mound of the celeriac on top and sprinkle with the walnuts.
SERVES 4

—————————————————

OPPOSITE: *(left) Pears in Tarragon Vinaigrette and (right) Hot Celeriac Purée*

FRIED PUMPKIN SLICES WITH DEEP-FRIED SAGE

Thinly sliced pumpkin, fried in olive oil until it is crisp on the outside, tender within, makes a quick, good starter. The crisp, deep-fried sage makes an attractive garnish, and is quick to do.

a little oil for deep-frying	*4 garlic cloves, peeled*
12 sprigs of fresh sage	*olive oil*
600g / 1¼ lb pumpkin, weighed with skin and seeds	*Maldon salt*
	freshly grated Parmesan cheese (optional)

First prepare the deep-fried sage for the garnish. Heat 2.5 cm/1 inch of oil in a small saucepan. When it is sizzling hot, put in some of the sage sprigs and deep-fry for a minute or two until they are crunchy, then drain them on kitchen paper and repeat the process with the rest. Keep on one side until required.

Peel the skin from the piece of pumpkin and remove the seeds and threads. Cut the flesh into long slim pieces something like 10 cm/4 inches by 2.5-4 cm/1-1½ inches, and not more than 5 mm/¼ inch thick. Crush the garlic to a paste in some salt. With a knife, smear this garlic paste very thinly on each side of the pumpkin slices to flavour them lightly.

Heat a little olive oil in a frying pan, and fry the pumpkin slices for about 3 minutes on each side, or until they are lightly browned and crisp and feel tender when pierced with the point of a knife. Take them out and drain them on kitchen paper. Serve them as soon as possible on warmed plates, sprinkled with a little crunchy Maldon salt and garnished with the deep-fried sage. Hand round the Parmesan cheese separately if you're serving this.
SERVES 4

Maldon salt is my favourite with its crunchy flakes that you don't need to grind. It can be bought from health shops and large high-class supermarkets.

FENNEL A LA GRECQUE

Pleasant either warm or chilled, this is good served with some bread to mop up the juices.

4 fennel bulbs	*1 × 400g / 14oz can*
2 tbls olive oil	*tomatoes*
1 tbls coriander seeds	*salt and freshly ground*
4 strips of lemon peel	*black pepper*
juice of 1 lemon	

Trim the fennel, saving any leafy bits. Pare off any chunky root part, and if the outer leaves look tough, either remove them or pare them a bit with a sharp knife, depending on how edible they look. Then cut the fennel down into eighths.

Heat the oil in a heavy-based saucepan and put in the fennel; turn it so that it all gets coated with the oil, then cover the pan and leave it to cook gently while you crush the coriander seeds roughly. A pestle and mortar is best for doing this; otherwise improvise by putting them into a small bowl and crushing them with the end of something like a rolling pin. Add the seeds to the fennel, along with the lemon peel and juice, and stir again.

Chop the tomatoes roughly then add them, and their juice, to the pan. Mix gently, cover and leave to cook gently for 15-20 minutes, or until the fennel is very tender and the tomato is reduced to a glistening crimson sauce. Remove from the heat, season with salt and pepper and leave to cool.

Add the reserved fennel leaves, chopped, just before serving.
SERVES 4

GOLDEN PEPPERS STUFFED WITH CHERRY TOMATOES

This is a pretty starter – red cherry tomatoes and green basil in golden pepper halves – and it's also easy to do. If you can't get cherry tomatoes, it can also be made successfully with ordinary tomatoes, chopped. It is equally good served as it is, or it can be lightly cooked.

2 golden peppers	*salt and freshly ground*
225g / 8oz cherry	*black pepper*
tomatoes	*olive oil (optional)*
1-2 tbls chopped fresh	
basil	

If you're planning to cook this starter, set the oven to 200°C/400°F/Gas Mark 6.

Halve the peppers, cutting through the stems and leaving these attached, then put the peppers shiny-side up on a grill pan and grill at full heat until the skin has blistered and begun to char. Move them halfway through the grilling so that all the skin gets done. Cover them with a plate to keep in the steam, and leave until they're cool enough to handle. Slip off the skins with a sharp knife – they'll come off easily – and rinse the peppers under the tap to remove the seeds. Finally, put them, the other way up this time, in a shallow casserole dish.

Skin the tomatoes by covering them with boiling water, leaving them for a few seconds until their skins loosen, then draining them and slipping off the skins. Halve or quarter the tomatoes, depending on their size, and mix them with the basil and some salt and pepper. Spoon this mixture into the pepper halves, dividing it between them. Trickle a little olive oil over each if you wish.

Serve the peppers as they are, or pop them into the oven and bake them for 15-20 minutes.

SERVES 4

SWEET POTATOES WITH HERB STUFFING

3 medium sweet	*1½ tsp chopped fresh*
potatoes, about	*thyme*
300g / 10oz each	*salt and freshly ground*
25g / 1oz butter	*black pepper*
2 tbls snipped chives	

Set the oven to 200°C/400°F/Gas Mark 6. Wash and prick the sweet potatoes. Place them on a baking sheet and bake for about 1 hour, or until they feel soft when squeezed. Holding them in a cloth, cut them in half horizontally, then scoop out the flesh into a basin with a teaspoon, being careful not to break the skins. Choose four of the best skins and place them in a baking dish, discarding the rest.

Add the butter to the scooped-out sweet potato flesh and mash well, then add the chives, thyme and salt and pepper. Spoon the mixture into the skins, piling them up well, then put them back into the oven for about 15 minutes to heat through.

They can be prepared in advance and heated through just before serving; if heating them through from cold, allow a bit longer: 20-25 minutes.

SERVES 4

WARMING MEALS

PUMPKIN AND GOAT'S CHEESE GRATIN

I love the contrast of the sharp flavour of the goat's cheese and the sweet creaminess of the pumpkin in this easy autumn gratin. I like to serve it with the Bitterleaf Salad with Walnut Dressing given opposite.

*900g / 2lb pumpkin,
    weighed with the skin
    and seeds*
25g / 1oz butter
*salt and freshly ground
    black pepper*

*225g / 8oz firm goat's
    cheese log or logs, cut
    into thin slices*
*50g / 2oz fresh
    Parmesan cheese,
    finely grated*

Set the oven to 200°C/400°F/Gas Mark 6.

Cut the skin from the pumpkin and remove the seeds and threads, then cut the flesh into even-sized pieces. Cook the pumpkin in boiling water to cover, or steam it until it is tender, then drain and mash it with the butter. (Keep the cooking water, which makes an excellent stock.) Season the pumpkin purée with salt and pepper and put half of it into a shallow gratin dish.

Cut the goat's cheese into thin slices and put these on top of the pumpkin in the dish, then spoon the rest of the pumpkin on top. Sprinkle with the Parmesan cheese and bake for about 30 minutes, or until the gratin is hot and bubbling and the cheese on top is golden brown.

SERVES 4

BITTERLEAF SALAD WITH WALNUT DRESSING

Put 2 tablespoons light olive oil, 1 tablespoon walnut oil, 1 tablespoon red wine vinegar and salt and pepper into a salad bowl and stir. Wash 2 heads of chicory, a radicchio and a small red oak-leaf lettuce, separating the leaves. Shake them dry, then tear them into the bowl. Add snipped chives.

Just before you want to serve the salad, toss the leaves so that they all get coated in the dressing, and add about 25-50g/1-2oz chopped walnuts.

GRILLED RED PEPPER AND AUBERGINE

Allow ½-1 red pepper and ½ medium-large (350g/12oz) aubergine for each person. Quarter the peppers, place them shiny-side up on a grill pan and grill at full heat until the skin has blistered and begun to char all over. Cover them with a plate and leave until they're cool enough to handle. Slip off the skins with a sharp knife and rinse the peppers to remove the seeds. Finally, slice the flesh.

Cut the aubergine into 5 cm/2 inch slices. Brush a little olive oil on a grill pan, put the aubergine slices on this (no need to salt them first) and brush the top surface with olive oil. Grill them until the tops are browned. You'll probably find that the bottoms are browned, too; if not, turn the slices over and do the other sides. The aubergines are done when they're browned on both sides and feel tender when pierced with a knife. Blot off any excess oil and serve them with the red pepper.

OPPOSITE: *Pumpkin and Goat's Cheese Gratin*

LENTILS AND CORIANDER WITH YOGURT SAUCE

If you can't get fresh coriander, use parsley-preferably flat-leaf if you can get it.

I use canned green lentils for this because they're so quick, although you could use dried ones if you preferred. If you do use dried lentils, you will need 100g / 3½oz; just boil them in plenty of water for 45–60 minutes or until they are tender – there's no need to soak them first, although if you do it will make the cooking time a bit shorter. And if you cook extra, for another time, they'll freeze perfectly in a suitable container. Serve with the Grilled Red Pepper and Aubergine dish on page 220 and a tossed green salad.

2 tsp olive oil
1 onion, peeled and
  sliced
2 tsp ground coriander
1 × 425g / 15oz can
  green lentils, drained
2 tbls chopped fresh
  coriander leaves

FOR THE SAUCE
1 small garlic clove,
  crushed
150ml / 5fl oz plain
  low-fat yogurt
salt and freshly ground
  black pepper

Heat the oil in a medium saucepan then put in the onion, cover and cook for 10 minutes, or until it is tender. Stir in the ground coriander and cook for a further 2 minutes. Add the drained lentils, stir gently, and cook for a few minutes until they're heated through. Then add the fresh coriander.

Meanwhile, make a quick sauce by stirring the garlic into the yogurt and seasoning with salt and pepper. Serve the lentils and sauce garnished with the grilled pepper and aubergine slices.

SERVES 2

SPICY CHICK PEAS WITH YOGURT AND PAPRIKA SAUCE

This is very quick, cheap, healthy and easy. I like it just as it is, but for a more substantial meal you can add some good bread – ciabatta or a Middle Eastern bread would be pleasant – or some cooked brown rice with some chopped herbs mixed into it.

2 × 425g / 15oz cans
  chick peas
6-8 plum tomatoes
8 sprigs of flat-leaf
  parsley
1 tbls olive oil
1 tsp cumin seeds
salt and freshly ground
  black pepper

FOR THE SAUCE
150ml / 5fl oz plain
  low-fat yogurt
small garlic clove,
  crushed (optional)
½ tsp paprika pepper

First make the sauce: mix together the yogurt and garlic, if you're using this, season to taste and leave on one side.

Drain the chick peas; wash and slice the tomatoes, wash the flat-leaf parsley and remove the leaves from the stems. Heat the oil in a large saucepan and add the cumin. Fry it for about 1 minute, until the seeds start to pop, then put in the tomatoes and chick peas. Stir over the heat for 2-3 minutes, until everything is heated through, then add the parsley and season to taste.

Serve the mixture on warm plates, pour on some of the sauce, and sprinkle the sauce with paprika. Or you can serve the sauce separately in a bowl, with the paprika sprinkled on top.

SERVES 4

OPPOSITE: *Spicy Chick Peas with Yogurt and Paprika Sauce*

SPAGHETTI WITH SPICY TOMATO AND RED PEPPER SAUCE

This quantity of sauce is right for two people or three at a pinch. If you're using wholewheat pasta, 75g/ 3oz per person will probably be enough, as it's more filling; otherwise, allow 125g/4oz per person.

175-225g / 6-8 oz
  spaghetti
olive oil
salt and freshly ground
  black pepper
FOR THE SAUCE
1 tbls olive oil

1 onion, peeled and
  chopped
1 red pepper
1 garlic clove, crushed
1 × 400g / 14oz can
  tomatoes in juice
1 dried red chilli,
  crumbled

First get the sauce started. Heat the oil in a medium saucepan and put in the onion; cover and cook gently for a few minutes while you wash, de-seed and chop the red pepper. Add this to the pan, along with the garlic, and cook for a further 5 minutes with a lid on the pan. Put in the tomatoes, together with their juice, and the red chilli. Mash the tomatoes a bit with a wooden spoon to make sure everything is well mixed, then cover and cook for about 15-20 minutes, or until all the vegetables are tender and the sauce is thick. Give the sauce a stir from time to time to make sure it isn't sticking.

Meanwhile, fill a large saucepan two-thirds full with water and heat it for the pasta. When the water is boiling, a few minutes before the sauce is ready, put the pasta into the water; give it a quick stir, let it come back to the boil and leave it to bubble away, uncovered, for about 8 minutes, or whatever it says on the packet.

Drain the pasta, then tip it back into the warm pan and add a little olive oil and some salt and pepper. Serve immediately, with the sauce.
SERVES 2

OPPOSITE: *(left) Chicory, Frisée and Watercress Salad and (right) Spaghetti Marrow with Gorgonzola, Cream and Walnuts*

SPAGHETTI MARROW WITH GORGONZOLA, CREAM, AND WALNUTS

Almost any salad goes well with this – the Chicory, Frisée and Watercress Salad given below is a particular favourite.

2 × 900g / 2lb spaghetti
  squash
25g / 1oz butter
150ml / 5fl oz double
  cream
125g / 4oz Gorgonzola
  cheese, grated

salt and freshly ground
  black pepper
50g / 2oz walnuts,
  roughly chopped
freshly grated
  Parmesan cheese

Bring to the boil two large saucepans of water: each pan should be big enough to hold one of the squash whole. Prick the squash in a few places, then put one in each saucepan, cover and boil for 30 minutes, or until the squash is tender when pierced with a skewer. Drain the squash and, holding them with a cloth, halve them and scoop out the 'spaghetti' into a hot saucepan. Add the butter, cream, Gorgonzola and some salt and pepper to taste. Stir quickly over a gentle heat, just to distribute all the ingredients.

Scatter over the walnuts, sprinkle with Parmesan and serve at once, on warmed plates.
SERVES 4-6

CHICORY, FRISEE AND WATERCRESS SALAD

Put 1 tablespoon red wine vinegar into a bowl with 3 tablespoons olive oil and some salt and a good grinding of pepper. Wash and dry 2 heads of chicory, ½ frisée lettuce and a packet or bunch of watercress. Tear the chicory and frisée into manageable pieces and put them into the bowl along with the watercress, on top of the dressing. Toss the salad just before you want to serve it.

I love those marrows which, when cooked, contain many strands, like spaghetti. You can cook them in many of the ways you'd cook spaghetti; but they're lighter, and, if you're food combining and not mixing starchy foods like pasta with proteins such as cheese, they're particularly useful as a pasta – replacement.

CABBAGE PARCELS WITH TOMATO SAUCE

As a variation, you could use large spinach or Swiss chard leaves instead of cabbage.

For this recipe you need cabbage leaves which are big enough to make into parcels, but tender. Young spring cabbage is ideal, although you'll be left with the heart of the cabbage; shredded and mixed with mayonnaise, yogurt and lemon juice, it makes a good salad. The cabbage parcels can be served on their own and this quantity, I found, was greedily consumed by two people; under more restrained circumstances, they can be served with another vegetable like French beans, and maybe some baby new potatoes, and made to serve four.

1 spring cabbage
2 tbls olive oil
2 onions, peeled and
 chopped
1 garlic clove, crushed
1 × 400g / 14oz can
 tomatoes in juice
salt and freshly ground
 black pepper

225g / 8oz button
 mushrooms
175g / 6oz Cheddar
 cheese, grated
50g / 2oz Parmesan
 cheese, preferably
 freshly grated

Set the oven to 200°C/400°F/Gas Mark 6.

First, half-fill a large saucepan with water and bring to the boil; while it's heating up, remove and discard any very tough leaves from the cabbage, then carefully ease off any that seem reasonably large and tender, aiming for eight. When the water boils, put in the cabbage leaves, pushing them down below water level. Cover and cook for 5 minutes or so, until they are tender but not completely soggy. Drain them into a colander and refresh them under a cold tap. Finally, spread them out on kitchen paper and blot them dry.

While the cabbage is cooking, heat the oil in another pan and add the onions; cover and cook gently for 5 minutes, then add the garlic and cook for a further 5 minutes. After this, put half the onion mixture into another pan and add the tomatoes and their juice, mashing them with a wooden spoon. Let them cook away for about 15 minutes until they form a thick sauce, then whizz them in a food processor and season with salt and pepper. Wash

and slice the mushrooms and add these to the pan containing the rest of the onion; fry for 3-4 minutes, until the mushrooms are tender, then remove from the heat and add the grated Cheddar cheese. Mix well, and put a bit of this mixture in the centre of each cabbage leaf; fold over the sides, and roll each leaf up into a neat parcel. Put the parcels into a shallow ovenproof dish, pour the tomato sauce over and sprinkle the grated Parmesan over the top in a fairly thick layer. Bake for 25-30 minutes, until it's hot and bubbling, and the top is golden brown and crisp.

SERVES 2-4

MEXICAN CHILLIES RELLENOS

This recipe can be prepared ready for baking ahead of time, and the best accompaniment, I think, is a simple, plain salad.

8 small green peppers,
 each about 75g / 3oz
175g / 6oz vegetarian
 Cheddar cheese,
 grated

FOR THE SAUCE
2 tbls olive oil

2 onions, peeled and
 sliced
2-4 garlic cloves,
 crushed
2 × 400g / 14oz cans
 tomatoes
chilli powder
salt and freshly ground
 black pepper

Set the oven to 200°C/400°F/Gas Mark 6.

Grill whole peppers at full heat until the skin has blistered and charred all over, turning the peppers around as necessary. Remove from the heat and leave them until they're cool enough to handle.

While the peppers are grilling, make the sauce. Heat the oil in a large saucepan and put in the onions; cover and cook gently for 5 minutes, add the garlic, cover again, and cook for a further 5 minutes. Put in the tomatoes, together with their liquid, and a good pinch of chilli powder, and cook, uncovered, for about 10 minutes, until much of the liquid has disappeared. Liquidize the mixture, then taste and add salt, pepper, and more chilli powder, as necessary.

With your fingers and a sharp knife, slip the skins off the peppers. Make a slit down one side of each pepper and, with kitchen scissors, snip out the main section of seeds – don't worry if some are left, they won't hurt. Next, stuff each pepper with some of the grated cheese. Pour some of the tomato sauce into a shallow casserole dish, put the peppers on top, then pour the rest of the sauce over them. Bake them, uncovered, for about 20 minutes.

SERVES 4

ARTICHOKE BASES STUFFED WITH MUSHROOM MOUSSE

For this recipe you need some big artichokes, which are usually available in the early autumn. Stuffed with a light mousse of mushrooms they're good either as a starter or, and I prefer them this way, as a main course. Some spinach, quickly steamed until it has wilted rather than cooked, goes well with them.

8 globe artichokes	salt and freshly ground
lemon juice	black pepper
900g / 2lb mushrooms	50g / 2oz pine nuts
50g / 2oz butter	
2-3 garlic cloves,	**FOR THE CHIVE AND**
crushed	**LEMON BUTTER**
2 tbls double cream	75g / 3oz butter
2 tbls chopped fresh	2 tbls lemon juice
parsley, preferably	1 tbls snipped chives
flat-leaf	

First prepare the artichokes by cutting off most of the leaves to reveal the choke, scraping this out, and trimming and tidying the remaining leaf-bases to form a neat shallow cup. Brush the cut surfaces with some lemon juice to preserve their colour, then cook them in a large panful of boiling water for 20-30 minutes, or until the bases are tender when pierced with a sharp knife. Put them upside down in a colander to drain. Meanwhile, wash the mushrooms, then chop them roughly. Melt the butter in a large saucepan, put in the garlic and mushrooms and cook, without a lid, for about 30 minutes, or until the mushrooms are tender and all their liquid has gone.

Set the oven to 200°C/400°F/Gas Mark 6. When the mushrooms are done, put them into a food processor and whizz to a purée. Add the cream, a squeeze of lemon juice, the parsley and some salt and freshly ground black pepper to taste.

Pat the artichoke bases dry with kitchen paper as necessary and put them, cup-side up, in a lightly greased shallow casserole. Spoon the mushroom mixture into them and top each with a teaspoon of pine nuts. Bake them, uncovered, for about 15 minutes, or until they are heated through and the nuts are golden.

While they're cooking, make the chive and lemon butter: melt the butter in a small saucepan, add the lemon juice, chives and a little salt and pepper as necessary. Serve the artichokes on warmed plates, with a pool of the sauce.

SERVES 4

For wilted spinach you need 450-700g/ 1-1½ lb tender spinach leaves, without much in the way of stem, for four people. Put into 6mm/¼ inch of boiling water in a large saucepan, stirring for a few seconds until the leaves have wilted. (You may need to do several batches). Transfer them to a warm dish, add salt, pepper, olive oil or butter.

MUSHROOMS

—— 🐚 ——

MUSHROOM 'CAVIAR'

To make melba toast triangles, toast pieces of bread from a sliced wholewheat loaf as usual then, with a sharp knife, slit each across. Cut these into triangles, and put them, untoasted side up, under a hot grill for a minute or two until golden brown and the edges are curling up.

As well as being good as a starter with some crisp Melba or plain toast, mushroom 'caviar' makes a good topping for canapés. Including some dried mushrooms in the mixture gives it extra flavour.

15g / ½oz dried morels or porcini mushrooms
450g / 1lb mushrooms
1 garlic clove, peeled
2-4 tbls chopped fresh parsley
25g / 1oz butter
squeeze of fresh lemon juice

salt and freshly ground black pepper

TO SERVE
a little soured cream
paprika pepper
sprigs of flat-leaf parsley
crisp toast triangles

First prepare the dried mushrooms by putting them into a bowl and adding boiling water just to cover them. Leave them to soak for about an hour. Drain the mushrooms, straining the liquid through a fine sieve or a piece of muslin to remove any grit. Reserve the liquid. If you have a food processor, put the dried mushrooms in that, along with the ordinary mushrooms, washed, the garlic and the parsley, and whizz until everything is finely chopped. Without a food processor, chop all these ingredients by hand; get them as fine as you can.

Heat the butter in a large saucepan and put in the chopped ingredients, stir, then cook uncovered for 15-20 minutes, or until any liquid which the mushrooms produce has boiled away. Pour in the reserved mushroom soaking liquid and a squeeze of lemon juice and cook for a few more minutes until the mixture is dry again. Remove from the heat and season.

Serve hot, warm or cold, on individual plates, with a heaped teaspoonful of soured cream, a sprinkling of paprika and a sprig of flat-leaf parsley on each. Accompany with crisp triangles of toast.
SERVES 4

WILD MUSHROOM DIP

If you've just got a few precious wild mushrooms, this dip makes the most of them, and the addition of some porcini intensifies the flavour.

10g / ¼oz dried mushrooms, porcini or morels
125g / 4oz wild mushrooms

25g / 1oz butter
225g / 8oz curd cheese
salt and freshly ground black pepper

Put the dried mushrooms into a bowl and add boiling water just to cover them. Leave them to soak for an hour. Drain the mushrooms, straining the liquid through a fine sieve or a piece of muslin, to remove any grit. Reserve the soaking liquid.

Wash the wild mushrooms, chop them with the dried porcini and cook them in the butter for 5 minutes, before adding the reserved soaking liquid. Let the mixture bubble away for 10 minutes or so until practically all the liquid has gone and the mushrooms are tender. Remove them from the heat.

When the mushrooms are cool, beat them into the curd cheese to make a creamy mixture, and season with salt and freshly ground black pepper. Serve with crudités or pitta fingers.
SERVES 4

OPPOSITE: *(top) Mushroom 'Caviar' and (bottom) Oyster Mushroom and Porcini Timbale (page 230)*

OYSTER MUSHROOM AND PORCINI TIMBALE

Because oyster mushrooms are flat, I thought they would look interesting if I layered them into a loaf tin, then set them in place with a light custard. This timbale is the result and I think it makes a really attractive and unusual main dish, good served with a red wine sauce and some seasonal vegetables like the Braised Celery on page 231.

10g / ¼oz dried mushrooms, porcini or morels	*1 garlic clove, crushed*
	salt and freshly ground black pepper
600g / 1¼lb oyster mushrooms	*2 eggs*
50g / 2oz butter	*150ml / 5fl oz single cream*

You can buy porcini in small packets. They're not cheap but they go a long way and the flavour is excellent.

Set the oven to 160°C/325°F/Gas Mark 3. Line a 450g/1lb loaf tin with a piece of non-stick paper to cover the base and extend up the short sides; grease the other sides. Put the dried mushrooms into a bowl and add boiling water just to cover them. Leave them to soak for an hour. While they are soaking, wash the oyster mushrooms, gently squeeze out excess water and pat them dry.

Melt the butter in a large saucepan and add the oyster mushrooms. Let them cook for about 20 minutes, without a lid on the pan, until they are very tender and have absorbed their liquid. Drain the dried mushrooms, straining the liquid through a fine sieve or a piece of muslin to remove any grit; chop the dried mushrooms finely. Add the chopped mushrooms and their liquid to the oyster mushrooms, along with the garlic, and cook for a further few minutes until they are again dry. Take them off the heat and season with salt and pepper.

Arrange the oyster mushrooms in the loaf tin in layers. Whisk together the eggs and cream, then pour this custard into the loaf tin, gently moving the oyster mushrooms with a knife and tipping the tin, to make sure that the custard seeps down between all the layers. Put the loaf tin in a roasting tin of boiling water and bake it for about 40 minutes, or until it is set and golden brown and a skewer inserted into the centre comes out clean. Run a knife around the edges of the timbale to loosen it, then turn it out on to a warmed serving dish.

This timbale cuts well both hot and cold, but you need to use a sharp, serrated knife.
SERVES 6

TOMATO AND RED WINE SAUCE

1 onion, peeled and sliced	*300ml / ½ pint red wine*
1 celery stick, chopped	*1 × 400g / 14oz can tomatoes*
1 garlic clove, crushed	
1 tbls olive oil	*salt and freshly ground black pepper*
sprig of fresh thyme	*15 g/ ½ oz cold butter*

Fry the onion, celery and garlic in the olive oil with the thyme for 10 minutes, browning them slightly, then add the wine and tomatoes. Bring to the boil, then let the sauce bubble away for about 5 minutes, to cook the tomatoes and thicken a bit. Liquidize the sauce, then pour it through a sieve into a saucepan. Season with salt and pepper.

Just before serving the sauce, bring it back to the boil then remove it from the heat and whisk in the butter, a little at a time, to make the sauce look glossy and thicken it a little more.

BRAISED CELERY

First trim off any roots from 2 heads of celery, then cut the stems down to about 15 cm/6 inches from the base. Now take a potato peeler and shave the outside stems of the celery to remove any tough threads. Cut the celery down into quarters and wash them well under the tap.

Heat 2 tablespoons olive oil in a large saucepan, add 1 teaspoon coriander seeds, a bay leaf, 6-8 peppercorns, and the pieces of celery. Turn the celery gently to coat it in the oil, add a sprinkling of salt, then pour in 600 ml/1 pint of water. Bring to the boil, cover and leave to cook gently for 1 hour, or until the celery is very tender. Remove the celery with a perforated spoon, put it into a shallow dish and keep it warm. Boil the remaining liquid hard to reduce it well and pour it over the celery. Sprinkle with some chopped parsley.

RAGOUT OF WILD MUSHROOMS

This is a dish to make when you've had a really successful mushroom hunt, or feel like a no-expense-spared special autumn meal. Alternatively, you can improvise by using a mixture of oyster, button and shiitake mushrooms instead of the wild ones (see opposite). Some baby sprouts and early chestnuts, below, go well with this, to make a complete meal.

1kg / 2¼lb wild mushrooms	*lemon juice*
	salt and freshly ground
75g / 3oz butter	*black pepper*
3 garlic cloves, crushed	*chopped fresh parsley,*
4 tbls double cream	*preferably flat-leaf*

Wash, trim and slice the mushrooms; pat them dry on kitchen paper. Melt the butter in a large saucepan and put in the mushrooms and garlic. Cook over a moderate heat, uncovered, until they are tender and any liquid that they make has bub-

bled away. The time varies according to the type of mushroom; it can be as little as 5 minutes, or as long as 20, but if you test the mushrooms with a sharp knife you'll be able to tell when they're tender.

Add the cream, a squeeze of lemon juice and some salt and pepper to season. Get the mixture really hot, sprinkle with parsley then serve at once.
SERVES 4

BABY SPROUTS AND EARLY CHESTNUTS

You'll need 450-700g/1-1½ lb sprouts for four people and 225-350g/8-12oz chestnuts, weighed before skinning. Really baby sprouts can be trimmed and cooked whole, but if they are larger, I think they're better if you cut them in half. The chestnuts need to be prepared in advance. The easiest way to skin them is to put them on a board on their flat side and make a sharp cut from top to bottom. Put them into boiling water, a few at a time, and boil for 3-5 minutes, or until the cut opens. Then take them out and peel off the skins. Once they're skinned, they need to be cooked in fresh water for about 15 minutes, or until they're tender.

Cook the sprouts in 1 cm/½ inch of fast-boiling water with a lid on the pan for 3-5 minutes, or until they're just done. Drain them (save the water as it makes good stock), add the hot cooked chestnuts with a little butter, and season with salt and freshly ground black pepper.

By wild mushrooms, I mean ceps (called porcini in Italy) or chanterelles (or morels in the spring) if you're lucky enough to get them; or oyster mushrooms or shiitake which are increasingly available from greengrocers and supermarkets.

PERFECT PUDDINGS

———————— ❧ ————————

APPLE AND BLACKBERRY LAYER

For this light pudding I like to use the sweetest apples and blackberries I can find, because the sweeter they are, the less additional sugar you need. You could use cooking apples if you prefer, sweetened with sugar or honey; and for a less-rich cream, you could use half whipping cream and half plain yogurt.

1kg / 2¼lb sweet apples
caster sugar, honey or
   no-added-sugar
   apricot jam
450g / 1lb blackberries

300ml / ½ pint
   whipping cream
25g / 1oz toasted
   flaked almonds

Peel, core and slice the apples, then put them into a heavy-based saucepan with 2 tablespoons of water. Cover and cook over a gentle heat for 10-15 minutes or until they have collapsed to a purée. Watch that they don't stick towards the end of the cooking time. Remove from the heat, taste the mixture, and add a little sugar, honey or no-added-sugar apricot jam to sweeten as necessary, then leave to get cold.

Wash the blackberries, put them into a saucepan without any water and cook them over a gentle heat for a few minutes until the juices run. Remove from the heat and sweeten as necessary, then leave until cold. (If they release a lot of juice, strain the fruit from the liquid with a slotted spoon.)

To assemble the pudding, first whip the cream until it forms soft peaks. Put a layer of blackberry mixture into a glass bowl, using about half the mixture; then put half the apples in an even layer on top, and spread half the cream over them. Repeat the layers, ending with a layer of cream, and keeping a few berries in reserve to decorate the top of the pudding. Chill until required – it will keep overnight, if covered with cling film and stored in the fridge. Sprinkle the toasted flaked almonds and reserved berries on top just before serving.

SERVES 4-6

SPICED QUINCE COMPOTE WITH ORANGE CREAM

Although this may not look amazing, being rather low-key in its colouring, it tastes good, especially if you serve it with the orange cream.

900g / 2lb quinces
3 cloves
½ cinnamon stick
50g / 2oz dark brown
   sugar

FOR THE ORANGE
CREAM

1 orange
150ml / 5fl oz thick
   Greek yogurt or
   double cream

Cut the quinces into quarters, remove the peel and cores and slice the flesh fairly thinly. Put the slices into a saucepan with the cloves, cinnamon, sugar and enough water to cover: I used 600ml/1 pint. Bring to the boil, then let them simmer until the quince is very tender and the liquid is reduced to a syrupy glaze. Remove from the heat and leave to cool – this compôte is good served warm or cold.

To make the orange cream, first remove a few long strands of peel with an orange zester for decoration, then grate enough peel to produce about a teaspoonful: finally, squeeze the orange. Add the grated peel to the yogurt or cream, along with 1-2 tablespoons of the juice, or enough to give a good flavour. If you're using cream, whisk it gently until it falls in soft peaks. (You can't use whipping cream for this recipe because the orange will prevent it from becoming thick.)

Serve the compôte in individual bowls, either with a spoonful of cream and some slivers of orange peel on top, which I think is prettiest; or, if not everyone wants cream, serve this in a separate small bowl, decorated with the orange peel slivers.
SERVES 4

OPPOSITE: *Apple and Blackberry Layer*

PEAR AND ALMOND TART

This is an unusual tart in which the base is made of ground almonds instead of pastry, and maple syrup is used for sweetening. Some lightly whipped cream with a dash of amaretto or poire william eau de vie would be the final touch for a special occasion.

700g / 1½lb sweet
  pears
6 tbls maple syrup
1 vanilla pod

1 tsp baking powder
1 tbls maple syrup
25g / 1oz butter
few drops real almond
  essence (optional)

FOR THE TART CASE

200g / 7oz ground
  almonds

Set the oven to 180°C/350°F/Gas Mark 4. Cut the pears into quarters and remove the peel and cores, then cut the flesh into thin slices. Put them into a heavy-based saucepan with the maple syrup and the vanilla pod and cook gently, uncovered, for about 10 minutes. The pears should be tender and almost transparent, and bathed in a glossy glaze after this time. Allow to cool.

Meanwhile, make the tart case: mix together, by hand or in a food processor, the ground almonds, baking powder, maple syrup, butter and, if you wish to intensify the almond flavour, a few drops of real almond essence. Press the somewhat sticky dough into a 20 cm/8 inch metal flan tin, pushing the mixture up the sides but being careful not to make it too thick. Prick the case all over and bake for 10 minutes, until the tart is crisp and golden brown. Remove from the oven and leave to cool.

Not more than an hour or so before serving the tart, arrange the pear slices on top of the pastry, removing the vanilla pod (rinse, dry and use again). Pour any glossy liquid from the pan over the pears; if it is watery rather than glossy, boil it up for a few minutes to reduce it before using.
SERVES 6

OPPOSITE: *Pear and Almond Tart*

FIGS WITH MASCARPONE

If you can get some perfect figs, this is a luscious way to eat them. I think they need a light red-fruit coulis to go with them; one made from raspberries is best if you can get them, otherwise you could use sweet ripe red plums.

raspberry coulis (see
  page 299)

8 sweet ripe figs
125g / 4oz mascarpone

First, make the coulis, which can be done well in advance – then leave it to get cool.

Just before you want to serve the pudding, pour a small pool of raspberry coulis on to four plates. Stand the figs on a board with their stalk uppermost, and cut them down, through the stalk, into sixths or eighths, keeping them attached at the base. Put a couple of figs on each plate and open out the cut sections like the petals of a flower. Spoon a little mascarpone into the centre of each 'flower', and trickle a little of the raspberry coulis on top.
SERVES 4

AUTUMN MENUS

MENU

HARVEST SUPPER PARTY FOR EIGHT

Pumpkin Soup

Aubergine, Tomato and Mozzarella Bake
Roasted Red Peppers Stuffed with Fennel
Autumn Green Salad with Toasted Hazelnuts

Fruit Salad with
Scented Geranium Cream
Apple Almond Cake

COUNTDOWN

Up to 1 day before:
Make the Pumpkin Soup, cover and keep in the fridge. Make the Apple Almond Cake and the filling, but don't assemble. Make the Aubergine, Tomato and Mozzarella Bake ready for baking.

2-3 hours before:
Make the Fruit Salad, cover; wash the salad and keep in the fridge.

1½ hours before:
Set the oven to 180°/350°F/Gas Mark 4. Prepare the Peppers and put them into the oven to cook. 30-40 minutes before you want to seve the meal, move the peppers to the coolest part of the oven and turn up the heat to 220°/425°F/Gas Mark 7. Put the Aubergine Bake into the oven. Cover the peppers with foil if they start to brown too much. Split and fill the cake; make the Geranium Cream; gently reheat the soup; finish making the salad.

PUMPKIN SOUP

Pumpkin makes a beautiful soup, golden and creamy, with a delicate flavour – and it couldn't be easier to prepare.

2.8kg / 6lb pumpkin, weighed with skin and seeds	salt and freshly ground black pepper fresh lemon juice
75g / 3oz butter	
2 large onions, peeled and chopped	TO GARNISH
4 garlic cloves, crushed	fresh chives
4 tbls single cream	flat-leaf parsley

Cut the skin from the pumpkin and remove the seeds and threads, then cut the flesh into even-sized pieces. Heat the butter in a large saucepan and put in the onion. Cook, covered, for 5 minutes, until it is beginning to soften, then add the garlic and pumpkin. Stir, then cover the pan again and cook for a further 5-10 minutes. Add 1.4 L/3½ pints water, bring to the boil, then half-cover the pan and let the soup simmer for 30 minutes, or until the pumpkin is very tender.

Liquidize the soup thoroughly, then pour it back into the saucepan, stir in the cream, and season with salt, pepper and a little squeeze of lemon juice to lift the flavour, if necessary.

Reheat and serve into warmed bowls, then snip some chives and parsley over each bowl.

OPPOSITE: *Dishes from Harvest Supper Party for Eight*

AUBERGINE, TOMATO AND MOZZARELLA BAKE

This warming casserole is as delicious to eat as it is easy to make; make sure you've got lots of crusty bread handy to mop up the juices.

2 small-medium aubergines, 450g / 1lb in all	glass of red wine (optional)
salt	salt and freshly ground black pepper
1 large onion	225g / 8oz Mozzarella cheese (packed in water)
olive oil	
2 garlic cloves	
2 × 400g / 14oz cans plum tomatoes	50g / 2oz fresh Parmesan cheese, grated
1 tsp dried oregano	

Set the oven to 220°C/425°F/Gas Mark 7. Cut the aubergine into 6 mm/¼ inch slices, discarding the stalk. Layer the slices into a colander, sprinkling each layer with kitchen salt. Put a plate and a weight on top and leave on the draining board for 10-30 minutes, depending on how rushed you are.

Meanwhile, make a rich tomato sauce. Peel and chop the onion then fry it in 1-2 tablespoons of olive oil for 5 minutes. Peel and crush the garlic and add to the pan, along with the tomatoes and their liquid, the oregano and the red wine if you're using it. Break up the tomatoes a bit with a wooden spoon, then leave the mixture to cook, uncovered, for about 15-20 minutes, or until the liquid has reduced considerably, leaving a thick, purée-like mixture. Stir from time to time. Season the sauce with salt and pepper.

Rinse the aubergines under the cold tap and pat the slices dry with a clean cloth or kitchen paper. Heat 2 tablespoons of olive oil in a frying pan and fry the aubergine slices in a single layer – you'll need to do several batches. After a minute or two turn the slices over, so that they get cooked and lightly browned on both sides. Lift them out on to a plate or baking sheet lined with kitchen paper and fry the next batch. Cut the Mozzarella cheese into slices about 6 mm/¼ inch thick.

To assemble the dish, put a layer of half the aubergine slices into a large, shallow casserole. Pour half the sauce on top and then lay the cheese slices on top of that. Cover with the remaining aubergine slices and the rest of the sauce, then sprinkle the Parmesan cheese on top. Bake for 30-40 minutes, or until the topping has turned golden brown and the mixture is bubbling. Serve at once.

ROASTED RED PEPPERS STUFFED WITH FENNEL

This is a slight adaptation of one of Delia Smith's recipes which I like very much. It can be served hot or cold as a first course or accompanying vegetable, and I also like it as a light main course with other vegetables. The red peppers need to be good medium-sized ones, rather square in shape; and the fennel bulbs need to be fairly small so that when cut into eighths two pieces will fit inside the peppers side by side.

2 fennel bulbs	salt and freshly ground black pepper
4 red peppers	
1 × 400g / 14oz can tomatoes in juice	1 tbls coriander seeds
	8 dsp olive oil

Set the oven to 180°C/350°F/Gas Mark 4. Bring 2.5 cm/1 inch of water to the boil in a medium saucepan. Cut the leafy tops off the fennel, trim the root ends and remove a layer of the white part if it looks as if it's tough. Cut the fennel down into quarters, then eighths, keeping them joined at the base. Cook the fennel in the water, with a lid on the pan, for 5-7 minutes, or until it's tender, then drain it. (Keep the water – it makes marvellous stock.)

Halve the peppers, cutting right down through the stalks, remove the seeds and trim the white part inside to make a good cavity. Arrange the peppers in a roasting tin or shallow casserole dish. Chop the tomatoes and divide the mixture between the peppers, adding a little of the juice as necessary. Season with salt and freshly ground black pepper, then

Any of the following would be good to drink with this supper: cider, an aromatic dry white wine such as Gewurztraminer, a light dry wine such as Muscadet, or a white Burgundy.

place two pieces of fennel side by side inside the peppers and on top of the tomato, with the root-end towards the stem end of the fennel; push them down neatly to fit and season again. Crush the coriander seeds in a pestle with a mortar or with the end of a rolling pin or wooden spoon, and sprinkle them over the top of the fennel. Finally, pour a dessertspoonful of olive oil over the top of each pepper half.

Bake the peppers, uncovered, for about 1 hour, or until they are very tender and beginning to brown. Serve hot or cold.

AUTUMN GREEN SALAD WITH TOASTED HAZELNUTS

When you're working out quantities for a party, one of the strange laws of life is that the more people present, the less salad they'll eat. So, under normal circumstances, I'd expect this salad to serve four salad-lovers, but for a harvest supper with more people (and lots of other food), it will be enough for about eight.

1 tbls hazelnut oil, if available	*½ frisée lettuce*
2 tbls olive oil or 3 tbls if you're not using hazelnut oil	*packet or bunch of watercress*
	1 celery heart
1 tbls wine vinegar	*2 tbls snipped fresh chives*
salt and freshly ground black pepper	*50g / 2oz skinned hazelnuts, toasted*
2-4 artichoke bases, cooked, cooled and sliced, or 1 avocado, peeled and sliced	*under the grill*

Mix the dressing straight into a salad bowl: put in the hazelnut oil, if you're using it, the olive oil, wine vinegar and some salt and freshly ground black pepper and mix together. Add the artichoke hearts

or avocado and mix gently. Wash the frisée and watercress, shake them dry, then put them into the bowl, tearing large pieces as necessary. Slice the celery heart finely, and add that to the bowl, too, along with the chives.

Just before you want to serve the salad, turn it gently so that all the leaves get lightly coated with the dressing, and add the chopped nuts.

FRUIT SALAD WITH SCENTED GERANIUM CREAM

Prepare the sugar for the geranium cream 3-4 days before you want to serve this pudding, to give the flavour a chance to develop.

450g / 1lb blueberries or bilberries	**FOR THE CREAM**
2 x 285g / 10oz jars no-added-sugar, high-fruit-content black cherry spread	*300ml / ½ pint whipping cream*
	2-3 scented geranium leaves, lemon or rose scent not mint
5 sweet russet apples	*caster sugar*
5 sweet pears	*extra geranium leaves to decorate*
5 sweet figs	

The geranium cream is made by sweetening the cream with sugar which has been flavoured with geranium. To make this sugar, bury several scented geranium leaves in a small jar of caster sugar and leave for 3-4 days or longer (like making vanilla sugar).

To make the fruit salad, wash the blueberries or bilberries and take out any damaged ones or stems. Put them into a heavy-based saucepan with the no-added-sugar spread and heat gently until the spread has melted and the fruit juices begin to run. Pour the mixture into a bowl and leave on one side to cool down. Meanwhile, peel, core, and thinly slice the apples and pears; wash and slice the figs. Add all these to the fruit mixture in the bowl and stir gently so that everything is distributed. Cover and leave until required.

Just before you want to serve the fruit salad, make the geranium cream. Whisk the cream until it makes soft peaks, then gently stir in a little of the geranium-scented caster sugar to flavour and sweeten. Transfer to a serving bowl. Garnish with a few scented geranium leaves and serve with the fruit salad.

APPLE ALMOND CAKE

This autumn cake consists of layers of light, quick-to-make almond-flavoured sponge cake sandwiched together with a thick purée of russet apples with amaretto. You can make both the sponge part and the apple purée a day or two in advance, but do not fill the cake until shortly before you want to eat it if you do. For a really luscious, richer, variation, you could spread each of the layers with whipped cream as well as apple purée.

FOR THE ALMOND SPONGE

175g / 6oz soft butter
175g / 6oz caster sugar
3 eggs
50g / 2oz ground almonds
1 tsp almond essence
175g / 6oz self-raising flour
1½ tsp baking powder
25g / 1oz flaked almonds

FOR THE APPLE FILLING

1kg / 2¼lb russet apples, peeled and sliced
3 tbls amaretto liqueur (optional)
no-added-sugar apricot jam, honey or sugar to taste

Set the oven to 160°C/325°F/Gas Mark 3. Line a deep 20 cm/8 inch round cake tin with greaseproof paper. To make the cake, put the butter, sugar, eggs, ground almonds and almond essence into a bowl, or the bowl of a mixer or food processor, then sift in the flour and baking powder. Whisk or process for a minute or two until the mixture is smooth and glossy, then add 3 tablespoons of water to make a mixture which is soft enough to drop reluctantly off a spoon. Spoon the mixture into the prepared tin, level the top, sprinkle with the flaked almonds and bake for 1-1¼ hours, until a cocktail stick inserted into the centre comes out clean. Cool for 10 minutes in the tin, then transfer to a wire rack. Remove the paper when the cake is cold.

To make the filling, put the apples into a heavy-based saucepan with 2 tablespoons of water. Cover and cook over a gentle heat for 10-15 minutes or until they have collapsed to a thick purée, stirring the mixture often to prevent it from sticking. Remove from the heat and allow to cool completely, then add the amaretto, if you're using it, and a little no-added-sugar jam, honey or sugar to taste.

Assemble the cake by cutting it across twice, to make three layers. Put the bottom layer on a plate and spread it with half the apple mixture, then put the next piece of sponge on top and press down. Spread with the rest of the apple purée and place the final layer, with the almonds in it, on top.

OPPOSITE: *Desserts from Harvest Supper Party for Eight*

MENU

HALLOWEEN PARTY FOR TEN TO TWELVE

Mexican Beanfeast with Tomato, Red Pepper and Avocado Salsas

❦

Pumpkin, Okra and Baby Sweetcorn Casserole

❦

*Maple Ice Cream
Chocolate Pecan Brownies*

❦

Party Cider Cup

MEXICAN BEANFEAST

*3 tbls olive oil
1 tbls cumin seeds
450g / 1lb onions, peeled and sliced
1 garlic clove, crushed
1 × 400g / 14oz can borlotti beans*

*1 × 400g / 14oz can red kidney beans
1 × 400g / 14oz can cannellini beans
1 × 400g / 14oz can black-eyed beans
chopped coriander to garnish*

Heat the oil in a large saucepan, then fry the cumin seeds for 30 seconds. Put in the onions and garlic and cook gently for 10 minutes, with a lid on the pan. Drain the beans, reserving the liquid. Add them to the saucepan, stirring very gently over a low heat to mix them all together, and heat them through without mashing them. Add a little of the reserved liquid if they are in danger of sticking.

Sprinkle with the chopped coriander and serve with Tomato, Red Pepper and Avocado Salsas, taco chips and a spoonful of soured cream.

COUNTDOWN

Up to 1 week ahead:
Make the Maple Ice Cream.

The day before:
Make the Chocolate Brownies.

Several hours in advance:
Make the Mexican Beanfeast, the Pumpkin, Okra and Baby Sweetcorn Casserole and the Tomato and Red Pepper Salsas.

1 hour in advance:
Make the Avocado Salsa. Gently re-heat the Mexican Beanfeast and the Pumpkin, Okra and Baby Sweetcorn Casserole. Remove the Ice Cream from the freezer 30 minutes or so before you want to serve it.

TOMATO SALSA

*700-900g / 1½-2lb tomatoes
juice of 1 lemon*

*4 tbls chopped fresh coriander leaves
salt and freshly ground black pepper*

Skin the tomatoes by covering them with boiling water, leaving for 60 seconds, then draining and slipping off the skins with a sharp knife. Chop the tomatoes coarsely, discarding any tough bits of stem, and put them into a bowl with the lemon juice, chopped coriander and salt and pepper to taste. Serve in a bowl, to accompany the beanfeast.

OPPOSITE: *Halloween Party for Ten to Twelve*

RED PEPPER SALSA

3 large red peppers
3 green chillis
juice of 1 lemon

salt and freshly ground
black pepper

Cut the red peppers into quarters, then put them shiny-side up on a grill pan, together with the chillis which can remain whole, and grill at full heat until the skin has blistered and begun to char. Move them halfway through the grilling so that all the skin gets done, then cover them with a plate to keep in the steam. Leave until they're cool enough to handle, slip off the skins and rinse the peppers under the tap to remove the seeds. Skin the chillis, too, then halve them and rinse away the seeds.

Put the pieces of pepper and chilli into a liquidizer with the lemon juice and some salt and pepper and whizz to a purée. Check the seasoning, and serve in a small bowl.

AVOCADO SALSA

1 lime
2 avocados
1 green chilli
1 garlic clove, crushed
(optional)

salt and freshly ground
black pepper
paprika pepper

Scrub the lime then, using a potato peeler, peel off a few pieces of rind and snip or cut them into shreds to make about a tablespoonful. Squeeze the juice from the lime and put it into a bowl. Remove the peel and stones from the avocados, cut into rough chunks and put into the bowl with the lime juice. Halve, de-seed and finely slice the chilli, being careful not to get the juice near your face or eyes (wash your hands afterwards), and add to the avocado, along with the garlic if you're using it, and the shreds of lime.

Mash all the ingredients together with a fork, to produce a mixture which is creamy without being

too smooth. Season with salt and freshly ground black pepper. Spoon the mixture into a small bowl and garnish with a sprinkling of paprika.

SPICED PUMPKIN, OKRA AND BABY SWEETCORN CASSEROLE

1kg / 2¼lb pumpkin,
weighed with skin
and seeds
50g / 2oz butter
2 tbls olive oil
2 large onions, peeled
and chopped
2 garlic cloves, crushed

1 cinnamon stick
225-350g / 8-12oz okra
225g / 8oz baby
sweetcorn
1 × 400g / 14oz can
tomatoes in juice
salt and freshly ground
black pepper

Remove the peel, seeds and threads from the pumpkin and cut the flesh into fairly thin slices. Heat the butter and oil in a large saucepan and put in the onions; cover and cook for 5 minutes, then add the garlic, pumpkin and cinnamon stick, broken in two. Stir well, then cover again and cook for a further 10 minutes.

Wash and trim the okra and sweetcorn, then either cut them into 1 cm/½ inch lengths, or leave them whole, whichever you prefer, and add them to the pan. Chop the tomatoes and add these, too, along with their juice. Season with some salt and pepper, cover and leave the casserole to cook for 20 minutes, or until the vegetables are all tender.

Check the seasoning and transfer the mixture to a warmed casserole dish.

Accompany this menu with either the party cider cup, or a medium-bodied French red wine such as Côtes du Rhône (domaine bottled).

MAPLE ICE CREAM

You don't have to stir this ice cream as it freezes in order to produce a smooth, velvety texture.

3 egg yolks	*300ml / ½ pint*
75ml / 3fl oz maple	*whipping cream*
syrup	

Put the egg yolks into a bowl and whisk until they are pale and thick, preferably using an electric whisk. Put the maple syrup into a small saucepan and boil for 2-3 minutes, until the syrup reaches 110°C/225°F on a sugar thermometer or a drop of it will form a thread when pulled between your finger and thumb. Remove from the heat immediately and pour the syrup on to the egg yolks while you whisk them. Continue to whisk for 2-3 minutes, until the mixture is cool and very thick and creamy. Whip the cream until it holds its shape, then fold it into the egg yolk mixture.

Pour the mixture into a plastic container and freeze until firm. Remove from the freezer about 15 minutes before you want to serve the ice cream to allow it to soften up a little, although it shouldn't get rock-solid in any case.

CHOCOLATE PECAN BROWNIES

Brownies always make a popular treat and are good to serve either as a cake or as a pudding. You can vary the nuts in these: skinned hazelnuts, brazil nuts or walnuts are also good.

300g / 10oz plain	*2 tsp vanilla essence*
chocolate, not too	*50g / 2oz barbados*
bitter, at least 50%	*sugar*
cocoa solids	*½ tsp baking powder*
125g / 4oz butter or	*125g / 4oz pecans,*
margarine	*roughly chopped*
4 eggs	

Set the oven to 180°C/350°F/Gas Mark 4. Line a 20 cm/8 inch square tin with a piece of greased grease-proof or non-stick paper. Break the chocolate into pieces, put it into a saucepan with the butter or margarine, and melt gently.

Meanwhile, put the eggs into a bowl with the vanilla and sugar and whisk at high speed in a mixer or with an electric hand-whisk for about 5 minutes, until they are very thick and pale. Whisk in the melted chocolate and stir in the baking powder and pecans. (There's no flour in this recipe, that's intentional!) Pour the mixture into the tin, easing it gently into the corners. Bake for 40 minutes. Cool in the tin, then cut into squares.

PARTY CIDER CUP

You can really make this cider cup to taste, adding more or less soda water and brandy as you prefer. It should be refreshing rather than too alcoholic and is a good thirst-quenching drink.

1 lemon	*100ml / 4fl oz brandy*
5cm / 2 inch piece of	*2 × 1L / 1¾ pints cider*
cucumber	*2 × 500ml / 1 pint*
1 red-skinned apple	*soda water*
6-8 sprigs of fresh	*ice cubes*
mint	

Slice the lemon and cucumber finely; wash the apple and cut it into chunky pieces about the size of a cherry. Bruise the mint by crushing it a bit with a rolling pin. Put all these ingredients into a bowl or very large jug (or divide the mixture between two), add the brandy, then cover and leave until just before the party.

When you're ready to serve the cup, add the cider and soda water to the bowl or jug(s), stir, add the ice cubes and serve at once

Look out for real maple syrup, not 'maple – flavoured' syrup.

WINTER

In winter, the sun's cycle reaches its nadir or lowest point; it never rises very high above the horizon, giving us short days and long nights. The earth lies dormant, the trees are bare, allowing us to see their stark and beautiful shapes against the muted browns, silvers and greys of the winter landscape. At the winter solstice, however, the sun starts its journey back towards us and, in the northern hemisphere, we celebrate the birth of the Christ child in the dark manger, linking this with the return of the life-giving force of the sun and with the awakening of the light within our own hearts.

Winter, for me, and I imagine for many other people in the northern hemiphere, falls into two distinct periods: a short one before Christmas and a more extended one afterwards. The time leading up to Christmas is one of excitement, anticipation and preparation. The shops are full of exotic and colourful items; thoughts are on parties, presents and preparations for the big meal of the year, Christmas dinner. I particularly enjoy the challenge of creating a vegetarian Christmas feast – such as the one on pages 266–69 with the Christmas Wreath as its centrepiece – which delights the senses and brings pleasure.

After Christmas we move into the second phase of winter which is longer and more extended, and often much colder. Without the excitement of Christmas to buoy us up, the warm days of spring seem far away. The sun never gets very strong or high in the sky, and we look to the stored sunshine in vegetables from the earth, dried seeds such as pulses, nuts, grains, stored and dried fruits, to give us energy while the earth lies dormant. We want warming food but, after the richness of Christmas eating, many people fancy simpler, filling, more homely bakes and casseroles, such as Golden Roulade of Lentils with Rich Mushroom Gravy (page 252) and Split Pea and Spinach Dhal (page 260).

Conversely, this is also a time when many people think about dieting and losing weight, an aspect of late-twentieth century living which goes totally against the rhythm of the seasons, when all the foods available suggest that this is a time when nature is encouraging us to gain a pound or two as protection against the cold. Constant worry about weight and the misery of being perpetually either on a diet or feeling one ought to be, is one of the sicknesses, I believe, of modern life in the affluent half of the world.

I used to be on this dieting switch-back – and being a cookery writer doesn't help. But I have found that, for me, the answer lies in compatible eating. That is, putting it at its simplest, not mixing concentrated protein foods – eggs, cheese, dairy produce (and, for meat eaters, meat, fish and poultry) – with concentrated carbohydrates or starches – bread, potatoes, pasta, flour, rice – at the same meal. Vegetables (except for potatoes, sweet potatoes and sweetcorn) go with everything. I've found that by eating compatible foods, yet at the same time having a wide range of possibilities open to me, there's no feeling of being 'on a diet' or of having to count calories; I simply do not get the cravings for certain foods – especially sweet ones and 'fattening' ones – that I used to.

SATISFYING SOUPS

WHITE WINTER SOUP WITH SUN-DRIED TOMATO PUREE

For a vegan version of white winter soup, replace the cream with a non-dairy cream which you can buy at some major supermarket chains.

The sunshine flavour of sun-dried tomatoes turns this simple soup into a winter treat. Puréed sun-dried tomato is available in jars, otherwise sun-dried tomatoes in oil, puréed in a blender, are similar.

225g / 8oz celeriac
225g / 8oz turnips
225g / 8oz leeks, white part only
1 tbls light olive oil
sprig of fresh thyme

4 tbls single cream
salt and freshly ground black pepper
4 tsp sun-dried tomato purée

Peel the celeriac and turnips and cut them into even-sized pieces; trim, wash and slice the leeks. Heat the oil in a large saucepan and put in the vegetables and the thyme. Cook the vegetables, with a lid on the pan, for about 10 minutes, then add 850 ml/1½ pints of water. Bring to the boil, turn down the heat and leave the soup to simmer for about 30 minutes, or until the vegetables are very tender.

Remove the thyme, liquidize a ladleful of the soup with the cream, then add this to the rest of the soup. Season the soup with salt and pepper, reheat gently, and serve into warmed bowls. Top each with a swirl of sun-dried tomato purée.

SERVES 4

STILTON SOUP

If you haven't any good home-made stock (which doesn't have to be made specially if you make a habit of saving the water in which vegetables are cooked, especially tasty ones like celeriac), it's much better to use water rather than a stock cube or powder. The celery, leeks and Stilton in this soup give it a good flavour in any case.

225g / 8oz outside celery sticks
225g / 8oz leeks
850ml / 1½ pints good vegetable stock or water
125g / 4oz Stilton cheese

salt and freshly ground black pepper
squeeze of lemon juice
1-2 tbls cream (optional)
snipped chives or parsley to garnish

Scrub the celery and run a potato peeler down each stick to remove any stringy bits; trim and clean the leeks. Chop the celery and leeks and put them into a large saucepan along with the stock or water; cover, bring to the boil and leave to simmer gently for 1 hour, or until the vegetables are very tender.

Put the soup into a food processor and crumble in the cheese, in rough chunks. Whizz to a purée, then pour the mixture back into the saucepan through a sieve, pressing through any lumps of cheese. Season with salt and pepper; add a squeeze of fresh lemon juice to sharpen the flavour slightly if necessary, and stir in the cream if you're using this. Reheat gently, without boiling.

Top each bowlful with some chives or parsley.

SERVES 4

OPPOSITE: *White Winter Soup with Sun-dried Tomato Purée*

CREAM OF CELERY SOUP

Apart from tasting good, this soup is an excellent way of using the tough outer sticks of celery which always get left and tend to lurk in the back of the fridge waiting to be thrown out.

2 tbls olive oil	*850ml / 1½ pints*
2 onions, peeled and	*vegetable stock or*
chopped	*water*
outside sticks of 1	*4 tbls cream*
head of celery, about	*salt and freshly ground*
450g / 1lb in all	*black pepper*

Heat the oil in a large saucepan and add the onions. Cover and cook over a gentle heat for 10 minutes, until the onions are soft but not browned.

Meanwhile, scrub the celery and run a potato peeler down each stick to remove any stringy bits. Chop the celery and add it to the onions, stir, cover, and cook for another 5 minutes. Add the stock or water, bring to the boil and leave the soup to cook gently for 1 hour, or until the celery is very tender.

Liquidize the soup and pour it through a sieve back into the saucepan to remove any remaining tough bits of celery. Stir in the cream and salt and pepper to taste and serve hot.
SERVES 4

MIDDLE EASTERN LENTIL SOUP

For a change, the lentil soup can be made with green lentils instead of split orange ones.

225g / 8oz split red	*1 tsp ground cumin*
lentils	*1 tbls olive oil*
2 onions, peeled and	*2 tsp ground coriander*
chopped	*juice of ½ lemon*
2 celery sticks	*salt and freshly ground*
1 garlic clove, crushed	*black pepper*

This is a quick and simple lentil soup with a topping of onion fried with ground coriander to make it crisp and spicy. Put the lentils into a large

saucepan with half the onions and 1 L/1¾ pints of water (or real vegetable stock if you have it). Run a potato peeler down the celery to remove any stringy bits, then chop the celery and add to the pan, along with the garlic and cumin. Bring to the boil, then let the soup simmer gently for about 1 hour, until the celery and lentils are very tender.

While the soup is cooking, fry the rest of the onion in the oil with the coriander for about 10 minutes, or until it is tender but lightly browned and crisp. Liquidize the soup, add the lemon juice, season with salt and pepper, then stir in the fried onion and coriander. Serve at once.
SERVES 4

GOLDEN ONION SOUP WITH CHEESE TOPPING

25g / 1oz butter	*1.2L / 3 pints vegetable*
1 tbls oil	*stock*
900g / 2lb onions,	*salt and freshly ground*
peeled and thinly	*black pepper*
sliced	*lemon juice*
2 garlic cloves, crushed	*125g / 4oz grated*
	Gruyère cheese

Heat the butter and oil in a large saucepan, add the onions and cook, covered, for 25-30 minutes until they're soft and golden, stirring them from time to time to prevent them from sticking. Stir in the garlic and cook for 2-3 minutes longer before adding the stock. Bring to the boil and let the soup simmer, uncovered, for 10-15 minutes. Season with salt and pepper and a dash of fresh lemon juice. Serve into individual bowls and put the cheese on top.
SERVES 4-6

BROCCOLI AND RED PEPPER SOUP

You can use purple sprouting broccoli, or the larger pieces of broccoli, for this cheering winter soup.

25g / 1oz butter
1 onion, peeled and
    chopped
450g / 1lb broccoli
1 small red pepper

2-3 tbls cream
    (optional)
salt and freshly ground
    black pepper

Melt the butter in a large saucepan, put in the onion, cover and cook for 5 minutes. Separate the broccoli florets from the stems, chop both and reserve a cupful of the florets. Put the rest of the broccoli, stems and florets, into the saucepan with the onion, cover and cook for a further 5 minutes, then add 600 ml/1 pint of water or vegetable stock. Bring to the boil, cover and simmer for about 15 minutes, or until the broccoli is very tender.

Meanwhile, in another pan, bring 300 ml/½ pint of water to the boil and cook the remaining florets for just a few minutes, until they are tender. Drain the liquid into the soup, put the florets into a colander and refresh under the cold tap so that they keep their bright colour. Also prepare the red pepper. Cut it into quarters and put these, shiny-side up, on a grill pan. Grill them for 10-15 minutes, until the skin has blistered all over and begun to char, turning them as necessary. Remove from the grill, cover them with a plate to keep in the steam, and leave until they're cool enough to handle. Slip off the skins with a sharp knife – they'll come off easily – and rinse under the tap. Cut into dice.

When the soup is done, whizz it to a smooth purée in a food processor or blender and return it to the pan. Adjust the consistency at this stage – add a little more water or some milk if it needs thinning, also the cream, if you're using it, along with the cooked florets and salt and freshly ground black pepper to taste.

Serve the soup in warmed bowls, with a spoonful of diced red pepper on top of each one.
SERVES 4

CREAM OF WINTER SWEDE SOUP WITH CINNAMON

Although you can make this soup for next to nothing, it tastes surprisingly luxurious with its velvety texture and hint of cinnamon.

25g / 1oz butter
1 onion, peeled and
    chopped
½ cinnamon stick
600g / 1¼lb swede
4 tbls single cream

salt and freshly ground
    black pepper
caramelized onion
    rings to garnish
    (optional)

Melt the butter in a large saucepan, put in the onion, cover and cook with the cinnamon stick for 10 minutes. Peel the swede and cut it into small dice, then add these to the pan. Stir, cover and cook gently for a further 5 minutes. Add 1.5 L/2½ pints of water and bring to the boil. Simmer for about 20 minutes, or until the swede is very tender.

Remove the cinnamon stick, whizz the soup to a smooth purée in a food processor, then pour it through a sieve back into the saucepan. Stir in the cream and season with salt and freshly ground black pepper. Garnish with caramelized onion rings which are made by frying onion rings in a little olive oil or olive oil and butter for 10-15 minutes, until they are brown and crisp. Drain them on kitchen paper and float a few on top of each bowlful of soup.
SERVES 4

Carrot can be used instead of swede for a change.

WINTER VEGETABLES AND HERBS

GOLDEN ROULADE OF LENTILS WITH SAGE AND ONION FILLING

This is really an interesting variation on a lentil loaf; the mixture is spread flat, then rolled up around a tasty filling of caramelized onions and chopped sage. It's good served with some cooked purple sprouting broccoli and roast potatoes.

Dried sage can be used instead of fresh although the colour is not so good, and you'll only need 2 teaspoons.

225g / 8oz split red lentils
50g / 2oz butter or margarine
450g / 1lb onions, peeled and chopped
2 tbls lemon juice
salt and freshly ground black pepper

2 tbls chopped fresh sage
butter or margarine for basting
sprigs of fresh sage to garnish

Set the oven to 200°C/400°F/Gas Mark 6. Put the lentils into a saucepan with 450 ml/¾ pint of water and bring to the boil. Reduce the heat, cover and leave to cook gently for 15-20 minutes, or until the lentils are tender, then beat in half the butter or margarine.

While the lentils are cooking, fry the onions in the remaining butter or margarine for 10-15 minutes, allowing them to brown, then remove from the heat. Add the lemon juice and salt and pepper to taste to the lentils, then spread the mixture out on a piece of non-stick paper to make a rectangle 17 × 28 cm/7 × 11 inches. Spread the onions evenly on top and sprinkle with the chopped sage.

Starting at one of the short ends, carefully roll up the lentil mixture, using the paper to help you. Keeping the roulade on the paper, lift it on to a baking sheet then remove the paper. Brush the surface of the roulade generously with soft butter or margarine, then bake for about 20 minutes, basting it again after 10 minutes, until the roulade is heated through. It should be brown and crisp on top, but be careful not to over-cook it or it will dry out.

Lift it on to a plate, garnish with a few sprigs or leaves of sage and serve at once, with the Rich Mushroom Gravy, below, or a Tomato and Red Wine Sauce (see page 230). Roast potatoes and winter vegetables such as leeks and carrots, or sprouts, make an excellent accompaniment.
SERVES 6

RICH MUSHROOM GRAVY

2 tbls olive oil
1 onion, peeled and chopped
1 garlic clove, crushed
175g / 6oz mushrooms, washed and chopped
2 tsp cornflour

2-4 tbls soy sauce
1 tsp vegetarian stock powder
½ tsp yeast extract
salt and freshly ground black pepper

Heat the oil in a medium saucepan, put in the onion and cook it, uncovered, for 5 minutes, so that it browns a bit. Add the garlic, some ground black pepper and the mushrooms, and cook for a further 5 minutes, continuing the browning process. Add 600 ml/1 pint of water and bring to the boil. Blend the cornflour with some of the soy sauce, add some of the boiling liquid, then tip the whole lot back into the pan. Add the bouillon powder and yeast extract, then let the mixture simmer gently for about 10 minutes, to thicken and give the flavours a chance to develop. Adjust the seasoning as necessary – you may not need any salt – and serve with the roulade.

OPPOSITE: *Golden Roulade of Lentils with Rich Mushroom Gravy*

ROASTED WINTER VEGETABLES WITH HORSERADISH SAUCE

Roasting brings out the flavour of winter vegetables in a delightful way. They make an excellent accompanying vegetable, but I like to eat them on their own, as a complete course, with lemon juice squeezed over them, a good sprinkling of crunchy salt flakes and a tangy horseradish sauce. Leave out the garlic if you wish, but when it's cooked, it becomes very mild and almost creamy and it's easy to pop the cooked garlic cloves out of their skins with a knife and fork.

350g / 12oz celeriac	**FOR THE SAUCE**
350g / 12oz parsnips	1-2 tsp horseradish
350g / 12oz swede	relish
350g / 12oz red onions	150ml / 5fl oz soured
25g / 1oz butter	cream or Greek
2 tbls olive oil	yogurt
1 garlic bulb	salt and freshly ground
lemon wedges	black pepper
(optional)	

Set the oven to 200°C/400°F/Gas Mark 6. Put a large pan of water on the stove to heat. Peel the celeriac, parsnips and swede, then cut them into chunky pieces. Trim the tops of the onions and peel off the outer skin without removing the root; cut them into quarters, still leaving the root, which will hold them together.

Put the butter and olive oil into a roasting tin and put it into the oven to heat up; meanwhile, put the vegetables into the pan of water and boil them for 5 minutes. Drain the vegetables and put them into the sizzling hot fat and put them into the oven.

Meanwhile, break the garlic into cloves. Add the unpeeled garlic to the vegetables after about 15 minutes, then roast them for a further 15-20 minutes, or until they are golden brown. Serve at once, garnished with lemon wedges, if using, and accompanied by the sauce.

OPPOSITE: *Roasted Winter Vegetables with Horseradish Sauce*

To make the sauce, simply stir the horseradish relish into the soured cream or yogurt and add seasoning to taste.

SERVES 2-4

VEGETABLE GOULASH

The idea behind this recipe was to make a vegetable version of a traditional goulash or, strictly speaking, paprikash (since it contains soured cream), using white root vegetables instead of white meat. It makes a warming yet light winter dish; I like it with buttered kale, and perhaps a baked potato.

900g / 2lb white root	½ tsp caraway seeds
vegetables: turnips,	salt and freshly ground
kohlrabi, celeriac,	black pepper
parsnips	150ml / 5fl oz soured
225g / 8oz onions	cream
25g / 1oz butter	
1 tbls mild paprika	
pepper	

First, prepare the root vegetables by peeling them, then cutting them into even, bite-sized pieces; peel and chop the onions. Melt the butter in a large saucepan, put in the onions, cover and cook gently for 5 minutes, then add the root vegetables, paprika and caraway and stir well. Pour in 100 ml/3½ fl oz water or vegetable stock and add a teaspoonful of salt. Cover tightly and leave over a gentle heat for 45-60 minutes, or until the vegetables are very tender and bathed in a glossy brick-red sauce. Keep an eye on it and add a tablespoonful of water if it looks as if it's sticking. Stir in 2 tablespoons of soured cream, check the seasoning, then serve, with the rest of the soured cream.

SERVES 2

To make buttered kale, allow 125 – 225g/4–8oz kale for each person. Remove any tough stems, then shred the kale. Bring 2.5 cm / 1 inch of water to the boil in a large saucepan, put in the kale, cover and cook for a few minutes, until the kale is just done. Drain, add butter, salt and freshly ground black pepper.

BABY WINTER SQUASH WITH SAGE, CREAM AND GRUYERE

This is based on a recipe in The Savoury Way, *by Deborah Madison. These baby squash or 'miniature pumpkins' as Deborah Madison calls them, make an excellent, easy meal. They are particularly good with the Frisée and Orange Salad which follows.*

4 baby squash (but not the tiny miniature ones with soft skins)	**4 sage leaves**
	150ml / 5fl oz single cream
salt and freshly ground black pepper	**125g / 4oz Gruyère cheese, grated**

Set the oven to 180°C/350°F/Gas Mark 4.

Slice the tops off the baby squash and scoop out the seeds. Sprinkle the insides with salt and grind in some pepper. Stand the squash in a casserole, snip a sage leaf into each one, pour in a spoonful of cream and divide the cheese between them, pushing it into the cavities. Replace the squash tops. Bake the squash until they're tender, around 35-45 minutes, but don't let them overcook and burst.

Serve immediately, with the salad.

SERVES 4

FRISEE AND ORANGE SALAD

For this simple, colourful salad, wash a head of frisée (or endive), shake it dry and put it into a bowl, tearing the leaves roughly as necessary. Then, holding them over the bowl to catch the juice, cut away the peel and pith from 4 oranges – ruby red oranges are lovely in this salad if you can get them – then slice them into thin circles and add them to

OPPOSITE: *Baby Winter Squash with Frisée and Orange Salad*

the bowl. Sprinkle in a little salt and grind in some pepper to taste. The salad can be left at this point, or you can add a tablespoonful or two of olive oil.

SPICED RICE WITH LEEKS AND RED KIDNEY BEANS

Serve this with a tomato and green bean vinaigrette.

225g / 8oz brown Basmati rice	**3 cloves**
	700g / 1½lb leeks
1 onion, peeled and sliced	**1 × 400g / 14oz can red kidney beans**
½ tsp cumin seeds	**1 tsp garam masala**
¼ tsp chilli powder	**salt and freshly ground black pepper**
½ tsp turmeric	
1 cinnamon stick	

Wash the rice in a sieve under the cold tap until the water runs clear, then put the rice into a heavy-based saucepan with the onion, cumin seeds, chilli powder, turmeric, cinnamon stick, broken in half, and the cloves. Pour in 600 ml/1 pint of boiling water and put over a moderate heat. Bring back to the boil, then put on a tight-fitting lid, lower the heat and leave to cook gently for 15 minutes.

Meanwhile, remove the roots and outer leaves from the leeks, and slit them down the sides so that you can open them up and wash them under the tap. Then cut them into 1 cm/½ inch lengths. After the rice has been cooking for 15 minutes, put the leeks into the pan on top – but don't stir. Cover and leave it to cook for a further 10 minutes, after which put the drained kidney beans into the pan on top of the leeks. Cover and cook for a further 5-10 minutes, until the kidney beans are hot, the leeks tender, the rice cooked and all the water absorbed.

Remove from the heat, sprinkle in the garam masala and season to taste. Fork through gently to mix everything and fluff the rice before serving.

SERVES 4

Some canned beans contain sugar, others do not. I prefer to use ones without sugar. If you would rather use dried beans, soak 100g/3½ oz overnight, drain, put into a pan with plenty of water, boil hard for 10 minutes, then leave to simmer for 1-1¼ hours, or until the beans are tender.

PUREE OF BUTTER BEANS WITH ROSEMARY AND BAKED ONIONS

This combination is very warming and good even though it's simplicity itself to put together. It makes a complete meal, although you could serve some steamed carrots or wilted spinach, too, for a bit of extra colour and flavour. I generally use canned butter beans to save time – I choose the ones that have been canned in water and salt but without sugar.

8 medium onions, unpeeled	sea salt, preferably Maldon, and freshly ground black pepper
2 × 425g / 15oz cans butter beans, or prepared dried butter beans	butter
	extra chopped fresh rosemary to garnish
good sprig of fresh rosemary	olive oil

Start by preparing the onions. Wash and dry them, then place them, unpeeled, on a dry baking sheet or in a roasting tin. Bake in a hot oven – 230°C/ 450°F/Gas Mark 8 – for 30–45 minutes, or until they feel tender when pierced with a sharp knife.

When the onions are almost done, prepare the purée. Put the butter beans into a saucepan (together with their liquid) and heat gently until they are very hot, then drain them but keep the liquid. Mash the butter beans or whizz them to a smooth purée in a food processor, adding enough of the reserved liquid to make a creamy consistency. Add the rosemary – you can whizz this with the butter beans if you're using a food processor, otherwise chop it by hand. It's best to add it a little at a time, as it's quite pungent. Season the butter bean purée with salt and pepper, then reheat it and keep it warm until you're ready.

Put two onions on each plate – you can leave them whole, or break them open – and put some butter, Maldon salt and freshly ground black pepper on each, along with the purée. Just before serving, top the purée with a bit more chopped rosemary and a spoonful of good olive oil.

SERVES 4

CURRIED ROOT VEGETABLES WITH CORIANDER RAITA

Any root vegetables can be used for this warming winter dish: carrots, kohlrabi, celeriac, parsnips, along with some cauliflower and spices. This is one of those dishes that is even better the next day, after the flavours have had a chance to develop thoroughly. Serve simply with the coriander raita or, for a more substantial meal, with some cooked rice.

900g / 2lb mixed root vegetables	1 × 400g / 14oz can tomatoes
4 tbls olive oil	1 small cauliflower
2 onions, peeled and chopped	1 tsp garam masala
1 green chilli	salt and freshly ground black pepper
walnut-sized piece of fresh ginger	
4 garlic cloves, crushed	FOR THE RAITA
½ tsp turmeric	300ml / ½ pint plain low-fat yogurt
2 tsp ground coriander	3-4 tbls chopped fresh coriander leaves
2 tsp ground cumin	

Peel the root vegetables and cut them into dice. Heat the oil in a large saucepan, put in the onions, cover and cook for 10 minutes. Halve, de-seed and slice the chilli, being careful to wash your hands afterwards and to keep the juice away from your eyes. Peel and grate the ginger, then add the chilli and ginger to the onions, together with the garlic, turmeric, ground coriander and cumin. Give it a good stir, add the root vegetables and stir again. Cover and let it cook gently for a minute or two while you open the tomatoes and drain and measure the juice. Chop the tomatoes and add them to the pan; make up the juice to 300 ml/10 fl oz, and add that too. Bring it to the boil, then cover and cook for 15-20 minutes, or until the root vegetables are almost tender.

Meanwhile, cut the cauliflower into quite small pieces and add to the pan; stir well, cover and cook for a further 10 minutes or so until the cauliflower is tender. Stir in the garam masala and add salt and pepper to taste.

To make the raita, simply mix together the yogurt and chopped coriander, stir well, then season with salt and pepper. Serve with the curry.
SERVES 4

CABBAGE TAGLIATELLE WITH CREAM CHEESE AND MUSHROOM SAUCE

In this recipe, spring greens are treated like tagliatelle and served with a creamy sauce, to make a delicious main course. The Tomato and Basil Vinaigrette which follows goes particularly well with it.

450g / 1lb spring greens	salt and freshly ground
125g / 4oz button	black pepper
mushrooms	
1 tbls olive oil	
75g / 3oz Boursin	
cream cheese with	
garlic and herbs	

Fill a medium-large saucepan with 5 cm/2 inches of water and put on the stove to heat up. Wash the greens, removing any tough stems or damaged leaves, then shred them into fine, long strips, like tagliatelle. When the water boils, put in the greens, cover the pan, and let them cook for 4 minutes or until just done.

Meanwhile, wash and slice the mushrooms and fry them in the olive oil for 3-4 minutes, until they are tender. Drain the greens, put them back in the hot pan with the mushrooms, and stir in the Boursin and a little salt and freshly ground black pepper to taste. Serve immediately.
SERVES 2

LEEKS PARMESAN

Another very simple dish which tastes really good. I like it as a quick and easy main course, but it also makes an interesting first course baked in little individual ramekins.

450g / 1lb leeks	*50g / 2oz Parmesan, freshly grated is best, but you can get away with ready-grated*

Set the oven to 200°C/400°F/Gas Mark 6. Trim the roots from the leeks, then cut off any tough-looking green parts. Slit them down the side then wash them under the cold tap, opening up the layers so that you get out all the grit. Cut the leeks into 2.5 cm/1 inch lengths. Bring 5 cm/2 inches of water to the boil in a medium saucepan, put in the leeks, cover, and cook for 7-10 minutes, or until they feel tender when pierced with the point of a sharp knife.

Drain the leeks – keep the liquid as it makes very good stock – and put them into a shallow ovenproof dish. Sprinkle the Parmesan cheese on top so that the leeks are covered, then bake for 20-30 minutes, until the top is golden brown and crisp. Serve at once, from the dish.
SERVES 2

TOMATO AND BASIL VINAIGRETTE

For this salad, which I shamelessly make all the year round now that firm tomatoes and fresh basil are available, simply slice 1-2 tomatoes for each person and put them into a bowl. Tear up some fresh basil leaves and add these to the bowl, along with a splash of red wine vinegar, a little olive oil and a seasoning of salt and a grinding of pepper. Mix it all together and serve.

You can also make a good vegan version of this by mixing the leeks with a knob of margarine before putting them in the dish, and by using ground almonds instead of grated Parmesan cheese for the topping.

WHOLEWHEAT PASTA TWISTS WITH BROCCOLI AND FROMAGE FRAIS

For a long time I avoided wholewheat pasta, having had some unfortunate experiences with it. However I've recently started experimenting with it again, and I've had some pleasant surprises, this dish being one of them. I find the nutty flavour of the pasta goes really well with the creamy, slightly sharp, sauce. I like to serve this with a tomato and basil salad like the one on the previous page.

225g / 8oz wholewheat pasta twists
15g / ½oz butter
salt and freshly ground black pepper

450g / 1lb broccoli
400g / 14oz fromage frais, very low fat or 8% fat

Bring a large pan of water to the boil, then put in the pasta, bring the water back to a fast boil, and cook the pasta for about 8 minutes, or as suggested on the packet, testing it just before the time given. Drain the pasta, return it to the pan and add the butter and salt and pepper to taste.

While the pasta is cooking, prepare the sauce. Bring 2.5 cm/1 inch of water to the boil in a large pan; wash the broccoli and cut into florets, removing tough stems. Put the broccoli into the boiling water, cover and cook for about 3 minutes, or until it is just tender. Drain, then add the fromage frais and salt and pepper to taste. Keep the sauce warm until the pasta is done, but don't let it get near boiling point or the fromage frais may separate.

Serve the pasta out on to warmed serving plates and spoon the sauce on top.

SERVES 4

SPLIT PEA AND SPINACH DHAL — WITH RAITA AND CHUTNEY

I find this a pleasant combination of flavours and colours just as it is; but for a more substantial meal you could add some fluffy cooked brown rice.

225g / 8 oz yellow split peas
1 onion, peeled and chopped
1 garlic clove, chopped
1 green chilli
2 tsp cumin seeds
½ tsp turmeric
225g / 8oz tender spinach leaves, stalks removed
1 tsp garam masala
squeeze of fresh lemon juice
salt and freshly ground black pepper

FOR THE RAITA
½ cucumber
300ml / ½ pint plain low-fat yogurt

FOR THE CHUTNEY
4 tomatoes
1 small onion, peeled and sliced
1 tbls lemon juice
1-2 tbls chopped fresh coriander leaves

Put the split peas into a medium-large saucepan with the onion and 850 ml/1½ pints of water, the garlic, the whole green chilli, cumin and turmeric. Bring to the boil, then let it simmer, half-covered, for about 45 minutes, or until the peas are very tender and the mixture is thick but not sticking. Put in the spinach and cook for a further few minutes, until the spinach is tender. Add the garam masala, lemon juice and salt and pepper to taste.

While the dhal is cooking, prepare the accompaniments. Peel the cucumber then cut it into small dice. Put these into a bowl and stir in the yogurt and some salt and pepper. For the chutney, slice the tomatoes and put them into a bowl with the onion, lemon juice, chopped coriander and salt and pepper. Stir, then leave on one side for the flavours to blend. Serve the raita and chutney with the dhal.

OPPOSITE: *Wholewheat Pasta Twists with Broccoli and Fromage Frais*

SEASONAL PUDDINGS

SATSUMA SYLLABUB

You can whisk these up in no time for a refreshing end to a meal. They're rich, so serve small portions – wine glasses make ideal containers for them.

4 satsumas
150ml / 5fl oz double
  cream
15-25g / ½-1oz caster
  sugar, or an apricot
  no-added-sugar jam
  to taste

TO DECORATE
curls of satsuma skin

Wash two of the satsumas, then grate the zest part of the rind finely into a bowl. Add the cream, stir, cover and leave for at least 30 minutes (or as long as overnight) for the flavours to infuse. Strain the cream through a nylon sieve into another bowl, pressing through as much of the oily rind as you can, to give flavour but to keep the texture of the syllabub smooth. Squeeze the juice from all the satsumas and add to the cream.

Half-whisk the cream, then stir in sugar or no-added-sugar apricot jam to taste. Whisk again, fairly gently to prevent curdling, until the mixture makes soft peaks, then spoon the mixture into small individual serving bowls or glasses.

Cover and chill until ready to serve, but don't make these too far in advance as the mixture may begin to separate after about an hour. Decorate with the satsuma curls before serving.

SERVES 4

ARMAGNAC PARFAIT

This parfait is a wonderful dessert for a special occasion; as it's rich it freezes to a velvet-smooth texture without any stirring, so you can put it straight into a mould and just turn it out for serving. The better the quality of the armagnac, the better the result. It makes an excellent Christmas pudding.

6 egg yolks
150g / 5oz caster sugar

600ml / 1 pint double
  or whipping cream
4 tbls armagnac

Put the egg yolks into a bowl and whisk until they are pale and thick, preferably using an electric whisk.

Prepare a syrup by putting the sugar into a medium saucepan with 4 tablespoons of water. Heat gently until the sugar has melted, then let it bubble for a minute or so until a drop of it on the back of the spoon forms a thread when pulled with a teaspoon. (It reaches this stage very quickly.) Immediately remove the pan from the heat and pour the syrup on to the egg yolks while you whisk them. Continue to whisk for 4-5 minutes, until the mixture is cool and very thick and creamy.

Whip the cream until it holds its shape, then fold it into the egg yolk mixture, along with the armagnac. Pour the mixture into a suitable container and freeze until firm. Remove from the freezer about 15 minutes before you want to serve the parfait, and serve in scoops.

SERVES 6

OPPOSITE: *Satsuma Syllabub*

RICH CHOCOLATE ICE CREAM

This is very rich and smooth. It's my favourite chocolate ice-cream recipe, and one of my all-time favourite chocolate dishes.

5 tbls cocoa powder
4 egg yolks
175g / 6oz caster sugar
1.2L / 2 pints single cream

200g / 7oz plain chocolate, at least 50% cocoa solids

Put the cocoa into a bowl with the egg yolks and sugar and blend to a smooth paste with some of the single cream. Put the rest of the cream into a saucepan and add the chocolate, broken into pieces. Heat the cream and chocolate over a gentle heat until the chocolate has melted and the mixture just comes to the boil. Pour some of it over the cocoa mixture, mix well, and pour the cocoa mixture back into the saucepan. Heat gently, stirring frequently, until the mixture thickens enough to coat the back of the spoon, but don't let it boil. (This only takes a minute or so.) Take it off the heat and let it cool, stirring from time to time to prevent a skin from forming.

Pour the cool mixture into a polythene container and freeze until it is solid around the edges. Then beat it well and put it back into the freezer until solid. Remove it from the freezer 15 minutes or so before you want to eat it, to give it a chance to soften up a bit.

SERVES 8

CRANBERRY AND CINNAMON CHEESECAKE

175g / 6 oz semi-sweet wholewheat biscuits
75g / 3oz butter
1 tsp ground cinnamon
200g / 7oz Philadelphia cream cheese
400ml / ¾ pint soured cream
1 egg and 1 egg yolk

75g / 3oz caster sugar
1 tbls lemon juice
½ tsp real vanilla essence

FOR THE TOPPING

125g / 4oz cranberries
75g / 3oz sugar

Set the oven to 160°C/325°F/Gas Mark 3.

Put the biscuits on a chopping board and crush them to crumbs with a rolling pin. Melt the butter in a medium saucepan, then mix in the crushed biscuits and cinnamon. Spread the mixture evenly over the base of a 20 cm/8 inch springform cake tin and press it down with a jam jar. Pop this into the oven for 10 minutes while you make the filling.

Put the cream cheese into a bowl and beat until it is smooth, then gradually beat in the soured cream, egg and egg yolk, sugar, lemon juice and vanilla, to make a smooth, fairly liquid mixture. Pour this into the tin on top of the biscuit crumb base and bake for 1-1¼ hours, or until the cheesecake is set, and a skewer inserted into the centre comes out clean. Turn off the oven but leave the cheesecake in there for 1 hour, then cool and, finally, chill it. The cheesecake benefits from several hours of chilling, or overnight.

To make the topping, wash the cranberries and remove any damaged ones. Put them into a saucepan with 1 tablespoon of water and cook gently for about 5 minutes, or until the cranberries are tender but not mushy. Add the sugar and heat gently until the sugar has dissolved. Boil for 1-2 minutes, until the mixture looks quite jammy, then remove from the heat and pour evenly over the top of the cheesecake.

SERVES 6-8

For a lemon and star fruit variation, omit the cinnamon. Add a good teaspoonful of grated lemon rind to the cheese mixture. Instead of cranberries, spread a small carton of soured cream over the top of the cheesecake after it is cooked, then leave it in the oven for 1 hour to cool down, as described. Decorate with star fruit, cut thinly to produce pretty stars.

OPPOSITE: *Cranberry and Cinnamon Cheesecake*

WINTER MENUS

———— ❧ ————

MENU

CHRISTMAS DINNER
FOR SIX

Watercress and Red Pepper with Mascarpone
❧

*Christmas Wreath with Cranberries
and Porcini Sauce
Carrots in Parsley Butter
Baby Brussels Sprouts
Cock's Comb Roast Potatoes (see page 363)
Christmas Salad with Truffle Oil*
❧

Armagnac Parfait (see page 262)

———— COUNTDOWN ————

Up to a week before:
Make the Armagnac Parfait.

The day before:
Make the Porcini Sauce and the Vinaigrette for the
salad. Prepare the Christmas Wreath ready for baking;
prepare the carrots, sprouts and potatoes, ready for
cooking. Grill and skin the peppers; wash the
watercress and the salad vegetables and store in
polythene bags in the fridge.

1½ hours before:
Set the oven to 160°C/325°F/Gas Mark 3. Parboil the
potatoes, heat oil in the oven, and put the potatoes on
to cook; put the Christmas Wreath into the oven about
1 hour before the meal. Assemble the Watercress
Starter; make the Christmas Salad but don't toss it.

10 minutes before:
Prepare pans for the carrots and sprouts; gently reheat
the sauce. Cook the sprouts and carrots just
before you sit down to the meal; drain them, put into
warmed serving dishes and keep warm.

WATERCRESS AND RED
PEPPER WITH
MASCARPONE

*The colours in this dish make it look like Christmas-
on-a-plate! If you prepare the pepper in advance, have
the watercress washed and the dressing already made
in a jar, the dish can be assembled in moments.*

*2 large red peppers
packet or bunch of
watercress
6 tbls olive oil
2 tbls wine vinegar*

*salt and freshly ground
black pepper
225g / 8oz mascarpone
cheese*

First prepare the red peppers. Cut them into quarters, then put them shiny-side up on a grill pan and
grill at full heat until the skin has blistered and
begun to char. Move them halfway through the
grilling so that all the skin gets done. Leave until
they're cool enough to handle, then slip off the
skins with a sharp knife – they'll come off easily –
and rinse the peppers under the tap to remove the
seeds. Cut the peppers into long thin strips, put
them into a shallow container, cover and keep cool.

Wash and remove stems from the watercress as
necessary; put into a polythene bag in the bottom of
the fridge until required. Make a quick vinaigrette
by putting the oil into a jar with the vinegar, some
salt and a grinding of pepper; shake well, then keep
until required.

To assemble the dish, put some sprigs of watercress on six small plates and arrange some red pepper on top, dividing it among the plates. Then,
using two teaspoons, put heaped teaspoons of mascarpone dotted around on top, about five to a plate.
Coarsely grind some black pepper over the mascarpone. Give the vinaigrette a quick shake, then
spoon a little over each plate.

OPPOSITE: *Christmas Dinner for Six*

CHRISTMAS WREATH WITH CRANBERRIES

To accompany this menu, choose either a medium – or full-bodied red such as Côtes du Rhône (domaine bottled), Claret or Chianti Classico ; or a medium – dry, fruity white such as Bouches-du-Rhône.

A dramatic centrepiece for a Christmas meal, this Christmas wreath goes well with all the traditional trimmings, and slices well both hot and cold. I love the strong taste of Stilton, but Cheddar, goat's cheese or even feta could be used for different flavours, according to your taste; and you can replace the broccoli with celeriac or other vegetables.

700g / 1½lb large leeks
700g / 1½lb broccoli
butter for greasing
250g / 9oz Stilton
  cheese, grated
150ml / 5fl oz single
  cream
4 eggs, beaten
3 tbls chopped fresh
  parsley
6 tsp chopped fresh
  thyme

salt and freshly ground
  black pepper

FOR THE CRANBERRIES

225g / 8oz cranberries
2 tbls all-fruit cherry
  and redcurrant soft-
  set fruit spread
sprigs of flat-leaf
  parsley and rosemary
sugar to taste

Trim the leeks and remove any tough leaves. Slit the sides of the leeks and rinse them thoroughly under the tap, then cook the leeks in a large saucepan of boiling water for about 20 minutes, or until they are very tender. Drain well – the water makes good stock for the sauce – refresh the leeks under the cold tap, and drain well again. Trim any tough stems from the broccoli, then chop it into fairly small pieces. (There should be 450g/1lb after trimming.) Cook the broccoli for about 5 minutes in boiling water until tender, then drain.

Set the oven to 160°C/325°F/Gas Mark 3. Grease a 1.5 L/2½ pint ring mould generously with butter. Lay single leaves of leek down the sides and base of the ring, going right round until it is all covered. Let the ends hang over the edge for the moment, don't cut them. Chop the rest of the leeks finely and mix with the broccoli, Stilton cheese, cream, eggs, parsley, thyme and salt and pepper to taste. Pour the mixture into the mould – it won't quite fill it, to allow the mixture to rise a little during cooking – and fold the overhanging leek leaves over the top.

Put the ring into a baking tin and pour boiling water around, to come halfway up the mould. Cover with foil and bake for 1 hour, or until the mould is set.

While the mould is cooking, prepare the cranberries for the decoration and sauce. Wash the cranberries, removing any bad ones. Reserve some for decoration, and put the remainder into a saucepan with the fruit spread. Cook gently for about 5 minutes, or until the berries are soft but not mushy. Remove from the heat.

When the mould is done, take it out of the oven and remove the foil. Loosen the edges of the mould, then turn it out on to a large round warm plate. If a small amount of liquid appears in the centre, blot it up with kitchen paper.

Arrange leaves of flat-leaf parsley and a few tiny sprigs of rosemary all round the top, to resemble a Christmas wreath, then arrange a few cranberries on top, at intervals, to resemble holly berries. Add a few cranberries and sprigs of rosemary around the base if you wish. Sweeten the rest of the cranberry mixture to taste as necessary, and serve it in a bowl or jug, to accompany the wreath.

PORCINI SAUCE

The wine makes this extra rich and tasty, but it is also extremely good without it – simply increase the amount of stock instead.

20g / ¾oz dried porcini
400ml / ¾ pint
  vegetable stock
50g / 2oz butter
300ml / ½ pint dry red
  or white wine

1 tbls Madeira wine or
  brandy
1 tbls double cream
salt and freshly ground
  black pepper

Put the porcini into a saucepan with the stock and bring to the boil; remove from the heat and leave them to soak for at least 1 hour, or even overnight. After this, strain the stock into a bowl through a very fine sieve or a piece of muslin. Chop the porcini finely, by hand or in a food processor.

Melt the butter in a medium saucepan and add the porcini; cook over a gentle heat for 5 minutes, then add the liquid you drained off the porcini, along with the wine. Bring to the boil, and let the mixture bubble away for several minutes until it is reduced by half. Stir in the Madeira or brandy and the cream, and season with salt and freshly ground black pepper. Serve with the Christmas Wreath.

CARROTS IN PARSLEY BUTTER

You can use baby carrots, or larger ones cut into matchsticks, allowing 700g/1½lb for six people. Scrape and cut the carrots as necessary – baby ones will just need washing – then cook them in boiling water to cover for 4-5 minutes, or until they are just tender. Drain, add a knob of butter, 1-2 tablespoons chopped parsley, a squeeze of lemon juice and salt and freshly ground black pepper to taste.

BABY BRUSSELS SPROUTS

If you can get really tiny Brussels sprouts, they can be cooked whole; otherwise, with larger ones, I prefer to cut them in half as I find they do not go soggy this way. Either way, you'll need 700g/1½lb for six people. Trim the sprouts as necessary, then cook in 1 cm/½ inch of fast-boiling water, with a lid on the pan, for 3-5 minutes, or until they're just done. Drain, add a little butter and some salt, freshly ground black pepper and grated nutmeg.

CHRISTMAS SALAD WITH TRUFFLE OIL

Some truffle oil (which you can buy at specialist delicatessens) makes this salad extra special. Choose tender salad leaves – ordinary lettuce, plus some lamb's lettuce (mâche) makes a good combination, or a good continental salad bowl mix. Have the leaves washed and ready, stored in a polythene bag in the fridge. Make up a vinaigrette by putting 3 tablespoons truffle oil into a jar with 1 tablespoon red wine vinegar, some salt and a grinding of pepper; shake well, then keep until required.

Just before you want to eat the salad, give the dressing a quick shake, then pour it into a salad bowl; put in the leaves on top of the dressing, toss the salad gently, and serve.

MENU

WINTER BUFFET FOR TEN TO TWELVE

A Trio of Dips - Roquefort, Goat's Cheese and Fresh Herb

Celeriac Terrine with Red Pepper Sauce
Warm Red Cabbage and Cherry Tomato Salad
Broccoli and Brie Bake
Little Gem and Watercress Salad

❧

Compôte of Exotic Fruits
Fruits Dipped in Chocolate
Chocolate Truffles

❧

Glühwein

COUNTDOWN

The day before:
Prepare and bake the Celeriac Terrine; make the Red Pepper Sauce. Prepare the Broccoli and Brie Bake ready for baking, cover well. Make the Chocolate Truffles and the Exotic Fruit Salad.

Several hours before:
Make the dips; cover and keep in a cool place. Make the Red Cabbage Salad but don't add the tomatoes. Wash the lettuce and watercress, keep in a polythene bag in the fridge; make the dressing. Prepare the Fruits Dipped in Chocolate.

10 minutes before:
Preheat the oven; 20-30 minutes before you want to eat, put in the Broccoli Bake. Make the Mulled Wine. Finish making the Red Cabbage Salad and the Lettuce Salad.

ROQUEFORT, GOAT'S CHEESE AND FRESH HERB DIPS

These dips are all simple to make and, I think, particularly good with some crudités, although crisps and tortilla chips are popular with them too.

FOR THE ROQUEFORT DIP	FOR THE FRESH HERB DIP
100g / 3½ oz Roquefort cheese	300ml / ½ pint soured cream
100g / 3½ oz fromage frais	3-4 tbls chopped fresh herbs: chives, marjoram, chervil, for instance, as available
FOR THE GOAT'S CHEESE DIP	salt and freshly ground black pepper
100g / 3½ oz goat's cheese log	
100g / 3½ oz fromage frais, a little milk or soured cream	

Either whizz the Roquefort and fromage frais to a cream in a food processor, or crumble the Roquefort into a bowl then mash with a fork, gradually adding the fromage frais until the mixture is smooth and creamy.

Make the goat's cheese dip in the same way; a food processor is probably best if the goat's cheese has a rind on it; or you could cut this off, depending on its state. If the dip seems a little dry when the ingredients have been mixed together, add a little milk or a little of the soured cream that you've got for the next dip, to soften it.

To make the fresh herb dip, put the soured cream into a bowl then stir in the chopped fresh herbs and some salt and freshly ground black pepper to taste.

OPPOSITE: *Dishes from Winter Buffet for Ten to Twelve*

CELERIAC TERRINE WITH RED PEPPER SAUCE

This is an excellent terrine which slices well either hot or cold and goes well with many autumn or winter vegetables.

700g / 1½ lb celeriac
25g / 1oz butter
125g / 4oz Cheddar
  cheese, grated
25g / 1oz freshly grated
  Parmesan cheese
4 tbls snipped chives
3 eggs
salt and freshly ground
  black pepper
cherry tomatoes and
  chives to garnish

FOR THE RED PEPPER
SAUCE

2 tbls olive oil
2 onions, peeled and
  sliced
2 red peppers
150ml / ¼ pint stock
salt and freshly ground
  black pepper
15g / ½ oz cold butter

Set the oven to 160°C/325°F/Gas Mark 3.

Line a 450g/1lb loaf tin with a piece of non-stick paper to cover the base and extend up the short sides; grease the other sides. Peel the celeriac, cut it into even-sized chunks and cook in boiling water to cover for about 15 minutes, or until the celeriac is tender. Drain – the water makes wonderful stock – then add the butter and mash, but don't purée because some texture is good in this dish. Mix in the Cheddar and Parmesan cheeses, the chives, eggs and salt and pepper to taste.

Spoon the mixture into the prepared tin and level the top. Bake for about 50 minutes, or until the terrine feels firm to the touch, looks golden brown and a skewer inserted into the middle comes out clean.

While the terrine is baking, make the red pepper sauce. Heat the oil in a saucepan, put in the onions and cook with a lid on the pan for 5 minutes. Meanwhile, wash the peppers and cut them into rough pieces – there's no need to remove the seeds because the sauce will be strained. Add the peppers to the onions, cover the pan again and cook gently for a further 5 minutes. Pour in the stock, cover and simmer for about 10 minutes, or until the peppers are tender. Liquidize the sauce, strain

it into a saucepan and season to taste.

When the terrine is cooked, remove from the oven and slip a knife around the sides to loosen, then turn it out on to a warmed plate. Garnish with halved cherry tomatoes and small strips of chives. Just before serving, bring the sauce to the boil, remove from the heat and whisk in the butter, a little at a time, to make the sauce glossy. Serve with the terrine.

WARM RED CABBAGE AND CHERRY TOMATO SALAD

Halfway between a cooked vegetable dish and a salad, this goes well with many winter dishes.

450g / 1lb red cabbage
1 onion
2 tbls olive oil
2 tbls red wine vinegar
225-350g / 8-12oz
  cherry tomatoes,
  halved

4 tbls snipped chives
salt and freshly ground
  black pepper

Wash and shred the cabbage as finely as you can; peel and slice the onion. Heat the oil in a large saucepan and put in the cabbage and onion, cover and cook gently for about 10 minutes, or until the cabbage is tender, stirring from time to time; finally, add the vinegar. This can be done in advance.

Just before you want to serve the salad, gently re-heat the cabbage; stir in the cherry tomatoes and chives, check the seasoning and serve.

As an alternative to- or as well as - the mulled wine, I'd suggest serving a light dry white wine such as Muscadet.

Other root vegetables such as carrots or parsnips could be used to make the terrine as a change from celeriac.

BROCCOLI AND BRIE BAKE

Although the flavour and texture of real Parmesan cheese cut from a block is best for many dishes, for this particular one, I prefer to use ready-grated Parmesan cheese from a carton. It makes a particularly dry, crunchy, golden-brown topping which contrasts well with the creamy sauce formed by the Brie melting into the cream in this dish.

700g / 1½lb broccoli
350g / 12oz Brie
150ml / 5fl oz single
  cream

75g / 3oz ready-grated
  Parmesan cheese

Set the oven to 200°C/400°F/Gas Mark 6.

Wash the broccoli and cut the florets into smallish pieces. Pare the stems with a sharp knife or potato peeler to remove the tough, outer layer, then cut the stems, too, into small pieces. Cook the broccoli in 2.5 cm/1 inch of boiling water, or in a steamer, for 4-5 minutes or a bit longer, until it is just tender. Put the stems in first and give them a minute or two before adding the florets which cook more quickly. Drain the broccoli and put it into a shallow casserole dish.

Cut up the Brie, including the rind, and add to the casserole, distributing evenly. Pour over the cream. Mash the broccoli and Brie into the cream a little with a fork, then sprinkle the Parmesan on top, to cover it evenly. Bake for 15-20 minutes, or until bubbly, golden-brown and crisp.

LITTLE GEM AND WATERCRESS SALAD

Three little gem lettuces and a bunch or packet of watercress will be ample for this buffet. Have the lettuce and watercress washed and ready, stored in a polythene bag in the fridge. Make up a vinaigrette by putting 3 tablespoons olive oil into a jar with 1 tablespoon red wine vinegar, some salt and a grinding of pepper; shake well, then keep until required.

Just before you want to eat the salad, give the dressing a quick shake, then pour it into a salad bowl; tear the leaves roughly and put them in on top, toss the salad gently, and serve.

COMPOTE OF EXOTIC FRUITS

Lychees make a fragrant base for this, well worth the effort of removing their hard skins and stones. To these I've added pawpaws, which are sweet and excellent as long as they're ripe – they should be flecked with yellow and give a little when lightly pressed. Sharon fruits are ripe when they feel quite soft to the touch. Together, these fruits make a compôte which is sweet but refreshing and needs absolutely no accompaniment.

700g / 1½lb lychees
2 large ripe pawpaws

4 ripe sharon fruits

Remove the hard skin and stones from the lychees; put the flesh into a bowl. Cut the paw-paws in half, scoop out the shiny black seeds, remove the peel and cut the flesh into pieces. Add to the bowl. Quarter the sharon fruits, cut off the skin and slice the quarters into pieces; put into the bowl with the rest of the fruit. Give it a stir, then cover and leave for an hour or so, or until required.

The flavours will blend and the juices will run, making a little natural syrup; if you leave it overnight in the fridge, this syrup will become almost jellied.

FRUITS DIPPED IN CHOCOLATE

Choose a selection of fruits for this, according to taste; grapes, strawberries and physalis are particularly good. You can use all plain chocolate, or a mixture of plain and white.

225g / 8oz plain
  chocolate, at least
  50% cocoa solids

about 700g / 1½lb
  assorted fruits

Break the chocolate into a bowl set over a pan of simmering water and heat gently until it has melted. Wash the fruits and dry them carefully, then dip them into the chocolate so that they are half-coated. Put them on a rack covered with non-stick paper and leave to set.

CHOCOLATE TRUFFLES

These are a bit fiddly to make, but they are a really special treat. This quantity makes about 30 truffles.

225g / 8oz plain
  chocolate, at least
  50% cocoa solids,
  broken up
300ml / ½ pint double
  cream

cocoa powder, icing
  sugar, finely chopped
  toasted hazelnuts to
  coat

Put the chocolate and cream into a bowl set over a saucepan of simmering water and heat gently until the chocolate has melted. Remove from the heat and cool quickly by placing the bowl in a bowl of cold water. Once it is cold and beginning to set, whisk it hard until it's thick and light – an electric whisk is best for this. (If it refuses to go thick, it isn't

cold enough yet. Put the bowl back in cold water and leave for a few minutes longer.) Put the whipped chocolate mixture into the fridge to chill until it's solid enough to shape.

Sprinkle a tablespoonful of cocoa on to a plate then, using two teaspoons, put generous teaspoonfuls of the chocolate mixture on top of the cocoa. Sift another tablespoonful of cocoa on top, dust your hands with more cocoa, then quickly roll the teaspoonfuls of mixture between your palms to make truffles, adding more cocoa to coat as necessary. Repeat the process using the other coatings in the same way. Put them on to a small plate and chill until needed.

GLÜHWEIN

Mulled wine, Austrian style, is warming and welcoming on a chilly night.

1 litre/1¾ pints cheap red wine
juice of 1 orange
juice of 1 lemon
1 teaspoon whole cloves
1 cinnamon stick, broken in half
75–100 g/3–4 oz caster sugar

Pour the wine into a large saucepan and add the orange juice, lemon juice, cloves and cinnamon. Add most of the sugar and heat gently, without boiling. Taste and add more sugar if necessary. If you don't like the whole spices, you can strain the Glühwein into a warmed serving bowl, or tie the spices in a piece of muslin and remove before serving.

OPPOSITE: *Sweets from Winter Buffet for Ten to Twelve*

275

I love Christmas. The fun, the memories, the spicy smells, the goodwill. Yes, like everyone else I deplore the exploitation and the pressures, the Christmas catalogues dropping through the letter box before the end of the summer and the carols being played in shops in November, but however much I may grumble about these things, the Christmas magic always gets to me in the end.

We always had especially wonderful Christmases when I was a child. My parents, sister and I, along with my aunt, uncle and cousins, always spent Christmas with my grandparents in their house in the country. This was great fun, with lots of excitement and racing around the house and garden, as well as singing – and listening to – carols, a beautiful service on Christmas Eve in the chapel there, and a short meditation at noon on Christmas Day. Then we had Christmas dinner, and opened all the presents which were kept under the tree until after the Queen's speech.

What really made Christmas special, though, was my grandmother's approach to it. My grandmother, Grace Cooke, was a very remarkable woman, a mystic and seer. Although she considered herself to be a Christian, and had a deep love and respect for Jesus, she thought of Christmas as being symbolic of an older, universal truth, not confined to the Christian church. She saw the birth of the baby Jesus in a dark cave or in a stable, as a symbol of the awakening of the light of love in every human heart.

It was her belief (and mine, too) that all of us have that light of love – the spark of divinity – within ourselves. We express it when we give and receive love, and it is at these times we feel happy within ourselves; but when we cut ourselves off from that centre, we become out of sorts with ourselves and others. We are probably most aware of this power when we fall in love – our heart really opens, and everything seems magical. We also notice it at Christmas, when we think about other people more than we usually do and there is a general feeling of goodwill and the dropping of barriers.

The sense of universality and brotherhood which this approach to Christmas gives appeals to me very much: no race or religious creed is excluded; the awakening of the light of love in our hearts is something which we can all experience and celebrate. For me it is especially significant that Christmas is at the time of the winter solstice when, in the northern hemisphere, the sun – or light – begins to get closer to us again.

All are reasons for celebration, of which preparing and eating wonderful meals together is a natural and important part. Christmas cooking is, for most people, the great culinary feast, not to say feat, of the year. Even people who do not do a great deal of cooking during the rest of the year find themselves doing so at Christmas and need good, reliable recipes. This is especially true if they find themselves having to cook for one or more of the increasing number of vegetarians!

This chapter aims to answer this need. It's a collection of all the tips, ideas and best recipes for Christmas that I've gathered over the years, as well as exciting new ones. So whether you've just one vegetarian to cater for, or a crowd, or just want some fresh and delicious ideas for festive food, I hope you'll find it helpful: a warm and practical cook's companion.

A
VEGETARIAN
CHRISTMAS

PLANNING & PREPARATION

One of the great pleasures of traditional Christmas cooking is that not only can it be done well in advance, but it's actually all the better for it. So when new supplies of plump dried fruit fill the shops, you can fill the house with the warm and spicy smells of Christmas and get the cake, pudding and mincemeat made and stored away, knowing that they will only improve with time. Shopping for ingredients and equipment, and the making of these delicious, traditional dishes, can be fitted in over several days and weeks, giving you a chance to produce them when it is convenient for you.

Good Christmas planning can begin as early as October, with the listing and buying of ingredients, the checking of tins and equipment, the making of menu plans and the gradual filling up of the store-cupboard and freezer. Done in this relaxed and gradual way, Christmas preparations can be enjoyed as the pleasure they really are. One of the bonuses is that there is time for other people, especially the children, to join in if they wish, which adds to the fun and sense of anticipation. Then, when Christmas arrives, with the majority of the work done, you can relax (mostly!) with everyone else, and have a really good time. I have found that the earlier I make my preparations, the more I enjoy them – and the more I enjoy Christmas itself.

Having said that, I must add that I know that Octobers don't always work out like that, nor Novembers, and there have certainly been times when I have been making a Christmas cake in the week before Christmas and icing it on Christmas Eve! So in this chapter you'll find a wonderful Last Minute Christmas Cake, as well as plenty of not-too-demanding but rather special recipes for every meal, since I know that even people who don't cook or entertain a great deal during the year find that they do so at Christmas, either through desire or necessity. I hope you'll enjoy them.

I've also considered the fact that many people are, I know, cooking for one or more vegetarians as well as for meat-eaters. Under these circumstances, there are two courses of action: sometimes everyone can enjoy a completely vegetarian meal; at other times, you can share the vegetables and accompaniments (as long as these are made without animal products like meat stock, gelatine or dripping etc), and the vegetarians can have their own main course.

Often, in practice, I've found that the meat-eaters like to share this, too, as a kind of extra side-dish to their meat, so you need to make enough. I rather like it when this happens; I certainly like to avoid a 'them' and 'us' approach, more a mutual acceptance of dietary preferences and a sharing of food. Of course, this does inevitably mean extra work for the cook, which is where advance preparation is such a help.

Most of the main courses in this chapter freeze really well, as do parts of the meal, such as crêpes, sauces, stuffings, pastry cases and so on, so that if you have some of these stashed away in the freezer, you can combine them with fresh vegetables, eggs, milk or cheese (if they eat these) and put together a delicious dish for one or two unexpected vegetarians in no time at all.

You'll find my specific freezer recommendations and standby recipes later in this section. But to begin the preparations, and get yourself into the mood early, I recommend that you stick with tradition and make the cake, the pudding and the pies first.

TRADITIONAL CHRISTMAS CAKE

700 g/1½ lb mixed dried
fruit
100 g/4 oz candied peel,
chopped
225 g/8 oz glacé cherries
150 ml/5 fl oz sherry or
orange juice
250 g/9 oz plain
wholewheat flour and
plain white flour, mixed
1 tsp baking powder
½ tsp mixed spice

¼ tsp freshly grated
nutmeg
250 g/9 oz butter or soft
vegetarian margarine
250 g/9 oz soft brown
sugar
4 eggs, lightly beaten
grated rind of 1 orange
grated rind of 1 lemon
50 g/2 oz ground
almonds
50 g/2 oz flaked almonds
2 tbls brandy

Put the dried fruit into a bowl with the candied peel. Rinse and halve the cherries and add to the bowl, along with the sherry or orange juice. Mix, then cover and leave for 1–2 days, stirring once or twice each day.

Line a 20 cm/8 inch round cake tin with a double layer of greaseproof paper, and tie a double layer of newspaper around the outside of the tin. Set the oven to 140°C/275°F/Gas Mark 1.

Sift together the flours, baking powder and spices. Cream the butter or margarine with the sugar until light and fluffy, then beat the eggs in a little at a time, adding some of the flour mixture if there is any sign of curdling. Fold in the flour mixture, then stir in the dried fruit, orange and lemon rind and the ground and flaked almonds. Spoon the mixture into the cake tin and bake for 4–4½ hours, until a skewer inserted into the middle of the cake comes out clean. Stand the cake in its tin on a wire rack to cool.

Remove the cake from the tin, strip off the paper, prick the cake all over with a skewer, and pour the brandy over it. Wrap in greaseproof paper and store in an airtight tin until needed. It will keep well for 1–3 months and 'mature' during that time. Sprinkle a little more brandy over the top occasionally if you like during storage.

MAKES ONE 20 CM/8 INCH ROUND CAKE

ALMOND PASTE

200 g/7 oz ground
almonds
200 g/7 oz caster sugar
200 g/7 oz icing sugar

1 tbls lemon juice
2 eggs, beaten
a few drops of almond
essence

Put the almonds into a large bowl with the caster sugar, then sift in the icing sugar. Add the lemon juice, then gradually mix in the beaten eggs, adding enough to make a stiff paste. Don't knead the mixture too much or it may get oily.

MAKES ABOUT 700 G/1½ LB, ENOUGH FOR A 20 CM/8 INCH ROUND CAKE

TO PUT THE PASTE ON THE CAKE

First prepare the jam for coating the cake to make the almond paste stick. If you are using apricot jam, sieve 2 tablespoonfuls into a small saucepan, or use redcurrant or other jelly, which avoids the need for sieving. Add a tablespoonful of water and heat gently until melted.

Use two-thirds of the almond paste to roll out a strip the height of the cake and the same length as the cake's circumference. Gather up the trimmings, and roll these, and the remaining almond paste, to make a circle just slightly larger than the top of the cake. You might prefer to use the cake upside down, as the base is usually flatter than the top. Brush this with some of the melted jam or jelly – don't do the sides yet. Holding the cake by the sides, put it, jammy-side down, on to the circle of almond paste. Now turn it up the right way, brush the sides with jam and, holding the top and bottom of the cake between your flat hands, place the side of the cake on the strip of almond paste and simply roll it along – the almond paste will stick to it.

Gently press together the join where the ends meet, then put the cake on a board and leave to dry for 24 hours.

OPPOSITE: (left) Traditional Christmas Cake with Royal Icing and (right) Traditional Christmas Cake with Fondant Icing (page 282)

ROYAL ICING

2 egg whites
2 tsp glycerine

700 g/1½ lb icing sugar,
sifted, plus extra for
dusting
juice of ½ small lemon

Beat the egg whites and glycerine together, then add the icing sugar, a little at a time, beating well after each addition. After adding half the icing sugar, add the lemon juice. Continue adding the remaining icing sugar, beating to incorporate, until the mixture forms stiff peaks.

MAKES ENOUGH FOR A 20 CM/8 INCH ROUND CAKE

VEGAN VERSION

For vegan icing, use a thick glacé icing (page 404).

TO ROYAL ICE THE CAKE

Spoon the icing on to the cake, on top of the almond paste. Use a spatula to draw the icing thickly and evenly all over the top and sides, then use it to flick up decorative peaks.

To decorate the Royal Icing Cake to the left in the photograph, I swirled about 12 thin red ribbons around the candle centrepiece, curling them so that they fell prettily over the cake. As a finishing touch, I arranged some holly sprigs (and berries) at intervals around the top outside edge, and tied a red ribbon round the sides.

FONDANT ICING

450 g/1 lb icing sugar,
sifted
50 g/2 oz liquid glucose

1 egg white
icing sugar for dusting

Mix all the ingredients together to make a stiff, mouldable paste. (If you wish, you can use bought fondant icing, in which case, you will need 2 × 450 g/1 lb packets to cover the cake.)

MAKES ENOUGH TO ICE AND DECORATE A 20 CM/8 INCH ROUND CAKE

TO FONDANT ICE THE CAKE

Roll the icing out, using sifted icing sugar to dust if necessary, to make a piece large enough to cover the top and sides of the cake. Lift this up carefully by putting your flat hands underneath it, then gently lower it over the cake, letting it fall down the sides. Ease the icing round the sides of the cake and press it gently into position. Trim all the extra icing away. Leave for 6–8 hours.

Meanwhile, gather up all the trimmings which you can colour if you like, re-roll and cut into interesting shapes with pastry cutters to decorate the top and sides of the cake.

For the Fondant Icing Cake on the right of our photograph, I cut out holly shapes and arranged them around the top outside edge of the cake and around the base, on the silver cake board. To add to the festive feeling, I put some small silver cake-decorating balls on top of each holly 'leaf' and some real holly leaves in a circle in the centre, surrounding the Christmas candle.

The final touch (beside each leaf) is the special Christmas jasmine flowers. To make them, use a fine brush to paint fresh jasmine flowers with a lightly whisked egg white (just enough to break it up – add a drop of two of water if it's too viscous). Then lightly sprinkle with caster sugar and leave to dry at room temperature or in a very cool oven. Just before serving, tie a ribbon round the cake to complete the decoration.

OTHER IDEAS FOR FONDANT ICING

Decorate the sides and top of the cake with interesting fondant shapes – and paint them with cake colourings. Angels round the sides with one on top would be appropriately festive; or you could stamp out lots of Christmas stars and scatter them over the top and sides of the cake.

A favourite fondant idea of mine is to ice the cake, then cut out some green fondant leaves (use green cake colouring to get the right colour) to go in the centre. Put a red candle in the middle of the 'leaves' and, around it, Christmas roses, also made from fondant icing. It's quite easy to mould them – stick five white 'petals' round a gold 'stamen' with egg white; about five 'roses' should fit nicely around the candle. Finish with a red ribbon around the centre.

OTHER CAKE DECORATIONS

You could use almond paste on its own. Flute it attractively around the top of the cake (as you'd flute a pie), perhaps lightly score in a criss-cross pattern with a knife. Then arrange a candle and holly, or marzipan fruit, in the centre and tie a toning ribbon round the outside.

Or try a jewel-bright topping of crystallized fruits and brazilnuts, halved pecans and whole cashew nuts or blanched almonds. Stick these on to the top of the cake in an attractive pattern with warmed clear honey, and brush over with more warmed honey to glaze. For a sparkling finish, brush over the whole cake with clear honey, then sprinkle with preserving sugar or even some coloured coffee sugar and little silver balls.

VEGETARIAN CHRISTMAS PUDDING

100 g/4 oz plain wholewheat flour
1 tsp baking powder
100 g/4 oz pure vegetable fat
100 g/4 oz dark brown sugar
450 g/1 lb mixed dried fruit
100 g/4 oz candied peel, chopped
100 g/4 oz soft breadcrumbs
25 g/1oz flaked almonds
grated rind of 1 orange
grated rind of 1 lemon
$\frac{1}{4}$ tsp ground ginger
$\frac{1}{4}$ tsp grated nutmeg
1$\frac{1}{2}$ tsp mixed spice
1 tbls black treacle
4 tbls whisky
150 ml/5 fl oz stout

Sift the flour and baking powder on to a plate and leave on one side. Put the fat and sugar into a large bowl and beat until creamy, then add all the remaining ingredients, including the flour, and mix very well, to a thick, creamy consistency. (Don't forget to wish!) Cover the bowl and leave overnight.

Next day, put the mixture into a lightly greased 1.2 l (2 pint) basin (or two 600 ml/1 pint basins), cover with a circle of greased greaseproof paper and put on a lid if the basin has one. If it doesn't, secure with some foil or a pudding cloth over the top of the basin. Steam for 6–8 hours. (The longer a pudding is steamed, the darker and more richly flavoured it will become.) Cool, then put a clean piece of greaseproof and new foil or a fresh pudding cloth on top of the bowl and store the pudding in a cool, dry place until required.

Steam for a further 3 hours before eating.
SERVES 6

TO FLAME A CHRISTMAS PUDDING
The important thing is to warm the brandy first. Put 4 tablespoons of brandy – or 2 tablespoons brandy and 2 tablespoons vodka, which is higher in alcohol so burns well – into a metal soup ladle and warm by holding over a gas flame or electric ring. Then quickly light the brandy and pour carefully over and round the pudding.

OPPOSITE: *Vegetarian Christmas Pudding, flamed with brandy*

MINCEMEAT

This deliciously moist and spicy mincemeat is fat free.

225 g/8 oz dried pears, chopped
grated rind of 1 lemon
grated rind of 1 orange
450 g/1 lb mixed dried fruit
100 g/4 oz whole candied peel, chopped
100 g/4 oz glacé cherries, halved
100 g/4 oz dates, chopped
50 g/2 oz flaked almonds
1 tsp mixed spice
½ tsp grated nutmeg
½ tsp ground ginger
100 ml/3½ fl oz medium sherry
100 ml/3½ fl oz brandy
100 ml/3½ fl oz water

Mix everything together in a large bowl and set aside for 1–2 hours to allow the flavours to mingle. Transfer to a casserole, cover and bake at 180°C/350°F/Gas Mark 4 for 1 hour. Cool, then store in an airtight jar until ready to use.
MAKES 1 KG/2¼ LB

MINCE PIES

1 quantity rich shortcrust pastry (see page 299)
450 g/1 lb mincemeat
caster sugar

Set the oven to 200°C/400°F/Gas Mark 6 and lightly grease a shallow 12-hole bun tin. On a lightly floured board, roll out the pastry thinly then cut out twelve 7.5 cm/3 inch circles and twelve 6 cm/2½ inch circles using a round cutter. Press one of the larger circles gently into each section of the bun tin, then put a teaspoonful of mincemeat on top and cover with the smaller pastry circles. Don't fill them too full, or they may ooze and burst as they cook. Press down at the edges, make a steamhole in the top, then bake for about 20 minutes, or until the pastry is lightly browned. Cool in the tin.

Freeze until required. Serve warm, sprinkled with caster sugar.
MAKES 12 PIES

MAKING THE MOST OF YOUR FREEZER

I find it a help to make, about six weeks in advance if I'm organized, a rough menu plan for the main meals to be cooked over the Christmas period so that I can freeze some of the dishes (as many as I have time to do) in advance. If you make your menu plan and list of dishes for the freezer in good time, it's easier and more enjoyable to fit in the extra cooking over the 4–6 weeks leading up to Christmas. You'll find ideas for menus for different types of meals on page 288 (The Twelve Days of Christmas), as well as notes of the individual recipes that freeze well in other parts of the book. Some of the most useful standbys for the freezer are listed below.

DIPS AND FIRST COURSES

These are the last thing you want to be bothered with when you're busy, so having some of these frozen is a real help. Dips such as hummus and aubergine freeze well (others, like soured cream and avocado, don't but can be whizzed up in moments). Most soups freeze beautifully, and it's particularly handy to have a supply of special garnishes, such as crisp Sesame Stars (served with Cream of Carrot Soup on page 369) or croûtons. Home-made Vegetable Stock (page 292) is another good standby. Although there are some quite good stock cubes and powders on the market, nothing can compare with the delicacy of home-made stock, and if I haven't got any I tend to use water. One way of getting good stock without any bother is to save the water in which vegetables have been cooked. I keep this, covered, in a jug in the fridge or freeze some if there's extra.

SAUCES

Sauces are a most useful freezer item, often enabling you to create a meal from a few ingredients you happen to have in, or providing the finishing touch to a meal without much effort. I find you can never have too much Fresh Tomato Sauce or Italian Tomato Sauce in the freezer. Thaw, heat and serve with pasta and you have a filling meal in minutes; spread on top of any number of different bases, such as French bread, baps or round pitta breads, top with slices of tomato, pepper, mushroom, or whatever you fancy and grated cheese and a few black olives for quick pizzas; pour over lightly cooked vegetables, such as fennel, top with Parmesan cheese and serve as a light main course; or serve with a vegetarian burger, croquette or savoury loaf to add lots of colour and moisture to the meal.

Traditional Christmas Sauces – Bread Sauce, Cranberry Sauce and Gravy (vegetarian style, of course) – all freeze perfectly, and if you're planning to serve these, it's a great help to get them done in advance. The same applies to sweet sauces and accompaniments such as Brandy Butter, Rum Sauce, Vegan Cream and Coulis.

VEGETABLES AND HERBS

On the whole, I prefer to use fresh vegetables for accompaniments, although there are some exceptions. It's always useful to have some Red and Green Peppers (page 331) in the freezer, either for a salad or to incorporate into another dish. Festive Red Cabbage (page 315) also freezes well and is a useful dish for the freezer because it's good with many savoury dishes. Make it into a light main meal with the addition of roast, baked or mashed potatoes, and perhaps some cooked chestnuts. Dishes that can be cooked straight from frozen are particularly useful so I always try to keep a stock – Light Gratin Dauphinois and Parsley Potato Stars (page 308) are two favourites in this category. In addition to all of these, I like to keep a stock of plain vegetables such as petits pois, sweetcorn, green beans, broad beans, leaf spinach and, sorry to admit this, oven chips. Chopped parsley is another good standby – in fact, most herbs freeze well and could be stashed away for times when they're difficult to find fresh.

OPPOSITE: *Cream of Carrot Soup with Sesame Stars,*
page 369

BREAD AND PASTRY

Home-made rolls keep well in the freezer, as of course does any commercial bread. I like to keep a supply of our normal favourite wholewheat loaf, plus specials like baguettes, croissants, pitta bread, perhaps some Italian Ciabatta bread. White and wholewheat bread-crumbs, stored in polythene bags which can be topped up whenever you have bread over, are always useful to have, but especially so when you're making Christmas recipes. And if you like Garlic Bread it's a great help to have some prepared and wrapped in foil ready for baking. Don't do too far in advance – no more than 1–2 weeks – the flavour of garlic mysteriously decreases in the freezer.

A packet of filo and home-made or bought puff pastry is handy to have, too, and I like to store flan/tart cases either uncooked or, more convenient, baked blind, for finishing with a quickly made filling. Many of the savoury pastry dishes in this book can also be frozen (see below and on the recipe pages for specific suggestions).

MAIN-COURSE DISHES

What main-course dishes you put in your freezer depends very much on your own taste and your menu plans. I find it useful to have some kind of frozen burgers (such as Kate's Butterbean Croquettes, page 320), so that I can take them out individually for giving kids suppers and snacks at odd times. They can be cooked quickly from frozen. Terrines, savoury bakes and loaves are also useful and can be frozen raw, cooked or partially cooked. They're best thawed before cooking.

Savoury pastry dishes such as Flaky Mushroom Christmas Tree (page 320), Chestnut and Red Wine Pâté en Croûte (page 352), and Christmas Savoury Strudel (page 365) freeze excellently; open-freeze them before baking, then wrap them well to protect any fragile garnishes. To use, loosen their wrappings and let them thaw completely, then bake as described in the recipe.

PUDDINGS

Ice creams and sorbets are useful freezer basics, and can be quickly made more special if you serve them with your own frozen fruit coulis or supply of purées and some thin, crisp biscuits or tuiles; or, a favourite with my children (as well as with adults), Meringue Nests (page 296). Already-made meringues are a particularly useful extra to have available at Christmas. Other made-up puddings will depend on your menus, but Chocolate Charlotte (page 380) as well as traditional Bûche de Noel (page 402) freeze well, as do most cheesecakes and traditional old-fashioned trifles. I find it useful to keep one or two sweet pastry dishes over and above mince pies as they are so popular with my family – the Gooseberry Tartlets (page 376) fit this bill; they are wildly out of season, and add a pleasantly refreshing contrast to the usual Christmas flavours.

CAKES

I'm not keen on giving up freezer space to foods that store well in other ways, so I never keep rich fruit cakes or gingerbread in the freezer, although both are good for Christmas. Both can be made in advance and kept in a tin, as can lighter cakes such as Madeira Cake (page 399), Vegan Chocolate Sponge Cake (page 398), Light Ginger Cake with Lemon Icing (page 401), if they're made just before you want them; but if you want to get ahead with these they freeze very well and can be made and decorated before freezing – open-freeze them so that they are hard before you wrap them, and pack them carefully to avoid damage.

THE TWELVE DAYS OF CHRISTMAS . . .

Christmas Eve though not, strictly speaking, one of the traditional 'twelve days', is, for most of us, the start of Christmas, as friends and family gather for this very special, and I think rather magical, night of the year.

The planning of the meal on Christmas Eve will, of course, depend on circumstances: whether people are arrriving late, from far away, perhaps; whether you're planning to go to Midnight Mass . . . In some families, the food on this night is as traditional as Christmas Dinner. I feel that the ideal meal for Christmas Eve is something festive, but different enough from Christmas Dinner not to rival it. Also, since however well organised you are Christmas Eve always seems to be a busy time of last-minute shopping, present-wrapping and beginning the preparations for Christmas Day, it should either be fairly easy to make, or something which you can freeze in advance and just heat through.

A meal that I think meets all these criteria is Christmas Eve Couscous (page 322). This consists of several bowls of different mixtures: the grain (couscous), the lightly spiced, colourful vegetable stew, and as many extras – such as chick peas, raisins, chutneys and pickles, pine nuts – as you want to serve. You can pass the bowls around the table and everyone can help themselves, which gets things off to a friendly start and somehow adds to the feeling of celebration. This meal is easy to do but all the extras make it look as if you've taken a good deal more trouble than you have. A simple first course, such as Stuffed Vine Leaves (page 302), or a dip like guacamole with some crisp fresh vegetables or warm pitta bread, goes well with this, as does a pudding such as Orange Slices with Flower Water (page 382). If people are going to church you might like to save the pudding for later and make it something warming and substantial to eat on their return, like hot Mince Pies (page 285), for instance, or Swedish Ring Cake (page 404). Or serve some good chunky bread or home-made biscuits with a good selection of cheese and pickles, nuts and fruit.

One of the Christmas Dinner menus in this book would also be ideal for a special Christmas Eve meal – I've given quite a variety of suggestions in a later chapter, so it's quite possible to use one on Christmas Eve and another for Christmas Day itself. Round the meal off with a light and delicious pudding such as an ice cream bombe (page 390), Rum-Marinated Fruits with Coconut and Lime Cream (page 386) or Lemon and Ginger Cheesecake (page 386). Another meal I'm fond of is the Flaky Mushroom Christmas Tree (page 320) with its fresh and tangy creamy herb sauce; or, for a festive yet light meal, I also very much like Chestnut-Stuffed Mushrooms (page 315) served with Festive Red Cabbage (page 315) and Potatoes with Lemon (page 307), or my own version of the French classic, creamy Light Gratin Dauphinois (page 308).

It's a good idea to decide on your Christmas Dinner menu – the most important meal of the year – first, before you plan any of the others, and choose your other meals accordingly. There are lots of ideas for this in the Christmas Dinner chapter, and each menu comes complete with countdown timetables to make sure that everything goes really smoothly, and that you enjoy the meal as much as everyone else. Whether you have Christmas Dinner at lunchtime or in the evening, you will probably want something light for the other meal of the day. My family is incurably traditional; having known only vegetarian Christmases, they always want the most traditional of vegetarian meals on Christmas Day: Cashew Nut Roast served with roast potatoes, gravy, cranberry sauce and all the other trimmings (page 348) – and they want it at lunchtime, followed by the Queen's speech and present-opening under the tree. I make enough of the roast to have it sliced cold in the evening with salad and pickles, followed by trifle, ice cream or hot mince pies.

Other ideas for a light yet Christmassy second meal of the day would be Festive Spring Rolls (page 302) (which can be frozen); Tagliatelle with Creamy Walnut Sauce (page 316), both of which I'd serve with a simple salad – mixed leaf, shredded lettuce or lettuce heart, for instance. If you're feeling really full, several dips of different colours, with some fresh vegetables such as radishes, spring onions and slices of lettuce heart, plus some bread, biscuits, crisps or tortilla chips, can be surprisingly successful and great fun to eat.

On the days following Christmas, fresh, light food seems to be what people fancy most – and it must either be quick and easy to make or eminently freezable. Some of our favourites are Clear Watercress Soup (page 306); Lemony Vegetables (page 311), served with light and creamy mashed potatoes or mixed rice; my daughter Kate's Butterbean Croquettes (page 320) or Little Brie and Hazelnut Bakes (page 337), both of which are delicious with some fruity home-made cranberry sauce; Avocado with Curried Brazilnut Stuffing (page 321); and Fennel Parmesan (page 308), which has a good, clean flavour. Puddings that are particularly good at this time are Lemon and Ginger Cheesecake (page 386); the refreshing Christmas Dried Fruit Salad (page 382); or Lychee Sorbet (page 385).

CHRISTMAS TIMETABLE

OCTOBER

- Find recipes for Christmas Cake, Pudding and Mincemeat.

- Make lists of ingredients needed and start buying items which store well, such as dried fruit.

- Check equipment: now is the time to buy new tins (the stronger and heavier the better), pudding basins, pastry cutters or anything special needed in Christmas recipes.

- Save jars for the mincemeat (and any other Christmas preserves).

- Check supplies of foil (the narrow type is most convenient), nonstick and greaseproof paper, polythene bags, clingfilm and labels for the freezer.

- If you're expecting to have a large party at Christmas and have limited freezer space, collect polystyrene boxes and packing, and get some freezer ice packs – these are good for keeping food cold for short periods of time when the fridge and freezer are full.

- Clear out the freezer and start using any items which need eating up to give you plenty of freezer space for Christmas.

OCTOBER/NOVEMBER

- Make the Christmas Cake, Pudding and Mincemeat. Keep them in a cool, dry place.

NOVEMBER

- Think about Christmas menus and any special dishes you want to try; check that you have the equipment needed.

- Make a plan of dishes to prepare for the freezer, and a rough timetable; most dishes keep well in the freezer for 4–6 weeks.

- Make any preserves, such as Kumquats in Brandy (page 414) or Mixed Vegetables in Oil (page 412), for eating at Christmas or giving as presents.

- From mid-November onwards, you can start freezing dishes for Christmas.

DECEMBER

- The more you can get into the freezer during the first fortnight the better.

- Make and freeze Mince Pies, Brandy Butter, Rum Sauce (see recipes in this chapter).

- Finalise Christmas Dinner menu. Make and freeze main courses and sauces as applicable. Some first courses, such as Iced Melon Soup with Violets can be frozen, too.

- During the second week, put almond paste and icing on your Christmas cake.

OPPOSITE: *Iced Melon Soup with Violets, page 352*

VEGETABLE STOCK

900 g/2 lb mixed
vegetables, for instance,
2 onions, 3 sticks of
celery, 2 carrots,
1 turnip, 2 broccoli
stalks
25 g/1 oz butter or white
vegetable fat

5 garlic cloves – no need
to peel, just halve
12 peppercorns
2 bay leaves
bunch of parsley, or just
the stalks
a few sprigs of thyme, or
1 tsp dried

Scrub and roughly chop the vegetables. Melt the butter or fat in a large saucepan, add the vegetables and fry for 10 minutes until soft. Add 1.5 l/2½ pints of water, the garlic, peppercorns, bay leaves, parsley and thyme. Bring to the boil, cover, and simmer very gently for about 40 minutes, until the vegetables are very soft. Leave the pot to stand until it's completely cold, then skim the fat from the surface. This stock keeps for a few days in the fridge and also freezes well: old cream or yogurt cartons make good containers.
MAKES ABOUT 1–1.25 L/1¾–2¼ PINTS

FRESH TOMATO SAUCE

Even in winter when tomatoes don't have that warm, sun-drenched flavour, I prefer this sauce to the more strongly flavoured kind made from canned tomatoes (see opposite), although both are useful. This one is good for serving with delicately flavoured foods, and my children love it with pasta of any shape! It's also good with boiled rice tossed with a few fresh herbs. In fact, I find I can't make too much of it. You can vary the basic sauce by adding chopped fresh herbs (basil and oregano are particularly good), sliced button mushrooms, crushed garlic or a dash of red wine.

1 medium-sized onion,
finely chopped
1 tbls olive oil

1 kg/2 lb 2 oz tomatoes,
skinned and roughly
chopped
salt and freshly ground
black pepper

In a large saucepan, fry the onion in the oil for 10 minutes, until soft but not browned. Add the tomatoes and cook for about 10 minutes, until they are soft but still bright in colour and fresh in flavour. Season with salt and pepper and freeze until required.

Usually I serve this sauce just as it is, which is fine for pasta and simple dishes, although it can be puréed in a food processor and then strained quickly through a sieve if you want a smooth sauce. Ideally it would be useful to keep both types, the chunky and the smooth, in the freezer!
SERVES 6

ITALIAN TOMATO SAUCE

This sauce has a stronger flavour which some people may prefer. I find it particularly useful as a topping for home-made pizzas. Spoon it on top of any bases which happen to be handy; home-made bread ones if there's time, otherwise split and toasted rolls or muffins, round pitta bread, or slices of bread which have been dried out in a cool oven, like the bases of Italian crostini.

1 onion, chopped
2 tbls olive oil
2 garlic cloves, crushed
2 × 400 g/14 oz cans
tomatoes
½ tsp dried basil

½ tsp dried oregano
1 bay leaf
150 ml/5 fl oz red wine,
stock or water
salt and freshly ground
black pepper

In a large saucepan, fry the onion in the oil for 10 minutes, until soft but not browned. Add the garlic, tomatoes and juice, basil, oregano, bay leaf and the wine, stock or water. Cook gently for 20 minutes, until the tomatoes have almost reduced to a purée. Remove the bay leaf, then purée the sauce in a blender or food processor. Season with salt and pepper. A little extra liquid can be added at this point for a thinner sauce. Freeze until required.
SERVES 6

CRANBERRY SAUCE

100 g/4 oz cranberries,   *50 g/2 oz sugar*
washed and picked over   *1 tbls port or orange juice*
3 tbls water   *(optional)*

Put the cranberries into a saucepan with the water. Bring to the boil, then simmer until the berries are tender; about 4–5 minutes. Add the sugar and cook gently until dissolved.

Remove from the heat and add the port or orange juice, if you're using these. Either serve warm or freeze until required.
SERVES 6

BREAD SAUCE

3 cloves   *15 g/½ oz butter*
1 onion, peeled   *2 tbls cream*
300 ml/½ pint milk   *salt and freshly ground*
1 bay leaf   *black pepper*
50 g/2 oz white bread,   *grated nutmeg*
crusts removed

Stick the cloves into the onion, then put the onion into a saucepan with the milk and bay leaf. Bring to the boil, then take off the heat, add the bread, cover and leave on one side for 15–30 minutes to allow the flavours to infuse.

Remove the onion and the bay leaf. Beat the mixture to break up the bread, and stir in the butter, cream and salt, pepper and grated nutmeg to taste. Either serve warm or freeze until required.
SERVES 6

VEGAN VERSION
Use vegan margarine instead of butter, soya milk instead of milk and omit the cream.

BECHAMEL SAUCE

This sauce will keep, well covered, in the fridge, for at least a few days.

25 g/1 oz butter   *6 black peppercorns*
25 g/1 oz flour   *a sprig of thyme*
600 ml/1 pint milk   *1–2 blades of mace*
piece of onion, celery and   *salt and freshly ground*
scraped carrot   *black pepper*
1 bay leaf   *grated nutmeg*

Melt the butter in a large saucepan. Add the flour, stir over the heat for a couple of minutes, then add the milk, a quarter at a time, mixing well between each addition. Add the onion, celery, carrot, bay leaf, peppercorns, thyme and mace and leave to simmer gently for 10–15 minutes. Strain the sauce through a sieve into a clean saucepan. Season with salt, pepper and grated nutmeg, and use as appropriate, with vegetables, pasta or other savouries.
MAKES 450 ML/¾ PINT

VEGAN VERSION
Use vegan margarine instead of butter and soya milk instead of dairy milk.

PARSLEY SAUCE
Add 2–4 tablespoons chopped parsley and a few drops of lemon juice (to taste) to the sauce after straining.

You may wish to make more Cranberry Sauce than the quantities given here, for serving with several meals over Christmas. Freeze in suitable sized containers and reheat gently before serving.

GARLIC BREAD

I love crisp, hot, buttery garlic bread and could eat it with almost any soup or salad. Assuming that others share my passion, I find it very useful to have some loaves already spread with butter, wrapped in foil and stored in the freezer, ready to pop straight into the oven. I've given quantities for one normal-size French stick here, but I generally make up more while I'm about it. It's sometimes convenient to freeze the bread in smaller amounts, perhaps a quarter of a loaf, firmly wrapped in foil. As the garlic flavour lessens during freezing, it's best not to keep it for more than 3–4 weeks, and 1–2 weeks is better.

1 French stick
75 g/3 oz soft butter or
vegan margarine

2–4 fat garlic cloves,
crushed

Cut the stick into 2.5 cm/1 inch diagonal slices without cutting right through to the base. Mash the butter with the garlic until it's thoroughly blended, then spread both sides of each slice of bread with the butter mixture. Press the loaf together and wrap in foil – or make two packages if this is more convenient and will fit your oven better. To use immediately, bake at 200°C/400°F/Gas Mark 6 for 20 minutes, or until it's hot inside and crisp on the outside; or freeze until required, then bake from frozen allowing 30 minutes.

FLAVOURED BUTTERS

Flavoured butters are a useful way of adding extra interest to vegetables and other dishes. Try parsley or lemon butter on top of plain steamed carrots, curry butter on boiled parsnips or spread on bread when making croûtons (see page 328), and paprika butter on open mushrooms before grilling.

OPPOSITE: *Garlic Bread with Paprika, Parsley and Lemon Butters*

PARSLEY BUTTER

75 g/3 oz soft butter

2 tbls finely chopped parsley

Beat the butter until creamy, then mix in the chopped parsley. Other herbs can also be used – chopped chives are good. Chill until firm, then wrap in foil and freeze until required.

LEMON BUTTER

75 g/3 oz soft butter

finely grated rind and juice of ½ lemon

Beat the butter until creamy, then mix in the lemon rind and juice. Chill until firm, then wrap in foil and freeze until required.

CURRY BUTTER

1 tbls olive oil
2 tsp curry powder

75 g/3 oz soft butter

Heat the oil in a small pan, then add the curry powder and stir over the heat for a few seconds, to release the flavour. Cool, then beat this into the soft butter. More or less curry powder can be used according to taste. Chill until firm, then wrap in foil and freeze until required.

PAPRIKA BUTTER

75 g/3 oz soft butter
2 tsp paprika

1 tbls lemon juice

Beat the butter until creamy, then mix in the paprika and lemon juice. Chill until firm, then wrap in foil and freeze until required.

BRANDY BUTTER

100 g/4 oz unsalted butter

100 g/4 oz soft brown sugar or icing sugar
2 tbls brandy

Cream the butter and sugar or icing sugar together until the mixture is fluffy, then beat in the brandy. Spoon into a serving dish, cover and chill until firm, then wrap in foil and freeze until required.
SERVES 6

Use vegan margarine for vegan flavoured 'butters'.

VEGAN CREAM

3 tsp cornflour
150 ml/5 fl oz
  unsweetened soya milk
1 vanilla pod

90 g/3½ oz soft pure
  vegetable margarine
2–3 tsp icing sugar
a few drops of vanilla
  extract (optional)

In a small bowl, blend the cornflour to a paste with a little of the soya milk. Put the rest of the milk into a saucepan with the vanilla pod and bring to the boil, pour over the cornflour mixture, stir, and return to the pan. Stir until the mixture thickens, then remove from the heat and leave until completely cold.

In another bowl, beat the margarine until it's light and creamy, then gradually whisk in the cooled cornflour mixture, avoiding the vanilla pod, which can be rinsed, dried and used again. It's important to add the cornflour mixture gradually, whisking well, to produce a beautiful light whipped cream. Add the icing sugar towards the end, a teaspoonful at a time, tasting the mixture to get it just right.

The delicate vanilla flavour can be enhanced with a drop or two of vanilla extract, or you can add a dash of brandy or rum, or orange or rose flower water, depending on what you're serving it with.
SERVES 4–6

MERINGUE NESTS

2 egg whites
pinch of cream of tartar

100 g/4 oz caster sugar

Set the oven to 150°C/300°F/Gas Mark 2 and draw six 7.5 cm/3 inch circles well apart on greaseproof or nonstick paper. Place the paper on a baking sheet, grease with butter or oil and sprinkle with flour.

Put the egg whites into a clean, grease-free bowl with the cream of tartar and whisk until stiff and dry. (You should be able to turn the bowl upside down without the egg whites falling out!) Whisk in half the sugar then add the remaining sugar and whisk well.

Put the mixture into a piping bag fitted with a large shell nozzle and pipe circles round and round within the circles on the paper, then a final circle on top of the outermost circle, to form a nest shape.

Put the meringues into the oven, then reduce the setting to 110°C/200°F/Gas Mark ¼ and bake for 1½– 2 hours, or until they are dried out. Turn the oven off and leave them to cool in the oven. Remove the meringues from the baking sheet with a palette knife. Either cool and use immediately or arrange carefully in a lidded container, cover and freeze until required.
MAKES 6

APRICOT COULIS

225 g/8 oz dried apricots   25 g/1 oz caster sugar

Put the apricots into a saucepan, cover with plenty of water and leave to soak overnight.

Next day, add the sugar and more water if necessary, so that the apricots are well covered. Bring to the boil, then let them simmer, uncovered, for about an hour, or until nearly all the water has gone and the apricots are very tender and bathed in a glossy syrup.

Cool, then liquidize thoroughly with some water to make a smooth purée. Add more water to thin the purée to a pouring consistency – like double cream, or even a bit thinner. Pour into suitable containers for freezing – old cream or yogurt cartons with a snap-on plastic lid are ideal – label and freeze. To use, thaw, then gently heat if you want to serve it hot.

OPPOSITE: *Gooseberry Tartlets, page 376, with Apricot Coulis*

RASPBERRY COULIS

450 g/1 lb raspberries   2 tbls water
(frozen are fine)   2 tbls caster sugar

Liquidize the raspberries with the water and sugar, then sieve. Turn the mixture into a saucepan, bring to the boil and boil for 1 minute, to make the sauce clear and glossy. Cool, then either serve warm or freeze as required.
SERVES 6

RUM SAUCE

25 g/1 oz butter or vegan   25 g/1 oz caster sugar
  margarine   4–6 tbls single cream
25 g/1 oz cornflour   2–3 tbls rum
600 ml/1 pint milk

Melt the butter or margarine in a medium-sized saucepan. Add the cornflour and stir for a few seconds before pouring in the milk, one third at a time, whisking well after each addition. Simmer for a couple of minutes, then stir in the sugar, cream and rum. Either use immediately or tip into a suitable container and freeze until required.
SERVES 6

RICH SHORTCRUST PASTRY

150 g/5 oz 85%   90 g/3½ oz butter
  wholewheat flour   1 egg yolk
pinch of salt   1 tbls water

OPPOSITE: *Flaky Mushroom Christmas Tree, page 320, made with Quick Flaky Pastry*

Sift the flour and salt into a bowl or food processor. Add the butter, cut into pieces, add the egg yolk and water, and either mix with a fork until combined or whizz for a few seconds without the plunger to let in more air, to make a medium-soft dough.

This pastry freezes excellently, both cooked and uncooked. To store, wrap loosely and freeze.
MAKES APPROX 250 G/9 OZ PASTRY

QUICK FLAKY PASTRY

250 g/9 oz strong brown   150 ml/5 fl oz ice-cold
  flour   water
1 tsp salt   squeeze of lemon juice
250 g/9 oz cold butter

Sift the flour and salt into a large bowl.

Cut the butter into 5 mm/¼ inch dice and add to the flour. Using a knife, mix the butter lightly into the flour so that the pieces just get coated with flour and are well distributed. Add the water and lemon juice and, again with a knife, quickly mix to a firm, soft dough.

On a lightly floured board, roll out into a rectangle, using short, quick movements, then fold the top over and over again. Give the folded pastry a quarter turn clockwise, so that the folded edges are now on your left. Roll again, sprinkling the pastry with some flour as necessary. Then fold and turn the pastry again. Keep repeating this rolling, folding and turning – the pastry we used in the picture of the Flaky Mushroom Christmas Tree (opposite) was rolled and turned seven times!

After the last rolling and folding, cover the pastry and chill it for at least 30 minutes. Or wrap loosely in foil and freeze until required. When you use, roll it out to about 2.5 mm/⅛ inch and bake in a hot oven preset to 230°C/450°F/Gas Mark 8 for 6–8 minutes, then reduce to 200°C/400°F/Gas Mark 6. Dampen the baking sheet, and remember to keep clear-cut edges for the pastry to rise from.
MAKES 350 G/12 OZ PASTRY

If you make the Rum Sauce in advance, cover with dots of butter to prevent a skin from forming.

LUNCHES, SUPPERS & SNACKS

Although we tend to think in terms of Christmas cooking as being the Dinner, in fact for most of us it involves a great deal more, especially now that the Christmas holiday seems to last longer and longer, requiring, I've found, food which is special and festive, but which is also refreshing and a good contrast to Christmas Dinner and the traditional pudding, mince pies and cake... So the recipes in the section are for all the other meals that Christmas cooking involves, apart from the big day itself and parties.

As far as I'm concerned, such meals must either be quick and easy to make or good for freezing, so that they need the minimum of time and effort to produce on the day. I hope you'll agree that the dishes which follow meet these criteria. There are recipes for light savouries and dips, which can be used as starters or, with the addition of some salad and bread, become snack meals in themselves. The same applies to the soups, which make particularly warming, filling winter meals, yet are easy on preparation and washing up.

If there are young children in the party, it's helpful to have some dishes in the freezer which enable you to take out a small portion and heat it up when required, for giving the kids an early supper before they go to bed, or snacks at odd times to fit in with their routine. Parsley Potato Stars or Kate's Butterbean Croquettes come into this category, as do the Christmas Sacks and Father Christmas Faces – all can be frozen in individual quantities, and the latter can also be put together quickly from fresh (non-frozen) ingredients.

Some of the recipes in this section could also be used for a vegetarian Christmas Dinner: the Flaky Mushroom Tree, perhaps served with traditional accompaniments from the Christmas Dinner section (pages 346 to 373), would be delightful, as would the Chestnut-Stuffed Mushrooms; or, for a real break from tradition, try the equally mouthwatering Avocados with Curried Brazilnut Stuffing.

STUFFED VINE LEAVES

When you're working with filo pastry, keep the rest of the pastry covered with polythene or a damp cloth to prevent it from drying out.

Stuffed vine leaves make a delicious starter or party nibble, either on their own or with some thick Greek yogurt.

1 × 227 g/8 oz packet of preserved vine leaves	50 g/2 oz raisins (optional)
225 g/8 oz long-grain brown rice	½ tsp powdered cinnamon or allspice
1 large onion, chopped	2 garlic cloves, crushed
2 tbls chopped parsley	salt and freshly ground black pepper
2 tomatoes, skinned and chopped	6 tbls olive oil
50 g/2 oz pine kernels	150 ml/5 fl oz water
	2 tbls lemon juice

Drain the vine leaves, cover them with cold water and leave to soak for 30 minutes or so, then rinse and drain them again, to remove some of the salt.

Blot the leaves dry, putting any torn ones aside. Half-fill a large saucepan with water, put in the rice and boil for 10 minutes, then drain and mix with the onion, parsley, tomatoes, pine kernels, raisins, if you're using them, cinnamon or allspice, garlic and seasoning. Put a spoonful of this mixture on each vine leaf, fold over the edges and roll the leaves up loosely, to allow space for the rice to swell.

Line a large frying pan with the torn leaves, then put in the stuffed vine leaves, side by side. Mix together the oil, water and lemon juice, and pour this over the leaves. Cover and cook over a very gentle heat for 2–2½ hours until the rice and leaves are tender. Keep an eye on the water level, and add a little more from time to time if necessary. Cool, then chill.

Serve cold.

MAKES ABOUT 36

FESTIVE SPRING ROLLS

FOR THE SAUCE	1 tsp grated fresh ginger
2 large red peppers	1 tbls Tamari
2–4 garlic cloves, peeled	salt and freshly ground black pepper
salt and freshly ground black pepper	1 x 350 g/12 oz packet filo pastry
	extra olive oil for brushing
FOR THE SPRING ROLLS	spring onion tassels, thin pepper slices and thin carrot curls, to garnish
2 onions, chopped	
2 carrots, diced	
1 tbls olive oil	
350 g/12 oz beansprouts	

First make the sauce, which can be done some time in advance and kept in the fridge. Quarter the peppers and remove the seeds. Place the peppers in a saucepan with the garlic cloves, cover with water and boil for 10–15 minutes, until the peppers are tender. Drain, liquidize, then pour the mixture through a sieve. Season with salt and pepper.

To make the spring rolls, if you're going to bake them straight away, set the oven to 200°C/400°F/ Gas Mark 6. In a frying pan, fry the onions and carrots in the oil for 7 minutes, until almost soft. Add the beansprouts and ginger and fry for a further 2–3 minutes, until all the vegetables are cooked. Add the Tamari and season with salt and pepper. Cool.

Cut a sheet of filo pastry in half, or divide it so that you have a piece measuring about 18 cm/7 inches square. Place a good heap of the mixture about 1cm/½ inch from the top and well clear of the sides, then fold over the top and the sides and roll up, to make a neat parcel. Place on a baking sheet which has been brushed with olive oil. Make the rest of the spring rolls in the same way and arrange on the baking sheet. Brush the spring rolls lightly with olive oil and bake for about 20 minutes, turning them over after about 10 minutes so that both sides get crisp.

Serve the rolls on individual plates on a pool of the red pepper sauce, garnished with spring onion, carrot and red pepper slices.

MAKES ABOUT 20 ROLLS

OPPOSITE: *Festive Spring Rolls*

WINTER VEGETABLE SOUP WITH ROUILLE AND CROÛTONS

The rouille on top of this soup adds a delicious, warming touch, but can be left off if you want a simpler version. You could stir in some soured cream or Greek yogurt instead, or top each bowlful with grated cheese, for a warming and filling winter meal.

1 large onion
2 leeks
225 g/8 oz celeriac or outer sticks of celery
2 tbls olive oil
1 × 400 g/14 oz can tomatoes in juice
1.2 l/2 pints water or vegetable stock
salt and freshly ground black pepper

FOR THE CROÛTONS
4 slices of wholewheat bread
25 g/1 oz butter

FOR THE ROUILLE
1 small or ½ large red pepper, seeded
1 red chilli, fresh or dried, seeded
50 g/2 oz white bread
100 ml/4 fl oz olive oil
salt and freshly ground pepper
chilli powder, to garnish

First make the croûtons, which can be done well in advance – they keep excellently in the freezer, too. Cut the crusts from the bread, then spread each side lightly with butter. Cut into small dice and place on a baking sheet. Set the oven to 150°C/300°F/Gas Mark 2 and bake for 40–60 minutes, or until they are crisp and crunchy.

Next, make the soup. Peel and chop the onion and clean, trim and slice the leeks, keeping as much of the green part as you can. Peel the celeriac and cut into 1 cm/½ inch dice or, if you are using celery, cut it into smaller dice as it takes a long time to soften. Heat the oil in a large saucepan, then put in all the vegetables. Cook over a gentle heat, with a lid on the pan, for 10–15 minutes, stirring every so often and not allowing them to brown. Add the tomatoes, with their liquid, and the water or stock, and bring to the boil. Then simmer gently for 30–40 minutes, or until all the vegetables are tender. Season with salt and pepper.

While the soup is cooking, make the rouille. Put the pepper into a pan of water and bring to the boil; simmer for about 10–15 minutes, or until the pepper is very tender, then drain thoroughly. Meanwhile, if you are using a dried chilli, soak this in a little boiling water. Put the cooked pepper, with any stalks removed, into a food processor with the fresh or soaked dried chilli, and whizz to a purée. Then add the bread, broken up into rough pieces, and whizz thoroughly, gradually adding the olive oil, whisking all the time, or after each addition. It's a bit like making mayonnaise, but much easier and less risky! As you add the oil, the mixture will thicken to a lovely smooth cream. Season with salt and a dash of chilli powder if you want it hotter. You can lighten the rouille mixture a bit by beating in a tablespoonful or two of boiling water if you wish.

Ladle the steaming hot soup into bowls and top each with a good spoonful of the rouille, some croûtons and a sprinkling of chilli powder – or let everyone help themselves to the extras.
SERVES 4

VARIATION
For a vivid yellow rouille, use a golden pepper instead of the red one.

OPPOSITE: *Winter Vegetable Soup with Rouille and Croûtons*

CAROL SINGERS' ONION SOUP

Surely this soup – a vegetarian version of the classic French Onion Soup – must be the most warming of them all? Wonderful to come in to on a cold night, whether you've been singing for your supper or not!

2 tbls oil
900 g/2 lb onions, thinly
  sliced
4 tsp sugar
salt and freshly ground
  black pepper
1.5 l/3 pints stock
2 garlic cloves, crushed

Tamari or Shoyu soy
  sauce
lemon juice
4–6 slices French stick
100 g/4 oz cheese,
  grated

Heat the oil in a saucepan, add the onions and fry for 10 minutes or until they are tender but not browned. Add the sugar and some salt and pepper, and continue to fry for a further 15–20 minutes, until the onions become a deep golden brown. Don't let them burn! Add the stock and garlic, bring to the boil and let the soup simmer for about 10 minutes. Add Tamari or Shoyu soy sauce to taste, and a few drops of lemon juice, salt and pepper as necessary.

When you're ready to serve the soup, have some piping hot bowls ready. Put the French stick on a grill pan, top with the cheese, and grill for a few minutes, until the cheese has melted. Ladle the soup into the hot bowls, top each with a piece of cheesy bread, and serve at once.

SERVES 4–6

CLEAR WATERCRESS SOUP

This easy-to-make, refreshing soup is a good alternative to Celery and Stilton Soup in the Christmas Dinner on page 360, if you want something lighter, and vegan. Adding the watercress just before serving gives it a lovely bright colour and fresh flavour.

2 leeks
1 tbls olive oil
1 l/1¾ pints water or
  stock
1 × 75 g/3 oz packet
watercress

Tamari or Shoyu soy
  sauce
salt and freshly ground
  pepper

Wash, trim and finely shred the leeks, using as much of the green part as you can. Heat the oil in a large saucepan, add the leeks, and fry gently for about 10 minutes, or until they are tender. Add the water or stock, bring to the boil, then simmer for about 10 minutes. Chop the watercress, then add this to the soup, along with Tamari or Shoyu to taste – probably 2–4 tablespoons. Season with a little salt and pepper if necessary. Reheat gently and serve.

SERVES 4–6

PASTA AND BROCCOLI BECHAMEL

225 g/8 oz broccoli
100 g/4 oz short
  macaroni, shells or
  other pasta shapes
300 ml/10 fl oz
  Bechamel Sauce
  (page 293)

salt and freshly ground
  black pepper
fresh breadcrumbs and a
  little butter or grated
  cheese for topping
  (optional)

Wash and trim the broccoli then divide it into smallish pieces. Cook it in 1 cm/½ inch of boiling water for 3–4 minutes, or until it is nearly tender. Drain and leave on one side.

Cook the pasta in a large panful of boiling water until that, too, is just tender – *al dente* – then drain it immediately.

Meanwhile, gently heat the bechamel sauce. Add the pasta and broccoli to the sauce, season, then stir gently over the heat until everything is really hot. Serve immediately or pour the mixture into a shallow heatproof dish, top with crumbs and a little butter or grated cheese and put under the grill until it's golden brown and crisp.

SERVES 2–3

VEGAN VERSION

Use a bechamel sauce made with soya milk and vegan margarine, and use margarine for the topping, if you're adding this.

CREAMY PARSNIP BAKE

This makes a pleasant, easy-going vegetable dish, which can be made in advance and reheated; I especially like it with any kind of crunchy burger, and it's also good for a light meal, with some watercress and sliced tomato.

900 g/2 lb parsnips
25 g/1 oz butter
150 ml/5 fl oz single
  cream
squeeze of lemon juice
salt and freshly ground
  black pepper

freshly grated nutmeg
buttered crumbs or
chopped walnuts or
hazelnuts for topping
(optional)

Peel the parsnips, then cut them into even-sized pieces. Put into a saucepan, cover with water, then bring to the boil and simmer, with a lid on the pan, until the parsnips are tender. Drain – the water makes good stock – then mash with the butter. When the parsnips are smooth, gradually beat in the cream.

Flavour with a squeeze of fresh lemon juice and salt, pepper and freshly grated nutmeg. You can then gently reheat the parsnip cream, stirring all the time over a gentle heat, and serve immediately; or you can spoon it into a shallow casserole, smooth the top, and sprinkle with some buttered crumbs or chopped walnuts or hazelnuts. It can then be reheated later in a moderate oven for 20–30 minutes, or in a microwave oven for 5–10 minutes.

SERVES 6

VEGAN VERSION

Use a vegan margarine instead of the butter, and soya milk instead of the cream. You could use a little extra vegan margarine to increase the richness – say 15 g/½ oz.

POTATOES WITH LEMON

The lemony tang is refreshing, and these potatoes are convenient to cook, because they can be prepared ready for baking, in advance, and don't need much attention once they're in the oven.

700 g/1½ lb potatoes
40 g/1½ oz melted butter
  or margarine

grated rind of 1 lemon
salt and freshly ground
  pepper

Choose even-sized potatoes and scrub them. Put them into a saucepan, cover with water and parboil them for 7 minutes or until they are almost tender. With a sharp knife, remove the skins and cut the potatoes in half lengthways. Melt the butter, then stir in the grated lemon rind. Brush this lemon butter all over the potatoes then put them in a single layer into a baking tin. Bake in the oven preset to 190°C/375°F/ Gas Mark 5, for about 45 minutes, or until they are golden and crisp, turning them over about half way through so they get evenly browned.

SERVES 6

You can use cavaway instead of lemon rind in this way.

307

LIGHT GRATIN DAUPHINOIS

This lighter version of the delicious classic goes well with many of the savoury dishes in this book. I often serve it for a light meal with just a good crunchy mixed vegetable salad or some stir-fried vegetables (like Lemony Vegetables on page 311).

900 g/2 lb potatoes
50 g/2 oz butter, melted
1 garlic clove, crushed
1 onion, thinly sliced

salt and freshly ground
 black pepper
grated nutmeg
150 ml/5 fl oz single
 cream

Set the oven to 180°C/350°F/Gas Mark 4.

Peel the potatoes and cut them into thin slices.

Grease a shallow wide gratin dish with half the butter, then spread the crushed garlic around the base and sides, too. Layer the potatoes and onion into the casserole, seasoning them with salt, nutmeg and freshly ground black pepper as you go, then pour over the cream and remaining butter. Cover with foil.

Bake for 1 hour, then remove the foil and bake for a further 30 minutes, or until golden brown.
SERVES 4

PARSLEY POTATO STARS

These are popular with children; they freeze well and can be grilled or baked from frozen.

900 g/2 lb potatoes
25 g/1 oz butter
25 g/1 oz chopped
 parsley

salt and freshly ground
 pepper
grated nutmeg
flour

Peel the potatoes and cut them into even-sized chunks, then boil in water to cover until they are tender. Drain really well, then dry a little over the heat. Mash with the butter, parsley and seasoning to taste, to make a smooth, very stiff consistency. Set the oven to 200°C/400°F/Gas Mark 6.

On a well-floured board, knead the mixture then press out to a depth of 1 cm/½ inch, and cut out star shapes. If you are using straight away, bake on a lightly oiled sheet for about 30 minutes until golden brown. If you are freezing them, bake for about 20 minutes until they are just set and beginning to brown, then cool and freeze.
SERVES 4–6

FENNEL PARMESAN

The slightly aniseed flavour of fennel makes it refreshing at any time, but particularly so, I think, at Christmas. This simple dish can be served as an accompanying vegetable, but I like it best as a simple lunch or supper, accompanied by a lovely big salad.

2 large fennel bulbs

100 g/4 oz Parmesan
 cheese, grated

Trim any tough outer leaves or stems from the fennel, then cut each bulb first in half and then into thin segments. Bring half a saucepanful of water to the boil, put in the fennel, and let it boil for 4 minutes or so, until it is just tender. Drain, keeping the liquid (which makes a delicious stock).

Heat the grill. Put the fennel in a single layer into a shallow flameproof dish and cover with the grated Parmesan cheese. Pour 6 tablespoons of the reserved liquid over the top of the cheese, then put the dish under a hot grill for about 5 minutes, or until the cheese has melted and browned lightly. Serve at once.
SERVES 4

OPPOSITE: *(top) Light Gratin Dauphinois and (bottom) Parsley Potato Stars*

LEMONY VEGETABLES

One of my favourite vegetable dishes, and a great hit with my family, this can be served as an accompanying vegetable, as a starter, or as a main course in its own right, perhaps with some cooked rice or a potato dish such as Light Gratin Dauphinois (page 308) or creamy mashed potatoes.

225 g/8 oz broccoli	1 lemon
175 g/6 oz mangetouts	1 bay leaf
2 onions	good pinch of dried thyme
2 red peppers	salt and freshly ground
1–2 fennel bulbs	black pepper
2 leeks	chopped parsley
75 ml/3 fl oz olive oil	

First prepare all the vegetables. Cut the thick stalks from the broccoli, then peel off the outer skin and cut the stalks into matchsticks. Separate the florets, halving any larger ones, so that they are all roughly the same size. Bring a large saucepan of water to the boil, put in the broccoli and blanch for 3 minutes, then drain into a colander and run under the cold tap. Pat dry with kitchen paper and leave on one side.

Top and tail the mangetouts, and blanch these in the same way for 1 minute; drain, refresh under cold water and pat dry. Peel and slice the onions; seed and slice the peppers; trim and slice the fennel into eighths or sixteenths, depending on the size of the bulbs; clean, trim and slice the leeks into 2.5 cm/1 inch lengths. (All this can be done in advance.)

When you are ready to make the dish, put the oil into a large saucepan or wok with the same quantity of water, the pared rind from half the lemon, the bay leaf and thyme. Put in the onions, red peppers, fennel and leeks and simmer for about 8 minutes, or until they are almost tender. Add the broccoli and mangetouts, and stir-fry for a further 2–3 minutes. Remove from the heat, add the grated rind of the other half of the lemon, and enough of the juice to give a pleasant tang. Season with salt and pepper, then serve, sprinkled with chopped parsley.

SERVES 4–6

OPPOSITE: *Lemony Vegetables*

SANTA'S SURPRISE PARCELS

The crêpes for this recipe can be made well in advance and frozen or kept in the fridge until needed. The following recipe makes 12 thin pancakes and each filling mixture is enough to fill about 4 pancakes.

FOR THE PANCAKES	1 tbls olive oil
50 g/2 oz plain white flour	2 eggs
50 g/2 oz plain wholemeal flour	300 ml/10 fl oz milk and water, mixed
good pinch of salt	oil for frying

To make the batter, if you have a food processor, simply put all the ingredients (except the oil for frying) into this; sift in the flours, as this helps to keep the mixture really light, and just tip in the final residue of bran from the sieve. Whizz without the plunger (to let in more air and lighten the pancakes), until everything is blended and you have a creamy mixture the consistency of double cream. Oil the base of a small frying pan (ideally measuring about 19 cm/7½ inches across the top) with a pad of kitchen paper and a teaspoon of olive oil, then heat it until a small drop of water flicked into it splatters immediately.

Pour about 2 tablespoons of the batter mixture into the pan and immediately tip so that the batter spreads all over the base. If it doesn't spread well, it may be too thick, so mix in a little water. After a few seconds, when the bottom of the pancake is lightly browned and the top set, flip it over using a palette knife and your fingers, to cook the other side for a few seconds, then lift it out on to a large piece of greaseproof paper.

Continue to cook more crêpes in this way until all the mixture is used, putting them side by side on the greaseproof paper. You will probably need to regrease the frying pan after every 2–3 crêpes. Leave them to cool completely, then cut the paper between them and stack the pancakes, on their paper, on top of each other. Keep in the fridge or freeze until required.

Serve with a selection of the fillings listed overleaf.

Make the fillings for these crêpes ahead of time, and you have a meal in minutes.

FOR VEGAN CRÊPES

Omit the eggs; add 3 tablespoons chick pea flour and a teaspoon of baking powder to the other flours. Use soya milk instead of dairy milk. You will need to add a little extra water to get this mixture to the right consistency. It's best to let this batter stand for about 30 minutes before using.

SPINACH AND RICOTTA

Cook 450 g/1 lb fresh spinach or 225 g/8 oz frozen leaf spinach. Drain well, really pressing out the liquid, then mix with 15 g/½ oz butter, 50 g/2 oz ricotta cheese, salt, pepper and grated nutmeg.

SWEETCORN AND CREAM CHEESE

Defrost 100 g/4 oz frozen sweetcorn kernels by putting them into a sieve and pouring boiling water over them. Put them into a bowl with 100 g/4 oz cream cheese or low-fat smooth white cheese. Mix well. Some chopped chives can be added.

AVOCADO AND TABASCO

Peel, stone and dice 1 ripe avocado. Sprinkle with lemon juice, salt, pepper and tabasco. A little crushed garlic, or some chopped chives can be added.

CAMEMBERT AND PINE NUTS

Dice 225 g/8 oz Camembert cheese and mix with 50 g/2 oz lightly toasted pine nuts.

RED PEPPER, TOMATO AND CHILLI

Grill then skin 1 large red pepper and, if you like the heat, ½ fresh red chilli (seeds removed). Chop and mix with a large skinned, seeded and chopped tomato. Season with salt and pepper.

COURGETTE AND TOMATO

Fry 1 small chopped onion in 1 tablespoon of oil for 10 minutes, then add 225 g/8 oz diced courgettes and 2 skinned, seeded and chopped tomatoes, and cook for about 5 minutes, or until the courgette is just tender. Add 1 tablespoon finely chopped parsley and some salt and pepper.

CREAMY MUSHROOM

Fry 100 g/4 oz washed and sliced button mushrooms in 15 g/½ oz butter for 15–20 minutes, or until all the liquid which they produce has boiled away. Then stir in ½ teaspoon cornflour and 100 ml/4 fl oz single cream. Stir well for about 2 minutes, until thickened, then remove from the heat. Season with salt and pepper, grated nutmeg and a squeeze of lemon juice.

TO FINISH THE DISH

Carefully arrange a good tablespoonful of the chosen mixture in the centre of each pancake and fold over the edges to make a parcel. Put this, seam side down, in a shallow gratin dish, packing in all the 'parcels' in a single layer. If you really want to play up the parcel idea you could even tie them with a long chive. They can be topped with 4–6 tablespoons of cream, or sprinkled with some grated Parmesan or, for vegans, fine breadcrumbs and dots of margarine.

Put them into a moderate oven preset to 180°C/ 350°F/Gas Mark 4 and bake for 20 minutes, just to heat them through.

Serve with Fresh Tomato Sauce (page 292) and cooked green beans or buttered broccoli; or a shredded lettuce or lettuce heart salad. Creamy mashed potatoes go well, too, if you want to make this a more substantial meal.

OPPOSITE: *Santa's Surprise Parcels*

CHESTNUT–STUFFED MUSHROOMS

I think these big, juicy mushrooms with their chestnut topping make a lovely festive dish. For extra crunch, I have arranged the mushrooms on crisp croûtes – but these are optional and can be omitted if you prefer. You can use either fresh chestnuts, vacuum-packed ones or, as a last resort, canned whole chestnuts. You will need about 450 g/1 lb fresh chestnuts to give the quantity used below.

8 large open mushrooms
olive oil for frying

FOR THE STUFFING
25 g/1 oz butter or vegan
  margarine
1 large onion, finely
  chopped
350 g/12 oz whole
  cooked chestnuts

fresh lemon juice
salt and freshly ground
  black pepper
grated nutmeg

FOR THE CROÛTES
8 slices of wholewheat
  bread
about 50 g/2 oz soft
  butter

If you're making the croûtes, it's a good idea to get them done in advance and out of the way. You can fry them, but I think they're much nicer baked to a crisp golden crunchiness in a slow oven. Set the oven to 150°C/300°F/Gas Mark 2. Stamp circles in the bread with a large pastry cutter; spread on both sides with butter and put them on a baking sheet. Bake for 1 hour, or until completely crisp and golden. Cool. These will keep in a tin for a few days.

To prepare the mushrooms, cut off any stalks so that the surface is level, then wash the mushrooms and pat them dry on kitchen paper. Fry them on both sides in the olive oil and drain well. Season them with salt and pepper, then leave on one side while you make the stuffing.

Melt the butter in a medium-large saucepan. Add the onion and fry for about 7 minutes, until soft. Chop up any pieces of mushroom stalk, add these and cook for a minute or two longer. Remove from the heat and add the cooked chestnuts, breaking them up

a bit as you do so to make a mixture which holds together but has some chunky bits in it. Add a dash of fresh lemon juice, and salt, pepper and grated nutmeg to taste.

To serve the dish, preset the oven to 200°C/400°F/Gas Mark 6, or preheat the grill to high. Put the croûtes on a baking sheet or in a shallow casserole, then place a mushroom on each one, black side up. Spoon the stuffing mixture on top. Bake or grill until heated through – about 10 minutes under the grill, 15–20 minutes in the oven.
SERVES 4

FESTIVE RED CABBAGE

This is a useful dish because it cooks slowly and won't spoil if you cook it too long or keep it waiting! It also adds a moistness to the meal which often avoids the need for a separate sauce – and it's delicious, especially if you reheat it the next day.

900 g/2 lb red cabbage
50 g/2 oz butter or vegan
  margarine
2 large onions, sliced
150 ml/5 fl oz red wine

150 ml/5 fl oz vegetable
  stock or water
salt and freshly ground
  black pepper
dash of sugar
2–4 garlic cloves, crushed

Shred the cabbage, discarding the tough core. Melt half the butter in a large saucepan or casserole and fry the onions for about 5 minutes; then put in the cabbage and stir well, to coat it thoroughly with the butter.

Pour in the wine and stock, and add a teaspoonful of salt. Bring to the boil, then either cover, turn the heat right down and cook for about 1 hour on top of the stove, or cover and cook in an oven preset to 170°C/325°F/Gas Mark 3 for about 1½ hours. The cabbage should be very tender.

Mix the rest of the butter with the crushed garlic and add to the cabbage, along with salt, pepper and a dash of sugar to taste.
SERVES 4–6

Try a Nordic version of this cabbage, too: add chopped apples and spices and take out the garlic.

OPPOSITE: *(right) Festive Red Cabbage and (left) Chestnut-Stuffed Mushrooms*

315

TAGLIATELLE WITH CREAMY WALNUT SAUCE

This is a lovely pasta dish to make at Christmas when there are good walnuts around. Get some help on cracking them — or use really fresh shelled ones.

1 tbls olive oil
450 g/1 lb tagliatelle or
  fettuccine
15 g/½ oz butter
freshly grated Parmesan
  cheese (optional)

FOR THE SAUCE
225 g/8 oz walnuts in
  their shells, or 100–150 g/
  4–5 oz shelled walnuts
1 garlic clove, peeled
150 ml/5 fl oz whipping
  cream
salt and freshly ground
  black pepper

To make the pasta, fill a large saucepan two-thirds full of water, add the oil, and bring to the boil.

Meanwhile, grind the walnuts and garlic in a food processor and gradually add the cream and some salt and pepper.

When the water boils, add the pasta, give it a quick stir, then leave to cook for about 6 minutes, or according to instructions on the packet. Don't let it get soggy! As soon as it's just done, drain it gently, add the butter and some salt and pepper, stirring very gently with a fork.

Add the sauce, mix quickly and lightly, and serve immediately, on warmed plates. Serve Parmesan cheese separately for those who want it; it's best grated straight on to the hot pasta.

SERVES 4

SANTA'S SACKS

Many other ingredients could be used with the potatoes for the filling here instead of sweetcorn and peanuts — I've used this combination because it's unfailingly popular with the kids I know. A can of chick peas, well drained, is good instead of sweetcorn, or chopped fried mushrooms, cheese or chopped nuts.

8 sheets filo pastry
4–6 tbls olive oil

FOR THE FILLING
1 onion, chopped
1 tbls olive oil

350 g/12 oz potatoes
50 g/2 oz frozen
  sweetcorn kernels
50 g/2 oz salted peanuts
salt and freshly ground
  pepper

First make the filling. In a medium-sized saucepan, fry the onion gently in the oil, with a lid on the pan, for 5 minutes. Meanwhile, cut the potatoes into small dice, add these to the onions, give them a stir, then cover and cook for 5 minutes. After that, put in 4 tablespoons of water, stir and cover, and continue to let them cook until the potatoes are tender — about another 5–10 minutes. Take the pan off the heat and stir in the sweetcorn, peanuts and seasoning to taste.

Set the oven to 200°C/400°F/Gas Mark 6. To make the sacks, take a piece of filo pastry and cut it into two squares about 15 cm/6 inches square. (Keep the rest covered with polythene or a damp cloth to prevent it from drying out.) Brush one of the squares with oil, then put the second one on top and brush with oil again. Put a good spoonful of the filling mixture into the centre, then dampen the edges with water and draw them up together, to make a sack. Brush the outside of the sack all over with more oil and put it on to a baking sheet. Continue like this until you have used up all the filling. (Any filo pastry which is left over can be put back in its wrappings — the packet will keep well in the fridge for at least a month if it's well sealed.)

Bake the sacks for about 20 minutes, or until they are crisp and golden all over, then serve at once.

MAKES 8

OPPOSITE: *Tagliatelle with Creamy Walnut Sauce*

OYSTER MUSHROOM RISOTTO

This makes a soothing and welcome meal at Christmas. It's easy to make and needs only a simple salad – sliced lettuce hearts, or tomatoes, for instance – to accompany it.

75 g/3 oz butter
1 large onion, chopped
1 garlic clove, crushed
300 g/10 oz arborio rice
150 ml/5 fl oz white wine – or use extra water

1 l/1¾ pints water or stock
100 g/4 oz oyster mushrooms
grated Parmesan cheese, to serve

Melt 50 g/2 oz of the butter in a large saucepan, add the onion and garlic and fry for 10 minutes, without browning. Put in the rice, some salt and the wine, then gradually add the water, mixing after each addition (it should moisten the rice each time) and bring to the boil. The mixture should cook for about 20 minutes in all.

Melt the remaining butter, stir in the oyster mushrooms, and add these, too, to the mixture. Bring back to a simmer, then leave the rice to cook for a further 15 minutes, stirring it often as the liquid is absorbed, to prevent it from sticking. The risotto is done when it is creamy in consistency, without any excess liquid, and the rice is tender. If the liquid is absorbed before the rice is quite done, either put a lid on the pan and leave it off the heat for 10–15 minutes, or add a little more liquid and continue to simmer it gently for a few more minutes. Season with salt and freshly ground black pepper. Serve with the grated Parmesan cheese.

SERVES 2–3 AS A MAIN COURSE

FATHER CHRISTMAS FACES

These can be made on lots of different bases, but here I have used soft white or brown salad rolls, which are about 10 cm/4 inches across – just right. Cut them in half and toast them, then cover the entire surface with home-made tomato sauce, or very finely chopped seeded tomato seasoned with salt and pepper. Then put a layer of grated Italian Mozzarella cheese around the top to make hair and fur, and around the base to make a beard (you'll need about 100 g/4 oz cheese).

Cut almost-halves of small black olives and position for shiny eyes, a piece of red pepper, cut curvy, for the mouth, and a round of it for the nose and a final slice or two above the cheese for his hat. Make some of the cheese into eyebrows.

Grill just to heat through – not too much or the cheese will melt too much and brown, and the effect will be lost. (If you don't have any Mozzarella, other white cheese, such as Wensleydale or Lancashire could be used, coarsely grated.)

OPPOSITE: *Father Christmas Faces*

319

FLAKY MUSHROOM CHRISTMAS TREE

350 g/12 oz Quick Flaky
  Pastry (page 299)
1 egg yolk, beaten with 1
  tbls water and a pinch
  of salt
FOR THE FILLING
25 g/1 oz butter
1 onion, sliced
1 garlic clove, crushed

450 g/1 lb mushrooms,
  sliced
75 g/3 oz cooked rice
75 g/3 oz cream cheese
1 tbls chopped parsley
1 tsp grated lemon rind
2–3 tsp lemon juice
salt and freshly ground
  black pepper

To make the filling, melt the butter in a small saucepan. Add the onion and cook for 5 minutes, then add the garlic and mushrooms. Fry until the mushrooms are tender and any liquid which they produce has gone – this can take 30 minutes. Add the rice, cream cheese, parsley, lemon rind and juice, and salt and pepper, stirring to mix well. Chill.

Set the oven to 200°C/400°F/Gas Mark 6. On a lightly floured board, roll out the pastry into a rectangle 30 cm/12 inches long by 40 cm/16 inches wide. Cut in half to give two rectangles of 30 cm/12 inches by 20 cm/8 inches. Fold each of these in half lengthways, then cut into a Christmas tree as indicated on the diagram below – or better if you can! – and unfold. Put one of the 'trees' on to a damp baking sheet. Spoon the filling on top, leaving a little gap – not more than 1 cm/½ inch – around the edges. Dampen the edges, then put the second tree on top, pressing the edges together to seal. Prick

![Diagram of Christmas tree cutting pattern with measurements: 9cm/3½", 4.50cm/1½", 4cm/1½", 7cm/3", 20cm/8", 30cm/12"]

lightly, then decorate with little cut-out pastry shapes, stuck on with cold water: a tiny angel or a star on the top, more little stars, hearts, teddy bears, crescents crackers, or whatever, all over. You can also write HAPPY XMAS diagonally across it, if you have the patience to cut the letters! Brush with egg yolk, salt and water and bake for 30 minutes, or until the pastry is nicely browned.

Serve piping hot, with the sauce.
SERVES 4–6

CREAM AND HERB SAUCE

150 ml/5 fl oz double
  cream
1 tbls lemon juice
salt and freshly ground
pepper

1 tbls chopped fresh herbs
  – parsley, chives,
  tarragon

Put the cream and lemon juice into a small pan and stir gently until hot. Add the seasoning and herbs, and serve.

KATE'S BUTTERBEAN CROQUETTES

My daughter Kate invented this dish, which is very simple to make and very popular with kids. It's very quick to whizz up too – but it also freezes well. You can add spices, such as a teaspoonful of cumin seeds and ground coriander, fried with the onion; or a dash of tomato chutney or chopped parsley, mixed in with the beans. They're good hot with Cranberry Sauce (page 293) or mango chutney; or cold, with yogurt and fresh herbs.

2 tsp olive oil
1 onion, chopped
2 × 425 g/15 oz cans
  butterbeans

salt and freshly ground
  black pepper
dried wholewheat
  breadcrumbs
olive oil for baking

Heat the oil in a large saucepan, add the onion and fry, with a lid on the pan, for about 10 minutes, or until it is tender and lightly browned. Remove the pan from the heat. Drain the butterbeans (you won't need the liquid) and add them to the pan, mashing them with a spoon or with a potato masher to make a lumpy mixture which holds together. Season with salt and pepper as necessary.

Divide the mixture into eight pieces, form into croquette shapes and coat in dried wholewheat breadcrumbs. Arrange them on a greased baking sheet. When you're ready to bake the croquettes, put them into an oven preset to 200°C/400°F/Gas Mark 6 and bake them for about 30 minutes, or until they are brown and crisp on the outside, turning them over after about 20 minutes.

MAKES 8 CROQUETTES, SERVING 4

AVOCADO WITH CURRIED BRAZILNUT STUFFING

These hot avocados make a good quick lunch or supper. They are quite rich, so go well with something plain and low in fat – like brown rice cooked so that it's nice and fluffy, with a few fresh herbs added.

2 large ripe avocados	*100 g/4 oz brazilnuts,*
juice of 1 lemon	*chopped*
6–8 spring onions	*salt and freshly ground*
1 tbls olive oil	*pepper*
2 tsp curry powder	*chilli powder*

Halve the avocados and remove the stones. Using a teaspoon, scoop out the flesh without damaging the skin. Cut the flesh into rough chunks, put them into a bowl and add enough lemon juice to coat the pieces.

Next, wash and trim the spring onions, then slice finely. Heat the oil in a medium saucepan, add the onions and curry powder and fry over a gentle heat for 4–5 minutes, or until the spring onions are tender. Remove from the heat and add the avocado, chopped brazilnuts, salt and pepper to taste, and a pinch or two of chilli to give it as much kick as you wish.

Heat the grill. Stand the avocado skins on a grill pan or flameproof dish, spoon the brazilnut mixture into the skins and grill for 5–10 minutes, or until the filling is heated through and the top is lightly browned.

SERVES 4

SHOPPER'S DELIGHT

¼ iceberg lettuce	*100 g/4 oz green pepper,*
4 wholewheat pitta	*sliced*
breads	
2 tsp olive oil	FOR THE GARLIC SAUCE
100 g/4 oz leek, finely	*150 ml/5 fl oz soured*
sliced	*cream or Greek yogurt*
100 g/4 oz cabbage,	*1–2 garlic cloves, crushed*
finely shredded	*salt and freshly ground*
100 g/4 oz button	*pepper*
mushrooms, sliced	

First make the garlic sauce by putting the soured cream or yogurt into a small saucepan with the garlic and seasoning with salt and pepper to taste. Leave on one side.

Finely shred the lettuce, and keep that on one side, too. Halve the pitta breads through the middle so that each one makes two pockets. Put these under the grill to warm through, but don't toast them.

Meanwhile, heat the oil in a large saucepan, add the leek, cabbage, mushrooms and green pepper and stir-fry for about 2 minutes, or until heated through. Gently heat the soured cream or yogurt and garlic, without letting it get anywhere near boiling.

Now fill the pitta pockets: put in a spoonful of shredded lettuce, then plenty of the stir-fried vegetables. Top with a good spoonful of the warm garlic sauce and finish with some more lettuce. Eat at once.

SERVES 4

CHRISTMAS EVE COUSCOUS

FOR THE VEGETABLE
 STEW
50 g/2 oz butter
450 g/1 lb onions, sliced
450 g/1 lb carrots, sliced
700 g/1½ lb acorn
 squash, peeled, seeded
 and diced
1 tsp ground ginger
½ tsp powdered cinnamon
½ tsp turmeric
¼–½ tsp ground white
 pepper
900 ml/1½ pints water or
 vegetable stock
450 g/1 lb courgettes,
 trimmed and sliced
450 g/1 lb frozen broad
 beans (or sweetcorn)
salt

squeeze of lemon juice
dash of sugar
chopped fresh coriander

FOR THE GRAIN
450 g/1 lb couscous
1 tsp salt
50 g/2 oz butter

FOR THE EXTRAS
1 tbls harissa sauce
1 x 425 g/15 oz can
 chick peas
1 tbls olive oil
1 tsp cumin seeds
150–175 g/5–6 oz
 raisins
100 g/4 oz pine nuts
225 g/8 oz Greek yogurt
a dusting of paprika

First make the stew. Melt the butter in a large saucepan. Add the onions and fry for 5 minutes, then add the carrots, squash and spices. Cook for a further 10 minutes, with a lid on, stirring from time to time, until all the vegetables are buttery and spicy. Add the water or stock and simmer for 10–15 minutes or until the vegetables are just becoming tender. Add the courgettes and broad beans and cook for a further 5 minutes or so. Season with salt, lemon juice and a little sugar if necessary. (This is best made in advance and reheated, as the flavours improve – it is particularly good after freezing.)

Now make the grain. This is an unusual way to cook couscous, but I find it gives the best results. Put the couscous into a baking tin and add 600 ml/1 pint of water; immediately drain this off and return the couscous to the tin. Leave it for 20 minutes, separating the grains with your fingers after 10 minutes, or more times if you're passing. Put the couscous into a sieve or steamer lined with a blue J-cloth. Set over a pan of simmering water (it doesn't have to be the stew) for 20 minutes. Tip the couscous back into the baking tin, and pour over 150 ml/5 fl oz cold water with the salt dissolved in it. Sift the grains with your fingers and leave for 15 minutes, then put back into the lined steamer and heat as above for a further 20 minutes. Sift with your fingers into a serving bowl and stir in the butter. Set aside while you put together the extras.

To assemble and serve, take a ladleful of liquid from the stew and add it to the harissa to make a thick paste. Put this into a small bowl. Drain the chick peas. In a small pan, heat the oil and add the cumin seeds, stirring for a moment or two, then add the chick peas and stir until heated through. Put into a second small bowl. Cover the raisins with boiling water, leave for 10 minutes or longer to plump, then drain and put into a third small bowl. Put the pine nuts into a fourth bowl – they can be lightly toasted if you like. Finally, put the yogurt into a fifth bowl and dust the top with some paprika.

To serve, ladle the stew over the couscous and garnish with chopped fresh coriander.
SERVES 6

OPPOSITE: *Christmas Eve Couscous*

PARTIES & BUFFETS

Christmas 'parties' cover a whole host of different occasions, ranging from a few simple nibbles with drinks to a full-blown buffet-style meal. This chapter, therefore, includes a variety of recipes to enable you to cope with all the very different festive entertaining you are likely to do. There are simple dips and savouries, as well as more substantial 'centrepiece' dishes and salads, along with some festive drinks, some with alcohol, some without. I hope you'll find something here to fit your particular needs – and don't forget to check other, appropriate sections, too: light savouries in Lunches, Suppers and Snacks (pages 300 to 322), which are good for drinks parties, for instance, while some of the main courses in Christmas Dinners (pages 346 to 373), could make very effective dishes for a buffet or fork supper.

One of the main problems when catering for a party is to know how much food to make. I generally go right back to basics and think in terms of individual portions – how much any one person would reasonably eat. For a drinks party, I think about five or six little savouries per person is about right, and it's nice if some of these are hot and some cold. Quite a few of the recipes I've given here can be made in advance and frozen, then cooked or heated and served with dips, crudités, crisps and small savoury biscuits, for a relaxed, hassle-free occasion. Along with the food, allow about half a bottle of wine per person, or the equivalent in other drinks, plus some non-alcoholic drinks as well. Mulled Wine (page 344) is a

particularly welcoming drink for a Christmas or New Year Party, although you should probably plan on serving wine at ordinary temperatures, too.

A buffet or fork supper can be as simple or as elaborate as you want to make it. You could serve just one really delicious main course with a salad, bread, cheeses and a pudding; usually, though, I think it's best to serve a choice of at least two main courses (most people will have a little of each, so allow for this when you calculate quantities), plus three or four salads and/or vegetables, of which people will have only a spoonful or so. One golden rule, when estimating amounts I've found, is that a group of people never, for some reason, eat as much salad as they would at a smaller gathering. Again, if you think in terms of what one person would eat and multiply up by the number of guests, you'll be on roughly the right track.

I haven't given separate pudding recipes in this section, although no real buffet is complete without one or two. There is, however, a whole range of spectacular and suitable offerings in Festive Puddings (pages 374 to 393). Perhaps the best idea is to choose two to finish your party in style: one that is rich (the Chocolate Charlotte with Chocolate Holly Leaves, page 380, or Bûche de Noel, page 402, would fit the bill nicely), and one that is refreshing (like Rum-Marinated Fruits with Coconut and Lime Cream, page 386, or Christmas Dried Fruit Salad, page 382).

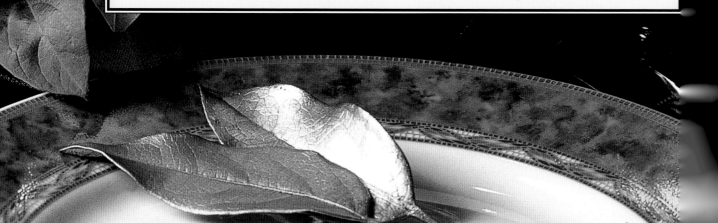

RED PEPPER AND GARLIC DIP

2 large red peppers
6 large garlic cloves,
  peeled
150 ml/5 fl oz light olive
  oil
1–2 tbls lemon juice

salt and freshly ground
  black pepper
25–50 g/1–2 oz soft
  white breadcrumbs
  (optional)

Quarter the peppers, removing the stems and seeds, then put into a saucepan with the garlic and water just to cover. Bring to the boil, then simmer for about 15 minutes, or until the peppers are very tender. Drain well and leave until cold.

Put the peppers and garlic into a food processor and purée, gradually adding the oil and lemon juice to make a soft, creamy mixture like mayonnaise. Season, then chill before serving.

The dip will thicken slightly as it stands, but if you wish you can thicken it a bit more by stirring in some breadcrumbs. Add these gradually, allowing them several minutes to swell and thicken the mixture before adding more.

SERVES 6–8 AS A FIRST COURSE

HUMMUS

This is a useful dip to have at Christmas, or almost any time, and makes a good creamy vegan salad dressing, too. Be sure to get the deliciously mild pale golden-beige tahini, not the dark brown one. It keeps for ages.

1 × 425 g/15 oz can
  chick peas
1 garlic clove, peeled
2 tbls tahini
5 tbls olive oil

juice of 1 lemon
salt and freshly ground
  black pepper
extra olive oil and
  paprika, to serve

Drain the chick peas, keeping the liquid. Put the chick peas into a food processor with the garlic and whizz to a thick purée, scraping down the sides as necessary. Add the tahini, oil, a tablespoonful of the lemon juice and a little of the reserved chick pea liquid, and whizz again. Keep on adding the reserved liquid until you have a smooth, creamy consistency, like lightly whipped cream. Taste the mixture and add more lemon juice if necessary then season with salt and pepper.

To serve, spoon the hummus into a bowl, swirl a little olive oil on top and sprinkle with paprika.

SERVES 4 AS A FIRST COURSE

AVOCADO DIP

Just about everyone's favourite, this is very easy to whizz up, and makes a lovely dressing for salad, too.

1 large ripe avocado
1 tomato
1 small green chilli
  (optional)

1–2 garlic cloves, crushed
juice of 1 lime or lemon
salt and freshly ground
  pepper

Halve the avocado, then remove the stone and peel. Mash the flesh roughly with a fork, or whizz it in a food processor if you want a thinner, creamier texture. Peel, seed and chop the tomato and add to the mixture.

Wash, seed and finely chop the chilli, if you're using this, and add it to the avocado, being careful to wash your hands afterwards; then add the garlic and enough lime or lemon juice to give the dip a good tang. Season with salt and pepper and serve as soon as possible.

This dip looks nice garnished with a leaf or two of fresh coriander or flatleaf parsley, a sprinkling of paprika pepper or a thin slice of lime or lemon.

SERVES 4–6

OPPOSITE: *A selection of party dips (from left to right) Avocado, Red Pepper and Garlic, Hummus and Smoky Aubergine, page 328*

SMOKY AUBERGINE DIP

Any of the dips on page 326 and here would make good toppings for Crostini.

3 medium aubergines	salt and freshly ground
1 garlic clove, peeled	black pepper
3 tbls olive oil	2–3 tsp red wine vinegar
juice of 1–2 lemons	chopped fresh parsley
	black olives

Cut the aubergines in half and place them, cut side down, under a hot grill for about 20 minutes until the skin is charred and the flesh feels soft. Leave them to cool, then remove the skin – it comes off very easily.

Put the flesh into a processor with the garlic, oil and a couple of tablespoons of lemon juice, and whizz to a smooth, creamy purée. Taste and season, adding more lemon juice and the red wine vinegar as necessary, to give a good piquant flavour.

Spoon the mixture into a small bowl, and serve sprinkled with chopped fresh parsley and garnished with some black olives.
SERVES 4

MASCARPONE AND HERB DIP

A rich and creamy dip for a party. You could make a less rich version by using curd cheese or, even less calorific, a skimmed milk smooth white cheese. Serve surrounded by crudités: radishes, baby sweetcorn, celery sticks, cauliflower florets, etc.

250 g/9 oz mascarpone	1–2 tbls chopped parsley
3–4 tbls plain yogurt	tabasco
2 garlic cloves, crushed	salt and freshly ground
1 tsp grated onion	pepper
1–2 tbls chopped chives	

Put the mascarpone into a bowl, add the yogurt, garlic and onion, and beat until creamy. Add the chives, parsley, a few drops of tabasco to taste, and some salt and pepper. Chill until needed.
SERVES 4–6

ASSORTED CROSTINI

These delicious crisp croûtons, with their colourful toppings, are very useful for parties. In keeping with the occasion, they can be hearty, in true Tuscan style, or delicate, depending on the size of the croûton bases.

A fairly slim French stick, sliced into rounds a bit less than 1 cm/½ inch thick, makes a good, average-size crostini; or, for mini ones, you can use bridge rolls, similarly sliced, to make smaller rounds. Put the rounds on baking sheets and put them in a coolish oven – 140–150°C/275–300°F/Gas Mark 1–2 – for about 20–30 minutes, or until they are dry and crisp. Half way through this process, brush on both sides with olive oil, then put back into the oven to finish crisping. Let them cool on the baking sheets.

For the toppings, you can use black olive pâté; a smooth soft goat's cheese and Tartex Swiss pâté, garnished with small sprigs of fresh herbs; pine nuts, capers, small pieces of grilled red pepper, or olives.

They're best assembled as near as possible to the time you're going to eat them so that the base remains crisp, but all the different parts, including the garnishes, can be prepared in advance.

GOAT'S CHEESE BALLS

450 g/1 lb soft medium-	2 tbls finely grated
fat goat's cheese	hazelnuts or roasted
2 tbls finely chopped	cashew nuts
chives	1–2 tbls paprika

Have three plates, one each for the chives, nuts and paprika. Break off small pieces of cheese – about the size of a marble – and divide them among the three plates. Roll them to coat the outside and form a smooth ball.

Chill, then serve piled up on a small plate.
MAKES ABOUT 15 BALLS

OPPOSITE: *Goat's Cheese Balls*

RED AND GREEN PEPPERS

3 large juicy red peppers
3 large juicy green
peppers
juice of 1 lemon

4 tbls olive oil
salt and freshly ground
black pepper
chopped fresh parsley

Cut the peppers into quarters, down from the stems. Place them, skin side up, under a very hot grill for about 15–20 minutes until the skin has blackened and blistered. As one area of the pepper gets blackened, turn them so that all the shiny skin gets done.

Remove from the grill and put them into a polythene bag, or between two plates, and leave them to get cold. Peel off the charred skins and rinse the peppers under cold water. Blot dry.

Cut the peppers into long thin pieces and put them into a shallow dish. Sprinkle them with lemon juice, oil and salt and pepper to taste. Leave them for a few hours if possible to allow the flavours to mellow and blend, giving them a stir from time to time. Check the seasoning, then sprinkle with parsley before serving.

SERVES 6–8 AS A FIRST COURSE

STUFFED BABY AUBERGINES

6 baby aubergines
1 tbls olive oil
1 medium-sized onion,
finely chopped
1 garlic clove, crushed
2 tomatoes, skinned,
seeded and chopped

25 g/1 oz pine nuts
1 tbls chopped parsley
dash of lemon juice
salt and freshly ground
black pepper
pine nuts, to garnish

Cut the aubergines in half, leaving the stalks on. With a small sharp knife and a teaspoon, carefully scoop out the flesh without breaking the skin. Set the skins

OPPOSITE: *(left) Red and Green Peppers and (right) Stuffed Baby Aubergines*

aside. Chop the flesh. In a saucepan, heat the oil and fry the onion for 5 minutes, with a lid on the pan. Add the chopped aubergine flesh, garlic and tomatoes, cover and cook for a further 10–15 minutes, or until tender and purée-like.

Set the oven to 180°C/350°F/Gas Mark 4. Blanch the skins in boiling water for 2 minutes, drain well and place in a greased shallow ovenproof dish. Add the pine nuts, parsley and lemon juice to the aubergine mixture, season and pile into the skins. Cover and bake for 20 minutes, or until browned and cooked. Serve cold, decorated with pine nuts.

SERVES 6 AS FIRST COURSE/OR 2–3 AS A LIGHT MAIN COURSE

GRILLED MUSHROOMS WITH GARLIC HERB CHEESE

These make a pleasant warm or hot nibble for a party, or, served with a salad garnish and some good bread, as a first course. You need small mushrooms, but not the very tight button ones.

225 g/8 oz mushrooms
olive oil

1 × 145 g/5 oz Boursin
garlic and herb cheese

Wash the mushrooms, then remove the stems by pushing them first one way and then the other – they should come out quite easily. Rub the mushrooms with a little olive oil, then place them, open-side down, on a grill pan or baking sheet.

Grill them for about 5 minutes, or until they are tender, then turn them up the other way and fill the cavity with the cheese. This can be done in advance. Just before you want to serve the mushrooms, put them under a hot grill to heat them through and melt and lightly brown the cheese.

Transfer them to a serving dish, or individual plates, and serve hot, or warm.

MAKES ABOUT 16; SERVES 3–4 AS A FIRST COURSE

BROCCOLI AND STILTON TART

The hot oil treatment of the pastry case and the preliminary cooking of the custard are tips I learned from a friend renowned for her wonderfully crisp flan bases. The contrast of the creamy custard and the crisp, light pastry is excellent.

75 g/3 oz plain white flour	FOR THE FILLING
75 g/3 oz plain wholewheat flour	225 g/8 oz broccoli florets
½ tsp salt	300 ml/10 fl oz single cream
75 g/3 oz butter	3 egg yolks
1 egg yolk	salt and freshly ground pepper
1 tbls cold water	100 g/4 oz blue Stilton cheese, thinly sliced
1½ tbls oil	

Set the oven to 200°C/400°F/Gas Mark 6.

Make the pastry by putting the flours, salt, butter and egg yolk into a food processor; whizz for a few seconds without the plunger to allow the air to get in until the mixture looks like breadcrumbs, then add the water and whizz again, briefly, until the mixture forms a ball of dough. Or make the pastry in the usual way by putting the flours and salt into a bowl, rubbing in the butter with your fingertips then adding the egg yolk and water to bind to a dough.

On a floured board, roll out the pastry as thinly as you can and press gently into a 23 cm/9 inch flan tin. Trim off the excess pastry, put a circle of greaseproof paper in the base and weigh it down with some crusts or dried beans. Bake the flan case for 7 minutes, then take out the greaseproof paper and crusts or beans and bake for a further 5–10 minutes, until the pastry base looks golden and feels set and firm to the touch. Just before you take the flan case out of the oven, heat the oil in a small saucepan until it is smoking hot. Pour this over the base of the flan case as soon as it comes out of the oven. It should sizzle and seem to 'fry' on the base of the flan. Now you can leave the flan case until you're ready to finish it.

To make the filling, bring 2.5 cm/1 inch of water to the boil in a saucepan. Put in the broccoli, cover, and boil for 2–3 minutes, or until it is just tender. Drain immediately into a colander, then put under the cold tap to cool the broccoli quickly so that it keeps its crispness and colour. Turn the broccoli on to a double layer of kitchen paper and blot-dry.

Put the cream and egg yolks into a saucepan and beat together. Season with a little salt and pepper, then stir over a gentle heat for a few minutes until the mixture just begins to thicken and coats the spoon. Remove from the heat immediately. Now put the broccoli and Stilton into the flan case and pour the custard over. Put into the oven, turn the heat down to 180°C/350°F/Gas Mark 4 and bake for 30–40 minutes.

SERVES 6

VARIATIONS

Brie is very good in this tart instead of the Stilton; so is Italian Mascarpone.

CELEBRATION WILD RICE WITH LEMON MAYONNAISE SAUCE

This is a pleasing mixture of flavours and textures; the chewiness and slightly smoky taste of wild rice is enhanced by the intensely flavoured porcini mushrooms, and the delicate, buttery avocado makes a complete contrast.

225 g/8 oz wild rice	LEMON MAYONNAISE
25 g/1 oz dried porcini mushrooms	150 ml/5 fl oz plain yogurt
2 ripe avocados	150 ml/5 fl oz soured cream
juice of 1 lemon	4 rounded tbls good quality mayonnaise, such as Hellman's
2 tbls chopped chives	
salt and freshly ground pepper	juice of 1 lemon
100 g/4 oz whole roasted cashew nuts, pine nuts or macadamia nuts	salt and freshly ground black pepper

First, make the rice. Put the rice into a saucepan with its height again in cold water and bring to the boil; let it simmer for about 45 minutes, or until it is tender and some of the grains have split open. Drain and put into a bowl.

Meanwhile, wash the porcini and put them into a saucepan with water to cover. Bring to the boil, then take off the heat and leave to steep for 30 minutes. After that, simmer the porcini gently for about 15 minutes, or until they are tender and all the water has been absorbed. Add the porcini to the wild rice.

Now make the lemon mayonnaise. Mix together the yogurt, cream and mayonnaise, then stir in the lemon juice, adding it a little at a time and tasting the mixture, to get the right amount of sharpness. Season with salt and freshly ground black pepper.

Halve the avocados and remove the stones and peel, then dice the flesh. Sprinkle the avocados with the lemon juice, and add these, and any extra juice, to the wild rice, along with the chopped chives. Season to taste with salt and freshly ground black pepper. Serve at once, or cover and refrigerate for up to an hour before serving. Just before serving add the nuts.

You can prepare this salad well in advance if you wish, as long as you leave out the avocado and nuts which should be added as near serving time as possible. Serve with the lemon mayonnaise.

SERVES 8–10 AT A PARTY

GNOCCHI ALLA ROMANA WITH CHAR–GRILLED VEGETABLES

Although gnocchi alla romana is usually served as a starter, I think it makes a delicious vegetarian main course, especially when accompanied by some grilled vegetables and perhaps some Italian tomato sauce (page 292). The gnocchi freeze excellently, either as separate cut shapes or assembled and sprinkled with Parmesan, ready for cooking.

1 l/1¾ pints milk	*salt and freshly ground*
1 bay leaf	*black pepper*
200 g/7 oz semolina	*freshly grated nutmeg*
2 egg yolks	*50 g/2 oz Parmesan*
100 g/4 oz cheese, grated	*cheese, freshly grated*

Put the milk and bay leaf into a large saucepan and bring to the boil. Add the semolina gradually in a thin stream, from well above the saucepan, stirring all the time. Bring the mixture to the boil, stirring, then let it cook gently for about 15 minutes until it is very thick. Remove from the heat and beat in the egg yolks and grated cheese. Season with plenty of salt, pepper and grated nutmeg. Spread the mixture out on an oiled baking sheet to a thickness of 1 cm/½ inch or a bit less, and leave to get cold and firm.

Cut the gnocchi mixture into shapes using a sharp pastry cutter, then assemble the dish. First put any odd shapes and trimmings onto a lightly greased shallow dish (a 30 cm/12 inch round ceramic pizza plate is ideal) and top with the remaining shapes. Sprinkle generously with the Parmesan cheese, then grill until the top is golden brown and bubbling, and the inside heated through.

Serve immediately.

FOR THE CHAR-GRILLED VEGETABLES
These can be grilled before the gnocchi, as they can be served warm. Remove the outer leaves from chicory and radicchio, then cut them downwards, halving the chicory and cutting the radicchio into sixths or eighths, depending on its size. Put the vegetables under a hot grill until they are lightly charred and wilted, but still crunchy, turning them over to do both sides. Put them into a serving dish, sprinkle with salt and pepper, and pour a little olive oil over them. I like to serve them with some chunky lemon wedges.

SERVES 6

MIDWINTER VEGETABLE TERRINE WITH MUSTARD VINAIGRETTE

This makes a striking dish for a buffet party. You can use other vegetables for the filling but they need to be of contrasting colours. I love the slightly sweet, nutty flavour of Jerusalem artichokes, which luckily I find I can eat without tiresome after-effects. I sometimes wonder whether it's fair to inflict them on visitors, though, delicious as they are, and use turnips instead! Parsnips, peppers, sweet potato, firm winter squash and courgettes would all taste and look good; leek could be substituted for spinach for the outside layer.

900 g/2 lb spinach
75 g/3 oz butter or vegan
  margarine
lemon juice
2 eggs
salt and freshly ground
  black pepper
450 g/1 lb carrots
700 g/1½ lb Jerusalem
  artichokes

FOR THE MUSTARD
VINAIGRETTE
3 tbls Dijon mustard,
  preferably Grey Poupon
3 tbls red wine vinegar
9 tbls olive oil

Wash the spinach thoroughly in three changes of water, then put it into a large saucepan with just the water clinging to it, and cook for about 10 minutes, or until it is tender. Drain it well, squeezing it really dry with your hands, or by pressing it against the sides of a sieve. Add 25 g/1 oz of the butter, a few drops of lemon juice, 1 egg, and mix well. Season with salt and pepper. Leave this on one side while you make the other two fillings.

Scrape or scrub the carrots and cut them into small dice; peel the artichokes as thinly as you can, and dice them. too. Divide the remaining butter between two pans, then put the carrots into one and the Jerusalem artichokes into the other. Cover and let them cook very gently for about 15 minutes, or until they are both tender. If they start to stick to the pan, add a tablespoonful of water. Then mash each roughly. Separate the remaining egg, and add the yolk to the carrots and the white to the Jerusalem artichokes. Mix well, adding salt, pepper and a little lemon juice to taste.

Set the oven to 180°C/350°F/Gas Mark 4. Line a 900 g/2 lb loaf tin (a long narrow one is best) with a long strip of nonstick paper to cover the base and ends, and oil the tin. Press the spinach mixture into the base and all the way up the sides, saving enough to cover the top. Put in the carrot mixture in a smooth layer, then the artichoke mixture, and finish with the rest of the spinach.

Stand the loaf tin in a baking tin and pour in boiling water so that it comes about two thirds up the sides of the tin. Bake for 50 minutes–1 hour until the top feels firm. Let it cool, then chill it. To serve, slip a knife around the edges, turn the terrine out on to a serving dish and strip off the paper. Decorate with cut-out Jerusalem artichoke stars and carrot shapes, and serve with the mustard vinaigrette.

To make the vinaigrette, put the mustard into a bowl with the vinegar, ¼ teaspoonful of salt and a grinding of pepper, and mix well. Gradually add the oil, mixing well after each addition to make a thick, emulsified dressing. Check the seasoning and add a little more salt if necessary before serving with the terrine.

SERVES 6–8

OPPOSITE: *Midwinter Vegetable Terrine with Mustard Vinaigrette*

LITTLE BRIE AND HAZELNUT BAKES

Quick, easy and delicious! Serve them with a crisp, simple salad such as lettuce, cucumber and tomato, or chicory, watercress and orange (as here), or celery and apple. They're also good with lightly cooked vegetables such as French beans, and I love them with the bitter-sweet fruity flavour of home-made Cranberry Sauce (page 293).

350 g/12 oz Brie	*50 g/2 oz hazelnuts, skinned*

Cut the Brie (including the rind) into 1 cm/½ inch chunky pieces and place close together in a single layer in four individual ramekins, or in a shallow ovenproof dish. Chop the hazelnuts roughly – I give them a quick whizz in the food processor – and sprinkle evenly over the top.

Place under a hot grill for about 10 minutes, until the Brie has heated through and half melted, and the nuts have toasted. Serve at once.

SERVES 3–4

CHUNKY HAZELNUT AND TOMATO TERRINE

25 g/1 oz butter or margarine	*100 g/4 oz fresh breadcrumbs*
1 onion, finely chopped	*1 tbls chopped parsley*
100 g/4 oz button mushrooms, chopped	*75 ml/3 fl oz water or stock*
2 tomatoes, skinned and chopped	*2 tbls Tamari or Shoyu soy sauce*
1 garlic clove, crushed	*1 tbls lemon juice*
1 tsp basil	*salt and freshly ground pepper*
200 g/7 oz skinned hazelnuts	

Set the oven to 200°C/400°F/Gas Mark 6 and line a 450 g/1 lb loaf tin with a long strip of nonstick paper to cover the base and narrow sides.

To make the terrine, melt the butter in a medium-large saucepan, then add the onion and fry for 7–8 minutes until soft but not browned; then add the mushrooms, tomatoes, garlic and basil, and fry for a further 5 minutes.

Meanwhile, chop the hazelnuts coarsely. Add these to the mixture in the saucepan, along with the fresh breadcrumbs, chopped parsley, water or stock, Tamari or Shoyu soy sauce and lemon juice.

Mix well, season with salt and pepper, spoon the mixture into the prepared tin and smooth the top level. Bake, uncovered, for about 40 minutes, or until the terrine feels firm to the touch. Leave it to cool completely in the tin, then chill.

Serve cold, thinly sliced, with warm Garlic Sauce (page 321).

SERVES 8 AT A PARTY

OPPOSITE: *Little Brie and Hazelnut Bakes*

MUSHROOM PÂTÉ WITH A HERBY CRUST

Cold and sliced, this makes a good pâté for a party – the Lemon Mayonnaise (page 332) goes very well with it, especially if you throw a few green peppercorns into it (about a tablespoonful). This pâté also makes a good first course and is an excellent sandwich filling, especially if you use a rather light granary bread.

25 g/1 oz butter
1 onion, chopped
700 g/1½ lb mushrooms
2 garlic cloves, crushed
50 g/2 oz fresh
  breadcrumbs
1 egg
salt and freshly ground
  pepper

FOR THE HERBY
  COATING
butter
dried wholewheat crumbs
1½ tsp mixed herbs

Set the oven to 180°C/350°F/Gas Mark 4 and line a greased 450 g/1 lb loaf tin with a long strip of nonstick paper to cover the base and narrow sides. Grease the paper very generously with butter, then sprinkle thickly with dried wholewheat crumbs and 1 teaspoonful of the mixed herbs, to form the herby coating.

To make the pâté, melt the butter in a large saucepan, add the onion and fry for 5 minutes; then add the mushrooms and garlic, and fry for about 30 minutes or until all the liquid has gone. Whizz the mushroom mixture to a purée in a food processor; add the breadcrumbs and egg, and whizz again briefly, to mix.

Pour the mixture into the prepared tin and smooth the top level. Sprinkle the top quite thickly with dried crumbs, sprinkle with the remaining mixed herbs and dot with a little butter. Bake, uncovered, for about 40 minutes, or until the pâté feels firm to the touch, and a knife inserted in the middle comes out clean. Leave it to cool in the tin, then loosen the sides, turn the pâté out and strip off the paper. If you want a crisper coating, pop the pâté back into the oven for 10 minutes or so, or until the outside is crisp.

Serve cold, thinly sliced.

SERVES 8 AT A PARTY

MINI CHESTNUT SAUSAGE ROLLS

These little 'sausages' are very popular with children. They freeze excellently, too, and can be baked from frozen – allow 5 minutes extra cooking time if you are doing this. They are good served with a dip, such as yogurt and herb, soured cream and horseradish, or with mango chutney.

225 g/8 oz quick flaky
  pastry (page 299)

FOR THE FILLING
1 x 250 g/9 oz can
  unsweetened chestnut
  purée
1 small onion, grated

1 garlic clove, crushed
1 tbls lemon juice
1 tbls soy sauce
100 g/4 oz soft
  wholewheat
  breadcrumbs
good pinch of chilli
  powder

First make the chestnut filling, by mixing together the chestnut purée, onion, garlic, lemon juice, soy sauce, breadcrumbs and chilli powder. Leave the mixture for a few minutes for the breadcrumbs to thicken it, then add a few more if necessary to make a soft mixture which you can roll into sausages.

Set the oven to 190°C/375°F/Gas Mark 5.

On a lightly floured board, roll out the pastry quite thinly, then cut across into long strips about 5 cm/2 inches wide. Roll pieces of the chestnut mixture into sausages about the width of a slim little finger and the length of the pastry strips, and lay on top of the pastry strips. Dampen the edges of the pastry with cold water, then roll them round the chestnut mixture, pressing the edges together. Prick the pastry with a fork, then cut into 2.5 cm/1 inch lengths and place, seam side down, on a baking sheet. Bake for about 10 minutes, or until the pastry is golden brown and crisp.

MAKES 48

OPPOSITE: *Mini Chestnut Sausage Rolls*

PARTY ROULADE

FOR THE ROULADE
50 g/2 oz soft white
  breadcrumbs
150 ml/5 fl oz single
  cream
2 tbls water
175 g/6 oz Gruyère
  cheese, grated
4 eggs, separated
salt and freshly ground
  black pepper
cayenne pepper

a little grated Parmesan
  for dusting

FOR THE FILLING
450 g/1 lb asparagus
2 tbls lemon juice
2 tbls olive oil
150 g/5 oz Lingot du
  Berry or other, similar
  soft medium fat goat's
  cheese
1 tbls chopped parsley

Set the oven to 200°C/400°F/Gas Mark 6 and line a
32 × 23 cm/13 × 9 inch Swiss roll tin with nonstick
paper.

First make the roulade. Mix together the breadcrumbs, cream, water, cheese and egg yolks. Season
with salt, pepper and a couple of pinches of cayenne.

Whisk the egg whites until stiff, then fold into the
egg yolk mixture. Turn into a tin, spreading into the
corners – get it level. Bake for 10–15 minutes or until
set and firm to a light touch. Leave it in the tin and
cover it with a tea towel that has been wrung out in
warm water. Set it aside to get completely cold.

To make the filling, trim the asparagus and cook
until just tender; drain. Cut off the tips and chop the
rest. Put it all in a shallow dish, sprinkle with the
lemon juice and oil and season. Leave to get cold.

To assemble the roulade, sprinkle a large sheet of
nonstick paper with grated Parmesan. Remove the
cloth from the roulade and turn the roulade out on to
the paper. Trim the edges. Spread the goat's cheese
all over the roulade. Remove 8 tips from the
asparagus and put the rest over the roulade, on top of
the cheese (don't use the dressing which may remain
with the asparagus). Sprinkle with the parsley.

Carefully roll up the roulade, using the paper to
help. Place on a dish and decorate with the reserved
asparagus tips, placed diagonally along the top.
SERVES 6

MIXED LEAF SALAD WITH ROCKET

This is a mixture of radicchio, frisée, lamb's lettuce,
some ordinary 'floppy' lettuce – not too much! –
rocket (which you can sometimes get growing in a
pot) and some freshly chopped herbs if available,
especially tarragon and chives. I usually serve with
a 'normal' vinaigrette, which I generally make with
1 tablespoon wine vinegar to 3 tablespoons olive
oil, a good pinch of sugar, about half a teaspoon
Dijon mustard, preferably Grey Poupon, and some
sea salt and pepper. Tear up the leaves, making sure
there's a nice mix of colours, with plenty of red.

CUCUMBER AND DILL SALAD

1 large cucumber
1 small onion (optional)
salt, sugar and freshly
  ground pepper

1 tsp white mustard seed
1 tbls chopped fresh dill
  or 1 tsp dried dill weed
2 tbls wine vinegar

Peel and thinly slice the cucumber and the onion, if
you're using this. Put the slices into a shallow dish
and sprinkle with a little salt, pepper and a dash of
sugar (about ½ teaspoonful). Mix in the mustard seed,
dill and vinegar, cover and leave until you need it.

The salad will make quite a lot of juice – that's
normal. Drain it off before serving, or not, as you
wish. It's nice mopped up with some bread.
SERVES 4

OPPOSITE: *Party Roulade*

LETTUCE HEART SALAD WITH FRESH HERB DRESSING

2 hearty lettuces, such as little gem
1 tbls chopped fresh herbs – tarragon is especially good if you can get it; otherwise chives or mint
½ tsp Dijon mustard
good pinch of sugar
salt and freshly ground black pepper
1 tbls red wine vinegar
3 tbls olive oil

Wash the lettuces, taking off the outer leaves but keeping the hearts intact; then slice. Put the herbs, mustard, sugar, some salt and pepper and the vinegar into a salad bowl – a glass one is nice – and mix together. Gradually stir in the oil. Cross salad servers over the top of the dressing and put the lettuce in on top. Gently toss the lettuce in the dressing just before you serve the salad.
SERVES 3–4

CHICORY, ORANGE AND WATERCRESS SALAD

The juice from the oranges provides a light dressing for this refreshing salad, although you can add 1–2 tablespoons of olive oil to make it into more of a vinaigrette-type of dressing if you prefer. Ruby oranges are particularly good if you can get them.

2 chicory
4 small sweet oranges
1 × 75 g/3 oz packet of watercress

Wash the chicory and cut it downwards into eighths and put it into a bowl. Holding the oranges over the bowl to catch the juice, cut the peel and pith, then slice them into thin circles. Add the watercress and toss all the ingredients together.
SERVES 4

COLESLAW

Coleslaw is so quick and easy to make, and the home-made version so good, that I wonder why people buy it ready-made . . .

450 g/1 lb white cabbage, finely shredded
225 g/8 oz scraped carrots, coarsely grated
150 ml/5 fl oz low fat plain yogurt
4 tbls mayonnaise
salt and freshly ground pepper
lemon juice (optional)

OPTIONAL ADDITIONS
2 onions, finely sliced
1 small green pepper, seeded and chopped
100 g/4 oz raisins

Put the cabbage and carrots into a large bowl, together with any of the optional extras. Add the yogurt, mayonnaise and salt and pepper to taste and mix well. Sharpen with a little lemon juice if you like, before serving.
SERVES 6

WATERCRESS AND RADISH SALAD

This is an easy salad to make – and a pretty, festive combination of colours, too. It tastes wonderfully fresh as is, but if you prefer, you can serve dressed with a light vinaigrette.

1 × 100 g/4 oz packet radishes
1 × 75 g/3 oz packet watercress

Wash the radishes, and halve them or leave them whole, as you wish. Give the watercress a quick swish through cold water, then shake dry and put into a bowl with the radishes.
SERVES 4

OPPOSITE: (left) Broccoli and Stilton Tart, page 332, and (right) Lettuce Heart Salad with Fresh Herb Dressing

MULLED WINE

5 oranges
5–6 cloves
1 cinnamon stick
1 bottle red wine

1 glass Cointreau or other
  orange liqueur
a little sugar to taste

Scrub the oranges, then stick the cloves into one and put all of them into a stainless steel or enamel saucepan with the cinnamon stick, wine and liqueur. Heat gently to just below boiling, then keep at this temperature for 10–15 minutes. Taste and add a little sugar as necessary, then ladle into warmed glasses.
SERVES 4–6

MULLED APPLE JUICE

Spices go well with apples, and this delightful, warming drink has something of the flavour of mulled wine, without any alcohol.

1 l/1¾ pints still apple
  juice
1 orange

6 cloves
1 cinnamon stick
demerara sugar

Pour the apple juice into a saucepan. Stick the cloves into the orange, then slice it fairly thinly and add to the apple juice, along with the cinnamon stick. Heat gently for about 30 minutes to draw out the flavour of the spices. Taste and add a little demerara sugar to taste, ladle into glasses and serve at once.
SERVES 6

GINGER PUNCH

3 lemons
3 oranges
6–8 mint sprigs
2 tbls caster sugar

1 l/1¾ pints ginger ale
1 l/1¾ pints soda water
12 ice cubes

Wash, then thinly slice the lemons and oranges. Put them into a large bowl and add the mint, bruising the mint a bit with a spoon to help bring out the flavour. Sprinkle over the caster sugar and leave to chill for at least an hour or two, or until you're ready to serve the punch.

Mix in the ginger ale, soda water and ice cubes, and serve at once.
SERVES 10–12

SLOE GIN AND TONIC

This is such a lovely festive drink that I had to include it, although it does need some advance preparation – in September or October, to be exact. If you're too late, you can buy it, but do try making it next year as it's so warming and festive. You can drink it undiluted as a liqueur, as well as with tonic.

450 g/1 lb ripe sloes
70 cl bottle gin
100 g/4 oz caster sugar

few drops almond
  essence or extract
tonic water, to serve

Wear an apron: the juice splatters and is indelible. Squish the sloes, or prick them with a darning needle, depending on how firm they are. Put them into a large empty plastic water bottle with the rest of the ingredients and shake. Leave for 2 months, shaking daily. Then strain twice through double muslin. Serve with tonic water. For a party, make up a jugful with tonic water and ice.

OPPOSITE: *Mulled Wine*

CHRISTMAS DINNERS

The Christmas dinners in this section are all for six people, although quantities could easily be reduced – sometimes individual recipes will make enough for six to have one serving hot and one cold, with salads and pickles. I've given a timetable for each meal, and if you're used to cooking turkey you'll see that a vegetarian Christmas dinner is actually much easier and quicker to prepare; the main thing you have to worry about is the roast potatoes, if you're serving them! Except for the Moulded Rice with Two Sauces menu, main courses can be made in advance and frozen, or made on Christmas Eve and kept overnight in the fridge – it's a great help to get the major dish done well ahead of time. The same applies to the basic sauces: if you want plenty of time to enjoy Christmas Day, I strongly advise you to make and freeze these as I've explained on page 286. For pudding, I would suggest choosing either something that can be taken care of in advance or something relatively straight-forward, like ice cream for the children or an exotic fruit salad – see the individual menus that follow for specific suggestions. All the puddings here, in fact, are served cold and benefit from being made in advance – I think the last thing the cook needs is yet another course to prepare on the day itself!

Christmas Pudding is an alternative to the pud-dings recommended in the menus – if the classic one is too heavy, try the Light Christmas Puddings on page 376. Much of the preparation for both of these can be done in advance.

I've suggested first courses, vegetables and accompaniments which I think go well with each of the main dishes given here and I've tried to avoid rep-etition, but My Favourite Way with Brussels Sprouts and Cranberry Sauce, for instance, would be delicious with the Chestnut and Red Wine Pâté instead of Julienne of Root Vegetables and Horseradish Sauce if prefer, and so on – so do change the menus to suit your own taste. If you're cooking for only one or two vegetarians, just reduce the quantity; most of them will adapt well. Or you can serve the vegetarian main course as an extra dish to the general meal, which the meat-eaters can share.

I've included a red and white wine suggestion for each menu but these are very much subject to personal preference. The usual rule of thumb I fol-low is that when I'm serving both white and red, I serve the white first; on the other hand, if you pre-fer it the other way round – go ahead and enjoy. I like dry wines with food but, again, semi-sweet or sweet is fine if those are your preferences. If you can't agree on the type of wine to have, you could always settle the argument (and add to the general festivity of the occasion) by serving sparkling wine or even Champagne!

For all the menus I've given timetables for lunch-time Christmas dinner, which is what most families, including my own, seem to like best, but they could, of course, easily be adapted if you're planning an evening feast.

MELON AND STAR FRUIT COMPÔTE

A melon with greenish flesh looks good with the yellow star fruit – either an ogen melon, or a honeydew, for instance. These are best bought a few days before you need them, so that they can ripen up. I choose the yellowest star fruit that I can find.

1 ripe melon	*clear honey*
juice of 2 oranges	*1 large ripe star fruit*

Halve the melon, remove the seeds, then cut the flesh into pieces or scoop it out with a parisienne cutter to make melon balls. Put the melon into a bowl with the orange juice and a little honey to taste, as necessary. If the melon is sweet you probably won't need any honey.

Cut the star fruit across – like slicing a cucumber – to produce thin star-shaped pieces. Add to the compôte, then divide the mixture betwen six bowls.

CASHEW NUT ROAST WITH HERB STUFFING

50 g/2 oz butter	*parsley sprigs and small*
1 large onion, sliced	*lemon slices, to garnish*
225 g/8 oz unroasted	
cashew nuts	
100 g/4 oz white bread,	FOR THE STUFFING
crusts removed	*100 g/4 oz white*
2 large garlic cloves	*breadcrumbs*
200 ml/7 fl oz water or	*50 g/2 oz softened butter*
light vegetable stock	*1 small onion, grated*
salt and freshly ground	*½ tsp each thyme and*
black pepper	*marjoram*
grated nutmeg	*25 g/1 oz parsley,*
1 tbls lemon juice	*chopped*

Set the oven to 200°C/400°F/Gas Mark 6 and line a 450 g/1 lb loaf tin with a long strip of nonstick paper; use some of the butter to grease the tin and paper well. Melt most of the remaining butter in a medium-sized saucepan, add the onion and fry for about 10 minutes until tender but not browned. Remove from the heat.

Grind the cashew nuts in a food processor with the bread and garlic, and add to the onion, together with the water or stock, salt, pepper, grated nutmeg and lemon juice to taste.

Mix the stuffing ingredients together and season.

Put half the cashew nut mixture into the prepared tin, top with the stuffing, then spoon the rest of the nut mixture on top. Dot with the remaining butter. Stand the tin in another tin to catch any butter which may ooze out, and bake for about 30 minutes, or until firm and lightly browned. (Cover the roast with foil if it gets too brown before then.)

Cool for a minute or two in the tin, then slip a knife around the sides, turn the nut roast out and strip off the paper. Decorate with sprigs of parsley and small slices of lemon, and surround with roast potatoes, if you're serving them.

OPPOSITE: *Christmas Dinner 1, with Cashew Nut Roast with Herb Stuffing*

ROAST POTATOES

1 kg/2 lb 2 oz potatoes   light olive oil

Set the oven to 200°C/400°F/Gas Mark 6.

Peel the potatoes and cut them into halves. Put them into a saucepan, cover with water, and parboil for 5 minutes, or until they are almost tender, but not showing any signs of breaking up.

When they are almost done, pour a thin layer of oil – 3 mm/⅛ inch – into a baking dish or tin and put into the oven to heat. Drain the potatoes thoroughly and, standing well back, put them into the oil, which should be smoking hot and sizzle and splutter as you put them in. Turn them with a perforated spoon, then put into the top of the oven.

Have a look at the potatoes after about 20 minutes and, if they're doing well, turn them over and continue to cook gently, alongside the nut roast or other main course. They will keep happily at this temperature for 45–60 minutes.

Drain them well on kitchen paper before serving with the nut roast.

CARROTS WITH PARSLEY BUTTER

700 g/1½ lb carrots
25 g/1 oz Parsley Butter
  (page 295)
or 25 g/1 oz butter or
  margarine and 1–2
  tbls chopped parsley
salt and freshly ground
  black pepper

Scrub or peel the carrots, then cut them into circles or sticks. Put the carrots into a saucepan, cover with boiling water and bring to the boil. Cover and cook for 5–10 minutes, or until they are just tender; don't let them get soggy.

Drain, add the parsley butter, salt and pepper, and serve immediately.

MY FAVOURITE WAY WITH BRUSSELS SPROUTS

I like Brussels sprouts which are only just done, nice and crunchy and green. I find that the best way to achieve this is to cut them in half – a trick I learnt from my mother.

700 g/1½ lb Brussels
  sprouts
25 g/1 oz butter
salt and freshly ground
  black pepper

Remove the outer leaves from the sprouts, then wash them and halve them. Just before you want to serve the meal, bring 1 cm/½ inch of water to the boil in a large saucepan. Put in the sprouts, cover with a lid, and boil for 4–5 minutes, or until they are just done. Drain and add the butter and salt and pepper.

VEGETARIAN GRAVY

3 tbls olive oil or melted
  butter
3 tbls wholewheat flour
600 ml/1 pint water or
  stock
3 tbls dark soy sauce, eg
  Tamari or Shoyu
salt and freshly ground
  black pepper

Heat the oil in a saucepan and add the flour. Stir over a moderate heat for a few minutes until the flour turns nut-brown. Standing well back, pour in the water or stock and stir until slightly thickened. Simmer for 10 minutes, then add the soy sauce and a little seasoning to taste if necessary.

FOR THE REMAINDER OF THE MENU

MENU 1 COUNTDOWN

MAKE IN ADVANCE

Cashew Nut Roast: freeze uncooked, for 2–4 weeks.
Vegetarian Gravy, Bread Sauce, Cranberry Sauce, Parsley Butter: all of these can be made in advance and frozen.
Meringue Nests: cook and freeze the nests unfilled.
Ice Cream: make up to 14 days ahead, cover well and freeze.
Mince Pies: cook a batch and freeze (it's easier to have a cooked batch for heating through on Christmas Day).

CHRISTMAS EVE

Remove from the freezer: Cashew Nut Roast, Vegetarian Gravy, Bread Sauce, Cranberry Sauce, Meringue Nests, Mince Pies. Put the Mince Pies on to a serving dish. Leave to thaw overnight.

Peel the potatoes and leave in a pan with cold water to cover. Prepare the sprouts and carrots; put them into separate polythene bags in the fridge.

Get together serving dishes – a large one for the nut roast and potatoes; vegetable dishes for the sprouts and carrots; gravy boats/jugs/bowls for sauces; a round serving plate for the Meringue Nests. Gather plates for the first course, main course and pudding.

CHRISTMAS DAY

11.00 am Lay the table. (This can be done on Christmas Eve if you're in the mood and don't need the table for breakfast.) Chill the white wine. Make the fillings for the Meringue Nests and pile into the nests. Store in the fridge.

11.15 am Set the oven to 200°C/400°F/Gas Mark 6. Prepare the Melon and Star Fruit Compôte; cover and chill in the fridge. Parboil the potatoes for about 5 minutes. Prepare the garnish for the nut roast.

11.40 am Heat the oil for potatoes at the top of the oven. Put the Cashew Nut Roast in towards the bottom of the oven. Put the potatoes into the oil and put the tin back into the top of the oven.

12.30 pm Open the red wine. Turn the nut roast out on to its plate; cover loosely with foil and put back into the oven. Reheat the sauces, then serve them out and keep them warm at the bottom of the oven.

12.45 pm Put the water on for the carrots and sprouts. Cook until they are only just done, then drain, put them into warmed vegetable dishes in the bottom of the oven to keep warm.

12.55 pm Open the white wine; light the candles; put the ice cream into the fridge.

1.00 pm Dinner is served!

After the starter Quickly serve out the sauces if you haven't already done so. Lift the potatoes out of the tin on to kitchen paper with a perforated spoon; quickly blot off excess oil, then put them around the Cashew Nut Roast; garnish. Put the Mince Pies, covered in foil, into the oven towards the bottom to warm through. Take main course dishes to the table.

After the main course Sprinkle the Mince Pies with caster sugar; take to the table with the pudding.

MENU 2

Iced Melon Soup with Violets

~

Chestnut and Red Wine Pâté en Croûte
Horseradish Sauce · Vegetarian Gravy
Light Mashed Potatoes
Julienne of Root Vegetables

~

Rum-Marinated Fruits with
Coconut and Lime Cream
or Chocolate and Vanilla Ice Cream

~

Mince Pies

~

WINES: *Chardonnay (white) Côtes du Rhône*
or Cabernet Shiraz (red)

ICED MELON SOUP WITH VIOLETS

2 ogen melons, or 1 large
  honeydew melon
2 tbls caster sugar

small bunch of fresh
  violets, washed and
  very gently shaken
  dry

Halve the melons and remove the seeds. Scoop out the flesh and liquidize until smooth, adding a little sugar if necessary. Chill in the fridge until ready to serve.

Serve the soup in chilled bowls, garnished with a few violet heads floating in each one. Or for extra effect, serve from one large bowl set over a larger bowl of crushed ice.

CHESTNUT AND RED WINE PÂTÉ EN CROÛTE

25 g/ 1 oz butter or vegan
  margarine
2 medium-sized onions,
  chopped
2 garlic cloves, crushed
50 g/ 2 oz button
  mushrooms, sliced
  (optional)
75 ml/ 3 fl oz red wine
75 g/3 oz soft fresh white
  or brown breadcrumbs

½ x 350 g/12 oz can
  unsweetened chestnut
  purée or mashed fresh or
  canned chestnuts
salt and freshly ground
  black pepper
450 g/1 lb Quick Flaky
  Pastry (page 299)
a little beaten egg to glaze
  (optional)

Melt the butter in a medium-large saucepan, add the onions and fry for about 10 minutes, until tender but not browned. Add the garlic and mushrooms, if you're using them, and cook for a further 2–3 minutes. Pour in the wine and let it bubble away for a minute or two until most of the liquid has gone; then remove from the heat and stir in the breadcrumbs, chestnut purée, and salt and pepper to taste.

Set the oven to 230°C/450°F/Gas Mark 8.

On a lightly floured board, roll out the pastry into two strips, one measuring about 15 × 30 cm/6 × 12 inches; the other 22 × 30 cm/9 × 12 inches. Put the smaller strip on to a baking sheet brushed with cold water. Spoon the chestnut mixture on to the pastry, keeping 1 cm/½ inch clear all round the edges, and piling it up well into a nice loaf-like shape in the middle. Brush the edges of the pastry with cold water, then ease the second piece of pastry on top; press down lightly and trim the edges. Cut the trimmings into holly leaves, Christmas trees, bells or whatever you fancy, and stick them on top of the pastry with water. Make a few small steam holes, then brush with beaten egg if you're using this.

Put into the oven and bake for 7–8 minutes, then reduce the temperature to 200°C/400°F/Gas Mark 6 and bake for a further 20–25 minutes.

OPPOSITE: *Christmas Dinner 2, with Chestnut and Red Wine Pâté en Croûte*

HORSERADISH SAUCE

Mustard Sauce is a pleasant variation of this sauce; use a little Dijon or whole-grain mustard instead of the creamed horseradish. A teaspoonful of drained, pickled green peppercorns or capers make a pleasant, piquant addition, too.

300 ml/10 fl oz soured	*1–2 tbls creamed*
cream or creamy plain	*horseradish*
yogurt	*salt*

Mix the soured cream or yogurt with enough creamed horseradish to give the sauce a good tang; season with salt before serving.

LIGHT MASHED POTATOES

1 kg/2 lb 2 oz potatoes	*salt and freshly ground*
25 g/1 oz butter	*black pepper*
4 tbls cream	

Peel the potatoes and cut into even-sized pieces, not too big. Put them into a saucepan, cover with water and boil until they are tender, about 15 minutes. Drain them, keeping the liquid, then mash them thoroughly using a potato masher or by pushing them through a vegetable mill – not in the food processor, or you'll end up with glue. Add the butter, cream and enough of the reserved water to make a very light consistency, like lightly whipped cream. Season with salt and pepper and serve immediately.

VEGAN VERSION
Use 40 g/1½ oz vegan margarine instead of the butter, and soya milk instead of the cream.

JULIENNE OF ROOT VEGETABLES

Choose a mixture of whatever root vegetables are available: some carrot gives a good basis, and kohlrabi adds a pleasant flavour if you can get it. Parsnip, swede and celeriac are other possibilities. Make sure that any alternative that you choose will cook in the same amount of time, or add the quicker-cooking vegetables, such as, for instance, courgette matchsticks, towards the end of the cooking time.

225 g/8 oz carrots	*squeeze of lemon juice*
225 g/ 8 oz kohlrabi	*salt and freshly ground*
225 g/8 oz turnips	*pepper*
25 g/1 oz butter	*grated nutmeg*

Scrub, scrape or finely peel the root vegetables, depending on their condition, then cut them into thin matchsticks. Cook them, covered in boiling water, or in a steamer, for 5 minutes, or until they are just tender.

Drain, add the butter, a squeeze of lemon juice, and salt, pepper and freshly grated nutmeg and serve immediately.

FOR THE REMAINDER OF THE MENU

MENU 2 COUNTDOWN

MAKE IN ADVANCE

Chestnut and Red Wine Pâté en Croûte: freeze, uncooked, for 2–4 weeks.

Vegetarian Gravy: make in advance and freeze.

Ice Cream: make up to 14 days ahead, cover well and freeze.

Mince Pies: cook a batch and freeze (it's easier to have a cooked batch for heating on Christmas Day).

CHRISTMAS EVE

Remove from the freezer: Chestnut and Red Wine Pâté en Croûte; sauces as required, including Vegetarian Gravy. Put the mince pies on to a serving dish. Leave everything to thaw overnight.

Peel the potatoes and leave in a pan with cold water to cover. Prepare the root vegetables; put them into a polythene bag in the fridge. Make the Horseradish Sauce, spoon it into a serving bowl or jug, cover and keep in the fridge.

Make the Coconut and Lime Cream, spoon into a bowl, cover and keep in the fridge.

Get together serving dishes – a large one for the Pâté; vegetable dishes for potatoes and root vegetables; gravy boats/jugs/bowls for sauces; a serving dish for the pudding. Gather plates for the first course, main course and pudding.

CHRISTMAS DAY

11.00 am Lay the table. (This can be done on Christmas Eve if you're in the mood and don't need the table for breakfast.) Chill the white wine.

11.45am Set the oven to 230°C/450°F/Gas Mark 8. Put the potatoes on to boil. Prepare the soup, put it into a bowl, cover and chill. Prepare and marinate the fruit for the pudding. Put the plates and dishes into the bottom of the oven to warm.

12.20 pm Mash the potatoes and put into the warmed serving dish; cover and put into the oven.

12.30 pm Put the Pâté into the oven. Open the red wine. Reheat the gravy, then serve out and keep warm at the bottom of the oven.

12.38 pm Turn the oven down to 200°C/400°F/Gas Mark 6.

12.45 pm Put the water on for the Julienne of Root Vegetables. Cook the vegetables until they are only just done, then drain, put into a warmed dish.

12.50 pm Pour the soup into bowls, garnish with the violets and take to the table.

12.55 pm Open the white wine; light the candles; put the ice cream into the fridge; check the Pâté.

1.00 pm Dinner is served!

After the starter Quickly serve the Vegetarian Gravy and Horseradish Sauce if you haven't already done so. Lift the Chestnut and Red Wine Pâté en Croûte on to a warmed plate. Put the Mince Pies, covered in foil, into the oven to warm through. Take all the main course dishes to the table.

After the main course Sprinkle the Mince Pies with caster sugar; take to the table, with the pudding.

CHERRY TOMATOES WITH HORSERADISH CREAM

450 g/1 lb cherry
tomatoes
salt and freshly ground
pepper
dash of sugar

4 tbls plain yogurt
1 tbls mayonnaise
1–3 tsp creamed
horseradish
fresh basil leaves

Cover the cherry tomatoes with boiling water; leave for a few seconds until the skins have loosened, then drain and cover the tomatoes with cold water. Slip off the skins with a small sharp knife. Put the tomatoes into a bowl and season with a little salt, pepper and a dash of sugar, if they need it. Chill until required.

Mix together the yogurt, mayonnaise and horseradish; season lightly and chill this, too.

Just before you want to serve this dish, put the tomatoes on to six individual serving dishes. Spoon the yogurt mixture over them and garnish with whole or shredded basil leaves.

STUFFED ACORN SQUASH

For this Christmas Dinner with an American flavour, you can either use small acorn squash, allowing half for each person, or one bigger one, depending on what is available. I think small ones are particularly good, but the combination of firm, buttery squash and light nutty filling is delicious either way.

2 small squash – about
350–450 g/12–16 oz
each, or 1 larger one,
700–900 g/1½–2 lb
25 g/1 oz butter or vegan
margarine
1 onion, chopped

1 small green chilli
(optional)
100 g/4 oz whole cashew
nuts, lightly chopped
2 tbls desiccated coconut
1 tbls chopped parsley
salt and freshly ground
black pepper

Halve the squash, scoop out the seeds and trim the bases a little as necessary so that they stand level. Cook them in water to cover for about 15 minutes – perhaps longer if you are using the bigger squash – or until you can pierce the flesh easily with a knife. Drain well and blot with kitchen paper. Stand the squash in an ovenproof dish or on a baking sheet and season with a little salt and pepper.

Next make the filling. Melt half the butter or margarine in a saucepan, add the onion and fry for 10 minutes, letting it brown a bit. Meanwhile, halve the chilli, if you're using this, and rinse away the seeds under the tap. Chop the chilli and add to the onion, along with the cashew nuts and coconut, and fry for a further 2–3 minutes. Season and pile the mixture into the squash. Cut the remaining butter into four pieces and put on top of the stuffing. Set the oven to 200°C/400°F/Gas Mark 6.

Cover the whole dish or tin with a piece of foil and bake the squash for about 15 minutes for small squash, 25–30 minutes for larger ones, or until heated through. Remove the foil and bake for a further 5–10 minutes, then serve immediately.

OPPOSITE: *Christmas Dinner 3, with Stuffed Acorn Squash*

GLAZED SWEET POTATOES

Get the type with delicious golden flesh – they make a marvellous Christmas vegetable – much easier to do than roast potatoes!

1 kg/2 lb 2 oz sweet potatoes	*25 g/1 oz light brown sugar*
25 g/1 oz butter	*2 tbls lemon juice*
	salt

Scrub the potatoes and cut into even-sized pieces, not too big. Put them into a saucepan, cover with water and boil until they are tender, 10–15 minutes. Drain them, cool and remove the skins.

Grease an ovenproof dish generously with half the butter, then put the sweet potato pieces in on top. Dot with the remaining butter and sprinkle with the sugar, lemon juice and a little salt. The sweet potatoes can be baked when it's convenient for you: they can wait in the fridge overnight, or you can keep them in the freezer.

Set the oven to 200°C/400°F/Gas Mark 6 and bake for 40–50 minutes. Have a look at them after about 30 minutes and turn them if necessary, so that they are golden brown and glazed all over.

BABY SWEETCORN AND MANGETOUTS

350 g/12 oz mangetouts	*15 g/½ oz butter*
350 g/12 oz baby sweetcorn	*salt and freshly ground black pepper*

Top and tail the mangetouts; just wash the sweetcorn. Fill a large saucepan two thirds full of boiling water.

Just before you want to serve them, throw the mangetouts and sweetcorn into the water – they should be covered and able to move around in it –

bring back to the boil, and boil for about 1–2 minutes, or until they are just tender.

Drain immediately into a colander, put them into a warmed serving dish with the butter and a little salt and pepper, and serve immediately.

PORT WINE SAUCE

3 tbls olive oil	*salt and freshly ground black pepper*
1 onion, finely chopped	
600 ml/1 pint red wine	*1–2 tsp redcurrant jelly or caster sugar (optional)*
1 tsp cornflour	
2–3 tbls port	*25 g/1 oz butter or vegan margarine, cut into pieces*

Heat the oil in a small saucepan, add the onion and fry for 10 minutes until it is tender but not browned. Pour in the red wine, bring to the boil, and leave to simmer, without a lid, for about 10 minutes, or until the mixture has reduced to 300 ml/½ pint.

Put the cornflour into a small bowl and mix to a thin paste with the port, then pour this into the wine mixture and stir briefly until it has thickened slightly. Taste the sauce, and add salt, pepper and a little redcurrant jelly or sugar as necessary.

Leave to one side until just before you want to serve the sauce, then quickly stir in the butter or margarine, to make it glossy.

FOR THE REMAINDER OF THE MENU

This sauce goes well with other Christmas Savouries, such as Cashew Nut Roast with Herb Stuffing, Yuletide Ring and also the Chestnut and Red Wine Pâté en Croûte, so it's worth having in the freezer.

MENU 3 COUNTDOWN

MAKE IN ADVANCE

Stuffing for Acorn Squash: freeze, uncooked, for 2–4 weeks.

Vegetarian Gravy, Port Wine Sauce, Cranberry Sauce: all can be made in advance and frozen.

Ice Cream: make 14 days ahead, cover and freeze.

Mince Pies: cook a batch and freeze (it's easiest to have a cooked batch for heating on Christmas Day).

CHRISTMAS EVE

Remove from the freezer: Stuffing for Acorn Squash, Vegetarian Gravy, Port Wine Sauce, Cranberry Sauce. Put the Mince Pies on to a serving dish. Leave everything to thaw overnight.

Peel and parboil the sweet potatoes. Put them into a well-greased shallow casserole, top with butter, sugar and lemon juice, cover and leave in a cool place. Prepare the mangetouts and baby sweetcorn; put them into a polythene bag in the fridge. Parboil the squashes, drain well and place on a baking sheet. Cover loosely with foil and leave in a cool place. Make the cheesecake, cover and put in the fridge.

Get together serving dishes – a large one to hold the squashes; one for the sweet potatoes; a dish for the mangetouts and sweetcorn; gravy boats/jugs/bowls for sauces; a plate for the cheesecake. Gather plates for the first course, main course and pudding.

CHRISTMAS DAY

11.00 am Lay the table. (This can be done on Christmas Eve if you're in the mood and don't need the table for breakfast.) Chill the white wine.

11.30 am Prepare the Cherry Tomatoes. Keep the tomatoes and sauce separate; chill.

11.50 am Set the oven to 200°C/400°F/Gas Mark 6. Put the plates and dishes into the bottom of the oven to warm.

12.10 pm Put the sweet potatoes into the oven towards the top.

12.20 pm Spoon the stuffing into the squash and put into the oven if you're using a large one; otherwise wait until 12.40. Open the red wine. Reheat the sauces, then serve them out and keep them warm at the bottom of the oven.

12.45 pm Put the water on for the mangetouts and sweetcorn. Cook until they are only just done, then drain; put them into the warmed vegetable dish and put them into the bottom of the oven to keep warm. Serve out the starter and take to the table, ready.

12.55 pm Open the white wine; light the candles; put the ice cream into the fridge.

1.00 pm Dinner is served!

After the starter Quickly serve out the sauces if you haven't already done so. Lift the squash out of the tin on to a serving plate; serve out the sweet potatoes, unless you're taking them to the table in the casserole (much easier!). Put the Mince Pies, covered in foil, into the oven towards the bottom, to warm through. Take all the main course dishes to the table.

After the main course Sprinkle the Mince Pies with caster sugar; take to the table, with the puddings.

add the cheese and reserved celery leaves. Stir gently until the cheese has melted into the soup.

Quickly check the seasoning (you probably won't need much as Stilton cheese is quite salty) and serve into warmed bowls.

YULETIDE RING

This makes a dramatic centrepiece to a Christmas Dinner — and there's enough here to feed 12 people, or one serving hot and one cold, for six. It consists of an outer layer of savoury brown nut roast followed by a lemony white layer, and a moist mushroom pâté. I like to fill the middle of the ring with herby stuffing balls, which are always popular.

FOR THE OUTER LAYER
50 g/2 oz butter or vegan margarine
1 large onion, chopped
90 g/3½ oz button mushrooms, chopped
1 tsp mixed herbs
2 tomatoes, fresh or canned
150 g/5 oz soft wholewheat breadcrumbs
150 g/5 oz cashew nuts, grated
150 g/5 oz walnuts, grated
1 tbls Marmite
2 tbls soy sauce
salt and freshly ground black pepper

FOR THE ALMOND AND LEMON LAYER
50 g/2 oz butter or vegan margarine
1 large onion, chopped
225 g/8 oz blanched almonds
100 g/4 oz soft white breadcrumbs
2 lemons

FOR THE MUSHROOM PÂTÉ
450 g/1 lb button mushrooms
25 g/1 oz butter
75 g/3 oz soft breadcrumbs
butter for greasing tin
slices of lemon and tomato, and sprigs of parsley, to garnish

---

MENU 4

Celery and Stilton Soup

~

Yuletide Ring with Parsley Stuffing Balls
Wild Mushroom and Madeira Sauce
Leeks Cooked in Spiced Wine
Cock's Comb Roast Potatoes · Carrot Purée

~

Exotic Fruit Salad and Lychee Sorbet

~

Mince Pies

~

WINES: *Fumé Blanc (white)*
Rioja or Shiraz (red)

CELERY AND STILTON SOUP

If you're going to freeze this soup, don't add the cheese. This can be grated, ready for adding, and frozen separately, to save time.

1 celery, or outside stalks from 2 heads of celery — about 450 g/1 lb in all
1 tbls olive oil
1 onion, chopped

1.5 l/2½ pints water or stock
150–175 g/5–6 oz Stilton cheese, grated
salt and freshly ground black pepper

Remove and reserve any leaves from the celery stalks; then chop the celery. Heat the oil in a large saucepan, add the onion and celery and fry gently, with the lid on the pan, for about 10 minutes, until tender but not browned. Add the water or stock, bring to the boil, and let the soup simmer for about 30 minutes, or until the celery is completely cooked and soft.

Liquidize the soup and pour it back into the pan through a sieve to remove any stringy bits. Heat the soup to boiling point, then remove from the heat and

---

OPPOSITE: *Christmas Dinner 4, with Yuletide Ring with Parsley Stuffing Balls*

First thoroughly grease a 22–23 cm/9–9½ inch ring mould, 1.2 l/2 pint capacity, with butter.

Since the basis of both nut mixtures is fried onion, you can melt the butter for both of them in a large saucepan, add both the onions and fry for 10 minutes, until tender but not browned. Put half the mixture into a bowl on one side. To complete the dark/outer mixture, add the mushrooms and mixed herbs to the pan. Skin the tomatoes, if you're using fresh ones, chop, and add to the saucepan, or just mash in the canned ones, without any juice. Let this mixture cook until all the liquid has gone, then remove from the heat and stir in all the remaining ingredients, and 50 ml/2 fl oz of water, to make a medium-soft mixture.

To complete the almond and lemon layer, grind the almonds and add to the other lot of fried onion, along with the crumbs and 200 ml/7 fl oz water, and flavour with lemon rind and juice. I like this mixture really lemony, and use the grated rind and juice of 1½ lemons; if that is too much for your taste, adjust the amount accordingly, and perhaps add a tablespoonful or two more water. The mixture should be quite soft but not sloppy.

To make the mushroom pâté, wash the mushrooms and chop them roughly. Melt the butter in a large saucepan, add the mushrooms and fry them, without a lid on the pan – they will soon make a great deal of liquid. Continue to cook them, uncovered, until all the liquid has gone – this may take as long as 30 minutes. Then liquidize with the breadcrumbs and season with salt and pepper.

Set the oven to 190°C/375°F/Gas Mark 5.

To assemble the ring, first press the dark nut mixture into the tin, to cover the base and all the way up the sides to within about 5 mm/¼ inch of the top (leave this clear to allow the mixture to rise a bit as it cooks). Next, put in the white mixture, over the dark one, to cover it. Add the mushroom pâté to fill the ring. When it is all in, gently press the top so that it is level, about 5 mm/¼ inch below the top. Cover with a piece of greased foil.

When you are ready to bake the ring, put it into the oven and bake for 1¼–1½ hours, or until the ring feels firm to the touch and a skewer inserted into the middle comes out clean. Let it stand for 2–3 minutes, then loosen the edges, put a large round plate on top

of it, and turn it upside down; hopefully it will come out in one piece. Fill the centre with stuffing balls; decorate the top with slices of tomato, lemon and parsley, and serve immediately.

PARSLEY STUFFING BALLS

350 g/12 oz soft white breadcrumbs	6–8 tbls chopped parsley grated rind of 1–2 lemons
175 g/6 oz softened butter	lemon juice
1 onion, grated	salt and freshly ground
2 tsp mixed herbs	black pepper

Mix all the ingredients together, adding grated lemon rind and juice and salt and pepper to taste. Roll the mixture into balls about the size of walnuts and put them, a little apart, in a greased baking tin. Bake them for about 25 minutes in an oven preset to 190°C/375°F/Gas Mark 5, turning them after about 15 minutes so that they become crisp all over.

WILD MUSHROOM AND MADEIRA SAUCE

10 g/¼ oz dried wild mushrooms	2 tsp cornflour
600 ml/1 pint water	2 tbls Madeira
25 g/1 oz butter	1 tbls Shoyu soy sauce
1 small onion, thinly sliced	salt and freshly ground black pepper

Wash the wild mushrooms to remove any grit, then put them into the water, bring to the boil and leave to soak for 30–60 minutes. Drain, keeping the liquid, and chop the mushrooms.

Meanwhile, melt the butter in a saucepan, add the onion and fry for 10 minutes, letting it brown. Add

This sauce goes well with a number of main courses, so you might like to make a larger quantity; 300 ml/ 10 fl oz portions are a good size for freezing.

the mushrooms and their soaking liquid and simmer for 30 minutes, until they are tender. Mix the cornflour with the Madeira and Shoyu, and add to the mushroom mixture; bring to the boil to thicken slightly. Season with salt and pepper.

LEEKS COOKED IN SPICED WINE

700 g/1½ lb thin leeks	*salt*
2 tbls olive oil	*150 ml/5 fl oz white or*
1 bay leaf	*red wine*
1 tsp whole coriander seed	*chopped parsley*
6 peppercorns	

Clean and trim the leeks and cut them into 5 cm/2 inch lengths. Heat the oil in a large saucepan and put in the leeks: stir-fry gently for about 5 minutes, then add the bay leaf and spices (which you can tie in a small piece of muslin or leave as they are), some salt and the wine. Cover and let the leeks simmer gently for 15–20 minutes, until they are tender. Check the seasoning then put the leeks and their liquid on to a serving dish, removing the bay leaf and spices. Sprinkle with chopped parsley and serve immediately.

COCK'S COMB ROAST POTATOES

1 kg/2 lb 2 oz potatoes	*salt*
50 g/2 oz butter	

Choose even-sized potatoes and scrub them. Put them into a saucepan, cover with water and parboil for 5 minutes or until they are reasonably tender. With a sharp knife, remove the skins and cut the potatoes in half widthways. Standing each potato on its cut surface in a baking tin, cut slits in the top, about 5 mm/¼ inch apart.

Melt the butter, brush this all over the potatoes then sprinkle them with salt. Bake in the oven preset to 190°C/375°F/Gas Mark 5, for about 45–60 minutes, or until they are golden and crisp.

CARROT PURÉE

700 g/1½ lb carrots	*salt and freshly ground*
25 g/1 oz butter or	*pepper*
margarine	*grated nutmeg*
150 ml/5 fl oz single	
cream	

Scrub or peel the carrots and cut into even-sized pieces. Put them into a saucepan, cover with water, bring to the boil, then cook, with a lid on the pan, until they are tender, about 15 minutes. Drain them, keeping the water, then mash or purée them thoroughly. Add the butter or margarine, cream or some of the reserved cooking water to make a soft purée, seasoning with salt, pepper and nutmeg.

If you're not serving this immediately, let it get cold, then reheat it over a very gentle heat, stirring often. Or put the purée into a vegetable dish, cover and bake in the oven preset to 190°C/375°F/Gas Mark 5 for 30 minutes, or until it's heated right through – it helps to turn the sides to the middle after about 20 minutes.

FOR THE REMAINDER OF THE MENU

Exotic Fruit Salad and Lychee Sorbet	*page 385*
Mince Pies	*page 285*

MENU 4 COUNTDOWN

MAKE IN ADVANCE

Celery and Stilton Soup: make 2–4 weeks ahead (without adding the cheese) and freeze.
Yuletide Ring and *Parsley Stuffing Balls*: freeze, uncooked, for 2–4 weeks.
Wild Mushroom and Madeira Sauce: can be made in advance and frozen.
Lychee Sorbet: make 14 days ahead, cover and freeze.
Mince Pies: cook a batch and freeze (it's easiest to have a batch for heating on Christmas Day).

CHRISTMAS EVE

Remove from the freezer: Yuletide Ring, Parsley Stuffing Balls, Wild Mushroom and Madeira Sauce, Soup; also Carrot Purée and Leeks in Spiced Wine, if you've managed to get them done. Put the Mince Pies on to a serving dish. Leave to thaw overnight.

If you haven't done the carrots and leeks you can do so now, then cool, cover and keep in the fridge overnight. Parboil, cut and butter the potatoes as described in the recipe, and leave in their tin, covered. Put the stuffing balls on to a baking sheet and cover.

Get together serving dishes – a large one for the Yuletide Ring; vegetable dishes for the potatoes, leeks and carrots; gravy boat for the sauce; a round serving dish for the fruit and sorbet. Gather plates for the first course, main course and pudding.

CHRISTMAS DAY

11.30 am Lay the table. (This can be done on Christmas Eve if you're in the mood and don't need the table for breakfast.) Chill the white wine.

11.00 am Set the oven to 190°C/375°F/Gas Mark 5. Prepare the garnish for the ring. Put the dishes into the bottom of the oven to warm.

11.30 am Put the ring into the middle of the oven.

12.00 pm Put the potatoes into the oven, towards the top. Make the Exotic Fruit Salad.

12.15 pm Reheat the vegetables, either by stirring gently in saucepans over the heat, or in a microwave. Put them into warmed dishes, cover, and put into the bottom of the oven.

12.30 pm Put the Parsley Stuffing Balls into the top of the oven. Open the red wine. Reheat the sauce, then serve out and keep warm in the oven (or in a baking tin of hot water, as for the vegetables).

12.50 pm Reheat the soup gently and stir in the grated cheese.

12.55 pm Open the white wine; light the candles; put the sorbet into the fridge. Serve the soup into warmed bowls and take to the table. Remove the ring from the oven and leave, covered, on one side.

1.00 pm Dinner is served!

After the starter Turn the ring out on to a warmed plate and fill the centre with stuffing balls; garnish. Quickly serve out the sauce if you haven't already done so. Serve out the potatoes. Take all the main course dishes to the table.

After the main course Sprinkle the Mince Pies with caster sugar; take to the table, with the puddings.

CHRISTMAS SAVOURY STRUDEL

The rich, wine-flavoured filling, the crunchy cashew nuts and the crisp, buttery pastry, are a very good combination here. Pecan or pine nuts are also delicious.

3 tbls olive oil	salt and freshly ground
2 onions, chopped	black pepper
2–3 garlic cloves, crushed	1 × 275 g/10 oz packet
2 × 400 g/14 oz cans	filo pastry
tomatoes in juice	100 g/4 oz butter, melted
1 tsp dried basil	90 g/3½ oz roasted
75 ml/3 fl oz red wine	cashew nuts, roughly
225 g/8 oz button	chopped
mushrooms, washed and	
sliced	

Heat the oil in a fairly large saucepan, add the onions and cook them, with the lid on the pan, for about 10 minutes, until they are tender but not browned. Add the garlic, the tomatoes together with their liquid, the basil and the wine. Let the mixture simmer gently without a lid on the pan, stirring from time to time, until the liquid has disappeared and it is quite thick – this will take about 20 minutes. Add the mushrooms and cook for a further 15 minutes or so, until they are tender and any liquid they make has boiled away. The mixture must be quite dry. Remove from the heat and season to taste.

When the filling mixture has cooled, you can assemble the strudel, which can then be cooked straight away, or kept in the fridge for a few hours until you're ready, or in the freezer for at least a month. I find it easiest to assemble the strudel directly on to a large baking sheet, which means you don't have to lift it later.

Set the oven to 200°C/400°F/Gas Mark 6.

If you have the type of filo pastry which is long and narrow – about 30 × 20 cm/12 × 8 inches – lay two sheets side by side, overlapping them slightly where they join. If you have the type which is quite large – about 30 cm/12 inches or so square – lay out one sheet. Either way, brush the surface with a little melted butter and then sprinkle with a third of the nuts. Put another layer of filo pastry on top, brush

MENU 5

Two-Pear Salad

⌣

Christmas Savoury Strudel
Port Wine Sauce
Celeriac and Potato Purée
Buttered Broccoli · Whole Baby Carrots

⌣

Christmas Dried Fruit Salad with Cream
or Chocolate and Vanilla Ice Cream

⌣

Mince Pies

⌣

WINES: *Graves or Sancerre (white)*
St Emilion or Pinot Noir (red)

TWO–PEAR SALAD

The combination of soft, sweet comice pear and buttery avocado is very good. Both pears need to be ripe; I find it best to buy them 5–7 days in advance and let them ripen up at room temperature.

2 large ripe comice pears	salt and freshly ground
2 large ripe avocados	pepper
juice of ½ lemon	½ × 75 g/3 oz packet
	watercress

Peel and core the comice pears, then slice them downwards into thin segments. Halve and peel the avocados and remove the stones. Cut the avocados, too, into long thin slices. Sprinkle the sliced pears with the lemon juice, salt and pepper.

Put a few watercress leaves on each plate, then arrange alternate slices of comice pear and avocado on top.

with butter, and scatter with nuts. Repeat with another layer, then a final layer of filo pastry, which you just brush with butter. Now tip the tomato filling mixture on top and spread it to about 2.5 cm/1 inch of the edges. Fold the edges over, to enclose the edge of the filling then, starting from one of the widest edges, roll the whole thing up like a Swiss Roll, trying not to let it break (although it's not the end of the world if it does). Brush with more melted butter, and garnish with some shreds or shapes of filo pastry.

Put the strudel into the oven and bake for 30 minutes, or until golden brown. Transfer carefully to a serving dish with the aid of two fish slices.

Cut the thick stalks from the broccoli, then peel off the outer skin and cut the stalks into matchsticks. Separate the florets, halving any larger ones, so that they are all roughly the same size.

When you are ready to cook the broccoli – just a few minutes before you want to eat it – bring 2.5 cm/ 1 inch of water to boil in a large saucepan. Add the broccoli, put a lid on the pan, and cook for 3 minutes; test it: it should be just tender when pierced with a knife. Immediately remove from the heat, drain – the water makes good stock – and put the broccoli back into the saucepan with the butter and some salt and freshly ground black pepper to taste.

CELERIAC AND POTATO PURÉE

225 g/8 oz celeriac	3–4 tbls cream or soya
450 g/1 lb potatoes	milk
25 g/1 oz butter or vegan	salt and freshly ground
margarine	black pepper
	parsley sprigs, to garnish

Peel the celeriac and potatoes and cut them into even-sized chunks. Put them into a saucepan, cover with water and boil until they are both tender, about 15 minutes. Drain them, keeping the liquid, then mash them thoroughly using a potato masher or by pushing them through a *mouli-legumes*. Add the butter or vegan margarine, the cream or soya milk, and enough of the cooking water to make a soft, creamy purée. Snip some parsley over the top.

BUTTERED BROCCOLI

450 g/1 lb broccoli	salt and freshly ground
25 g/1 oz butter	black pepper

WHOLE BABY CARROTS

450 g/1 lb baby carrots,	squeeze of lemon juice
scrubbed	salt and freshly ground
25 g/1 oz butter	black pepper

These carrots are delicious cooked in a steamer, over another vegetable, such as potatoes. Watch them carefully as they cook quickly if they are really tiny – the timing will depend on the size, but could be as little as 4–5 minutes for really baby ones, while bigger carrots could take up to 15 minutes.

Drain the carrots, then return to the hot saucepan or put into a warmed serving dish. Add the butter, seasoning and a squeeze of lemon juice, and mix gently to distribute the butter.

FOR THE REMAINDER OF THE MENU

Port Wine Sauce	*page* 358
Christmas Dried Fruit Salad	*page* 382
Ice Creams	*pages* 388 *and* 393
Mince Pies	*page* 285

OPPOSITE: *Christmas Dinner 5, with Christmas Savoury Strudel*

MENU 5 COUNTDOWN

MAKE IN ADVANCE

Christmas Savoury Strudel: freeze, uncooked, for 2–4 weeks.

Port Wine Sauce: can be made in advance and frozen.

Celeriac and Potato Purée: can be frozen for 2–4 weeks.

Ice Cream: make up to 14 days ahead, cover well and freeze.

Mince Pies: cook a batch and freeze (it's easiest to have a batch for heating on Christmas Day).

CHRISTMAS EVE

Remove from the freezer: Christmas Savoury Strudel, Port Wine Sauce, Celeriac and Potato Purée. Put the Mince Pies on to a serving dish. Leave everything to thaw overnight.

Prepare the broccoli and carrots; put them into separate polythene bags in the fridge.

Make the Christmas Dried Fruit Salad, cover and put in the fridge. If you like, put scoops of ice cream into a serving dish and refreeze, to make serving easier.

Get together serving dishes – a large one for the strudel; vegetable dishes for the celeriac and potato purée, broccoli and carrots; a gravy boat and bowl for the sauce and cream; a round serving dish for the dried fruit salad. Gather individual plates for the first course, main course and pudding.

CHRISTMAS DAY

11.30 am Lay the table. (This can be done on Christmas Eve if you're in the mood and don't need the table for breakfast.) Chill the white wine.

12.00pm Set the oven to 200°C/400°F/Gas Mark 6. Prepare the Two-Pear Salad; cover and chill in the fridge, either in a large bowl for serving later or, if there's room in the fridge, on individual plates. Pour single cream into a jug; keep in the fridge.

12.30pm Put the strudel into the top of the oven and the plates into the bottom, to warm. Open the red wine. Reheat the Celeriac and Potato Purée and the sauce, then serve out and keep warm in the oven. (If there isn't room, keep them in their pan over a very low heat or stand them in a baking tin of steaming water over a very low heat.)

12.45 pm Put the water on for the vegetables. Cook them until they are only just done; then drain them, put them into the warmed vegetable dishes with butter, cover with foil (or lids) and put them into the bottom of the oven to keep warm. Serve out the starter and take to the table.

12.55 pm Open the white wine; light the candles; put the ice cream into the fridge.

1.00 pm Dinner is served!

After the starter Quickly serve out the sauce if you haven't done so. Lift the strudel on to a large, warm serving dish. Put the Mince Pies, covered in foil, towards the bottom of the oven to warm through. Take all the main course dishes to the table.

After the main course Sprinkle the Mince Pies with caster sugar and take to the table, along with the puddings and cream.

Place on a baking sheet and bake for 1 hour, or until completely crisp and golden. Cool.

Meanwhile, make the soup. Melt the butter in a large saucepan, add the onion and fry for 5 minutes without browning. Then add the carrots and potato, cover, and cook gently without browning for 10 minutes. Add the water, cover, and simmer for about 20 minutes, or until the vegetables are tender.

Liquidize the mixture, then pass quickly through a sieve and back into the rinsed-out pan. Add more water to make a nice light consistency, then add the cream, and lemon juice, salt, pepper and nutmeg to taste. Garnish with fresh herbs – dill would be particularly nice – and a swirl of cream, if you wish, and serve with the sesame stars.

MOULDED RICE WITH TWO SAUCES

This is basically a simple mixture of three types of rice. The hot cooked rice is pressed into a mould – either a large one, or six individual ones – then turned out on to a plate or plates and served with the Red Pepper and Green Sauces.

100 g/4 oz brown rice
50 g/2 oz wild rice
100 g/4 oz white Basmati rice
salt and freshly ground black pepper
4 spring onions, finely chopped
fresh herbs or spring onion tassels, to garnish

FOR THE SAUCES
3 large red peppers
salt and freshly ground black pepper
25–50 g/1–2 oz fresh basil
50 g/2 oz pine nuts
1 garlic clove
8 tbls olive oil
8 tbls boiling water

First make the sauces, which can be prepared well ahead and kept in the fridge until you need them. For the red pepper sauce, halve, then quarter the red peppers, removing the stalks and seeds. Place these quarters, shiny-side up, on a baking sheet or grill pan and place under a very hot grill until the skin is blackened and blistered. Cover the pieces with

---

MENU 6

Cream of Carrot Soup with Sesame Stars
~
Moulded Rice with Two Sauces
Favourite Stir-Fried Vegetables
Christmas Salad
Creamy Potato Salad
~
Christmas Bombe
~
Mince Pies
~
WINES: *Pinot Grigio or Riesling (white)*
Tavel (rosé) or Bardolino (red)

CREAM OF CARROT SOUP WITH SESAME STARS

FOR THE SOUP
25 g/1 oz butter
1 onion, chopped
700 g/1¼ lb carrots, sliced
225 g/8 oz potato, diced
1.5 l/2½ pints water
150 ml/5 fl oz single cream
squeeze of lemon juice
salt and freshly ground black pepper

grated nutmeg
fresh herbs or extra cream, to garnish

FOR THE SESAME STARS
3–4 tbls sesame seeds
6 slices white or wholewheat bread
25–50 g/1–2 oz soft butter

First make the sesame stars, which can be done in advance and kept in a tin for a few days. Set the oven to 150°C/300°F/Gas Mark 1. Sprinkle about half of the sesame seeds on to a plate. Cut the bread into stars, using a pastry cutter. Spread one side of the stars with butter, put them buttered-side down on the plate of sesame seeds, then spread butter on the other sides and sprinkle with the remaining seeds.

polythene or a plate, leave to get completely cold, then peel off the charred skin. Liquidize the pepper, adding a little water if necessary, to make a smooth purée the consistency of double cream. Season with salt and pepper.

To make the green sauce, put the basil, pine nuts and garlic into a blender and whizz to a purée, then add the oil and lastly the water.

Now for the rice. Wash the brown rice and the wild rice by putting them together in a sieve and rinsing under the cold tap. Put them into a saucepan with 450 ml/15 fl oz water and a good pinch of salt, and bring to the boil. Then cover the pan, turn the heat down very low and leave the rice to cook for 40 minutes, when it should be tender and all the water absorbed. If there's still some water, put the lid back on the pan and leave it to stand, off the heat, for another 15 minutes.

Meanwhile, wash the Basmati rice in the same way. This is best cooked in a panful of water, so put about 1.2 l/2 pints of water into a medium-large saucepan and bring to the boil, then add the rice and a good pinch of salt. Let the rice boil, uncovered, for about 10 minutes, or until it is just tender. Drain into a sieve and rinse with hot water. Add this rice to the brown rice mixture, together with the spring onions and salt and pepper as necessary. Mix it all gently with a fork, to avoid mashing the rice. Keep the rice warm over the lowest possible heat, perhaps using a heat-saving pad under the pan, or by standing the pan in an outer pan of boiling water.

To serve the rice, have ready a 1.2 litre/2 pint mould or six 175–200 ml/6–7 fl oz moulds – darioles or little ramekins – lightly brushed with olive oil. Spoon in the rice and press down gently, then immediately turn it out on to a warmed serving plate or individual plates. Spoon the sauces in separate pools beside the rice and garnish with a spring onion tassel or sprigs of fresh herbs.

FAVOURITE STIR-FRIED VEGETABLES

4 globe artichokes
lemon juice
450 g/1 lb asparagus
200–225 g/7–8 oz shiitake
  mushrooms
225–250 g/8–9 oz oyster
  mushrooms

3 tbls olive oil
salt and freshly ground
  black pepper
90 g/3½ oz pine nuts,
  lightly toasted under the
  grill

First prepare the artichokes and asparagus, which can be done well in advance. Cut the leaves, stem and hairy choke from the artichokes, leaving just the bases. Squeeze a little lemon juice over the bases to preserve the colour, then put them into a saucepan, cover with water and simmer until just tender, about 15 minutes. Drain, cool, and cut into eighths.

While the artichokes are cooking, cut the tough stems off the asparagus, cut off the tips, and slice the stems slantwise into 2.5 cm/1 inch lengths. Bring 5 cm/2 inches of water to the boil in a saucepan and put in the asparagus. Boil it for about 2 minutes, or until it is bright green and still quite crisp. Drain both into a sieve and run the asparagus under cold water. Put the asparagus and the artichoke pieces into a bowl and cover with clingfilm until you need them.

To complete the stir-fry, wash and slice the shiitake mushrooms; just wash the oyster mushrooms and pat dry on kitchen paper. Heat the oil in a large saucepan or a wok if you have one, then put in the mushrooms. Cook for about 10 minutes or until the mushrooms have softened and any liquid has boiled away. Add the asparagus and artichokes and stir-fry gently for about 5 minutes or until they are heated through. Add a squeeze of lemon juice and salt and pepper to taste, then serve, sprinkled with the pine nuts.

OPPOSITE: *Christmas Dinner 6, with Moulded Rice with Two Sauces*

CHRISTMAS SALAD

It is important that the cherry tomatoes are really firm, so that you can remove the skins without the tomatoes collapsing. If you can't get them, use 225 g/8 oz firm normal-size tomatoes instead, with the skin and the pulp removed, and the flesh cut into large dice. It's best to assemble this salad just before you want to serve it.

1 large creamy ripe avocado	*a few fresh basil leaves, roughly torn*
lemon juice	*1 tbls olive oil*
1 × 400 g/14 oz can palm hearts	*salt and freshly ground black pepper*
225 g/8 oz cherry tomatoes, skinned	

Peel, stone and slice the avocado; put the slices into a bowl and sprinkle with a little freshly squeezed lemon juice. Drain the palm hearts, cut them into 2.5 cm/1 inch slices, and add to the avocado, together with the tomatoes, basil, oil and some salt and pepper to taste.

Mix gently and serve immediately.

CREAMY POTATO SALAD

This salad is surprisingly light and delicate given its ingredients. Use either home-made mayonnaise or a good-quality bought one, such as Hellman's; if you can't find chives, use the green parts of spring onions very finely chopped.

700 g/1½ lb baby new potatoes	*1 tsp red wine or tarragon vinegar*
2 tbls mayonnaise	*1 tsp Dijon mustard*
2 tbls soured cream or thick yogurt	*salt and freshly ground black pepper*
	2 tbls finely chopped chives

Scrub the potatoes, and halve or quarter them unless they are very small. Put them into a saucepan, cover with water, bring to the boil, and boil for 7–10 minutes, or a bit more, depending on the size of the potatoes. They should be tender but not breaking up. Drain and set aside to cool (the water makes a very good stock).

To make the dressing, mix together the mayonnaise, soured cream or yogurt, vinegar, mustard and seasoning, then pour this over the potatoes; stir gently so that they are all coated. Put the mixture into a shallow dish and sprinkle with the chives.

The potato mixture can be covered and kept in the fridge for 12–24 hours, but add the chives just before serving.

FOR THE REMAINDER OF THE MENU

Christmas Bombe	*page* 390
Mince Pies	*page* 285

MENU 6 COUNTDOWN

MAKE IN ADVANCE
Cream of Carrot Soup: freeze for 2–4 weeks.
Sesame Stars: freeze for 2–4 weeks.
Red Pepper Sauce: freeze for 2–4 weeks.
Christmas Bombe: make up to 14 days ahead, cover well and freeze.
Mince Pies: cook a batch and freeze (it's easiest to have a batch for heating on Christmas Day).

CHRISTMAS EVE
Remove from the freezer: Cream of Carrot Soup, Sesame Stars, Red Pepper Sauce. Put the Mince Pies on to a serving dish. Leave to thaw overnight.

Prepare the vegetables for the stir-fry; put them into separate polythene bags in the fridge. Toast the pine nuts. Make the rice mixture; keep in a glass or metal bowl (making it easier to reheat), cover. Cook the potatoes for the salad then cool before combining with the rest of the ingredients.

Make the Green Sauce; put into a serving dish, cover and keep in the fridge.

Get together serving dishes – a large one to hold the rice, either in little timbales or turned out of a large mould; jugs/bowls for the sauces; a round plate for the Christmas Bombe. Gather individual plates for the first course, main course and pudding.

CHRISTMAS DAY
11.00 am Lay the table. (This can be done on Christmas Eve if you're in the mood and don't need the table for breakfast.) Chill the white wine.

11.45 am Set the bowl of rice, covered with foil, over a pan of simmering water, to reheat. Prepare the garnish for the Moulded Rice.

12.15 pm Make the Christmas Salad; cover and keep in a cool place.

12.30 pm Open the red wine. Reheat the sauces, then serve them out and keep them warm in their pans over a very low heat. (Or stand the pans in a baking tin of steaming water over a low heat.) Turn the rice into small oiled dariole moulds, or one large mould. Keep warm in hot water over a hot plate or in a cool oven set to 150°C/300°F/Gas Mark 1.

12.45 pm Make the stir-fried vegetables. When they are done, turn off the heat. Put the Christmas Bombe into the fridge to soften it a bit.

12.55 pm Reheat the soup; put the sesame stars into a serving dish; open the white wine; light the candles.

1.00 pm Dinner is served!

After the starter Quickly serve out the sauces if you haven't already done so. Turn the heat on under the stir-fry and give the mixture another quick stir as it reheats (it should still be quite hot), then serve out and sprinkle with the pine nuts. Turn the rice out on to a warmed serving dish. Put the Mince Pies, covered in foil, towards the bottom of the oven to warm through. Take main course dishes to the table.

After the main course Sprinkle the Mince Pies with caster sugar and take to the table. Turn out the bombe and take it to the table.

FESTIVE PUDDINGS

Even if you eat abstemiously most of the year – perhaps, especially if – I think it's good to have something a bit different once a year at Christmas. At the same time, many Christmas main courses are quite rich and filling, and for these, a light yet still festive, pudding is required. So the recipes in this section range from the simple and refreshing, such as Lychee Sorbet, Christmas Dried Fruit Salad, Orange Slices with Flower Water, Exotic Fruit Salad and Figs with Rosemary Coulis, which are great to round off a substantial meal, to the luxurious and indulgent, such as Chocolate Charlotte with Chocolate Holly Leaves, Christmas Bombe and Meringue Nests with Several Fillings – all wonderful and wicked for those special occasions!

The dishes here can be mixed and matched with recipes in the rest of the book to make up menus suitable for various occasions over Christmas. For a balanced menu, it's best (though not essential, of course) to avoid serving a fruity pudding if you're having a fruit-based first course; and to avoid having a creamy pudding if the starter and/or main course contain cream, or are particularly rich. And it's probably not a wonderful idea to serve a particularly filling nut

roast with a scrumptiously hearty dish like Lemon Surprise Pudding. If you're uncertain which to aim for, you could solve the dilemma by providing a choice so that your guests can decide for themselves.

Some of these puddings make excellent alternatives to the traditional Christmas Pudding on Christmas Day (I've even included a special Light Christmas Pudding so that you can be both traditional and modern/healthy!); and a choice of two or more contrasting dishes will provide a great finale to a buffet or fork party. I'm not usually a pudding person, but sometimes for a special occasion over Christmas, I quite like having a portion of favourite pudding instead of a main meal, perhaps with some good strong black coffee – a real treat.

Your choice of 'big day' and party/buffet puddings is up to you, but you will make life easier for yourself if you choose something that doesn't require last-minute preparation. As with the savoury recipes in this chapter, most of the puddings here either freeze well or are easy to whizz up very quickly from fresh and/or storecupboard ingredients. The accent throughout is on minimal preparation – and maximum enjoyment!

LIGHT CHRISTMAS PUDDING

This pudding freezes well either cooked or uncooked – if you freeze cooked, defrost then cook for 45 minutes for large 35 minutes for small.

I've adapted this deliciously light, fruity pudding without any flour from Doris Grant's Christmas pudding recipe in Food Combining For Health. *Unlike a traditional Christmas pudding, you make it just before you want to eat it (although you need to soak the prunes two days before), and steam for about three hours. Serve with Rum Sauce (page 299).*

90 g/3½ oz prunes
300 g/11 oz sultanas
200 g/7 oz large raisins, such as Lexia
75 g/3 oz finely chopped walnuts
juice of 1 small orange, and grated rind if untreated
100 g/4 oz ground almonds
90 ml/3 fl oz brandy
2 egg yolks
1 tsp mixed spice (optional)

Cover the prunes with plenty of water and leave them to soak for 2 days.

Drain them, saving the water, remove their stones and put the prunes into a food processor with half the sultanas and all but 50 g/2 oz of the raisins. Whizz to a purée. Tip the mixture into a bowl and add the remaining sultanas and raisins, the chopped walnuts, juice of the orange and rind if you're using this, the ground almonds, brandy, egg yolks and 150 ml/5 fl oz of the reserved prune water. For a spicy, traditional Christmas pudding flavour, add the mixed spice; without it, the pudding tastes rich and fruity. Mix well to a medium-soft consistency.

Grease the pudding basin(s) with butter, then spoon in the pudding mixture, leaving plenty of room at the top for it to rise. Cover with a circle of greaseproof paper, put on a lid if the basin has one or secure with some foil, or a pudding cloth over the top. Stand the pudding or puddings in a saucepan with boiling water to come two thirds of the way up the sides, and steam for 3 hours for the large pudding and 1½ hours for the small ones.

Loosen the edges and turn out on to a warmed serving dish or individual plates.
MAKES ONE 1.2 L/2 PINT PUDDING OR SIX 175 G/6 OZ ONES

GOOSEBERRY TARTLETS

These tartlets, a memory of sunny days past and a reminder of those to come, are good for post-Christmas eating, being a complete contrast to mince pies and other Christmas flavours. Serve with Apricot Coulis (page 296) to make it a real pudding.

1 quantity (250 g/9 oz) Rich Shortcrust Pastry (page 299)
1 x 680 g/1½ lb jar gooseberries (about 350 g/12 oz drained weight)
caster sugar
1 tsp arrowroot or cornflour

Set the oven to 190°C/375°F/Gas Mark 5 and lightly grease six to eight 6–7 cm/2½–3 inch loose-base fluted flan tins with butter. On a lightly floured board, roll out the pastry thinly, and line the tins. Prick the bases lightly, then bake for 10–15 minutes, or until the pastry is set and golden brown. Remove from the oven and cool.

To make the gooseberry filling, drain the gooseberries well, keeping the liquid. Sweeten them if necessary with a little sugar – they should still have a nice sharp tang to them. Just before you want to serve the tartlets (but not too soon, or the gooseberries may make the pastry soggy), fill each pastry base with gooseberries.

Blend the arrowroot or cornflour with 150 ml/5 fl oz of the reserved gooseberry liquid, again sweetening to taste. Bring this to the boil in a small saucepan, stir for a minute or two until it has thickened, then take it off the heat and pour a little over the fruit in each tartlet. It will set almost immediately, and they are then ready. To serve them as a pudding, heat through in a moderate oven and serve warm on individual plates, with a pool of apricot coulis beside them.
MAKE 6–8 TARTLETS

OPPOSITE: *Light Christmas Pudding with Rum Sauce, page 299*

FLOATING ISLANDS

I love this light and delicately flavoured pudding, which I find perfect for serving during the Christmas season, a welcome contrast to Christmas Pudding. It's excellent served just as it is or can be topped with some cinnamon-flavoured caramel (as here).

2 egg whites	300 ml/10 fl oz single
100 g/4 oz caster sugar,	cream
preferably from a jar	300 ml/10 fl oz milk
with a vanilla pod in it	1 vanilla pod
	4 egg yolks
	2 tsp cornflour

Whisk the egg whites until they stand in stiff peaks, then whisk in all but 1 tablespoonful of the sugar. Put the cream and milk into a large saucepan with the vanilla pod and bring to simmering point. Drop walnut-sized pieces of the meringue mixture into the milk and cream, allowing room for them to double in size. Simmer gently for about 3 minutes, until the meringues are set and firm. Carefully lift them out with a perforated spoon, and place on kitchen paper. Continue until all the egg white is used – you will probably end up with about 18 meringues.

Now put the 4 egg yolks into a small bowl with the cornflour and the remaining sugar. Add a little of the milk and cream from the pan, mixing until smooth, then tip this in with the rest of the milk and cream. Stir over a gentle heat until the mixture will coat the back of a wooden spoon – don't let it boil – then remove from the heat and pour into a shallow glass serving dish. Put the meringues on top.

Leave until cool, then chill for at least 30 minutes before serving – several hours is better.

If you want to add a caramel topping, heat 50 g/2 oz granulated sugar in a small pan until melted and golden brown, then remove from the heat, stir in ½ teaspoon powdered cinnamon, and pour over the meringues before chilling.

SERVES 6

OPPOSITE: *(right) Floating Islands and (left) Christmas Dried Fruit Salad, page 382*

SNOWY TRIFLE

I don't make trifle very often, but when I do, I like to make it with a home-made Swiss roll and proper, vanilla-flavoured, egg custard. The result is a light, delicate, very 'snowy' and absolutely delectable dessert.

1 raspberry Swiss roll	4 egg yolks or 1 egg and
(page 402)	2 yolks
4 tbls sherry or sweet	40 g/1½ oz caster sugar
wine	2 tsp cornflour
	300 ml/10 fl oz whipping
FOR THE CUSTARD	cream
600 ml/1 pint milk	50 g/2 oz flaked almonds,
1 vanilla pod	toasted

First, make the custard. Put the milk into a saucepan with the vanilla pod and bring to the boil. Remove from the heat, cover and leave to infuse for about 15 minutes.

Meanwhile, whisk together the eggs, sugar and cornflour, just to blend. Strain the milk on to the egg mixture, then pour the whole lot back into the saucepan and stir over a gentle heat for a few minutes until the mixture thickens – don't let it boil. It's done when it's thick enough to coat the spoon thinly. When you get to that point, take it off the heat and leave on one side for the moment. (Wash and dry the vanilla pod – it can be used many times.)

Cut the Swiss roll into slices, put these into a wide shallow dish, preferably glass, and sprinkle the sherry on top. Strain the custard over the top, then put it into the fridge to chill for about an hour, and to allow it to set a bit. Once this has happened, whip the cream and spread it lightly all over the top.

Chill until required; sprinkle the toasted almonds on top just before serving.

SERVES 6

CHOCOLATE CHARLOTTE WITH CHOCOLATE HOLLY LEAVES

This amount is right for a 20 cm/8 inch loose-base tin, serving 14 people – a real party piece. For a smaller charlotte, to serve 6, use a 15 cm/6 inch tin and halve all the ingredients except for the sponge fingers; you'll still need more than one packet. The holly leaves are quite difficult to make. Use very flat leaves if you can find them, and get the chocolate really thick. They need to be as cold as possible to peel off, but can't be put in the fridge. If you find them really impossible, an alternative is to cut holly leaf shapes from a thin sheet of melted chocolate – but those lack the pretty curves and veins of the actual leaves. I found Menier cooking chocolate worked particularly well.

FOR THE HOLLY LEAVES
100 g/4 oz plain
  chocolate
10 or more holly leaves,
  not too hard or curvy

FOR THE CHARLOTTE
2 × 200 g/7 oz packets of
  sponge finger biscuits

6 tbls rum
450 g/1 lb plain
  chocolate, broken up
600 ml/1 pint single
  cream
150 ml/5 fl oz whipping
  cream, whipped with 1
  tablespoon rum, to
  decorate

The holly leaves can be made some time in advance if you wish; they will keep in a tin, with greaseproof paper between the layers. The leaves should be clean and completely dry. Melt the chocolate then, holding a leaf by its stem, pull it through the chocolate, until the top is covered. Make sure it is really thick. Leave it, chocolate side up, until completely cold and set – overnight is best. (Don't put the leaves into the fridge, or you might get white spots on them.) Once they are completely set, peel the leaves away from the chocolate.

To make the charlotte itself, first prepare the tin. If you haven't got a loose-base tin, line an ordinary one by pressing foil into it to cover the base and sides. Arrange sponge finger biscuits all round the edge of the tin, then sprinkle half the rum in the base and arrange more sponge fingers over the base, to cover it, more or less, breaking them as necessary to fit. They don't have to be neat. Sprinkle the rest of the rum evenly on top.

Next, make the filling. Put the chocolate and single cream into a bowl set over a saucepan of simmering water and heat gently until the chocolate has melted. Remove from the heat and cool quickly by placing the bowl in a bowl of cold water. Once it is cold and beginning to set, whisk it hard until it's thick and light – an electric whisk is best for this. (If it refuses to go thick, it isn't cold enough. Put the bowl back in cold water for a few minutes longer.)

Carefully spoon the chocolate mixture into the tin, pushing the sponge finger biscuits back against the sides of the tin if they flop forwards. Chill in the fridge until firm.

To serve, remove the charlotte from the tin. If you've used the tin lined with foil, carefully lift the foil out, then peel down the sides. Slide a fish slice under the charlotte and lift it on to a serving dish.

Decorate with whipped cream and holly leaves and a dusting of grated chocolate; add a ribbon around the outside of the Charlotte, too, if you want an extra festive touch.

SERVES 14

OPPOSITE: *Chocolate Charlotte with Chocolate Holly Leaves*

ORANGE SLICES WITH FLOWER WATER

This deliciously refreshing salad is best made ahead of serving to allow the flavours to mellow – it can be made a day or two in advance and kept in the fridge, well covered. Remove from the fridge for an hour or so before serving. Serve with Vegan Cream (page 296) for a luxurious yet light pudding.

9 oranges   orange flower water
honey – Greek, or orange
flower if possible

Scrub one of the oranges thoroughly then, preferably with a zester, pare off long thin strips of peel. Keep on one side.

Holding the oranges over a bowl, use a sharp, serrated stainless steel knife to cut away the peel and zest together, round and round, like peeling an apple in one go. Slice the orange flesh into thin circles or segments. Add the zest. Sweeten to taste with a little honey and add the orange flower water.

Cover and leave until ready to serve.
SERVES 6

CHRISTMAS DRIED FRUIT SALAD

Add a tablespoon of orange flower water to this dried fruit salad to give it extra fragrance.

This is very easy to make and good to eat – it's lovely with Floating Islands (page 379) or with thick Greek yogurt. You can either buy packets of mixed dried fruit or make your own combination, including raisins, figs or whatever you fancy.

450 g/1 lb mixed dried   1 cinnamon stick, broken
fruit – peaches, apricots,   in half
prunes, pears, apples   6 tbls rum or brandy
50 g/2 oz soft brown or   90 g/3½ oz blanched
demerara sugar   almonds

Wash the dried fruit, then put it into a bowl, cover with plenty of water and leave to soak overnight. Next day put into a saucepan with its soaking water and more, if necessary, to make it just level with the top of the fruit. Add the sugar and cinnamon stick and bring to the boil. Let the mixture simmer away, without a lid on the pan, for about an hour, or until nearly all the liquid has boiled away.

Remove from the heat and add the rum and nuts. Leave to cool, then serve at room temperature.
SERVES 4–6

MERINGUE NESTS WITH SEVERAL FILLINGS

12 Meringue Nests   FRUIT FILLING
(page 296)   fresh fruit, such as
                    strawberries, kiwi,
ORANGE LIQUEUR AND   grapes, etc
GLACÉ FRUIT FILLING   150 ml/5 fl oz whipping
150 ml/5 fl oz whipping   cream
cream
1 tsp grated orange rind
2 tbls orange liqueur   GINGER FILLING
red and yellow glacé   150 ml/5 fl oz whipping
fruits, to decorate   cream
chopped angelica, to   25 g/1 oz chopped stem
decorate   ginger
                    chocolate curls and grated
                    chocolate, to decorate

To make the orange liqueur and glacé fruit filling, beat the cream until thick, then stir in the orange rind and liqueur. Pile into four meringue nests and decorate with glacé fruits and angelica.

To make the fruit filling, chop your selection of fresh fruit and whip the cream until thick; divide between four nests.

To make the ginger filling, beat the cream until thick, then stir in two-thirds of the stem ginger. Spoon into the remaining nests and use the rest of the ginger and the chocolate to decorate the tops.
SERVES 3–6

OPPOSITE: *Meringue Nests with Several Fillings*

LYCHEE SORBET

This is a pudding which can be whizzed up in no time at all, and it is fragrant and refreshing.

2 × 410 g/14 oz cans
  lychees in syrup
juice and grated rind of 1
  lemon

2 egg whites
fresh violets, jasmine, or
  mint leaves, to decorate

Drain the lychees, keeping the liquid. Put the lychees into a food processor with the lemon juice and rind and 300 ml/10 fl oz of the reserved liquid, and whizz to a purée. Pour this into a shallow container and freeze until the mixture is half-frozen, about 2 hours.

Whizz again in a liquidizer. Whisk the egg whites until stiff, then beat in the lychee purée. Pour the mixture back into the freezing container, and freeze for about 3 hours, until firm.

Remove the sorbet from the freezer about 45 minutes before you want to eat it, then put several scoops into individual glass dishes.
SERVES 6

VEGAN VERSION
Simply omit the egg whites and whisk extra vigorously!

FIGS WITH RASPBERRY COULIS

An out-of-season treat ... If you can get fresh ripe figs at Christmas, and have some Raspberry Coulis (page 299) stashed away in the freezer, this pudding is light, easy and delicious.

You need one fresh fig for each person, 2–3 tablespoons of raspberry coulis and, if you like, a good heaped dessertspoonful of thick Greek yogurt. Wash the figs and pat them dry on kitchen paper. Cut

OPPOSITE: *(top) Lychee Sorbet and (below) Exotic Fruit Salad*

them downwards, through the stem but not completely through the base, making three cuts, so that you end up with six segments still attached to the base. Serve with a little pool of coulis and yogurt if you're using this.

EXOTIC FRUIT SALAD

This is one of the simplest, prettiest and most refreshing puddings, and makes a lovely contrast to some of the richer and more filling Christmas and winter dishes. Choose your own selection of fruits, aiming for plenty of different colours and textures. I think they look best arranged on a round glass plate, and they are delicious eaten on their own, or with thick Greek yogurt or, best of all, a scoopful of Lychee Sorbet (left).

6 lychees
1 ripe paw-paw or 2
  pomegranates
1 nectarine
2 figs
50 g/2 oz Cape
  gooseberries

225 g/8 oz strawberries
100 g/4 oz raspberries,
  golden or red
1 star fruit
a few sprigs of fresh mint,
  to decorate

Using a stainless knife which won't give the fruit a metallic flavour, peel the lychees and paw-paw, and remove the stones. Remove the stone from the nectarine. Cut the flesh into neat pieces, not too small. If you are using pomegranates, halve them then, holding each half over a bowl to catch the delicious crimson juice, ease out the seeds with a small pointed teaspoon (a grapefruit spoon is ideal), or the point of a knife. Discard the skin. Slice the figs into thin circles. Pull back the petals on the Cape gooseberries, wash the strawberries and raspberries – and wash, then thinly slice, the star fruit. Arrange each type of fruit in a pile on a large platter, then decorate with a few sprigs of fresh mint.
SERVES 6

LEMON AND GINGER CHEESECAKE

I call this cheesecake, but really it's a bit of a cheat one, because it doesn't contain cheese – just a beautifully smooth, lemony cream (which sets like a cheesecake), on a crisp ginger-biscuit base. It's easy to make and an unfailingly popular party dessert. It's rich, so a little goes a long way.

200 g/7 oz ginger biscuits
75 g/3 oz butter
½ tsp ground ginger
300 ml/10 fl oz double cream

1 × 218 g/8 oz can condensed milk
grated rind and juice of 1 lemon
slivers of lemon peel and chopped preserved ginger, to decorate

Put the biscuits in a polythene bag and crush to coarse crumbs with a rolling pin. Melt the butter in a medium saucepan, then stir in the crushed biscuits and ground ginger. Press this mixture into the base of an 18–20 cm/7–8 inch springform cake tin – the base of a jam jar is useful for pressing the crumbs firmly into the tin. Put into the fridge to chill.

Now make the filling: whisk the double cream until it is almost fully whipped, then add the condensed milk and whisk again, until very thick. Finally, stir in the lemon rind and juice. The mixture may look as if it's going to separate at first, but don't worry, it won't; just keep on stirring gently until it is very smooth and thick.

Spoon this mixture on top of the ginger base, then smooth and level it with the back of a spoon or a spatula. Cover and chill for several hours, then remove the outside of the springform tin and decorate the top of the cheesecake with lemon peel and ginger before serving.

This cheesecake can be made at least 24 hours in advance; it keeps very well for several days in the fridge, but keep it tightly covered so that it doesn't absorb any other flavours.

SERVES 8–12

RUM–MARINATED FRUITS WITH COCONUT AND LIME CREAM

1 ripe pineapple
2 bananas
1 ripe paw-paw
grated rind and juice of 1 lime
50 g/2 oz brown sugar

4 tbls brown rum
100 g/4 oz coconut cream
300 ml/10 fl oz boiling water
extra sugar or honey to taste

Cut the skin from the pineapple, making sure you've taken out all the little black bits, remove the central core and cut the flesh into dice. Peel the bananas and slice into chunks, peel, seed and slice the paw-paw and add them to the pineapple, with half the lime juice, the sugar and rum. Cover and leave the mixture to marinate for at least 1 hour, stirring gently from time to time.

Meanwhile, make the cream. Cut up the coconut cream and put into a small saucepan with the boiling water. Stir until dissolved, heating gently if necessary. Then remove from the heat and leave until completely cold.

Stir in the lime rind and remaining juice, and a little sugar or honey to taste. It will thicken as it gets cold, especially if you chill it in the fridge. Serve with the fruit.

SERVES 6

OPPOSITE: *Rum-Marinated Fruits with Coconut and Lime Cream*

VANILLA ICE CREAM

I've made many vanilla ice creams over the years, some with a light egg custard base, delicately flavoured with a vanilla pod; and others using the meringue method, with a sugar syrup poured on to eggs . . . But the one my family always ask for is the simplest of them all: just whipping cream and condensed milk.

All you do is whisk the cream until it's almost fully whipped, then whisk in the condensed milk and 2 tsp vanilla extract. Pour the mixture into a suitable container and freeze, without a lid, until solid. The proportions I use are 600 ml/1 pint whipping cream to one 405 g/14 oz can of skimmed condensed milk. This makes a lot, but it keeps very well in the freezer.

For a simple but luxurious pudding, I love this ice cream served with Raspberry Coulis (page 299), which gives just the right touch of sharpness, and some baby macaroons or ratafias.

You can add other flavourings to the basic ice cream: a coffee version is particularly good, as the coffee cuts the sweetness of the condensed milk. For this I use a good-quality instant coffee – 1–2 tablespoons – dissolved in a little boiling water and added with the condensed milk.

LEMON CURD ICE CREAM

This tangy, refreshing ice cream can be made in moments. If you have some home-made lemon curd, this is a delicious way to use it; otherwise buy the best-quality pale-coloured lemon curd, or lemon cheese, that you can find. This ice cream is good served with Raspberry Coulis (page 299).

1 × 312 g/10 oz jar   300 ml/10 fl oz whipping
lemon curd   cream
600 ml/1 pint natural
low-fat yogurt

Put the lemon curd into a bowl and mix until smooth, then gradually beat in the yogurt then the cream, to make a smooth, creamy mixture. Pour this into a polythene container and freeze until firm. The ice cream sets very hard, so you need to remove it from the freezer in good time – let it stand at room temperature for 30–45 minutes, or in the fridge for at least an hour before you want to serve it.
SERVES 6

PASSION FRUIT AND LIME SORBET

This sorbet is easy to make and has a wonderful flavour. I like it with the passion fruit seeds left in, because they give a good crunchy texture and pretty speckled appearance; however most people, including my own family, prefer it when they've been sieved out.

350 g/12 oz caster sugar   12 passion fruits
600 ml/1 pint water   1 lime

Dissolve the sugar in the water over a low heat, then bring to the boil and boil for 3–4 minutes to make a sugar syrup. Remove from the heat and set aside to cool.

Scoop all the pulp and seeds out of the passion fruits, pass them through a nylon sieve to remove the seeds (if you wish) and add the purée to the cooled sugar syrup. Wash the lime, then remove long thin shreds of peel; put these into a polythene bag and keep until needed.

Squeeze the lime and add the juice to the passion fruit mixture. Transfer the mixture to a polythene container and freeze, uncovered, until solid – about 6 hours, or overnight. Cut the mixture into small chunks and put these into a food processor. Whizz for a minute or two until the sorbet is soft and fluffy, then put back into the container and freeze again.

When the mixture is frozen but not too hard, put small scoops of it on to a plate and refreeze. This makes the sorbet easier to serve. Decorate with the lime rind just before serving.
SERVES 6

LEMON SURPRISE PUDDING

This is an easy-to-make, popular family pudding, and another one which contrasts pleasantly with spicy Christmas foods. The mixture separates as it cooks, resulting in a light lemon sponge on top of a sharp, citrus sauce.

100 g/4 oz butter or
  margarine
100 g/4 oz caster sugar
100 g/4 oz self-raising
  flour
grated rind of 1 lemon
2 eggs
a little milk

FOR THE SAUCE
75 g/3 oz caster sugar
2 tbls cornflour
juice of 1 lemon

Set the oven to 190°C/375°F/Gas Mark 5.

Make the sponge mixture by creaming together the butter or margarine, sugar, flour, lemon rind and eggs. Beat well for about 2 minutes, until smooth and glossy, adding a little milk or water – about 2 tablespoons – if necessary for a soft consistency. Spoon the mixture into a lightly greased shallow baking dish; it should only half fill it.

Now make the sauce. Put the sugar and cornflour into a bowl with the lemon juice and mix together, then gradually add 300 ml/10 fl oz of boiling water, stirring all the time. Pour this sauce over the sponge mixture in the dish, then bake for about 40–45 minutes, or until the mixture has risen and feels firm to the touch.

Serve hot or warm.

SERVES 4–6

CINNAMON TORTE

100 g/4 oz self-raising
  flour
1 tsp powdered cinnamon
100 g/4 oz ground
  almonds
100 g/4 oz caster sugar

100 g/4 oz butter or
  margarine
grated rind of 1 lemon
225 g/8 oz raspberry jam
icing sugar

Sift the flour and cinnamon into a bowl or food processor, then put in the ground almonds, sugar, butter or margarine and grated lemon rind. Process, without the plunger (to let in more air and make the mixture light), or rub the fat into the other ingredients with your fingers. Either way, the result will be a soft dough. You can roll this out straight away, but it's easier to handle if you wrap it in polythene and chill it for 30 minutes.

Set the oven to 180°C/350°F/Gas Mark 4. On a lightly floured board, roll out two-thirds of the almond mixture, to fit a 20 cm/8 inch flan tin. Put the pastry into the tin and trim the edges. Spread the jam over the pastry, then roll out the remaining pastry, including the trimmings, and cut long strips to make a lattice across the top of the jam. Bake the torte for 30 minutes, or until the pastry is set and lightly browned. Serve hot or cold, with a snowy topping of sifted icing sugar.

SERVES 6

I like lemon curd or apricot jam instead of raspberry jam sometimes in Cinnamon Torte.

CHRISTMAS BOMBE

When you cut this snowy white ice cream bombe, a golden inner layer flecked with brightly-coloured crystallized fruits is revealed. It's wonderful as an alternative Christmas pudding, or for a party, and it's easy to make. You need to allow plenty of time for the freezing – it's better to start making it the day before you need it, or it can be made up to four weeks in advance and stored in the freezer. It looks good with extra Cointreau-soaked crystallized fruits on top, but this makes the pudding quite boozy, so drivers should be warned!

FOR THE WHITE LAYER
4 egg whites
225 g/8 oz caster or vanilla sugar
150 ml/5 fl oz water
450 ml/15 fl oz whipping cream
a few drops of vanilla essence

FOR THE GOLDEN LAYER
225 g/8 oz crystallized fruits, in a variety of colours
2 tbls Cointreau or other orange liqueur
4 egg yolks
4 tangerines or satsumas
100 g/4 oz caster sugar
150 ml/5 fl oz whipping cream
extra glacé fruit, to decorate

First turn your freezer to its coldest setting and chill a 1.7l/3 pint ice cream bombe mould or pudding basin, preferably metal.

Now for the white ice cream. Put the egg whites into a bowl and whisk them until they are very stiff, as if you were making meringues. Put the caster sugar into a saucepan with the water and heat gently until the sugar has dissolved, then bring to the boil and boil hard for 3 minutes. Take off the heat and immediately pour this mixture on to the egg whites, whisking them at the same time. An electric table or hand whisk makes this operation easier. Next, whisk the cream until it will stand in soft peaks, then whisk it into the egg white mixture, together with a few drops of vanilla essence. Pour the whole lot into the bombe mould or bowl and freeze until firm – this may take 5–6 hours. Meanwhile, prepare the crystallized fruits; cut them into 1 cm/½ inch chunks then put them into a shallow container and sprinkle with the Cointreau.

Now make the tangerine ice cream for the 'golden' layer. Put the egg yolks into a bowl with the grated rind of two of the tangerines and whisk until pale and beginning to thicken. Squeeze the juice from all the tangerines and put this into a saucepan with the caster sugar. Heat gently until the sugar has dissolved, then boil hard for 3 minutes. Immediately pour this mixture over the egg yolks, whisking at the same time. When it has all been added, continue to whisk the mixture for about 5 minutes until it is very thick and light. Whisk the cream to the soft peak stage, then whisk this into the tangerine mixture. Put it into the freezer and freeze for 2–3 hours, or until it is beginning to solidify but is still soft enough to stir. Add the crystallized fruits and orange liqueur to the tangerine ice cream, together with any liquid that's left over.

Hollow out the inside of the white ice cream to make a cavity for the tangerine ice. Push the bits of ice cream that you scoop out of the centre up the sides of the bombe, aiming for a thickness of about 1cm/½ inch, although this will depend on the exact shape of your mould or bowl. Spoon the tangerine mixture into the centre and finish by smoothing any remaining white ice cream on top. Put the bombe back in the freezer and freeze for several hours until the layers are completely firm.

Unmould the bombe by dipping the mould into a bowl of hot water for a few seconds, then loosening the edges with a palette knife and turning the ice cream out on to a plate. Smooth the top with a palette knife, then put the bombe back into the freezer until you need it. Decorate with a few pieces of glacé fruit on top. It can be served straight from the freezer as it soon softens.
SERVES 8

OPPOSITE: *Christmas Bombe*

BOOZY VEGAN ICE CREAM

This is a simple vegan chocolate ice cream, which has always been a favourite with my kids, dressed up for Christmas with the addition of some dried fruits, nuts and booze. It makes a good frozen Christmas pudding if you freeze it in a plastic pudding basin.

1 tbls cornflour
900 ml/1½ pints soya milk
1 vanilla pod
2 tbls sugar
50 g/2 oz vegan
  margarine
100 g/4 oz plain
  chocolate

100 g/4 oz glacé cherries
50 g/2 oz whole mixed
  peel, chopped
50 g/2 oz raisins or
  sultanas
4 tbls rum or brandy
25 g/1 oz flaked almonds

Put the cornflour into a bowl and blend to a paste with a little of the milk. Put the rest of the milk into a saucepan with the vanilla pod, sugar, margarine and the chocolate, broken into pieces. Heat gently to boiling point, then pour over the cornflour and mix until combined.

Return the mixture to the saucepan and bring to the boil, stirring. Remove from the heat. Cover and leave until cool, then remove the vanilla pod (wash and dry it – it can be used many times) and liquidize the mixture. Pour it into a container and freeze until it is solid around the edges. Whisk and return to the freezer. Repeat this process, this time whisking in the fruits, rum or brandy and almonds, and let the ice cream freeze until solid.

Make sure this ice cream is well-softened before you use it, as it freezes very hard – an hour at room temperature is not too long. Then beat it before serving, or simply turn it out of a pudding bowl, like a Christmas pudding.

SERVES 6–8

CHOCOLATE ICE CREAM

2 egg whites
150 g/5 oz caster sugar
8 tbls water

100 g/4 oz dark
  chocolate, broken up
300 ml/10 fl oz
  whipping cream
extra dark or white
  chocolate, to decorate

Whisk the egg whites until they are stiff, as if you were making meringues. Next, put the sugar and water into a small saucepan and heat gently until the sugar has dissolved. Raise the heat and let the mixture boil for 2 minutes. Remove from the heat, and pour this over the egg whites, whisking at the same time.

Melt the chocolate in a bowl set over a pan of simmering water, or in the microwave, and add carefully and gradually to the egg white mixture. Whip the cream until it is standing in soft peaks, then fold quickly into the mixture.

Turn the ice cream into a polythene container and freeze until firm.

To serve, remove from the freezer 10–15 minutes before you need it, to soften it a little, and scoop into sundae glasses.

Decorate with extra chocolate (white makes a nice contrast, shaved into curls on a potato peeler, as here) and serve with biscuits, such as Macaroons (page 418).
SERVES 6

OPPOSITE: *Chocolate Ice Cream and Macaroons, page 418*

CHRISTMAS BAKING

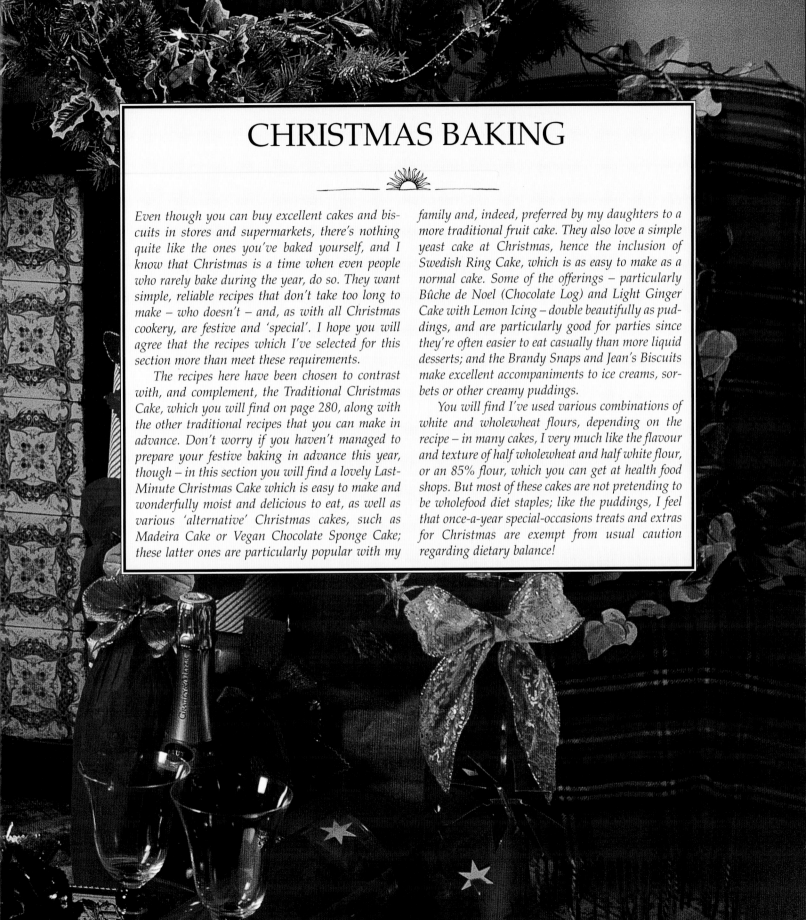

Even though you can buy excellent cakes and biscuits in stores and supermarkets, there's nothing quite like the ones you've baked yourself, and I know that Christmas is a time when even people who rarely bake during the year, do so. They want simple, reliable recipes that don't take too long to make – who doesn't – and, as with all Christmas cookery, are festive and 'special'. I hope you will agree that the recipes which I've selected for this section more than meet these requirements.

The recipes here have been chosen to contrast with, and complement, the Traditional Christmas Cake, which you will find on page 280, along with the other traditional recipes that you can make in advance. Don't worry if you haven't managed to prepare your festive baking in advance this year, though – in this section you will find a lovely Last-Minute Christmas Cake which is easy to make and wonderfully moist and delicious to eat, as well as various 'alternative' Christmas cakes, such as Madeira Cake or Vegan Chocolate Sponge Cake; these latter ones are particularly popular with my family and, indeed, preferred by my daughters to a more traditional fruit cake. They also love a simple yeast cake at Christmas, hence the inclusion of Swedish Ring Cake, which is as easy to make as a normal cake. Some of the offerings – particularly Bûche de Noel (Chocolate Log) and Light Ginger Cake with Lemon Icing – double beautifully as puddings, and are particularly good for parties since they're often easier to eat casually than more liquid desserts; and the Brandy Snaps and Jean's Biscuits make excellent accompaniments to ice creams, sorbets or other creamy puddings.

You will find I've used various combinations of white and wholewheat flours, depending on the recipe – in many cakes, I very much like the flavour and texture of half wholewheat and half white flour, or an 85% flour, which you can get at health food shops. But most of these cakes are not pretending to be wholefood diet staples; like the puddings, I feel that once-a-year special-occasions treats and extras for Christmas are exempt from usual caution regarding dietary balance!

LAST–MINUTE CHRISTMAS CAKE

If you can't find small cake tins, make the little cakes by cutting the big square one into quarters then carefully sculpting into rounds.

575 g/1¼ lb mixed dried fruit
225 g/8 oz sultanas
225 g/8 oz Lexia raisins grated rind and juice of 1 lemon
1 tbls black treacle
150 ml/5 fl oz port or sherry

250 g/9 oz wholewheat flour and plain white flour, mixed
1 tsp mixed spice
1 tsp powdered cinnamon
225 g/8 oz butter
225 g/8 oz dark brown sugar
4 eggs
175 g/6 oz glacé cherries
25 g/1 oz flaked almonds

Put the mixed dried fruit, sultanas, raisins, rind and juice and treacle into a saucepan with the port and bring to the boil. Remove from the heat, cover and leave to get cold. (This process can be speeded up if you stand the pan in a bowl of cold water.)

Meanwhile, set the oven to 150°C/300°F/Gas Mark 2 and line a 20 cm/8 inch square tin or four 10 cm/ 4 inch round tins with greaseproof paper.

Sift the flours with the spices, on to a plate. Cream the butter and sugar until very light, then alternately beat in the fruit, eggs and flour. Finally, stir in the cherries and almonds. Spoon the mixture into the tin or tins, hollowing out the centre very slightly so that the surface will be flat. Bake the large cake for 2–3 hours and the small ones for 1½–1¾ hours, or until a skewer inserted in the middle comes out clean. (It took 2 hours 30 minutes to cook the large one, 1½ hours for the small ones in my oven.) Leave to cool in the tin(s).

MAKES ONE 20 CM/8 INCH SQUARE CAKE OR
FOUR INDIVIDUAL 10 CM/4 INCH ROUND CAKES

TO PUT A NUTTY TOPPING ON THE SQUARE CAKE

This is a very quick, easy and effective topping for a Christmas Cake, especially nice if you aren't too keen on almond paste and icing. The nuts should be put on the cake before it's baked.

Hollow out the centre of the cake slightly so that it will be flat when it's cooked, then arrange the nuts attractively in diagonal rows on top; be careful not to press them into the mixture or they may sink and disappear as it bakes! For a 20 cm/8 inch cake with a separate row of each one, you will need about 50 g/2 ounces of blanched almonds, brazilnuts, skinned hazelnuts, pecan nuts or walnuts. Glacé cherries would make an attractive centre row. Finish with a flourish by tying a bow of red ribbon around the sides.

TO DECORATE THE LITTLE ROUND CAKES

Cover the cakes with almond paste (page 280), then make one recipe of Fondant Icing and use it to decorate the cakes (page 282).

For the mini-cakes shown here, I decorated the top of one cake with marzipan fruits (page 423), another with a mixture of glacé cherries, strips of angelica and crystallized orange segments and a third with a candle and some holly. For the fourth cake, I rerolled the fondant icing trimmings and cut into star shapes, using a pastry cutter, then used them to decorate the sides and top, dusting the top one with a little fine brown sugar. The final flourish is acheived by pinning an appropriately festive ribbon round the sides.

OPPOSITE: *Little Christmas Cakes*

LITTLE CHRISTMAS BUNS

This is another recipe with children in mind. They want something special and partyish but often dislike the rich, spicy flavours of Christmas cake and mince pies, and these little buns are always popular. You can let your imagination go when you decorate them – or, if you've got the time, let the children have the fun of doing it themselves. I think the buns are pretty decorated with marzipan shapes such as crackers or holly leaves and berries (see page 423), or stars cut out of fondant icing and adorned with silver balls, but children really prefer using (and eating!) Smarties, dolly mixtures and bits of chocolate flake.

175 g/6 oz 85%
wholewheat self-raising
flour
100 g/4 oz soft butter or
margarine
100 g/4 oz caster sugar
2 eggs

paper cake cases
sweets, marzipan
   shapes, etc, to decorate

FOR THE GLACÉ ICING
100 g/4 oz icing sugar

Set the oven to 190°C/375°F/Gas Mark 5.

Sift the flour into a bowl, then add the butter or margarine, sugar and eggs. Beat well with a wooden spoon or an electric mixer until the mixture is thick and slightly glossy-looking. Put heaped teaspoonfuls of the mixture into paper cases, which can be put into deep bun tins with a flat base, or on to a baking sheet. Bake for 15–20 minutes, until the cakes have risen and spring back to a light touch. Set aside to cool on a wire rack.

To decorate, make some glacé icing by mixing the icing sugar with about a tablespoonful of water; spread a little of this on top of each bun, then decorate with sweets, marzipan shapes, etc, as desired.

MAKES 15 BUNS

VEGAN CHOCOLATE SPONGE CAKE

Actually this cake could be flavoured in other ways, according to your taste (just replace the cocoa with the same amount of flour), but I think it needs quite a strong flavour. Whatever you do, don't leave out the lemon juice, which is there not for flavour, but for acidity, to help the cake to rise. The result is a light sponge, luscious when sandwiched and topped with vegan buttercream.

175 g/6 oz self-raising
flour
175 g/6 oz caster sugar
¾ tsp bicarbonate of soda
40 g/1½ oz cocoa powder
40 g/1½ oz soya flour
juice of 1½ lemons
150 ml/5 fl oz groundnut
oil
1 tsp vanilla essence

FOR THE BUTTERCREAM
100 g/4 oz vegan
margarine
200 g/7 oz icing sugar
2 tbls cocoa powder
a little plain chocolate, to
decorate

Set the oven to 180°C/350°F/Gas Mark 4 and grease two 18 cm/7 inch round sandwich cake tins, lining each with greased nonstick or greaseproof paper.

Sift all the dry ingredients – the flour, sugar,

bicarbonate of soda, cocoa powder and soya flour – into a large bowl. Put the lemon juice into a measuring jug and make it up to 350 ml/12 fl oz with cold water; mix with the oil and vanilla essence. Pour all this liquid into the dry ingredients and quickly mix with a wooden spoon to a smooth batter.

Pour the batter into the two tins and bake for about 35 minutes, or until the cakes spring back to a light touch. Cool them on a wire rack, then sandwich them and ice the top with a buttercream made by beating together the margarine, icing sugar, cocoa and enough hot water to make a light, fluffy consistency. Decorate with some shavings of plain vegan chocolate, if you wish.

MAKES ONE 18 CM/7 INCH CAKE

MADEIRA CAKE

This is another favourite cake which my daughters always ask for at Christmas – in fact they prefer it to fruit cake! I like to use half 100% wholewheat flour and half white, so either the plain flour or the self-raising could be wholewheat.

175 g/6 oz plain flour	*4 large eggs, beaten*
175 g/6 oz self-raising	*2–3 tbls milk (optional)*
flour	*2–3 thin slices candied*
250 g/9 oz butter	*citron peel*
250 g/9 oz vanilla sugar,	
or caster sugar with 1½	
tsp vanilla extract	

Set the oven to 180°C/350°F/Gas Mark 4 and grease and line a 20 cm/8 inch round cake tin with greased greaseproof paper.

Sift the flours together on to a plate, adding any bran left in the sieve. Leave this on one side while you cream together the butter and sugar until they're light and pale – you can use an electric whisk for this – then whisk in the beaten eggs, about a tablespoonful at a time, and the vanilla extract, if you're using this. Put the flour on top and fold this in very gently with a metal spoon, to keep as much air in the mixture

as possible. Add a spoonful or two of milk if necessary to make a soft, dropping consistency, and spoon the mixture into the prepared tin.

Bake for 20 minutes, then carefully lay the peel on top of the cake and bake for a further 40 minutes, or until a warmed skewer inserted into the centre comes out clean. Turn out on to a wire rack to cool.

MAKES ONE 20 CM/8 INCH CAKE

DRENCHED LEMON CAKE

175 g/6 oz self-raising	*2 free-range eggs*
flour	*2–4 tbls milk*
1 tsp baking powder	
175 g/6 oz caster sugar	FOR THE SYRUP
100 g/4 oz soft butter or	*juice of 1 lemon*
margarine	*100 g/4 oz caster sugar*
grated rind of 1 lemon	

Set the oven to 180°C/350°F/Gas Mark 4 and line a 900 g/2 lb loaf tin with a strip of nonstick paper to cover the base and come up the narrow sides. Grease the remaining sides of the tin.

Sift the flour and baking powder into a bowl, then add the sugar, butter and lemon rind, and crack in the eggs. Beat vigorously with a wooden spoon or with an electric whisk until the mixture is thick, smooth and slightly glossy-looking – about 2 minutes by hand. Add a little milk to make a soft dropping consistency, and mix again, then turn the mixture into the prepared tin.

Bake for 40 minutes, or until the cake springs back to a light touch.

While the cake is cooking, make the syrup by mixing together the lemon juice and sugar. As soon as you take the cake out of the oven, pour the syrup evenly over the top, then leave it to get completely cold in the tin. Finally, remove the cake from the tin and strip off the paper.

MAKES ONE 900 G/2 LB CAKE

LIGHT GINGER CAKE WITH LEMON ICING

I think this light ginger cake, with its tangy lemon icing, is nicer at Christmas than the more usual dark gingerbread because it's so different from Christmas Cake. It's very quick to make.

100 g/4 oz 85%
wholewheat self-raising
flour
1 tsp baking powder
2 tsp ground ginger
100 g/4 oz caster sugar
100 g/4 oz soft butter
2 eggs

50–100 g/2–4 oz
preserved stem ginger,
roughly chopped

FOR THE LEMON ICING
100 g/4 oz icing sugar
1–2 tbls freshly squeezed
lemon juice
zest of lemon, to decorate

Set the oven to 170°C/325°F/Gas Mark 3 and line a 450 g/1 lb loaf tin with a strip of nonstick paper to cover the base and narrow sides; grease the uncovered sides with butter.

Sift the flour, baking powder and ginger into a food processor, mixer or bowl, then put in the sugar, butter and eggs. Whizz, whisk, or beat everything together until it is light, thick and slightly glossy looking. This will take about 3 minutes by hand, less time in a processor or with an electric whisk or mixer. Stir in the chopped stem ginger.

Spoon the mixture into the tin and gently level the top with the back of a spoon. Bake for 1 hour to 1 hour 10 minutes, or until the cake is risen, has shrunk a little from the sides of the tin, and the centre springs back to a light touch. Cool for a few minutes in the tin, then turn out on to a wire rack to finish cooling.

To make the icing, sift the icing sugar into a bowl, then gradually mix in enough of the lemon juice to make a stiff mixture. Put this on top of the cake, spreading it gently to the edges. Use a zester to make long thin strips of lemon peel, or shave off pieces of peel and cut them into long strips with a knife. Scatter these over the top of the cake.
MAKES ONE 450 G/1 LB CAKE

OPPOSITE: *Light Ginger Cake with Lemon Icing*

PARKIN

This parkin is a favourite recipe which has appeared before, but I wanted to include it as it's a useful cake for Christmas, contrasting well with other flavours and storing well – it can be made at least a week in advance and just goes on improving. One reader tells me that she always makes this parkin for her Christmas cake! It can be jazzed up with some glacé icing, and I love it with bits of chopped candied peel and preserved ginger in it (the kind in a pretty jar) but my kids all prefer it plain.

100 g/4 oz plain 100%
wholemeal flour
2 tsp baking powder
2 tsp ground ginger
100 g/4 oz medium
oatmeal
3 rounded tbls real
barbados sugar
100 g/4 oz black treacle
100 g/4 oz golden syrup
or honey

100 g/4 oz butter or
vegan margarine
175 ml/6 fl oz milk or
soya milk

OPTIONAL EXTRAS
50 g/2 oz preserved
ginger, chopped
50 g/2 oz whole candied
peel, chopped

Set the oven to 180°C/350°F/Gas Mark 4 and line a 20 cm/8 inch square tin with greased greaseproof paper.

Sift the flour, baking powder and ginger into a bowl, adding the residue of bran from the sieve, as well, and also the oatmeal. Put the sugar, treacle, golden syrup and butter or vegan margarine into a saucepan and heat gently until melted. Let the mixture cool until tepid, then add the milk to it. Pour the whole lot into the dry ingredients, and add the preserved ginger and candied peel if you're using these. Mix well, then pour into the prepared tin.

Bake for 50–60 minutes, or until the parkin is firm to the touch. Lift the parkin out of the tin, on its paper, and put it on a wire rack to cool. When it's cool, cut the parkin into pieces and remove the paper.
MAKES 12–16 PIECES

FAVOURITE SWISS ROLL

This is a very light Swiss roll and it's very quick and easy to make if you have an electric whisk.

100 g/4 oz caster sugar	*1 tbls cornflour*
4 eggs	*225 g/8 oz raspberry jam*
50 g/2 oz self-raising flour	*extra cornflour and icing sugar, to dust*

The classic way to make a whisked sponge like this is to whisk the eggs and sugar over a pan of steaming water. However if you heat the sugar for a few minutes in the oven and then add this to the eggs, you can do away with the pan of water. So, first set the oven to 200°C/400°F/Gas Mark 6 and line a 22 × 32 cm/9 × 13 inch Swiss roll tin with greased greaseproof or nonstick paper. (Even nonstick paper needs to be greased for this recipe.)

Put the sugar on to a baking sheet and pop into the oven for 4–5 minutes to heat up. Break the eggs into a bowl or the bowl of an electric mixer, then tip in the sugar. Whisk for about 5 minutes, or until the mixture is very pale, light and fluffy, and the mixture will hold the impression of the whisk for several seconds. Then sift the flour and cornflour in on top, and fold them in carefully with a metal spoon or thin plastic spatula.

Pour the mixture into the prepared tin and bake for 7–8 minutes – it's done when the centre springs back to a light touch. While it's cooking, lay a piece of greaseproof paper or nonstick paper out on the working surface and dust it with cornflour, then turn the Swiss roll straight out on to this. Trim the short edges with a sharp knife.

Warm the jam gently in a saucepan, then pour and spread this all over the Swiss roll and quickly roll it up from one of the long edges. Brush off any excess cornflour, and dust with a little icing sugar.

MAKES ONE SWISS ROLL

BÛCHE DE NOEL (CHOCOLATE LOG)

4 eggs	*150 ml/5 fl oz water*
175 g/6 oz caster sugar	*2 egg yolks*
50 g/2 oz cocoa powder	*100 g/4 oz plain chocolate, melted*
2 egg whites	*100 g/4 oz soft unsalted butter*
FOR THE SPECIAL BUTTERCREAM	*icing sugar for dusting*
100 g/4 oz caster sugar	

Set the oven to 200°C/400°F/Gas Mark 6 and line a greased 23 × 32 cm/9 × 13 inch Swiss roll tin with a piece of greased greaseproof paper.

First make the buttercream. Boil the sugar and water for 5 minutes. Meanwhile, whisk the egg yolks then pour in the sugar mixture and whisk well; add the chocolate, then gradually whisk in the butter. Chill then whip before using.

To make the log, whisk the eggs and sugar together in a bowl set over a pan of simmering water until they are pale and fluffy. Remove from the heat and stir in the cocoa. Whisk the egg whites until stiff, then fold these gently into the mixture.

Pour the mixture into the prepared tin, spreading it out to the edges. Bake for 15 minutes. Cool mixture in the tin for 10 minutes, then cover with a damp teacloth and leave for a further 10 minutes. Remove the cloth and turn the cake out on to a piece of greaseproof paper that has been dusted with icing sugar. Remove the greaseproof paper from the top of the cake and leave to cool completely.

When the log is cold, trim the edges and spread the top with the whipped buttercream, then carefully roll the cake up like a Swiss roll, using the paper to help: don't worry if it cracks! Sprinkle with more icing sugar. This log will keep well in the fridge for several hours, and can also be frozen successfully.

SERVES 6–8

OPPOSITE: *Bûche de Noel (Chocolate Log)*

SWEDISH RING CAKE

This makes a pleasant change from the rich and spicy food of Christmas, while still looking festive. It is also, for some reason I've never quite been able to understand, extremely popular with all children. (They might prefer it without the cinnamon – mine certainly do.)

75 g/3 oz butter
¾ tsp sugar
¾ tsp salt
200 ml/7 fl oz milk and
 boiling water, mixed
350 g/12 oz strong white
 flour
1 sachet easy-blend yeast
a little oil

50 g/2 oz demerara sugar
1 tsp powdered cinnamon
 (optional)

FOR THE GLACÉ ICING
225 g/8 oz icing sugar
squeeze of lemon juice
red and green glacé
 cherries, to decorate

Melt the butter without browning it, and leave to cool. Add the sugar and salt to the milk and water mixture, and stir until they have dissolved. Put the flour into a large bowl and sprinkle in the easy-blend yeast. Make a well in the centre. When the melted butter is tepid, pour this into the well, along with most of the milk and water mixture, which should also be tepid: too hot and it will kill the yeast, too cold, and it will take ages to work! Mix the flour into the liquid, adding the rest as necessary, until you have a sticky dough.

Now, either turn the dough out on to a lightly floured surface and knead it for 10 minutes, or divide it into batches and process it in a food processor with a dough blade for 1 minute. In either case, it's ready when it's smooth and has lost its stickiness. It should still be fairly soft. Oil the base of your mixing basin, put the ball of dough into this, then turn it up the other way so that the oily side is on top, to prevent a skin forming.

Put the bowl in a large carrier bag, closing it to exclude draughts, then leave it in a warm place. I generally stand it on a folded towel on a radiator and sometimes wrap a thick towel around it, too. Leave it for 1–2 hours, or until it has literally doubled in bulk. Then turn it out on to a lightly floured surface and knead it very briefly. Now press the dough out into a large rectangle, about 40 cm/16 inches long and 20

cm/8 inches across. Sprinkle the surface with the demerara sugar and the cinnamon if you're using this, then roll it up from one of longer edges and press the ends together to make a circle.

Place the ring on a baking sheet then, with scissors, make slanting cuts in the outer edge. Put the baking sheet inside the plastic bag again – or two bags, if it's large – and leave in a warm place for a further ¾–2 hours, or until the ring is very fat and puffy. It's really important to let it rise enough, then you'll get a lovely light, springy cake like the one pictured here.

About 20 minutes before you think this stage is reached, set the oven to 190°C/375°F/Gas Mark 5. Bake the cake for 30–35 minutes, then remove from the oven and set aside to cool on a wire rack, with a cloth over it to soften the crust.

Make the icing by mixing the icing sugar with a squeeze of lemon juice and enough cold water to make a thick, just-spreadable consistency. Spread this over the top of the cake, and decorate with slices of red and green glacé cherries.

MAKES ONE 20 CM/8 INCH RING

OPPOSITE: *(left) Swedish Ring Cake and (right) Little Christmas Buns, page 398*

POPPY SEED ROLLS

Home-made rolls, made with a rich dough, are a delicious treat. They freeze well and can be warmed through from the freezer. The dough also makes an excellent base for pizza.

450 g/1 lb strong plain flour
1 tsp salt
1 tsp sugar
1 sachet easy-blend yeast
100 g/4 oz butter or margarine, melted and cooled

350 ml/12 fl oz tepid water, or milk and water mixed
oil
a little milk or beaten egg, to glaze
poppy seeds

If you have the chance to warm the flour by placing it in a coolish oven, or on a radiator beforehand, this will speed up the action of the yeast. Anyway, sift the flour into a bowl and add the salt, sugar and yeast. Make a well in the centre and pour in the melted butter or margarine, then start pouring in the liquid, mixing the flour into it, to make a soft dough.

Put this dough into a food processor and process, without the plunger, for 1 minute – you may need to do the dough in two batches. Or knead the dough by hand, for 10 minutes. Either way, you will end up with a lovely smooth, elastic dough. Put this into a warm, oiled bowl, then turn it up the other way, so that the oily surface is on top. Cover the bowl with a polythene carrier bag, put it into a warm place, and leave it until the dough has doubled in size – this takes 1–1½ hours, or longer if it's in a coolish kitchen.

Knead the mixture briefly, then divide it into 24 pieces, and roll these into rounds or sausages, or make them into knots, and place well apart on greased baking sheets. Cover again with polythene carrier bags and put into a warm place to rise. The rolls should be doubled in size, well-risen and puffy, so that they will be light. This will take 45–60 minutes, or more if the kitchen is cool.

About 20 minutes before the rolls are ready, set the oven to 220°C/425°F/Gas Mark 7. Brush the tops of the rolls lightly with milk or beaten egg, sprinkle with poppy seeds and bake for 10–15 minutes.

MAKES 24 ROLLS

CHOCOLATE BISCUIT SLICES

These no-bake, easy-to-make slices can be completely vegan if you choose biscuits, margarine and chocolate which don't contain any dairy produce.

50 g/2 oz butter or margarine
50 g/2 oz golden syrup

200 g/7 oz plain chocolate
200 g/7 oz plain biscuits, such as rich tea

First, line a Swiss roll tin with nonstick paper. Put the butter or margarine into a heavy-based saucepan with the golden syrup and half the chocolate, broken into pieces. Heat gently until everything has melted.

Meanwhile, put the biscuits in a polythene bag and crush to coarse crumbs with a rolling pin. Add the biscuits to the chocolate mixture and mix well until they are all coated. Spoon the mixture into the tin and press it down with the back of a spoon.

Melt the rest of the chocolate in a bowl over a pan of simmering water and spread over the top of the biscuit mixture. Leave until cold and set, then cut into serving pieces.

MAKES 24 BISCUITS

JEAN'S BISCUITS

100 g/4 oz soft margarine
50 g/2 oz caster sugar
100 g/4 oz porridge oats
25 g/1 oz plain flour
25 g/1 oz semolina

25 g/1 oz desiccated coconut
½ tsp bicarbonate of soda
175–225 g/6–8 oz plain or milk chocolate, melted (optional)

Set the oven to 140°C/275°F/Gas Mark 1.

Put the margarine and sugar into a bowl and beat until creamy, then beat in all the other ingredients, except the chocolate, to make a stiff dough. On a lightly floured board, roll out this dough making it as thin as you can. If you find it too crumbly to work, add a drop or two of water, but don't over-do it. Stamp into rounds with a cutter and lift on to a baking sheet – they'll hardly spread at all, so can be quite close together.

Bake for 20 minutes. Let them cool on the sheet until you can handle them then, if you wish, dip each one in melted chocolate to half-coat it on the front and back. Leave on a wire rack to finish cooling and let the chocolate set.

MAKES 24 BISCUITS

PEPPERMINT STARS

An easy recipe which children enjoy making, or helping to make. You can get oil of peppermint at the chemist. For a rather more elaborate version, the stars can be half-dipped in melted plain chocolate.

1 egg white	*extra icing sugar for*
350 g/12 oz icing sugar	*rolling out*
a few drops of oil of	*silver balls (optional)*
peppermint	

Put the egg white into a large bowl and whisk until it is frothy and well broken up. Sift in about half of the icing sugar and beat until smooth; continue in this way until you have a stiff, creamy mixture, and all, or nearly all, the icing sugar has been used. You may find it easier to use your hands to knead in the icing sugar as the mixture gets thick.

Flavour the mixture with a few drops of peppermint oil, then sift some icing sugar over a board and roll out the mixture quite thinly – to about 5 mm/¼ inch – and cut into stars with a small cutter. Decorate each star with some silver balls, to make sparkly stars, if you wish, then put the stars on to a baking sheet lined with a piece of nonstick paper and leave them near a radiator or in a warm kitchen for a day or so until they have dried out.

Pack them into pretty boxes or in twists of coloured cellophane.

MAKES 30–40 STARS

THIN SESAME CRACKERS

These thin, savoury crisp crackers are particularly good with soft cheeses.

200 g/7 oz brown bread	*50 g/2 oz butter or*
flour	*margarine*
50 g/2 oz sesame seeds	*extra flour for rolling*
1 tsp salt	

Set the oven to 150°C/300°F/Gas Mark 2. Have ready some large baking sheets – they don't need to be greased.

Put the flour, sesame seeds, salt and butter or margarine into a bowl or food processor and blend together until the fat is mixed with the flour and the mixture looks like breadcrumbs. Add enough boiling water to make a dough – it should be soft enough to roll out, but not sticky.

Divide the dough into three or four pieces. Take one of these pieces and put the rest in a polythene bag. Roll the piece of dough out on a lightly floured board, making it as thin as you can. Cut it first into squares, then cut each across into a triangle. Taking each of these triangles in turn, roll them to make them as thin as possible, and place them on a baking sheet. Continue in this way until you have used up all the dough.

Bake the crackers for 15–20 minutes, or until they are crisp but not browned. If they are browning, turn the oven down a setting.

Let them cool on a wire rack, then store in an airtight tin.

MAKES ABOUT 60 CRACKERS

CHRISTMAS 'FLOWERS'

This is a great favourite with my family, particularly the kids. The 'flowers' are crisp biscuits, moulded into shape over a small cup while they are still warm; and the goodies inside can be as plain or partified as you like.

FOR THE 'FLOWERS'
25 g/1 oz butter or vegan
  margarine
50 g/2 oz icing sugar
25 g/1 oz plain flour
2–3 tbls double cream
1 egg white
icing sugar for dusting

FOR THE FILLING
vanilla ice cream
whipped double cream
sweets
seedless grapes,
  raspberries, blueberries,
    nectarines, etc

Set the oven to 200°C/400°F/Gas Mark 6. Draw four 10 cm/4 inch circles on a sheet of nonstick paper to fit a baking sheet.

Melt the butter, then mix it in with the icing sugar, flour, cream and egg white, beating well to make a smooth batter. Put a teaspoonful of this mixture on one of the circles, and spread it out carefully to cover the circle thinly. Make three more in the same way, then bake them for about 5 minutes, or until they are lightly browned. Set the unused mixture aside (you will use it later).

Have ready four small cups or jars (the size of mustard jars). Lift the biscuits off the paper and on to the inverted cups or jars, pressing the top to flatten it – this will be the base of the 'flower' and needs to be level so that it will stand well. Curve the edges round the cup or jar to shape. Leave to cool, then remove the biscuits. While the first lot are cooling, make more in the same way. These will keep for a day or two in an airtight tin, or carefully packed in a rigid container in the freezer.

To complete the 'flowers', stand them on a serving plate, or on individual plates and fill with tiny scoops of vanilla ice cream – a melon-baller is good for making these – lightly whipped cream and some little sweets or pieces of fruit.

MAKES 8 'FLOWERS'

BRANDY SNAPS

Everyone loves brandy snaps, and they're surprisingly easy to make. They harden as they cool, so the trick is to lift them off the paper as soon as they're firm enough to handle, but before they get too brittle to roll – so keep testing them. If they do get too hard, just pop them back in the oven for a few seconds to soften them up again. You can fill them with cream or ice cream, or serve them plain, with a creamy fool, fruit compôte or sorbet.

50 g/2 oz golden syrup
50 g/2 oz sugar
50 g/2 oz butter or
  margarine

50 g/2 oz plain flour
1 tsp ground ginger
1 tsp lemon juice

Set the oven to 200°C/400°F/Gas Mark 6, then line a large baking sheet with nonstick paper.

Put the golden syrup into a saucepan (you can measure it straight into the pan, if you have the kind of scales you can adjust), with the sugar and butter or margarine, and melt over a gentle heat. Take the pan off the heat and stir in the flour, ground ginger and lemon juice.

Put heaped teaspoons of the mixture well apart on the baking sheet (you'll probably need to do at least two batches). Bake for 4–6 minutes, or until the brandy snaps are an even mid-golden brown, then remove from the oven and leave to cool on the paper for 2–3 minutes.

As soon as the brandy snaps are firm enough to pick up with a fish slice, lift them off the paper and mould each around the handle of a wooden spoon, or some other suitable cylinder shape. When the brandy snaps are cool and crisp, remove them and keep them in an airtight tin until you need them. To serve them, fill with cream which has been whipped with a little brandy, or with vanilla ice cream.

MAKES 12 SNAPS

OPPOSITE: *Christmas 'Flowers'*

SWEETS & PRESENTS

The recipes in this section concentrate on those little extras which you can make to enhance your own Christmas or give as presents. They're delicious and a bit frivolous, but fun to make and give – a collection of festive biscuits, some of which can be hung on the tree on a suitable branch as decorations (well out of the way of dogs!); easy-to-make sweets and petits fours and some good but simple pickles, preserves, jellies and relishes. Some of the cakes in Christmas Baking (pages 394 to 405), particularly the Little Christmas Cakes on page 396, would also make perfect presents, as would Mincemeat (page 285), prettily displayed in a decorative jar and festively wrapped.

I think that making presents, decorations and treats adds to the pleasure and fun of Christmas, especially if you have children, and they can join in. I liked to involve my kids in this kind of preparation; they usually loved helping and it's educational as well as fun – a great way to help children learn to weigh and measure, recognise shapes and colours, and so on. Not to mention being a useful way of using up their pre-Christmas energy and excitement! But don't set your standards too high, and be prepared for lots of mess and fairly inedible offerings at the end of it – depending, of course, on the age of the child, you'll probably end up with fairly grey, misshapen biscuits, wobbly marzipan teddy bears (which must, of course, be sincerely praised and appreciated) and a sticky kitchen. You may find yourself making another batch of Stained Glass Windows to hang on the tree after your young helpers are safely in bed but, for sheer pleasure and fun involved, it will have been worth it....

If you are giving the biscuits or other treats as presents, the way you package and wrap them can make all the difference. Crunchy cellophane is excellent for wrapping biscuits, sweets, cakes and little jars of preserves. Make sure that the jars are sparkling bright and attractively labelled, perhaps with a ribbon round the top. Sometimes I also include a few ideas for using the preserve, and the recipe, too, if it seems appropriate.

MIXED VEGETABLES IN OIL

This is an adaptation of one of Nicola Cox's delicious recipes from her lovely book Country Cooking. *You will need some jars with plastic-lined or glass lids; wash and sterilize the jars as described for Apricot Chutney (right). Choose a selection of the vegetables listed below.*

50 g/2 oz sea salt for each 450 g/1 lb prepared vegetables
450 g/1 lb baby carrots, halved or quartered downwards if fat
1 cucumber, cut into chunky matchsticks
450 g/1 lb French beans, topped and tailed
1 cauliflower, broken into small florets

1 red pepper, seeded and sliced into thin lengths
1 green pepper, seeded and sliced into thin lengths
12 baby pickling onions, peeled
1 fennel, trimmed and cut into lengthwise strips
fresh parsley sprigs
600 ml/1 pint spiced vinegar (see below)
oil or grapeseed oil

Make up a brine by dissolving 50 g/2 oz of sea salt in a pint of water for every pound of vegetables. Put the vegetables into a deep glass or china bowl and pour over the brine to cover them. Put a plate and weight on top to keep the vegetables under water. Leave them there for 12–24 hours, then drain them and rinse them well under cold water.

Arrange the vegetables attractively in the sterilized jars, adding some fresh parsley sprigs too, and packing them firmly to within an inch of the tops of the jars. Then whisk 1 part spiced vinegar with 1 part light (not best virgin) olive oil and 1 part grapeseed oil and pour into the jars, to cover the vegetables and come right up to the top. Put on the lids, and leave for at least several days, preferably longer.

Take out the vegetables as you need them, making sure that the remaining vegetables are always covered by an inch of oil. (Later, the oil can be used in salad dressings, etc.)

MAKES ABOUT 1 KG/2 LB 2 OZ PICKLE

If you overcook this Apricot Chutney and it gets too thick and syrupy stir in some cider vinegar to thin it.

SPICED VINEGAR

To make spiced vinegar, put 600 ml/1 pint of white wine vinegar into a saucepan with a couple of peeled garlic cloves, 12 peppercorns, 3 cardamom pods if available, a good pinch of dried marjoram, 1–2 teaspoons sugar, $\frac{1}{2}$ teaspoon dill seeds, a few stalks of parsley and a bay leaf. Bring to the boil, then leave, covered, until cold. Strain before using, although you can add the seeds, pods and herbs to the jars.

APRICOT CHUTNEY

225 g/8 oz dried apricots
2 large onions, chopped
1 garlic clove, crushed
100 g/4 oz sultanas
350 g/12 oz demerara sugar

2 tsp salt
450 ml/15 fl oz malt or cider vinegar
juice of 1 lemon
1 tbls pickling spice

Cover the apricots with water and let them soak for a few hours, or overnight. Then drain them, keeping the liquid.

Chop the apricots roughly, then put them into a large saucepan with the onions, garlic, sultanas, sugar, salt, vinegar and lemon juice. Add the pickling spice, which can be tied in a piece of muslin if you wish – I leave them loose, as I like the crunchiness. Measure the reserved apricot liquid and if necessary make up to 300 ml/10 fl oz with water, and add that, too, to the pan. Bring to the boil, then let the mixture simmer gently, uncovered, for about 1 hour, or until it is thick and glossy.

While the chutney is cooking, prepare some special chutney jars by washing them well, then drying and sterilizing them in an oven preset to 140°C/275°F/Gas Mark 1 for 30 minutes. Spoon the chutney into the jars, cover with non-metal, vinegar-proof lids, and label.

MAKES ABOUT 1 KG/2 LB 2 OZ

OPPOSITE: *Mixed Vegetables in Oil*

CRANBERRY CONSERVE WITH PORT

To me, this glossy red conserve really smells and tastes of Christmas . . . It's good with puddings as well as savouries; try it spooned over ice cream or cheesecake; or with Greek yogurt.

225 g/8 oz cranberries
300 ml/10 fl oz water
450 g/1 lb granulated
 sugar

juice of 3 oranges
3 tbls port

Wash the cranberries, then put them into a medium-large saucepan with the water and let them simmer gently until they are tender – about 4–5 minutes. Add the granulated sugar and orange juice, and heat gently until the sugar has dissolved, then let the mixture boil steadily until it reaches setting-point: 105°C/221°F on a sugar thermometer, or when a little of the liquid dropped on to a cold saucer wrinkles when you push it with your finger. Remove from the heat and stir in the port.

Pour the mixture into clean jars that have been warmed and sterilized in an oven preset to 140°C/275°F/Gas Mark 1 for 30 minutes.
MAKES ABOUT 1 KG/2 LB 2 OZ

CHEDDAR CHEESE AND BRANDY DIP

A good cheese dip, packed into an attractive container, such as a pretty pâté dish or even a special mug tied up with cellophane and ribbon, makes a thoughtful gift. This cheese dip is easy to make, tastes good, and keeps for several weeks.

100 g/4 oz Cheddar
 cheese, finely grated
25 g/1 oz soft butter

1 tbls brandy
freshly ground pepper

Put the cheese and butter into a bowl and beat together; gradually beat in the brandy and a small amount of water, if necessary, to make a creamy

I use horseradish jars to store Kumquats in Brandy if I don't have any mustard ones handy.

consistency. Add a little pepper to taste.

Pack the mixture into your chosen container, cover, and refrigerate until needed.
MAKES ABOUT 175 G/6 OZ

KUMQUATS IN BRANDY

These tiny oranges, preserved in a brandy syrup, make an attractive gift – I generally add a handwritten label to the jar with a few ideas for using them. They're delicious spooned over thick yogurt, cream or ice cream; added to a fruit salad or, in small quantities, on their own or with a few whole, blanched almonds. You can eat them after a week, but they're much nicer if you can leave them for 4–6 weeks to mellow and mature.

350 g/12 oz kumquats
225 g/8 oz granulated
 sugar

3 tbls brandy

First choose a suitable jar or jars. This amount will fill one 600 ml/1 pint jar or two or three small ones, like old mustard jars. Wash the jars well, then dry and sterilize them by putting them into an oven set to 140°C/275°F/Gas Mark 1 for 30 minutes.

To prepare the kumquats, first wash them, then prick them all over with a darning needle or skewer. Put the sugar into a saucepan with 300 ml/10 fl oz water and heat gently until the sugar has dissolved, then bring to the boil. Add the kumquats, cover and simmer for about 15 minutes, or until the kumquats are tender and shiny-looking.

Spoon the fruit into the sterilized jars, then add the brandy and enough of the cooking liquid to cover the kumquats. It's important to put plenty of fruit into the jar or jars, or the fruit will rise when you add the syrup. Screw on the lids. Store in a cool, dry place until required.
MAKES THREE 200 ML/6 FL OZ JARS

OPPOSITE: *Kumquats in Brandy*

CINNAMON SHORTBREADS

These cinnamon shortbreads are delicious with Chocolate Ice Cream (page 393) or Christmas Dried Fruit Salad (page 382), as well as being good on their own, with tea or coffee.

100 g/4 oz plain wholewheat flour	*2–3 tsp powdered cinnamon*
100 g/4 oz plain white flour	*225 g/8 oz soft butter or vegan margarine*
50 g/2 oz cornflour	*100 g/4 oz caster sugar*
50 g/2 oz semolina or ground rice	

Set the oven to 170°C/325°F/Gas Mark 3 and grease a 19 cm × 29 cm/7½ inch × 11½ inch shallow tin with butter.

Sift the flours, semolina or ground rice and the cinnamon into a large bowl or food processor, adding the residue of bran from the sieve. Then put in the butter or margarine and the sugar. Whizz, or beat, all the ingredients together until they form a soft dough which leaves the sides of the bowl clean.

Press this into the tin, levelling the surface by pressing with the back of a metal spoon. Then prick the surface all over with a fork. Bake for about 45 minutes, until the shortbread is set and quite crisp on top and very lightly tinged with gold. It's more tricky to tell when these are done than with normal shortbreads because they are already rather brown! If you are in doubt, you can cut the shortbread and very carefully lift up one of the end pieces and look underneath it to see if it looks done. If not, carefully put it back and let the shortbread cook for a bit longer. When it's done, cut it into sections and leave it to cool and crisp up in the tin.

This shortbread keeps well in a tin for several days, if it gets the chance, and also freezes well. It defrosts very quickly; you can use it almost straight from the freezer.

MAKES 24 SHORTBREADS

OPPOSITE: (left) Greek Shortbreads and (right) Cinnamon Shortbreads

GREEK SHORTBREADS

These are a cross between a sweet and a biscuit and make a lovely petit four, or, prettily packed, an attractive gift. Once they have been coated with rose water and icing sugar and then dried, they keep very well. I find the best place to buy rose water is from a Middle Eastern shop if there is one near to you — ask them which is the best. Otherwise some supermarkets and chemists have it; if you get it from the chemist, make sure it is suitable for cooking.

225 g/8 oz soft butter	*about 6 tbls triple-distilled rose water*
50 g/2 oz caster sugar	*350–450 g/12 oz–1 lb icing sugar*
1 egg yolk	
275 g/10 oz plain flour	
50 g/2 oz cornflour	
90 g/3½ oz ground almonds	

Set the oven to 170°C/325°F/Gas Mark 3 and line two large baking sheets with nonstick paper.

Put the butter and sugar into a bowl or food processor and whizz, or beat, them together until they are light, then beat in the egg yolk. Sift the flour and cornflour into the bowl, add the ground almonds, and mix gently until everything is combined.

Break off small pieces of the dough, about the size of a marble, and form them into crescents or barrel shapes. Put them on to the baking sheets, leaving a little space around them: they will expand a bit, but not too much. Bake for about 25 minutes, or until they are set but not coloured. Cool on a wire rack.

When the shortbreads are cool, put 6 tablespoons of rose water into a small bowl and sift the icing sugar into another bowl. Dip each shortbread quickly first into the rose water, then into the icing sugar. Return them to the wire rack and leave in a warm room for several hours. Pack them in a tin, or in boxes, sprinkling extra icing sugar between the layers, and on top.

MAKES ABOUT 70 SHORTBREADS

VEGAN VERSION

Just leave out the egg yolk, and use a vegan margarine instead of the butter.

MINI FLORENTINES

50 g/2 oz butter
50 g/2 oz caster sugar
50 g/2 oz glacé cherries,
  finely chopped
75 g/3 oz hazelnuts,
  finely chopped

25 g/1 oz mixed peel,
  finely chopped
2 tsp lemon juice
100 g/4 oz chocolate, use
  half plain and half white

Melt the butter in a saucepan, then add the sugar and bring to the boil, stirring all the time. Remove from the heat and stir in the cherries, hazelnuts, peel and lemon juice. Allow to cool slightly while you line two baking sheets with nonstick paper.

Set the oven to 180°C/350°F/Gas Mark 4.

Put little heaps of the mixture, about the size of a hazelnut, on the sheets, leaving room for them to spread. Bake for 5–6 minutes, until they are a light golden brown. Push the edges in with a knife to neaten, then leave them to cool on the paper.

Melt the chocolate in two separate bowls set over saucepans of simmering water, or in a microwave for 3–4 minutes, then spread over the smooth side of the florentines. Just before the chocolate sets, make wavy lines with a fork. Leave to cool completely.

MAKES ABOUT 60

MACAROONS

100 g/4 oz ground
  almonds
175 g/6 oz caster sugar
a few drops of almond
  essence

2 egg whites, lightly
  whisked
granulated sugar
6–7 almonds, blanched
  and halved

Set the oven to 180°C/350°F/Gas Mark 4 and line a baking sheet with nonstick paper.

Put the ground almonds into a bowl with the sugar and almond essence, then mix in enough of the egg white to make a stiff mixture. (You may not need all the egg white.) Either put teaspoonfuls of. the mixture well apart on the baking sheet, or pipe small

mounds, using a piping bag with a 1 cm/½ inch plain nozzle, allowing room to spread. Sprinkle with sugar and top with half an almond.

Bake for 15–20 minutes, or until set and golden brown. Allow to firm up on the paper, then lift off on to a wire rack to finish cooling.

MAKES 12–14 MACAROONS

SHAPED BISCUITS

175 g/6 oz butter or vegan
  margarine
50 g/2 oz icing sugar
100 g/4 oz plain white
  flour

100 g/4 oz wholewheat
  flour
glacé icing (page 404),
  sweets, hundreds and
  thousands, melted
  chocolate, etc, to decorate

Set the oven to 180°C/350°F/Gas Mark 4 and line two large baking sheets with nonstick paper.

Put the butter or margarine into a bowl with the icing sugar and beat together until they are light and creamy. Add the flours and beat again to make a dough. You can add flavourings at this point: some grated lemon rind, cinnamon, ginger or a drop or two of real vanilla essence are good. On a lightly floured board, roll out the dough to 2.5 mm/⅛ inch, then cut into all kinds of Chrismassy shapes – stars, angels, Christmas trees, and so on. Put the biscuits on the baking sheets – they won't spread much.

Bake for about 10 minutes, or until the biscuits look golden brown, set and are browning a little more at the edges. Leave to cool on the sheets, then decorate, using glacé icing, little sweets, hundreds and thousands, some melted chocolate, to make them look really colourful. The children will probably love to help with this. If you're planning to hang them on the tree, punch a hole on an outside edge before baking so that you can thread them later.

MAKES 18–20 BISCUITS

OPPOSITE: *Mini Florentines, made with light and dark chocolate*

418

SNOWFLAKES

The children will love to help with all of these biscuits - baking them and hanging them on the tree afterwards.

2 egg whites
100 g/4 oz caster sugar
15 g/½ oz finely chopped
  skinned hazelnuts

15 g/½ oz preserving
sugar

Set the oven to 150°C/300°F/Gas Mark 2 and line two large baking sheets with nonstick paper.

Whisk the egg whites until stiff, as for meringues, then gradually whisk in the sugar. Put the mixture into a piping bag fitted with a shell nozzle – about 5 mm/¼ inch across. Pipe blobs of meringue on to the baking sheets in the form of snowflakes – with six points. Don't make them too high as they will rise a bit.

Mix together the nuts and preserving sugar and sprinkle these over the top of the snowflakes. Bake for about 1 hour, until they have dried out and are crisp. Leave to cool on the sheets.

These are extremely popular with children and look very pretty on the tree. Make a little hole in the middle of your snowflake before baking so that you can thread them.

STAINED GLASS WINDOW BISCUITS

75 g/3 oz plain white
flour
75 g/3 oz wholewheat
flour
100 g/4 oz butter or
vegan margarine

40 g/1½ oz icing sugar
about 24 boiled sweets of
different colours: red,
orange, green, yellow and
purple

Set the oven to 180°C/350°F/Gas Mark 4 and line two large baking sheets with nonstick paper.

Beat together the flours, butter or margarine and icing sugar, to make a dough. On a lightly floured board, roll out the dough to a depth of 2.5 mm/⅛ inch. Cut out shapes which are large enough to take a

boiled sweet in the centre, allowing for the sweet to spread a bit. Then cut a circle out of the middle of the biscuits, about the size that the sweet will spread to. I use the round end of a piping nozzle for this. Put the biscuits on the baking sheets – they won't spread much – and pop a boiled sweet into each centre.

Bake for about 10 minutes, or until the sweets have melted and the biscuits look golden brown, set and are browning a little more at the edges. Leave to cool on the sheets, but before they get completely firm, make a little hole in the top of each, well away from the edges, through which you can thread some cord to hang them on the tree.

MAKES ABOUT 24 BISCUITS

GINGER BEARS

50 g/2 oz butter
25 g/1 oz caster sugar
50 g/2 oz plain white flour
50 g/2 oz wholewheat flour
1 tsp baking powder

1 tsp ground ginger
1 tbls golden syrup
glacé icing (page 404),
  sweets, melted chocolate,
  etc, to decorate

Set the oven to 180°C/350°F/Gas Mark 4 and line two large baking sheets with nonstick paper.

Put the butter or margarine into a bowl with the caster sugar and beat together until they are light and creamy. Add the flours, baking powder, ginger and syrup, and beat again to make a dough. On a lightly floured board, roll out the dough to 2.5 mm/⅛ inch, then cut into teddy bears. Put the biscuits on the baking sheets – they won't spread much.

Bake for about 10 minutes, or until the biscuits look golden brown, set and are browning a little more at the edges. Leave to cool on the sheets, then decorate, using glacé icing, little sweets, hundreds and thousands, some melted chocolate.

MAKES ABOUT 10–12 BEARS

OPPOSITE: A selection of Christmas tree biscuits: Snowflakes, Stained Glass Window Biscuits, Ginger Bears and Shaped Biscuits, page 418

MARZIPAN SWEETS

These are fun to make with children – like play dough, but more satisfactory because you can eat the results! Although you can use home-made almond paste, I find bought white almond paste/marzipan is better because it is less likely to get oily when rolled and moulded.

To colour the marzipan, take a small amount of marzipan, roll it into a ball, then break it open and put a few drops of colouring in the centre. Knead it until it is evenly coloured. When the shapes have dried a little you can paint on extra details if you wish. Put a little cake colouring on a piece of greaseproof paper, dip a clean, fine paint brush into this and paint the models as required.

To make Santa's sack, colour a piece of marzipan brown, flatten it, then gather up the edges to make a sack. Fill this with 'presents' made from pieces of coloured marzipan – squares, rectangles and other shapes – with bows and cords made of small pieces of marzipan. If you feel up to it, you can make a yellow teddy bear (or other appealing toy!) to stick out of the top of the sack. Use a cylinder of yellow marzipan for the body, a ball on top for the head (pulled out to a point for the nose) and stick on little ears and long 'sausages' to make arms and legs. Some red and green crackers look nice as part of the display, too: for these, use cylinders of marzipan, indented to make the part you pull, and fringed with a cocktail stick. Leaves of holly can be cut from green marzipan with a holly cutter, and decorated with a few red marzipan berries.

To make marzipan fruits, roll out balls of orange marzipan to make oranges, running them over a fine grater to get an orange-peel texture: finish with a clove stuck in the end to make the stalk. Make apples and pears by shaping light greeny-yellow marzipan and sticking the pointed end of cloves into the tops to make stems. The apples can be painted with a flush of red when they have dried a bit. For bananas, roll out 'sausages' of yellow marzipan, then curve them round and join several together to make a bunch. These can be painted with some flecks of brown (cake colouring or cocoa mixed with a little water) when they have set a bit. Grapes are made from purple or green marzipan, rolled into tiny balls and stuck together to make a bunch.

OPPOSITE: *Marzipan Sweets*

VEGAN FUDGE

The secrets of making good fudge, vegan or otherwise, are to use a really large saucepan and not to try to make too much fudge at once; and to use a sugar thermometer, which takes all the guesswork out of it. This is a basic vegan fudge which you can flavour in different ways. For a chocolate version, beat in 100 g/ 4 oz plain chocolate, broken up, when you take the fudge off the heat and start beating it.

700 g/1½ lb caster sugar
600 ml/1 pint soya milk
100 g/4 oz vegan
  margarine

2 tsp vanilla essence
100 g/4 oz walnut pieces
  (optional)

First line an 18 cm/7 inch square tin with nonstick paper.

Put the sugar, soya milk and margarine into a large, heavy-based saucepan and heat gently until the margarine has melted and the sugar dissolved. Bring to the boil and let it simmer steadily until the temperature reaches 120°C/240°F on a sugar thermometer, or a small piece dropped into a cup of cold water forms a soft ball. Remove from the heat immediately and add the vanilla essence and walnuts if you are using them, then cool it quickly by placing it in a bowl of cold water.

Beat the mixture for a few minutes, until it thickens and is on the point of setting, then pour it into the prepared tin and leave to set.

When the fudge is firm, cut it into squares using a sharp knife.

MAKES ABOUT 40 SQUARES

COCONUT ICE

This is a tradional recipe for pink-and-white stripy coconut ice, and it's vegan. It's particularly easy to make if you have a sugar thermometer.

450 g/1 lb granulated
  sugar
150 ml/5 fl oz water
1 tsp vanilla essence

100 g/4 oz desiccated
  coconut
red vegetable colouring

First line an 18 cm/7 inch square tin with nonstick paper.

Put the granulated sugar and water into a medium-sized, heavy-based saucepan and heat gently, without boiling, until the sugar has dissolved. Bring to the boil and let it simmer steadily until the temperature reaches 120°C/240°F on a sugar thermometer, or a little of the syrup dropped into a cup of cold water forms a soft ball. Remove from the heat immediately and add the vanilla essence and desiccated coconut.

Stir the mixture for 5–10 minutes, or until it begins to thicken and set, then pour half of it into the prepared tin and smooth it level. Colour the remaining half pale pink with a drop or two of colouring, then pour this on top of the white coconut ice, spreading it to the edges and making sure it's level. Press it all down quite firmly with the back of a spoon, and leave it to harden.

Turn the coconut ice out and cut it into squares using a sharp knife.

MAKES ABOUT 700 G/1½ LB

INDEX